Herself Beheld

Adolescence, Gerald Leslie Brockhurst; Etching, National Gallery of Art, Washington, D.C., Rosenwald Collection.

Herself Beheld

The Literature of the Looking Glass

Jenijoy La Belle

CORNELL UNIVERSITY PRESS
Ithaca and London

Cornell University Press gratefully acknowledges
a grant from the Andrew W. Mellon Foundation
which aided in bringing this book to publication.

First published 1988 by Cornell University Press.
Second printing 1989.

International Standard Book Number 0-8014-2202-7
Library of Congress Catalog Card Number 88-47734
Printed in the United States of America
Librarians: Library of Congress cataloging information appears on the last page of the book.

The paper in this book is acid-free and meets the guidelines for permanence and durability of the Committee on Production Guidelines for Book Longevity of the Council on Library Resources.

For Bob

Contents

Acknowledgments

A character in Margaret Atwood's *Lady Oracle* remarks, "I went into the mirror one evening and I couldn't get out again." There have been times in the last few years when I felt very like that woman, and I am indebted to those friends who sometimes accompanied me. To Marjorie Perloff I record my gratitude for reading a draft of my manuscript and offering valuable suggestions. Many friends, including Warren Dennis and Nicholas Warner, brought to my attention mirror scenes that I might otherwise have missed. Special thanks are due Jinx Brown, Carlye La Belle, and Aymalee Roderick for their support, John Heaney for providing a typewriter, Betty Hyland for her expert secretarial assistance, and Morris Eaves for his advocacy. I am particularly grateful to Bernhard Kendler of Cornell University Press for his generous encouragement of my work. The readers' reports acquired by the Press were most helpful in making this a better book. My deepest gratitude is to Robert N. Essick for his counsel during all stages of composition. The dedication of this book to him is scarcely adequate recompense.

I am beholden to Pomona College and the American Council of Learned Societies for the Graves Award in the Humanities, given to aid my early researches on this project. A preliminary version of my remarks on *Jane Eyre* and *The Mill on the Floss* appeared as "Mutiny against the Mirror" in *Pacific Coast Philology* in 1985. The frontispiece is reproduced courtesy of the Rosenwald Collection, National Gallery of Art, Washington, D.C. (with additional thanks to Ruth Fine for locating the Gallery's splendid impression of Gerald Leslie Brockhurst's 1932 etching *Adolescence*).

Permission to quote from the following works has been granted by their copyright holders:

Margaret Atwood, *Lady Oracle,* copyright © 1976 by Margaret Atwood, reprinted by permission of Simon and Schuster, Inc.; the Canadian publishers, McClelland and Stewart, Toronto; the British publishers, André Deutsch Ltd., London.

"Man Alone," copyright © 1923, 1929, 1930, 1931, 1933, 1934, 1935, 1936, 1937, 1938, 1941, 1949, 1951, 1952, 1954, 1957, 1958, 1962, 1963, 1964, 1965, 1966, 1967, 1968 by Louise Bogan. From *The Blue Estuaries* by Louise Bogan, published by the Ecco Press in 1977. Reprinted by permission.

Eva Figes, *Waking,* copyright © 1981 by Eva Figes. Published by Pantheon Books, a Division of Random House, Inc., 1981. All rights reserved.

A Mother and Two Daughters by Gail Godwin. Copyright © 1982 by Gail Godwin. All rights reserved. Reprinted by permission of Viking Penguin Inc.

Erica Jong, *Fear of Flying* (1973), *Half-Lives* (1971), copyright © 1973, 1971 by Erica Mann Jong. Published by Henry Holt and Company, Inc., 1973, 1971. All rights reserved.

Excerpts from "Morality," "Intimates," and "Know Deeply, Know Thyself More Deeply" from *The Complete Poems of D. H. Lawrence,* Collected and Edited by Vivian de Sola Pinto and F. Warren Roberts. Copyright © 1964, 1971 by Angelo Ravagli and C. M. Weekley, Executors of the Estate of Frieda Lawrence Ravagli. All rights reserved. Reprinted by permission of Viking Penguin Inc., and Laurence Pollinger Ltd., England, and the Estate of Mrs. Frieda Lawrence Ravagli.

Doris Lessing, *The Summer before the Dark,* copyright © 1973 by Doris Lessing. Published by Alfred A. Knopf, Inc., and Random House, Inc.; the British publishers, Jonathan Cape Ltd., 1973. All rights reserved.

Alison Lurie, *The War between the Tates,* copyright © 1974 by Alison Lurie. Published by Random House, Inc., 1974. All rights reserved.

Laura Mullen, "Mirror, Mirror" (1982), with permission from *Poetry Northwest.*

The Diary of Anaïs Nin, Volume Two, ed. Gunther Stuhlmann, copyright © 1967 by Anaïs Nin. Published by Harcourt Brace Jovanovich, Inc., 1967. All rights reserved.

Susie Orbach, *Fat Is a Feminist Issue,* copyright © 1978. Quoted by permission of the author.

"Words of Comfort To Be Scratched on a Mirror" from *The Portable Dorothy Parker* by Dorothy Parker. Copyright 1928, renewed © 1956 by Dorothy Parker. All rights reserved. Reprinted by permission of Viking Penguin Inc.; the British publishers, Gerald Duckworth and Company Ltd.

Sylvia Plath, *The Bell Jar,* copyright © 1971, Harper and Row, Publishers, Inc. Reprinted by permission of the publisher and the Estate of Sylvia Plath.

Sylvia Plath, "Mirror," *The Collected Poems,* ed. Ted Hughes, copyright © 1981, Harper and Row, Publishers, Inc. Original copyright © 1963, *The New Yorker;* reprinted by permission of Harper and Row, Publishers, Inc., and the Estate of Sylvia Plath.

John Updike, "Mirror," copyright © 1957 by John Updike. Reprinted from *The Carpentered Hen and Other Tame Creatures* by John Updike, by permission of Alfred A. Knopf, Inc. Originally appeared in *The New Yorker.*

Alice Walker, *The Color Purple,* copyright © 1982 by Alice Walker. Published by Harcourt Brace Jovanovich, Inc., 1982. All rights reserved.

"Before the World Was Made" (1933) and "The Hero, the Girl, and the Fool" (1928). Reprinted with permission of Macmillan Publishing Company from *The Collected Poems* by W. B. Yeats. Copyright © 1928, 1933 by Macmillan Publishing Company, copyright renewed 1956, 1961 by Bertha Georgie Yeats; and A. P. Watt Ltd. on behalf of Michael B. Yeats and Macmillan London Limited.

Anne Hébert, "Life in the Castle," trans. A. Barnstone and W. Barnstone; Hsüeh T'ao, "Spring-Gazing Song," trans. Carolyn Kizer; Lady Ise, "Even in My Dreams," trans. Etsuko Terasaki with Irma Brandeis; Tada Chimako, "Mirror," trans. Kenneth Rexroth and Ikuko Atsumi. From *A Book of Women Poets from Antiquity to Now,* ed. Aliki Barnstone and Willis Barnstone, copyright © 1980 by Schocken Books. Reprinted by permission of Pantheon Books, a Division of Random House, Inc.

JENIJOY LA BELLE

California Institute of Technology
Pasadena, California

A Note on Citations

In order to avoid a multitude of interruptive footnotes, I have cited works in my text by author (or author and title when necessary) and page number in parentheses. See the list of Works Cited for full bibliographic entries.

Herself Beheld

Introductory Reflections

For there was never yet fair woman
but she made mouths in a glass.
Lear's Fool

My subject is the confrontation between a woman and her reflection in a mirror. Let me begin with the concluding stanza of Sylvia Plath's "Mirror," a poem in which the looking glass is also the speaking glass:

> Now I am a lake. A woman bends over me,
> Searching my reaches for what she really is.
> Then she turns to those liars, the candles or the moon.
> I see her back, and reflect it faithfully.
> She rewards me with tears and an agitation of hands.
> I am important to her. She comes and goes.
> Each morning it is her face that replaces the darkness.
> In me she has drowned a young girl, and in me an old woman
> Rises toward her day after day, like a terrible fish. (174)

The mirror claims for itself a voice, a separate identity, and a power over the woman who looks into it. That power comes from an irreducible honesty, the truthfulness of outline, which the mirror itself contrasts to those chiaroscurist liars, the candles and the moon. The mirror has the ability to show the woman what she cannot otherwise see—her face, her back—and perhaps even more hidden prospects of her being. The importance of the mirror is demonstrated by the woman's anguished response. This is, of course, a reaction to her own image. Or is it? Is the seemingly immaterial image of her material body herself or not herself? Is that question another way of asking if the body is the woman? The woman, the body? I think most of us would come to any poem about a mirror with the assumption that the mirror image does not capture the soul of a person but does reflect the outward human form. Yet in Plath's poem we are led to that disturbing "terrible fish," a creature lacking not only a human soul but a human body. The presence in the mirror has become utterly inhuman, an otherness that shakes our faith in the similitude of the body and its reflection.

Over the last several years I have been reading lyric poems and passages in many other genres in which women look into mirrors searching for what they really are. Among the hundreds of looking-glass scenes I have collected are many that, like Plath's poem, reveal an intimate and significant relationship between the mirror and a woman's conception of what she is, what she has been, and what she will become. At those times in the lives of female characters when they are most concerned with their self-identities, or when crises in their lives throw them back on their sole selves, they turn with remarkable frequency to the contemplation of their images in the glass. Such literary events suggest that often, for a woman, the mirror is an important tool not just for beholding her face and form or for seeing how the world views her as a physical object, but also for analyzing and even creating the self in its self-representations to itself. Indeed, these passages have led me to an even odder hypothesis—one that places the mirror at a historical focus of female identity and questions dichotomies between self and reflected image, between spirit and flesh, between psychological presence and physical body. These are the very oppositions basic to representations of masculine selfhood which underlie a great deal of Western thought. I did not begin this study with the intention of questioning the bastions of male ontology, but I have found in these encounters of female characters with their mirrors a key to some of the distinctions, social and psychological, between men and women, particularly as they are portrayed in the literature of the last one hundred and fifty years.

As I've just suggested, the words "identity" and "self" will appear frequently throughout this book. These are troubling terms with multiple meanings subject to ideological tensions between competing schools of thought. My purpose here is not to engage all issues pertaining to self-identity but to consider the role that mirroring plays in what specific women, real and fictive, think about themselves. Thus my perspective is, broadly speaking, phenomenological and open to a variety of definitions of "identity" as these evolve in different texts. I approach the "self" not as an *entity* but as an *activity*, a continual process that gives rise to concepts by which an individual both distinguishes herself from others of her species and situates herself in relation to these other "selves." Although often taken to be a transcendental category of consciousness, a secular substitute for "soul," the self will be viewed in this book as a reification of specific sensate and material acts of enormous complexity.[1] These acts must necessarily take on a semiotic function as signifiers to contribute to a woman's own definition of what *her* self is. And it must be remembered that, in the vast majority of cases, the phenomenon of self-conception unfolds for women without the slightest pretensions about what the "self" is as a philosophical issue.

From childhood through old age, female characters have been mesmerized by mirrors. This book is in no sense a catalogue or a chronology of this pervasive motif, but let me present here a few brief examples. A five-year-old in Alice Adams's *Rich Rewards* spends a long trip giggling at her reflection in the car's dashboard, a reflection that deforms the oval shape of her head, making it round (63). In *Dreams of Sleep*, a six-year-old girl perches on the edge of the bathroom sink, looking into the mirror, just beginning what the author Josephine Humphreys calls "that lifelong interrogation" (127). A scrawny child in Hilma Wolitzer's *In the Palomar Arms* preens and tap-dances "in front of every surface that would give back her own image" (71). The diminutive Miss M. of Walter de la Mare's *Memoirs of a Midget* recalls surveying herself "with endless satisfaction" on the Christmas morning after her ninth birthday and smiling at her reflection, "as if to say, 'So this is to be my companion, then'" (14). Some of these characters regard themselves hurriedly; others inspect themselves for hours at a time. Anne Brontë's young governess in *Agnes Grey* spends "as

1. By calling the self a reification, I do not mean to reduce the concept to an ontological absence. The deconstructive notion that such reifications are self-mystifications still assumes the presence of a self that can be mystified.

much as two minutes" (110) in contemplation of herself, while a teen-ager in Ann Beattie's *Falling in Place* stares so long into the glass that her eyes ache. In Angela Carter's *The Magic Toyshop,* a girl passes almost the whole of her fifteenth summer "behind a locked door in her pastel, innocent bedroom," posing and poring over "herself, naked, in the mirror of her wardrobe" (1–2). Adolescents (like the young woman in Brockhurst's print that serves as a frontispiece to this book) look for themselves in mirrors not only in private but also in public and in groups. When the bell rings to end the class Miss Brigson teaches in Ruth Adam's *I'm Not Complaining,* there "would be a flutter of dirty powder-puffs and a sudden flashing of thirty little mirrors" (272). Neither does glass-gazing know any economic boundaries. An affluent mother and daughter in an Anita Brookner novel, while waiting for coffee in the salon of a Swiss hotel, survey "their faces sternly in the mirrors of their respective compacts" (34). In James Stephens's *Mary, Mary,* we find a charwoman and her daughter who often stand together in their bare room "before the little glass that had a great crack running drunkenly from the right-hand top corner down to the left-hand bottom corner" (31). Sometimes, as in Elizabeth Spires's poem "Mascara," it is sisters who "cheek to cheek, . . . stare for one / bright moment in the mirror" and "share each other's / face" (58). Even aging and aged women continue their dialogues with the glass. As a widow in an Elizabeth Jolley novel comments, "I must say I like a mirror, . . . it's company, isn't it" (57). In *Crampton Hodnet,* Barbara Pym describes a resilient old lady of nearly eighty taking "a little mirror out of her reticule" at a tea party (120). "Even in my coffin, I should hate to look dreary," announces a woman in Ellen Glasgow's *Vein of Iron* to her face in the glass (327).

Some fictive women approach the mirror gently and sensuously, like Kitty, in Rebecca West's *The Return of the Soldier,* who bends "over her image in her hand-mirror as one might bend for refreshment over scented flowers" (15). Others become fierce, even cruel, as they stare at themselves. According to M. J. Farrell in *Mad Puppetstown,* "It is in cloak rooms that a strange streak of the savage comes uppermost in the female. Here is revealed her deepest buried, most primitive resolve—the resolve towards beauty. A woman's beloved friend may sink dying and ignored in the queue for a cloak-room mirror, while in any other place she would be mourned with every fantastic circumstance of grief" (216–17).

Female characters view themselves in various kinds of mirrors. They peer at their reflections in wavy-surfaced mirrors, examine themselves from every angle in swinging mirrors, nod to their faces in silver-backed hand glasses, twirl in front of triple mirrors. They regard themselves in the demoralizing glasses in ladies' rooms. They lean close to mirrors studded with incandescent bulbs. Passing shops, they catch glimpses of themselves in polished panes. They pull thin rectangular mirrors out of their pocketbooks. They use windows as dark mirrors when the daylight dies. They inspect themselves in convex pier glasses that, as Margaret Atwood points out in *The Handmaid's Tale*, bulge outward like eyes under pressure (49). They discover that there are "good" and "bad" mirrors. Leonora's fruitwood mirror in Pym's *The Sweet Dove Died* is a flattering one: "The glass had some slight flaw in it, and if she placed it in a certain light she saw looking back at her the face of a woman from another century, fascinating and ageless" (87). On the other hand, the glass in poor Miss Bolby's room in Laura Talbot's *The Gentlewomen* is "a mean sort of mirror, singularly unflattering; spots, brown constellations that transfixed themselves on to the face, were splashed across its surface" (1). Even when Miss Bolby leaves the boarding house and accepts a post as governess at Rushford Hall, she is dogged by blemished looking glasses: "it was not a good mirror. . . . there were smudges; she tried to efface them with a corner of *The Times*" (51). Some characters gaze at themselves in small mirrors and yearn for large ones; some do just the opposite—or wish for no mirrors at all. A young girl in F. Tennyson Jesse's *The Lacquer Lady* looks into a "ridiculous little postage-stamp" of a glass and longs "for the day when she would be able to see herself full length in a great mirror with a gilt frame" (69). In contrast, Colette's aging courtesan Léa in *Chéri* plans to replace the large looking glasses in her bedroom with painted panels. At the end of the novel, however, the mirrors remain; Léa watches "an old woman" repeating her movements in the long pier glass and wonders "what she could have in common with that crazy creature" (130). Some characters use more than one glass, like the actress from a James McCourt story who scans her face "reiterated to the vanishing point" in a mirror set up against an opposite mirror, "creating the endless-passage effect she'd favored since childhood" (23–24). Or like the Vicar's youngest daughter in May Sinclair's *The Three Sisters*, who, allowed to use her father's full-length looking glass only twice in every two years, sneaks into the Vicar's bedroom and experiments lavishly with both the long glass *and* his large and perfect hand glass (88–89).

Of course, when a character feels the need for a mirror, she can make any smooth, reflecting surface serve. A stark naked teen-ager in Margaret Drabble's *Jerusalem the Golden* stands and stares at her watery image in a wet tiled floor. She is truly moved by the sight of herself from this "unexpected angle"—especially by the view of "the undersides of her breasts, never before seen" (58). In Elizabeth Taylor's *Blaming*, a woman picks up a spoon that has fallen off the salt-cellar and studies her reflection "longways, sideways, convexly, concavely" (77). One of Joyce Carol Oates's adolescents in her novella "A Sentimental Education" tries to look at herself in a knife blade.[2] It is a brass bedwarmer hanging beside a fireplace that allows a girl in a Jean Stafford short story to observe her face (409). The female molecular geneticist in Perri Klass's *Recombinations* "likes seeing herself in the polished metal side of a lab refrigerator, or in the shiny door of an incubator" (13). Jean Rhys describes a young nun from Ireland "looking at herself in a cask of water, smiling to see if her dimples were still there" (46). In *The Curate's Wife* by Emily Hilda Young, a woman stares in a dark cistern at her pale face "as though she could wrest from it some solacing wisdom, or as though she must take the message it had come to give her" (222). Kitchens and pantries do not normally contain mirrors, but bright surfaces can almost always be discovered there. Jean, in Jayne Anne Phillips's *Machine Dreams*, watches "her reflection hover over a single yellow plate" in a glass cupboard (115). In Wolitzer's *Hearts*, Linda scrutinizes her semblance in a toaster and in the black glass door of the wall oven. Another character in the same novel holds her teaspoon up, "seeking her own tiny inverted reflection in its bowl" (283). To seek one's image in a spoon is to

2. This act is a sign of the character's emotional disturbance, but a recent issue of *Mademoiselle* (August 1985) advises its female readers, "If you're out to dinner and want to check for an eye-makeup or lipstick smudge, be discreet! No one will notice if you use the blade of your knife as a mirror!"

seek a warped reflection, but, for some women, even a distorted representation is better than none. Certain women, of course, are always prepared for confrontation. Fay Moon in Humphreys's *Dreams of Sleep* has a mirror on the kitchen cabinet, "one of many that she keeps in the apartment, at least one mirror in every room" (19).

Even without taking such precautions, characters with a strong mirror compulsion usually manage to find a mirror wherever they are—and not just in the domestic female world of the kitchen but in the masculine world of war and its trophies. Little Pearl and her mother in Nathaniel Hawthorne's *The Scarlet Letter* study themselves in the burnished breastplate of a suit of armor hanging in the central hall of the Governor's mansion. At Auschwitz, in the Commandant's house, a young Polish woman in William Styron's *Sophie's Choice* gazes deeply "at her duplicate self" in "the protuberant glass eyeballs" of an antlered stag (481). Walking into the hardware section of a large store, a character in Wolitzer's *In the Palomar Arms* finds "a saw blade in which she can see her reflection" (282). If a mirror cannot be found, one can be created. When Tess's mother is dressing her daughter to send her off to work for the d'Urbervilles in Thomas Hardy's novel, she handily converts a window into a looking glass: "Mrs. Durbeyfield hung a black cloak outside the casement, and so made a large reflector of the panes, as is the wont of bedecking cottagers to do" (40). Because the panes are both a window and a mirror, they suggest that Tess is embarking on a double journey into the world and into herself.

The relationships of actual women with their mirrors are just as complex as those of fictional characters. Maud Gonne's biographer, Samuel Levenson, explains that although the adolescent Maud "refused to attend the special class given to instruct debutantes how to curtsy and manage their trains, she spent hours practicing in private before the long mirror in her room" (23).[3] According to French actress Jeanne Moreau, Lillian Gish put a mirror next to the camera when she worked in silent films so she could study her own close-ups (6). In *An Unfinished Woman*, Lillian

3. Perhaps this is what Yeats had in mind when he recommended (in "Discoveries") that an awkward girl learn "before all else the heroic discipline of the looking-glass" (270).

Hellman remembers her visits to the house of a great dancer "who, wherever she sat, always faced a mirror, her eyes unwavering" (155). The ballerina Gelsey Kirkland reveals in her autobiography how difficult it is "to resist the habit of the mirror" (72). Every chapter of her story finds her embarking on yet "another round of warfare with the looking glass" (169). Throughout the early phases of her career, the glass becomes "seductive to the point of addiction" (72). Later, when the dancer descends into cocaine abuse, she still leans over a mirror as she inhales lines of white crystals. Virginia Woolf suffered all her life from what she terms in "A Sketch of the Past" her "looking-glass shame" (68). At the other extreme is the flamboyant Violet Trefusis, who delighted in looking glasses and, according to her biographers Philippe Jullian and John Phillips, collected magnificent mirrors "surrounded with colored Venetian glass, with silver Stuart frames, with mahogany Chippendale pagodas" (83). Simone de Beauvoir and Anaïs Nin both write about their interchanges with the glass at every stage of their lives. We are not surprised when a young man pastes a small piece of mirror between Nin's eyes: "Your third eye," he calls it (*Diary* 4: 47).

And what about intriguing mixtures of fact and fiction? Did Elizabeth I actually order that all the looking glasses around her be covered so that she could not see her ruined face? Or are we just confusing history with Bette Davis screaming, in *The Private Lives of Elizabeth and Essex*, "Break every mirror in the palace! I never want to see one in Whitehall again!" The "real" Ana de Mendoza y de la Cerda, princess of Eboli and duchess of Pastrana, born in 1540, lost an eye in a duel when she was fourteen. Alone in the night, did she, as Kate O'Brien writes in her historical novel *That Lady*, take off her black diamond patch and stare "in the mirror at her hungry, long face, so halved and split into blankness, and at the closed and dark-stained empty socket of her eye" (129)? Michael Korda claims that his novel *Queenie* is a work of fiction, but we all know that he is the nephew of Merle Oberon. Is it an imagined creature or the movie star herself who learns to analyze her extraordinary beauty in front of magnifying mirrors: "She searched endlessly for flaws and found few, self-absorbed in a task that was almost as fascinating as sex, and not always easily distinguishable from it" (259). And how many modern authors who write extensively about their central characters' experiences while gazing in the glass—Margaret Atwood, Margaret Drabble, Gail Godwin, Erica Jong, Doris Lessing, Alison Lurie, Katherine Mansfield, Sylvia Plath, May Sarton, Elizabeth Taylor, Antonia White—are describing an archetype of female self-consciousness in which they themselves share, as does much of their audience? Are most women caught, to borrow a phrase from Allen Tate, "in the deep suspension of the looking-glass" (38)? "Captured," as Simone de Beauvoir writes in *The Second Sex*, "in the motionless, silvered trap" (701)? Are we all daughters of Milton's Eve, whose initial act on earth was to bend over the still water and gaze upon the first "herself"?

In the following chapters, I attempt to substantiate my conviction that an understanding of mirror scenes in literature will tell us much about feminine consciousness in its relation to body and to world. Through the mirror, we can gain insight into the reciprocal interchanges between interiority and exteriority as these create what a woman is to herself and to her culture. The reflection in the glass is at once both the self and a radical otherness, an image privileged with a truth beyond the subjective and at the same time taken to be the very essence of that subjectivity. Defined biologically, a female is not, of course, a creature who looks into mirrors. And there are women who have created themselves outside the world established by the glass through what they do as workers, as mothers, as artists. Yet in European culture for at least the last two centuries a female self as a social, psychological, and literary phenomenon is defined, to a considerable degree, as a visual image and structured, in part, by continued acts of mirroring. Many women have accepted such definitions, and as a result their self-identities have an exteriority—and hence a vulnerability—greater than masculine egos. What women do with mirrors is clearly distinct from and psychically more important than what men do with mirrors in their pursuit of generally utilitarian goals. I think it is significant that in my search for mirror scenes I have found precious few in which men use the mirror for acts of self-scrutiny. Men look at their faces and their bodies, but what they *are* is another matter entirely—ultimately, a transcendental concept of self. To refer again to Plath's poem with which I began, women explore the reaches of the mirror for what they really are.

The French psychoanalyst Jacques Lacan has drawn attention to mirroring as an essential part of the early formation of self-consciousness. His "mirror stage" begins in the first eighteen months of childhood when the infant recognizes "as such his own image in a mirror" (1). The child is thereby initiated into a "primordial form" of the "symbolic matrix," and his fragmentary sense of his own bodily presence starts to coalesce into a unitary concept of identity (2). This mirror phase, however, is for Lacan a single, originary event. I have found that, for women, mirroring is not a stage but a continual, ever shifting process of self-realization. And while the self-other paradox inherent in the catoptric experience bears a structural parallel with Lacan's sense of the unavoidable alienations of self-consciousness, I have based my discussions of self-division on a broad historical context reaching back to Plotinus.[4] Perhaps this approach lacks some of the political punch of a study directed by a more single-minded ideology, but such a perspective would not be sufficiently responsive to the wide variety of texts considered here.

The organization of this book is, I hope, self-explanatory in the main. I have purposely excluded from my study the generally allegorical presentations of the mirror in Medieval and Renaissance literature in order to concentrate on the presence of the glass in nineteenth- and twentieth-century works. Most of these texts are products of and reflect upon European and American culture. Further, most of the characters are middle or upper middle class and heterosexual; and although I make use of a few important examples beyond these parameters, I am not attempting to extend my conclusions about female psychology into other cultures and times. Although selective quotations could be marshaled to produce a sense of historical development, I have found a surprising continuity in the uses of the mirror topos over the last one hundred and fifty years. One might expect a diminishing of the mirror's importance in this century, but some of the most important revolts against the mirror and what it represents appear in Victorian nov-

4. I deal with this concept and its historical background in Chapter 2. I have made no attempt to juxtapose my own views on ego formation and deformation with Lacan's very different outlook.

els, while some of the female characters most subservient to its powers are inventions of our own times. Accordingly, chapters are divided conceptually, not chronologically, with each centering upon a different pattern in the ratios of dominance between the woman and the glass. In the first three chapters I demonstrate the importance of mirroring as a literary motif and begin an investigation of the mirror's complex duality, with an emphasis on those women who identify intensely with their reflections. The fourth chapter presents a consideration of the temporal dimension of the glass and its different uses at various stages of a female's life. In the next two chapters I move to the other half of the mirror's double nature and explore what happens when women fail to recognize their own images. While disruptions of the normative self/reflection equation often signal profound psychic disturbances (Chapter 6), a willful dissociation can also constitute a revolt against the mirror and the patriarchal values it has so frequently represented (Chapter 7). Many of the catoptric confrontations treated throughout the book raise questions about how an ocular reflection can act as a sign. This general theoretical issue becomes the core of Chapter 8. It is only in very recent times that we witness a significant historical shift in approaches to the mirror, a development I examine in the final chapter. This revisionary return to the looking glass maps out the way women can use its exteriority as a means for constructing a feminist and nonpatriarchal consciousness incorporating body into mind.

I have taken my examples from a liberal range of literary forms, extending from well-known classics to contemporary self-help books, and a few of these have required quotation at length. Some readers may find that this potpourri pays insufficient heed to qualitative differences, but the full investigation of my subject requires a broad base and a hermeneutics that emphasizes the values and pleasures of variety more than a rush to aesthetic judgment. My methodology is inductive and eclectic, drawing on several literary, semiotic, and psychological strategies as each proves useful in illuminating different facets of my subject. Although broadly feminist in perspective, this book was not written according to any ideological agenda. I have included several important male writers who have spoken to the issues at hand. To ignore their contribution, or to segregate them into a separate section, would equate gender differences among authors with differences among their female characters. The actual patterns of differences and similarities would only be disguised by such easy classifications. I have also intermingled fictive women and real women, and I fear that advocates of the (old) New Criticism might charge me with treating the former as if they were the latter. I would claim, rather, that I am dealing with both types as texts, for the "self," whether historical or fictive, is treated as a semiotic phenomenon in the context of this book.[5] Although I maintain the commonsensical distinction between "real" women and fictive characters, and ultimately grant importance to fictions because they reveal how we represent life, all selves are known to us only through signifying media. Indeed, even the knowledge of one's own self is dependent upon the silent narratives of consciousness, those stories we tell ourselves to become ourselves.

I focus throughout the book on women in front of real mirrors, and not on the mirror as a metaphor for acts not requiring the physical presence of the glass.[6] In a few cases, women look into magic mirrors, and some of these encounters are within the frame of my study. There are, however, some notable literary uses of the mirror, including Lewis Carroll's *Through the Looking-Glass*, omitted here. Although Carroll offers us a mirror, he does not provide the other crucial element—a female looking into it and thinking about how she looks and who she is.

My interest in this subject has been stimulated by several tantalizing studies that have touched upon women before their mirrors. In *The Second Sex*, Simone de Beauvoir was one of the first critics to treat the matter seriously. Patricia Meyer Spacks's *The Female Imagination* contains concise and suggestive analyses of mir-

5. For a more traditional claim that the real and the fictive are a seamless fabric, see Katherine Dalsimer, *Female Adolescence: Psychoanalytic Reflections on Literature*. Relying on the mimetic and representational powers of language, Dalsimer writes that "a work of literature that continues to be read—for other than historical or scholarly interest—must resonate with enduring features of psychological reality" (3).

6. The topic of the mirror as metaphor and emblem in the Middle Ages and Renaissance has been dealt with extensively in such studies as those by Herbert Grabes and Frederick Goldin. Grabes includes a synoptic listing of mirror titles from the thirteenth century to the end of the seventeenth century in English literature.

ror scenes involving a few famous women, both real and fictive. Another predecessor is Anne Hollander's chapter "Mirrors" in *Seeing through Clothes*. Hers is primarily a study of the pictorial arts, but some of the methodology that Hollander develops is relevant to my literary investigations. Also of importance are the many recent critical studies that do not mention mirrors but are deeply concerned with the self-reflexive artifact and the metaphysics of presence. While these theoretical perspectives have to some extent shaped my own, I have tried not to impose them on my materials but rather to allow general considerations of self-consciousness and its semiotic habits to evolve out of the engagement with specific texts.

1.

Powers of the Mirror

One night the mirror people invaded
the earth.
Jorge Luis Borges

In *The Devil's Dictionary*, Ambrose Bierce writes, "To men a man is but a mind. Who cares / What face he carries or what form he wears? / But woman's body is the woman" (15). Let us assume that the devil's definition has a truth to tell, and that in some important ways women in Western culture have been defined—have even defined themselves—in a more visual, material, and outward way than have men. One method for testing this hypothesis is to study how women relate to their images in mirrors, those tools so useful for the literal representation of one's physical presence. Do women find in their mirror images more than an accurate but ultimately inconsequential exteriority? Do they find a power in the glass which transforms it into a vehicle of self-representation, even self-creation? In European literature through the eighteenth century, a woman looking in a mirror only rarely escapes its traditional emblematic meaning—vanity. But, in the works of a few acute novelists in the nineteenth century, we find writers investigating more than the Vanitas motif: we begin to see the psychological processes that come into play when a woman looks in the glass.

In George Eliot's *The Mill on the Floss* (1860), pretty Lucy Deane manages to come upon a mirror shortly after a visit from the man who is courting her: ". . . and you will not, I hope, consider it an indication of vanity predominating over more tender impulses, that she just glanced in the chimney-glass as her walk brought her near it. The desire to know that one has not looked an absolute fright during a few hours of conversation, may be construed as lying within the bounds of a laudable benevolent consideration for others. And Lucy had so much of this benevolence in her nature that I am inclined to think her small egoisms were impregnated with it . . ." (322). Lucy's glancing in the chimney-glass is not an act of vanity because Eliot, with her penetrating insight, realizes that it is male society that has promoted that emblematic meaning of looking in a mirror, and the author understands the far more intricate and complex roles a mirror plays in the process of recognition, identity, and self-consciousness. Eliot explicitly directs us *not* to read this scene in the traditional way established by hundreds of years of male-dominated literature and art. Lucy is indeed asking—how do I look and how have I looked?—but Eliot suggests that a woman can glance in a mirror for that purpose without being vain. Lucy's interest is in finding out how she appeared to someone else who is important to her. The vain woman who looks in a mirror (to apply makeup, for instance) does it before the confrontation with the male world; here, Lucy looks in after the encounter. Her act is more momentary and more subtle than the result of personal satisfaction. It addresses the issues of self-conception and the recovery of information about how other people have conceived of her. This is a very gentle and tender passage. It does admit Lucy's "small egoisms," but the whole activity is filled with something other and more than vanity. And sweet Lucy's little egoisms become part of her charm—like her little mouth, her little hands, even her silly little dog.

The Italian novelist Sibilla Aleramo presents a far less benign scene in *A Woman* (1906). The young narrator and her father are dressed and ready to leave for an important dinner: "But Mother hovered in front of the mirror. . . . She was passing the powder-puff across her face over and over again, when father, irritated by the delay, appeared once more in the doorway to their room. I can still hear, quivering in the air, a phrase hurled like a knife: 'Must I conclude, then, that you are nothing but a flirt?'" (18). The man thinks that all his wife is doing before the mirror is creating a superficial, flirtatious appearance that is denigrating her by giving so much attention to this shallow activity and delaying matters of more import. But for the woman, this time in front of the glass is her preparation of her identity—not to flirt with someone, but to take possession of her sense of self. It is an instructive moment for the girl who is learning a decided difference between male and female. This incident also exemplifies how men in this masculine world use women's interest in the mirror to criticize and subjugate them, to brand their use of the mirror as purely a matter of vanity and flirtatiousness.

But men also desire what they censure. When the narrator in Aleramo's novel is fourteen, she states, "It was my father who first made me examine myself anxiously in the mirror. One evening I heard him say to himself, in joy and amazement, 'She's going to be a beauty . . .'" (28). The two responses of the father—one to criticize the mother, the other as a means to create the daughter—show two significant sides of the male view of the glass. Further, the mirror plays a major intermediary role between the girl's relationship with the father and her relationship with other males. The "beauty" she will become is defined by men, at first by her father, and later by suitors, lovers, and even anonymous strangers. Since this latter group may not be as straightforward as the father in proclaiming—and thus creating—the girl's beauty, she must consult the mirror, compare the image with social norms, and thereby test her beauty against an instrument offering full (although silent) disclosure. The glass will always be there as the father—to reassure or criticize.

Beyond vanity, and even beyond social definition, the mirror can reflect and project an otherworldly ideal. The "world" in W. B. Yeats's "Before the World Was Made" is a temporal, fallen place in which beautiful women grow old. Applying makeup before the mirror, the speaker strives to become even more lovely than she already is. She displays not pride but a quest for a transcendent beauty. Her performance before the glass is almost neo-Platonic, for her pursuit of a beautiful face is not the worship of self but the worship of an ideal:

> If I make the lashes dark
> And the eyes more bright
> And the lips more scarlet,
> Or ask if all be right
> From mirror after mirror,
> No vanity's displayed:

I'm looking for the face I had
Before the world was made. (266)

This woman is also very much the artist who, like Yeats in some of his aesthetic moods, aims at perfection. The woman's physiognomy is but a shadow version of the perfect face of beauty. She wants men who love her to love the idealization she can contemplate and work toward before her glass. The phrase "From mirror after mirror" gives a sense of the process of striving after the ideal. The continuation of the attempt shows the dedication of the artist. This stanza in its stateliness—as well as in the ideas it invokes—is beautiful, optimistic, and hieratic. Nature by definition is fallen and can be redeemed or overcome only through artifice, a product of the transcendent imagination.

Since the self, like Yeats's ideal face, is never fully achieved, it is necessary to look in the glass to see how one is doing in the process of constantly reinventing the self. Others may assume that the person looking in the mirror is doing so out of vanity, but this is not always the case. Carrie Meeber in Theodore Dreiser's *Sister Carrie* (1900) possesses "an innate taste for imitation" (117). She spends a great deal of time in front of mirrors, but she is not just adoring herself, as her lover Charles Drouet thinks; she is creating herself out of an implicit theory of mimesis. Drouet believes that Carrie frequently admires herself in the mirror, but she is actually "recalling some little grace of the mouth or of the eyes which she had witnessed in another. Under his airy accusation she mistook this for vanity and accepted the blame with a faint sense of error, though, as a matter of fact, it was nothing more than the first subtle outcroppings of an artistic nature, endeavouring to re-create the perfect likeness of some phase of beauty which appealed to her" (117). Carrie, unlike the woman in Yeats's poem, is not the artist but the artifact. The self that is doing the creating has no existence independent of those things she imitates and follows.

When women of the nineteenth and twentieth centuries look in mirrors, it is not—essentially or necessarily—an act of vanity. Sometimes, as in Nancy Mitford's *The Pursuit of Love* (1945), it is from an almost opposite emotion. As adolescents, Polly Hampton and Linda Radlett are already trained in the knowledge that it is the relationship with the mirror which is preeminent. After sneaking away from home one afternoon to visit some undergraduates at Oxford, they stop in a ladies room to check their rather rudimentary attempts at applying cosmetics: "We gazed and gazed, hoping thus, in some magical way, to make ourselves feel less peculiar. Presently we did a little work with damp handkerchiefs, and toned our faces down a bit. We then sallied forth into the streets, looking at ourselves in every shop window that we passed" (70). Mitford adds, parenthetically, "I have often noticed that when women look at themselves in every reflection, and take furtive peeps into their hand looking-glasses, it is hardly ever, as is generally supposed, from vanity, but much more often from a feeling that all is not quite as it should be" (70). The sense of repeated gazing at oneself, and of the relation between mirroring and the attitudes a woman has toward her self, distinguishes the modern woman of the mirror from the vain females of the emblematic tradition. A brief passage from Margaret Atwood's poem "Marrying the Hangman" states plainly the centrality of mirroring in the formation of female identity. A woman has been put in jail and is "living selflessly": "To live in prison is to live without mirrors. To live without mirrors is to live without the self" (49).[1] Rather than dismiss Atwood's proposition as idiosyncratic, or accept it as a truism, we need to test it against other texts and attempt to discover how and why mirrors can take on such an extraordinarily important role in women's lives.

Margaret Drabble's 1977 novel *The Ice Age* reveals the way mirrors can fulfill some of the same functions as society in the creation of a self. Alison Murray has always lived in a world where people corroborated her sense of identity. But now she has had to fly to some obscure Balkan country behind the Iron Curtain because her teen-age daughter has been arrested for dangerous driving. For hours Alison has been sitting on a hard chair, waiting to see a

1. See also Atwood's recent novel *The Handmaid's Tale* (1986). It is set in the future in a grim, restrictive society ruled by men. Almost all of the mirrors in this world have been removed entirely or, in a few cases, replaced with "oblongs of dull gray metal" (72). Within the political dynamics of this visionary allegory, the imposed absence of mirrors is part of the male regime's subjection of women. In the play "Pandora's Box" by German dramatist Frank Wedekind (1864–1918), a female prisoner does manage to use the back of a new dustpan as a mirror. "The tin didn't flatter me," she reports, "but it did me good all the same. . . . One feels so frightened when one hasn't seen oneself for months" (124).

psychiatrist whom she hopes to persuade to visit her daughter in a prison hospital. She is not used to being ignored, and she must do something "to maintain her own status in her own eyes" (53). She takes her powder compact out of her handbag, opens it, and looks at herself in the small oval mirror: "There she still was. But Alison found . . . that there was very little kick left in her own face. It was still there, but it didn't do much for her. She put the compact back in her bag, and went on waiting" (53). In this strange, hostile country where no one confirms her sense of ego, Alison falls back on that always available, useful tool for the reaffirmation of her identity. Lacking a social context in which Alison can use the reaction of others to determine the quality of her individual presence, she substitutes her mirror for such a world and, quite literally, measures "her own status" with "her own eyes." "There she still was"—not just physically, but psychologically. Yet this experience has started to shake the foundations of her self-possession.

The one thing humans always try to cling to—even in sickness or old age—is this sense of self. Someone who is seriously ill and is losing touch with the world still tries to maintain an identity. Even as a person is losing language (a primary medium of interchange between oneself and the world), even then, at that extreme moment of loss, he or she desperately grasps for self-conception. In Hilma Wolitzer's *Hearts* (1980), Linda's mother has suffered a major stroke that has impaired her speech and makes it difficult for her to name familiar objects: "Wanting a mirror, her mother had drawled, 'White flash,' and then, not understood, had grown angry. 'Ohhh, face box!' she cried. Linda ran around the room bringing the wrong things: comb, magazines, handkerchief, water, becoming as frantic as her mother" (165). This woman "who was losing the names of the things in the world" wants that crucial tool for self-definition—the "white flash," the "face box," the mirror.

"The Flight of Betsey Lane" (1893), a short story by Sarah Orne Jewett, is about an old woman who lives in a poorhouse. One day she receives a visit from a member of the family in whose household she used to work:

> "Is there anything I can do for you?" asked Mrs. Strafford kindly. . . .
>
> "Yes, there is one thing, darlin'. If you could stop in the village

> an' pick me out a pritty, little, small lookin'-glass, that I can keep for my own an' have to remember you by. . . . that's the only thing I feel cropin' about." (190)

The mirror is associated with Betsey Lane's sense of identity; she can use it not only "to remember" Mrs. Strafford, but also to remember herself. The one thing she chooses to have, to own, is a looking glass, that instrument for self-possession and creation even when other media and points of reference begin to fail.

The importance of the role assumed by mirrors in some versions of female consciousness can be defined more distinctly through contrast with masculine uses of the mirror. Shakespeare's King Henry V states most succinctly and clearly the traditional male attitude toward the mirror. In his blunt wooing of Kate ("I speak to thee plain soldier"), he describes himself as "a fellow . . . that never looks in his glass for love of any thing he sees there" (*Henry V*, 5.2.147–48). Henry associates his mirror with directness and honesty. A man, he suggests, does not define himself through the image in the glass, or look in it because of vanity. This common notion is not just descriptive, but often prescriptive: a man *should* not define himself through mirrors. Dependable Harold Eastwood (L. P. Hartley, *A Perfect Woman*, 1955), traveling by train on business, is representative of this view: "He put aside his dispatch-case and looked out of the window, but the November murk pressed so thick and close against it that he could see little but his own reflection. . . . Harold, as conventional as his face, had been told in childhood that a man should never be caught studying his reflection in a glass and he . . . turn[ed] away" (4). The temporary lapse is an indulgence in an essentially feminine activity. Accordingly, the voice of male consciousness, instilled in Harold at an early age as part of his socialization as a "man," calls him back to his proper role.

The speaker in Alan Dugan's poem "The Mirror Perilous" visits the "Garden of Love." He informs us that there is a sign by the central pond that reads: "Property of Narcissus. / Trespass at your own risk":

> I looked in that famous mirror perilous
> and it wasn't much: my own face,

> beautiful, and at the bottom,
> bone, a rusty knife, two beads,
> and something else I cannot name. . . .
> I could take it or leave it, go or stay,
> and went back to the office drunk,
> possessed of an echo but not a fate. (35)

The speaker converts the mirror into a window, the reverse of what we will find women doing. He looks through the reflection to the bottom of the pool and not at that paradoxical image which is both self and other. "I could take it or leave it," he says, indicating that the mirror is not essential to him, the reflection not something that fates a certain self-conception.

When a man stands before a mirror, he is usually there for a practical purpose. For example, the speakers in Robert Graves's "The Face in the Mirror" (1958) and in Christopher Isherwood's *A Single Man* (1964) are both shaving. The person revealed in the glass in Graves's poem is, not surprisingly, a self created elsewhere. His face preserves a "record" of his archetypally masculine exploits, such as "low tackling" in football matches and "old-world fighting." One brow droops "because of a missile fragment still inhering" (339). These past events constitute the vale of self-making for the man. Looking at himself in the glass can offer a way of checking on the physiognomic record of the history through which the man has come into his present being, but is not itself part of the process of self-production.[2] The speaker in Graves's poem refers to himself in the first person. In contrast, he addresses his reflection as "the mirrored man" and refers to that figure as "he." The dissociation between identity and image, signaled by the third-person pronoun, holds a quite different meaning for a man from the one it holds for a woman. As we shall see,

2. John Ashbery's "Self-Portrait in a Convex Mirror" is I believe another, albeit highly complex, example of this type of male use of the mirror. Although he begins with, and sporadically returns to, a man looking into a mirror, this act very quickly becomes a metaphor for the relations between signs (preeminently paintings and texts) as outer surfaces and personalities (the products of memory and interior experience) as depths. Ashbery uses the mirror metaphor ("The surface is what's there / And nothing can exist except what's there" [70]) within deconstructive turns against depth, but such eruptions of otherness and nothingness are equally corrosive of *any* concepts of the mirror as a scene of self-creation.

when a woman feels a disunity between herself and the image in the mirror, it is often a sign of revolt or the beginning of a psychological disorientation. For a male, the split is normative.

The protagonist of *A Single Man* speaks of his body and everything revealed in the glass as other than himself. Using the mirror as a practical tool, he is not involved in an act of ego formation, but an act of preparation for others. At the beginning of Isherwood's novel, George's body "levers itself out of bed," "shambles" into the bathroom, empties its bladder, and "then to the mirror":

> What it sees there isn't so much a face as the expression of a predicament. Here's what it has done to itself, here's the mess it has somehow managed to get itself into during its fifty-eight years. . . .
>
> Staring and staring into the mirror, it sees many faces within its face—the face of the child, the boy, the young man, the not-so-young man—all present still, preserved like fossils on superimposed layers, and, like fossils, dead. (7–8)

George sees a face that is an expression of a particular life history. But that face has been created through a man's activities that have no intimate connection with the physical act of mirroring per se. The mirror is used merely as a tool to see the exterior evidence of an immaterial being we call "character" or "personality." There is no implication that the reflection (or even the face) *is* the character or the personality or the self. The external presence registered by the glass can never be more than a sign of a reality which is within, but different in kind from, that sign. What is remarkable, then, about so many women in front of mirrors is that the image in the glass *is* the character, the personality, the soul.

There is no doubt for a moment in John Updike's poem "Mirror" that the mirror image is not the self:

When you look   kool uoy nehW
into a mirror   rorrim a otni
it is not   ton si ti
yourself you see,   ,ees uoy flesruoy
but a kind   dnik a tub
of apish error   rorre hsipa fo
posed in fearful   lufraef ni desop
symmetry.   .yrtemmys (77)

The reversed half of the poem indicates the meaninglessness of the catoptric experience. It is no accident that male poets, such as Updike, Jonathan Swift, and Byron, rhyme "mirror" with "error," since for them the glass does not directly reveal the self. For the female poet, such as Sylvia Plath, "mirror" corresponds with "terror."[3] When she looks into a mirror it is herself she sees and, if it is not, then she experiences a sense of fear, not of fallacy. For her, the mirror *is* "perilous."

There are, of course, some male characters in literature who use mirrors in a way our culture defines as feminine. In Olive Schreiner's *The Story of an African Farm* (1883), Gregory Rose is a young Englishman who has been working for about six months on a Boer farm in South Africa. He sits down to write a letter to his sister, to whom he always writes when he is miserable. First he takes up a white sheet of paper, but then decides that pink is more suitable to "the state of his feelings." He begins:

> MY DEAR JEMIMA,—
>
> Then he looked up into the little glass opposite. It was a youthful face reflected there, with curling brown beard and hair; but in the dark blue eyes there was a look of languid longing that touched him. He re-dipped his pen and wrote:
>
> *When I look up into the little glass that hangs opposite me, I wonder if that changed and sad face—*
>
> Here he sat still and reflected. It sounded almost as if he might be conceited or unmanly to be looking at his own face in the glass. (175)

The fact that the young man's relation to the mirror includes a sense of the otherness of the image in the glass establishes a typically masculine attitude, yet there is the hint that he somehow defines himself through that relation. Like the pink paper, his self-contemplation in the mirror reveals a feminine component to his psyche which purely practical uses of the mirror would not suggest. Because of this passage, we are not terribly surprised that in a later chapter, titled "Gregory's Womanhood," the young man actually dresses up in women's clothing to disguise himself as a nurse: "He drew from his breast pocket a little sixpenny looking-

3. See Swift's "Daphne" (3:907); Byron's *Don Juan*, canto 6, stanza 89; and Plath's "Tale of a Tub" (24).

glass and hung it on one of the roots that stuck out from the bank. Then he dressed himself in one of the old-fashioned gowns and a great pinked-out collar. Then he took out a razor. Tuft by tuft the soft brown beard fell down into the sand, and the little ants took it to line their nests with" (270). The masculine act of shaving is here changed into a process of gender transformation as the male becomes a female—not, of course, biologically, but functionally in his social context. Even the fallen hairs are converted to domestic uses. The presence of the mirror as a special instrument of self-conception or feminization is altogether appropriate, given its gender associations in Western culture.

Susan Sontag has written that men look in mirrors less frequently than women do, for it is women's "duty to look at themselves—to look often. Indeed, a woman who is not narcissistic is considered unfeminine" (34). Sontag's implication that looking into a mirror is a superficial activity overlooks the motivation for the act. Many women sense a "duty" to look at themselves because that is the way they create themselves. Sontag is right when she adds, "Women do not simply have faces as men do" (35). All men *have* faces; many women *are* their faces.

For some women, their consciousness that they exist at all is dependent on seeing themselves in the glass. The absence of the mirror can create an anxiety of nonreflection. In Gwyneth Cravens's short story "Vision" (1975), her character goes down into a subway station. "On the platform she moves from candy machine to candy machine, looking in the mirrors. In the spaces between the mirrors, her whole life falters; she fails, for a few seconds, to exist" (168). Later in the story, the young woman actually states that it is these visits to the candy machine mirrors that "keep her alive" (172). In "the first lonely days" after her breakup with her lover, a twenty-four-year-old woman in Wolitzer's *In the Palomar Arms* (1983) finds herself "going frequently to the mirror, not out of sudden vanity, but to say, see, *I'm* still here" (289). A similar and equally direct statement of this fundamental version of mirror consciousness is presented in Sylvia Plath's *The Bell Jar* (1963): "She stared at her reflection in the glossed shop windows as if to make sure, moment by moment, that she continued to exist" (81–82). A teen-age girl in Judith Rossner's *August* (1983) tells her psychiatrist, "I had a friend . . . who took acid and looked in the mirror and couldn't see her own reflection. That's the most terrifying thing that ever happened to anyone" (95).[4] Such experiences can be just as horrific when the absence of self-reflection results from merely mechanical difficulties, as is dramatized by a twelve-year-old girl in Susan Kenney's *In Another Country* (1984): "I hold my mother's hand mirror over my shoulder and look at my reflection in the full-length mirror in the upstairs hall. But something goes wrong with the angle, and for a moment I can't see myself, only what looks like a hole in the mirror, or a tunnel into it. My stomach goes all cold and splintery as I look down the endless tunnel. *Why, that's eternity*, I think to myself as I stand there, *that's death*" (36). The inability to perceive the reflection, even if only momentary, is here equated with the utter absence of self-presence.

Although all of these characters happen to be young, this self-substantiating dependence on the mirror may be felt by older women too. In her journal *At Seventy,* May Sarton remembers her friend Jean Dominique telling her that "when she had become too blind to see her own face in a mirror,. . .it was a strange alienation, as though she did not exist because she could no longer meet *herself* as others saw her" (307). The aging female speaker in Horace Gregory's poem "The Postman's Bell Is Answered Everywhere" asks, "Since I'm a woman, . . . / how can I close my eyes before a mirror. . . ?" (104).If she is unmirrored, she will stop being a woman to herself and to the world. The old lady in Edith Sitwell's "Mademoiselle Richarde" is a gray, grim, empty creature who feels nothing. The mirror—the instrument that might permit her to develop an identity—is kept from her. All the looking glasses are

> Placed just beyond her reach for fear that she
> Forget her loneliness, her image see
> Grown concrete, not a ghost by cold airs blown.
> So each reflection blooms there but her own. (143)

4. Compare with a character's nightmare in Elizabeth Taylor's *The Soul of Kindness* (1964). A woman dreams that she walks into the drawing room of her own house, "and the glass over the fireplace was blank when she looked in it. Terror mounted in her" (179). The protagonist of a Penelope Mortimer novel states, "one way of scaring myself stiff is to imagine looking into a mirror and finding no reflection" (7).

Everyone and everything else are presences, but this woman, like a phantom, is not reflected in the mirrors. Thus she does not exist within the realm of human consciousness, not even her own.

These are all extreme examples of mirror consciousness, but it is important to realize that they are extensions of a fundamental paradigm of female self-definition in Western culture. If we define "existence" in a metaphysical sense, then the perception of one's image in a glass cannot literally create that existence. But if we conceive of "being" in a psychological and cultural sense, as existing as a person to oneself and to others—the two modes interdependent—then these women have a perspective which, although exaggerated, is not necessarily pathological. Indeed, as we shall see, the pathology of female self-conception is often signaled not by intense identification with the mirror image but by a fracturing of that relationship.

It is perhaps a commonplace that the culture in which women find their identities, or have those identities imposed on them, is dominated by patriarchal structures and powers. That dominance extends to the mirror. In Hawthorne's *The Scarlet Letter* (1850), Hester Prynne, afraid that her child, Little Pearl, the result of her adultery, may be taken from her, goes with her daughter to the Governor's mansion for an interview. There Hester encounters a gleaming suit of armor and sees herself in "the polished mirror of the breastplate." Because of its convex shape, the mirror greatly exaggerates the size of the scarlet letter on the breast of her gown, and Hester seems "absolutely hidden behind it" (101). Thus, for this reflective exemplar of the masculine, Hester has disappeared behind the classification "Adulteress." Even her self-conception is being subordinated to this social category imposed by males. Earlier in life, Hester looked into the mirror to behold her beauty; now she looks in to observe her sin.[5] What the woman has become is imaged in the parts of this giant mailed male. The mirror reflects a kind of truth, but a truth that must be rejected because it is outwardly but not inwardly true. A revolt of the inner against the outer is Hester's challenge.

Although the mirror is seldom so manifestly and glaringly male

5. When Hester stands on the scaffold of the pillory, she recalls looking into the "dusky mirror" to see her "girlish beauty" (58).

as it is in Hawthorne's scene, over and over we find an identification between the man and the mirror. Sometimes, as in Dreiser's *Sister Carrie*, the male becomes a mirror, telling the female how to compose her outer self. Carrie Meeber leaves home at eighteen. Without money and unable to find a job, she accepts the offer of a "loan" from Charles Drouet, a traveling salesman and man of the world. Drouet buys Carrie some clothes, tells her how to wear them and how pretty she looks under his management, and shows her about the town. Drouet fills Carrie's hours "with sight-seeing," and the main sight she sees is herself through his eyes (58). He acts as a mirror, forcing her to create a new outer self. When she finally looks into an actual mirror, she sees what he has created for his own beholding. Dreiser presents a good example of the continuum between what women perceive in the glass and what the masculine world creates. Because Carrie looks "quite another maiden," she is "quite another maiden" in the eyes of the mirror and the eyes of the man, which are cohorts in their influence on the woman's sense of social and self-identity. Carrie, admiring herself in the glass, feels "her first thrill of power" (58). This feminine power comes through acceptance. Although this kind of female force is always edged with irony, it doesn't make the power any less effective, for it is the potency of weakness and the control that the created may eventually gain over the creator. When Carrie thinks, "Drouet was so good" (58), she realizes that he is "so good" at creating her. She prefers this to her own production, which is nil.

Both the man and the mirror can command the woman, as is demonstrated in Colette's short story "The Judge." Madame de La Hournerie has come home, after devoting half a day to a hairdresser who has talked her into an unaccustomed coiffure. The change precipitates, in this woman's eyes, a veritable destruction of her previous self, and this new person is intensely foreign to her. We see a woman before the glass trying to come to terms with this new self. Will she reject or accept it?

> She took a hand-mirror and admired the large knob of polished hair and the arrow of brilliants at the back of her neck.
>
> "I must say, it's smart," she said aloud to reassure herself. . . . But faced by this lady with the lacquered skull, the slightly sunk-

> en broad cheeks, loose mouth and enlarged nose, she did not recognize herself and felt uneasy. (35–36)

The word "skull" makes it clear that the mirror is revealing something beneath the surface—a presentiment of death. The change this woman made in pursuit of the beautiful and as a way of masking the inevitability of aging has, in this case, resulted in an expression of decay.

When Madame de La Hournerie goes downstairs to dine and her male servant Marien contemplates her with an "indescribable expression of horror and shame" (37), she runs to her triple mirror and orders her maid to make an immediate appointment with the hairdresser. Colette identifies Marien's severe eyes with the power of the looking glass by describing them as "mirrors for soubrettes." What his eyes reflect are women who are obeisant to him—shopgirls and maidservants. But included in that company is the elegant Madame de La Hournerie, for she defers to him as she defers to her mirror. The relation between this servant and the mirror is a similitude approaching identity: he is another mirror having control over her, another representative of the world that creates her by perceiving or reflecting her visual presence.

Even though Marien is a mere servant (like a mirror), he is (also like a mirror) a male. Both have enormous influence. Colette is stressing her point by *not* presenting the male as an authority figure like a father or a husband. Even a man who is a servant has this power of reflection, mental or visual, over Madame de La Hournerie. The image of the new self is so frightening to this woman that one might expect her to revolt against the glass and search for an alternative means of creating herself. But such a recourse does not occur to her and thus she searches for a substitute mirror in Marien. Both the mirror and the servant are masters. Her solution will be through the offices of yet another servant-master, the hairdresser.

At times, the mirror is used as the stand-in for a man or for male-dominated society in general—as in Jane Shapiro's short story "Life without Martin" (1979). When a husband and wife separate because of marital problems, the woman heads for the local shopping mall and begins trying on new clothes:

> I stood in the dressing room watching myself stand around in jeans outfits, marked way down, while on either side of me other women shifted their weight in identical garments. The women intently eyed their own flanks, then looked for long minutes over their shoulders at their own backs, preparatory to going home to husbands. . . .
>
> In half an hour anxiety had risen up in me, but I wrenched myself into forgetfulness, showing the mirror my stuff, kicking higher than the other ladies. . . . Men tossed me fascinated glances like fish to a seal, which I snapped up. (29–30)

The speaker shows her "stuff" to the mirror as she would to a man. The mirror is not just a tool by which one sees one's appearance; the whole revery of herself being looked at by many men evolves out of her looking in a mirror.[6] This mature woman, at a moment of transition, acts out the adolescent performance of trying to please the glass and of becoming both male spectator and female actor in a little drama of self-presentation verging on self-creation.

For the woman in Anne Hébert's *Kamouraska* (1970), the mirror is the presence of the missing man, a supplement required by that absence: "Madame Rolland draws herself up, straightens the pleats in her skirt, smooths back her hair. Over to the mirror, to find her own reflection, her best defense. My soul—my musty, mildewed soul—off somewhere. Held prisoner, far, far away. And yet I'm pretty. Still pretty. Let everything else come falling down around my head, why should I care? One thing is clear. One thing that keeps me going through all the nagging fears, all the horror of my days. To stay pretty forever, for him" (8). Madame Rolland defines herself through her relationship, actual or only hoped for, with a man. To compensate for his absence, she turns to the mirror. It is the glass that tells her she is still pretty, and thus like a male it substantiates her sense of being. The mirror renews her, rejuvenates her psychically: "the mirror, come to life like a bub-

6. A stanza of Erica Jong's "The Girl in the Mirror" (1971) stresses the close identification of the world of mirrors and men: "you are lying in a room / where everything is silver. / The ceiling is mirrored, / the floor is mirrored, / & men come out of the walls" (163). The plural "men" in the final line indicates the social dimension of the mirror, the way it is the stand-in not just for a single and specific man—a lover, a husband—but for those masculine observers in the aggregate who constitute the world at large.

bling spring" (132). Her sense of a nonexterior self, a "soul" not defined visually and in relation to the mirror / man, is vague, distant, and unhelpful in this moment of crisis. If this "soul" exists at all, it too is a "prisoner" of forces outside of and beyond her control.

By the third grade, Sasha Davis, the narrator of Alix Kates Shulman's *Memoirs of an Ex-Prom Queen* (1972), comes to realize that there is only one thing worth bothering about—becoming beautiful. She sits before her three-way mirror studying herself by the hour. At twenty-four, however, she has trouble interpreting the statement the mirror is making. Since she lacks a strong sense of self, she needs more than just the glass to tell her she is beautiful. Further, she thinks it is too late to find some way of defining self other than through appearance. One day she goes to bed with a customer of the New York office where she works as a receptionist. Afterward, he tucks some money into her coat pocket. Sasha is exhilarated by the thought of this money:

> All the way back, my heart pounding in time with the clicking of my heels on the pavement, I kept thinking: *if he thinks I'm beautiful it will be twenty dollars at least.* Twenty struck me as a very large amount. . . .
>
> It was a fifty-dollar bill. I was jubilant. I looked in the mirror. I *am* beautiful, I thought.
>
> But when my customer came back from his lunch a couple of hours later and acted as though he didn't know me, I was quite as uncertain of how I looked as I had been in the morning. There was really no way to tell. (199)

Sasha has had three signifiers of her beauty—the man, the money, the mirror. All are part of, and synecdoches for, the culture that defines this ex-prom queen through its responses to her physical appearance. Sasha needs constant reinforcement since her sense of self is so vulnerable to external forces. When the man doesn't acknowledge her, Sasha's uncertainty over how she looks becomes so profound that neither the money nor the mirror seems sufficient. The chain of mutually supporting signs of her beauty has broken, and she is left without resources for answering the questions of who and what she is.

Tolstoy's Kitty Shcherbatsky is more certain of her beauty than

Sasha is. In *Anna Karenina* (1877), he describes the eighteen-year-old princess as she enters a ballroom and catches sight of herself in a looking glass: "Her eyes sparkled and she could not keep her red lips from smiling at the consciousness of her own attractiveness" (91). A transference takes place in this scene. Kitty does not need actual responses from others. Like all true votaries of the mirror, she believes so strongly in it that, as long as she looks good to herself, it suffices as a realization and registration of what others will see. Such a woman makes two psychological suppositions—that the mirror substitutes for other people and that one is capable of an astounding degree of objectivity. Kitty believes she can evaluate her own mirror image as fairly and dispassionately as the world will evaluate her appearance to determine what she is. She sees the image as the self, yet simultaneously appraises it with the impartiality she brings to the evaluation of things outside the self. People may lie; the mirror—or, more accurately, the girl's radical honesty before the mirror—never lies. The psychological processes are similar to those of artists who must look at their own productions with enormous objectivity.

For many women, how they look is who they are. Astonishingly lovely women always know this. They are aware that they exist *as* shining creatures, that they have no being other than their beauty. Aphrodite is said to have a servant who walks before her carrying a mirror so that she may constantly look at herself. The goddess gazes in the glass not because she is vain, but because she needs to see that she is still beautiful. She only exists for herself (and for the world) as a beautiful being. If the woman totally identifies her center, her self, with her appearance (as Aphrodite does), then her appearance takes on psychological and existential importance. As Laura Riding writes in one of her short stories about a beautiful woman, "If she was at all, she was beautiful; but she was not beautiful, she was not, unless she was known to be beautiful" (135).

It is not just spectacularly attractive women who define themselves through how they look. Many women almost automatically make an equation between self-conception and physical appearance. Sociologist Lillian B. Rubin in *Women of a Certain Age: The Midlife Search for Self* recounts her interviews with 160 women between the ages of thirty-five and fifty-four—"women who come from all walks of life and represent a cross-section of 'women of a certain age' in America today" (11). She asked each of them the following question: "I wonder if you could briefly describe yourself in some way that would give me a good sense of who and what you are?" She reports that most started "with some description of their physical attributes . . . testifying to the primacy of their appearance in their image of self" (54). In some cases, the assumptions implicit in a researcher's questions can reveal as much as the answers. In her book *Unfinished Business: Pressure Points in the Lives of Women*, psychiatric writer Maggie Scarf interviews a woman named Anne. She is trying to find out from Anne what the word *mature* means to her. "What would you look like," she asks, "if you went to your bathroom mirror one morning, and saw yourself as a totally mature and adult person?" (34) Scarf's formulation of her question assumes the validity of the self / mirror-image equation. Many women simply accept this underlying assumption that appearance and something as unphysical as the psychological condition of being an "adult person" are linked.

Because of this exteriority of self-conception, what a woman looks like can become more important than what she feels. Martha in Doris Lessing's *A Proper Marriage* (1952) can "forget how she had *felt* in her previous incarnations, but she could not forget how she had looked" to herself in the mirror (22). Sometimes a woman only knows what she's feeling by seeing in the mirror how she's looking. Edith in Ada Leverson's "Love's Shadow" (1908) takes a walk through her entire flat, going into every room and studying herself in every glass: "She appeared to like herself best in the dining-room mirror, for she returned, stared into it rather gravely for some little time, and then said to herself, 'Yes, I'm beginning to look bored'" (4). Being bored is not essentially a matter of appearance; yet this woman so conceives of herself by and through the mirror that she first realizes her dissatisfaction by seeing the physiognomy of ennui in the glass. There is for Edith no distinction between the self and what she sees in the mirror. Thus she enacts a female abnegation of ego to other: what counts is not how one feels, but how one looks, in the mirror or in the eyes of others.

The image in the mirror can create a significant alteration in self-conception for some women. Leverson describes a small circle of people at a party who are all "most pleasing to the eye" (29).

Especially lovely is a young woman named Hyacinth. "Of course," writes Leverson, "she looked her best. Women always do if they wish to please one man when others are there, and she was in the slightly exalted frame of mind that her reflection in the mirror had naturally given her" (29). Hyacinth's reflection has changed her psychic condition, for the physical form she can observe in the mirror has exalted her "mind." I have not been able to find many scenes in literature in which a man looks into the mirror and by so doing alters the way he thinks or how he structures his identity. But, Leverson implies, this is exactly what happens "naturally" for the woman. Leverson's language goes beyond saying that Hyacinth felt good because she looked good, for the operative faculty is not a personality extrinsic to the mirror but the person in the mirror. It is the "reflection" framed in the glass which has "given," has created, the "frame of mind."

Of course the equation between self-conception and physical appearance can work in the opposite direction. When a woman begins not to look her best, she loses faith in herself. Cate in Gail Godwin's *A Mother and Two Daughters* (1982) sits brushing her hair in front of her dressing table—shortly before her fortieth birthday and shortly after breaking one of her teeth while eating peanut brittle:

> From time to time she looked up, quickly, into the mirror, trying to catch sight of the old hag who awaited her somewhere on the other side of forty; and then she wondered if she were deluding herself, out of sheer familiarity with her own face, that she still looked good.
>
> She opened her mouth, revealing the new hole; there, now she looked less good. . . . There was nothing like a lost tooth, or even a piece of one, to remind you that Old Father Time was chip-chipping away at the cherished edifice of self. (77–78)

For the last word of the last sentence, one might think that "body" or "face" or "appearance" would suffice, but the word "self" is chosen. Although it is tied to appearance, "self" means more than just face. When Cate sees her looks growing unpleasant, she realizes that the "edifice of self" has been eroded. Identities are constructed in and through experience and, for this woman, in front of and by mirrors. Since Cate's awareness of her body was an important part of the construction of that edifice, the broken tooth, the symbol of the decay of the body, means that the ego is harmed, or at least there is a prophecy of harm. The verb "chip-chipping" is continuous. The discrete event (chip) is part of an unremitting process eating away at this self she has created. Cate's is not just a dental difficulty, but a transcendental one which reveals the potential powers that the mirror has over many women, fictive and real. They have given to the glass, to an exterior object, an extraordinary degree of control over their self-conceptions.

Godwin's movement from exterior appearance to "self" presupposes a direct and revelatory relationship between visible body and inner being. In that sense, the mirror is an essential instrument in a physiognomic interpretation. In Booth Tarkington's *Alice Adams* (1921), twenty-two-year-old Alice, yearning to escape from her lower-middle-class family and knowing that her destiny depends on her looks, devotes much of her time to posturing and practicing expressions before the mirror. One evening she spends several hours preparing to attend a dance. She finally stands in front of her glass, "completed, bright-eyed, and solemn" (73). The word "completed" intimates that this is not just the perfection of a particular costume but the completion of an ego. Alice has to create and realize a self, and the mirror is the tool she uses to test whether or not she has succeeded. "Have a good time," her father says to her. "I mean to!" she cries.

> "What was he talking about?" her mother inquired, . . . "What were you telling him you 'mean to'?"
>
> Alice went back to her triple mirror for the last time, then stood before the long one. "That I mean to have a good time to-night," she said; and as she turned from her reflection to the wrap Mrs. Adams held up for her, "It looks as though I *could*, don't you think so?" (74–75)

Alice's last remark shows the connection between the purely exterior phenomenon and the condition—both present and future—of the self. Alice assumes that there is a continuum between what she looks like and what she's capable of feeling.

When women sense an alteration of any sort in their lives, frequently they look into the glass. For instance, Linda, a character in

Wolitzer's *Hearts*, notices, as she is traveling cross-country, gradual and then dramatic changes in the scenery: "The vegetation in New Mexico was sparser than it had been a little further east, in Texas. And what did grow was tougher-looking, spiky and aggressive, defiant of the dry, penetrating heat. Linda pulled down the sun visor and looked at herself in the little mirror to see if she, too, was toughening to accommodate the altering climate of her life" (218). A straightforward belief in the influence of the environment on one's emotional state suggests to Linda that she may be "toughening" in response to the landscape. To this notion she adds an implicit belief in the physiognomic powers of the mirror, and thus checks on any changes in her psychology not through self-reflection (i.e., simply becoming conscious of her feelings) but through literal reflection. Linda believes that the mirror is a more trustworthy register of personal change than her own cognitive powers of self-conception. Indeed, the language of this passage undercuts our usual notions of an inner / outer duality: the "toughening" is simultaneously both an emotional and a facial phenomenon.

Certain women, who have invested much faith in the mirror's ability to reveal the self, are shocked when what they feel is not immediately disclosed by the glass. In a moment of anger, Lewis Dodd, in Margaret Kennedy's *The Constant Nymph* (1924), tells his wife Florence that he loves another woman. Florence goes to the dressing table and begins rapidly to pin up her hair. As she glances furtively into the glass, she is astonished to see that "this mortal wound had, as yet, written no history on her face" (280). In like manner, when a woman in Godwin's *A Mother and Two Daughters* decides to embark on a love affair, she "was surprised to see that her face in the mirror still retained its precise shape, for she felt all blurry and melted down" (140). Because the relationship between identity and appearance in the mirror is so strong for many women, when the self has a feeling, the presumption is that the feeling will be recorded by the mirror. What is interesting about this cliché is the expectation. It's almost an automatic reflex for some women to turn to the glass when emotions have transformed how they feel about themselves. If the face changes, the self will change. Thus they suppose that the equation works with equal force in the opposite direction: a change in the self will alter the face. That this is not necessarily the case indicates the driving force behind the causal relationship—an unquestioning belief in the hegemony of visual presence over self-conception, which by its very nature cannot empower an insubstantial ego to transform substantial appearance.

At times the definitiveness of the mirror goes beyond other tools of physical measurement. Almost every woman has witnessed or played the leading role in a scene similar to the one Kim Chernin describes in *The Obsession: Reflections on the Tyranny of Slenderness* (1981):

> The locker room of the tennis club. Several exercise benches, two old-fashioned hair dryers, a mechanical bicycle, a mirror, and a scale.
>
> A tall woman enters, removes her towel; she throws it across a bench, faces herself squarely in the mirror, climbs on the scale, looks down.
>
> A silence.
>
> "I knew it," she mutters, . . .
>
> "Two pounds," she says,. . ."Two pounds." And then she turns, grabs the towel and swings out at her image in the mirror, smashing it violently, the towel spattering water over the glass. "Fat pig," she shouts at her image in the glass. "You fat, fat pig." (20–21)

It is interesting that the woman doesn't hit the weighing machine. How does she know she has gained two pounds? The scale tells her. But she doesn't smash it; she lashes out at the mirror. For a woman, weight is how you look. The incident, and even the pronoun "you," indicates once again the exteriority of female self-conception. Perhaps this woman's actions are based on the assumption that what the scale registers might be kept secret, but what the mirror registers is unavoidably revealed to the world.

In fact, the mirror is such a powerful tool of self-perception that even if a mirror is distorted and the woman rationally *knows* that it is distorted, there is still a tendency to accept the image in the glass as the true self. For instance, in Godwin's witty but serious short story "Death in Puerto Vallarta" (1971), a woman goes off by herself on a trip after her lover tells her he doesn't intend to leave his wife. She records her experiences in a notebook, always referring to herself in the second person. In her hotel room, she discovers that the full-length mirror in the bathroom is defective, swelling and thereby disfiguring the shape of her reflection:

> The first evening you make a joke about it. "I've left my good body at home with him while this fatwoman and I carouse beneath the whispering palms and fortify our egos with sun baths and the hot eyes of appreciative peasants," you say. . . .
>
> You squat in front of your distorted mirror and make the fatwoman swing her breasts, tremble her haunches, and do a very obscene dance. (144–45)

The speaker is already starting to characterize herself in her own imaginative world as the mirror's fat woman. The misshapen image is taking on a forceful presence, a reality with the power to influence the woman's thoughts about who and what she is.

> Second night. . . . You rub shoulders with the fatwoman, study her intimately. How funnily she billows out from a foreshortened waist into a massive blob of hips and thighs. Just where exactly does the mirror part company with reality? Maybe you've been kidding yourself and your mirror at home is the one that's distorted. A sand flea has bit you / her unbecomingly on the right buttock just below the bikini line. (Will it heal before HE sees it again?) (146)

The fact that this mirror is warped increases the sense of ambiguity between self and other, a duality embodied in the "you / her" play of pronouns. The complexity of that ambiguity is multiplied by the woman's uncertainty about the boundary—if indeed there is one—between the real and the reflected. Yet even in this distorted condition, the mirror image is beginning to insinuate itself into her self-conception, as though the power of the glass transcended mimetic fidelity. For this woman, and perhaps for many others, that power resides not in the mirror's ability to reflect what is already present, but in its projective imaging of what those under its spell will become.

It is as if some women discover that their mirrors are fragments from the demon's glass in Hans Christian Andersen's "The Snow Queen." His "grinning" mirror enlarges whatever is ugly and shrinks almost to nothing whatever is good and beautiful (117). In an even more famous fable about mirrors, the Grimm brothers'

"Snow White" (1812), the mirror goes beyond the power to grin and takes on the power of speech:

> "Mirror, mirror, on the wall,
> Who is the fairest one of all?"
> And the mirror replied:
> "Lady Queen, you are the fairest one of all."
> Then she was content, for she knew that the mirror told the truth.
> (55)

The mirror speaks to the Queen's vanity, but it also is a literalized version of the Renaissance metaphor of the steel glass that always images the truth. In the end the evil Queen dies—killed by being forced to dance in red-hot iron shoes, but already destroyed beforehand by the veracity of the steel glass when it tells her she is no longer the fairest. The fables of the mirror's tremendous powers are not as fabulous as one might at first think; rather, they are exaggerations of psychological patterns found in more realistic genres—and in life.[7]

Randall Jarrell in his poem "The End of the Rainbow" alludes to the Grimm fairy tale and plays on the word *fair*: "Who is the fairest of us all? / According to the mirror, it's the mirror" (225). The woman wishes to know who is the most beautiful; Jarrell's mirror is interested in determining who is the fairest in the sense of the most just. As we have seen time and time again, looking into the mirror is for the woman intensely personal and subjective, but Jarrell suggests that the mirror itself is dispassionate and objective. In the first stanza of her poem "Mirror," Sylvia Plath suggests that the power of the mirror comes from this very impersonality. As in "Snow White," the glass speaks:[8]

> I am silver and exact, I have no preconceptions.
> Whatever I see I swallow immediately
> Just as it is, unmisted by love or dislike.

7. The common ground between fable and novel is intimated by a simile in Marilyn French's *The Women's Room* (1977): "Women don't get even the respect of fear. What's to fear, after all, in a silly woman always running for her mirror to see who she is? Mira lived by her mirror as much as the Queen in *Snow White*. A lot of us did: we absorbed and believed the things people said about us" (14).

8. For other poems with speaking mirrors, see Thomas Hardy's "The Lament of the Looking-Glass" and Herman Melville's "Madam Mirror." In Louise Bogan's "Little Lobelia's Song," it is the girl's reflection that does the speaking.

> I am not cruel, only truthful—
> The eye of a little god, four-cornered.
> Most of the time, I meditate on the opposite wall. (173)

The radical exactness and objectivity of the mirror generate its value as a corrective for the subjectivity that women bring to the glass. It is indeed a "god" elevated above the mortal world, its serene silence broken only by utterances of absolute truth and enormous rhetorical potency.

Another power sometimes granted to the mirror is a will of its own. Gwendolen, in George Eliot's *Daniel Deronda* (1876), catches "the reflection of her movements" in a glass panel. As she advances toward the mirror, it appears to her as though it is the reflection that has the power to move forward: "Seeing her image slowly advancing, she thought, 'I *am* beautiful'" (294). Although it is actually she who is advancing, Gwendolen attributes this movement, and even the will to move, to the mirror image. In Antonia White's aptly titled novel *Beyond the Glass* (1954), her character Clara Batchelor finds not simply independent motion but menace in her mirror image. Usually the reflection is "friendly," but occasionally it becomes "mocking": "Clara would smile placatingly and the other would return a sneering grin. Gradually the other would take charge, twisting its features into grimaces she was compelled to imitate" (31). This is a total reversal of what is normally accepted as fact, that is, the mirror image following what the self does. But the problematics of what constitutes the self, where it resides, and how it comes to be through objectification, introduce the possibility for overthrowing such norms. Another young woman, Alice in Tarkington's *Alice Adams*, has an experience with the mirror similar to Clara's. For her, too, the mirror ceases to be an agent and becomes a master:

> The apparition before her had obeyed her like an alert slave, but now, as she subsided to a complete stillness, that aspect changed to the old mockery with which mirrors avenge their wrongs. The nucleus of some queer thing seemed to gather and shape itself behind the nothingness of the reflected eyes until it became almost an actual strange presence. If it could be identified, perhaps the presence was that of the hidden designer who handed up the false, ready-made pictures, and, for unknown purposes, made Alice ex-

> hibit them; but whatever it was, she suddenly found it monkey-like and terrifying. (160)

Alice begins by recognizing the otherness of the image. She starts to feel that the mirror has a great deal of control and is forcing a series of "pictures" on her. She's right in a way. What the mirror stands in place of (men, society, the world) does impose on the woman these various faces she exhibits. The medium of reflection *does* have enormous power, the power of the world to determine self. Alice's is almost a vortex experience. She has spent years identifying with the image in the glass, but eventually that concentration produces its opposite. Instead of identification, there is a rebound effect in which the mirror becomes an alien force, its reflection less an embodiment of ego than a locus of demonic energies. As Dylan Thomas writes, "Still a world of furies / Burns in many mirrors" (60).

All of these texts reveal an exploitation of the otherness of the mirror. What we usually see in the glass is ourselves, but in these passages a wholly different personality is grinning or boasting or moving or mocking or draining all presence from the self and giving it to the mirror.[9] One final absurdist expression of the mirror taking over as subject and the woman becoming the object occurs in Samuel Beckett's play *Happy Days* where Winnie says, "'Ah yes, things have their life, that is what I always say, *things* have a life.' (*Pause*). 'Take my looking-glass, it doesn't need me'" (54).

Many of the examples in this chapter raise complex issues about difference and similitude as they pertain to the woman and her reflection. In some cases, the woman immediately identifies the image with herself; in others, she finds something that startles her with its alterity. We need to look more closely at this paradoxical quality of the mirror image and consider the extent to which paradox is inherent in mirroring and in the evolution of self-consciousness.

9. In Lois Gould's *A Sea-Change* (1976), a woman is afraid to remain before her mirror "lest it read her thoughts" (25). In this instance, the glass takes on powers even greater than those of the person using it.

2.

The Differential Image

Likeness tells the doubting eye
That strangeness is not strange.
Laura Riding

The following traditional riddle appears in *The Puffin Book of Nursery Rhymes* collected by Iona and Peter Opie:

> I've seen you where you never were,
> And where you ne'er will be,
> And yet within that self-same place
> You can be seen by me. (109)

The intriguing part of the riddle is not the answer to the question "where is *where*?"—which is, of course, "in a mirror." The heart of this conundrum is "who is *you*?" The *I* and the *you* are the same being in this verse, yet splitting it into two words suggests a division in the unity of the ego. Looking at oneself in a mirror can, in a disturbingly ambiguous way, bring up the whole question of the nature of identity. Is that image I see in the mirror I or isn't it? Am I one with what I see in the glassy surface or is the self to be defined as some immaterial thing not caught by the reflection?

In thinking about this riddle, we confront problems in general semiotics. Neither the word *apple* nor a picture of one is the same thing as the object apple; yet, within the confines of referential systems, the difference must be muted by the users of those systems. In the riddle, *you* is the self, but this self is also an otherness, as indicated by the two words *I* and *you* and, in the last line, *you* and *me*. The jesting doubleness of the grammar nicely captures the sense of the mirror image as a signifier necessarily different from its signified—and yet a signifier with a peculiarly (perhaps even uniquely) intimate, direct, and complete relationship with the signified. Further, this signified is one with the perceiver participating in the semiotic phenomenon of mirroring.[1]

The children's riddle leads us to an essential paradox in the mirror experience. The image in the glass is always at once the self (at least in the visual sense) and not the self. The reflection is, of course, not flesh and blood, only photons bouncing off atoms of silver. Yet, in daily practice men and women take their images in the glass to be, in important and various ways, identical with their selves. Thus, the mirror is inescapably "oxymoronic"—a term I will use instead of "paradoxical" because mirroring is, quite literally, a mode of figuration or figuring-forth an image which, like metaphor, is inscribed with both identity and difference. The two traditional versions of the Narcissus myth exemplify the double character of the mirror image. As the legend is told by Ovid, the beautiful youth falls in love with his own reflection in a pool (3.83–87). In Pausanias's version of the story, Narcissus is in love with his twin sister. When she dies, he goes to the pool, sees his reflection, but believes that he sees the image of his sister (bk. 9, chap. 31). In Ovid, Narcissus falls in love with the self; in Pausanias, with the other. The two stories present the contradictory modes of response to the mirror; one version assumes the identity of self and image, while the other offers an extreme example of difference. Few literary encounters between women and mirrors portray the opposite ends of the spectrum in such absolute terms. But as we shall see, the oxymoronic nature of the self / image relationship underlies the phenomenon of mirroring presented in many texts, even when the mirror's double identity as both ego and other never rises to an explicit level of consciousness.

Eva Figes's *Waking* (1981) invites the reader into seven mornings in a woman's life from early childhood to old age. Each part, except for the very first and the very last, explores the woman's relationship with the glass. In the psychological theories of Jacques Lacan, the "mirror stage" is a single event; but for this speaker describing the seven ages of woman, all her world is a mirror

1. Umberto Eco's contention that a mirror reflection is only nascently semiotic will be discussed in Chapter 8.

stage. The teen-age girl in her secret room studies her reflection, defining herself as someone who is looked at and who derives pleasure from being looked at. The otherness of the mirror actually helps the adolescent's psychic development. Her new body is so strange to her that at first she says, "this is she." Only later can she say, "here I am." What she will become to herself is already physically presented by the body she can see in the mirror:

> . . . I exult in the way my breasts have grown like those of an adult, the curve of my hips gives me pleasure. I study the line of neck and shoulder as though it belonged to somebody else, and as though it was somebody else looking back at me from the mirror I appraise the line of her chin . . . and those remarkable eyes which look back at me so seriously. So this is she, I say, watching the apparition. And sometimes . . . I say to the world of the empty garden and the houses beyond: this is she, here I am. (22)

This brief passage goes through the entire oxymoronic cycle. In the beginning, the girl looks in the mirror as a utilitarian process of seeing what her body looks like. Next she begins to develop a little narrative based on the otherness of the mirror image. She starts with the "that's I" half of the oxymoron and soon afterward plays an interesting, complex game on the "that's not I" half. Through her psychic games with the latter, she comes full circle back to identity. The experience with the mirror allows her to say "this is she" in reference to herself and then to move toward an internalization of the reflected image and an identification of ego with what had begun as an otherness. In this brief scene, Figes has shown in gradual and discrete steps the oscillations of the oxymoronic mirror, the movements between image as self and image as other, which can (and often do) occur with great rapidity in actual experiences of mirroring and even in texts about those experiences.

The young girl in *Waking* hates her parents and wants a world of her own, "allowing in only what is beautiful" (25). She presents this ideal realm in chiaroscuro—"moonlight riding the dark shadows across ghostly lawns"—because these are images that have yet to take on distinct outlines. Her desires are general and unspecific in their object, since her self-conception is equally imprecise. She refers to "my own haunting image in the murky mirror" and "the shadow which looks out at me from the oval mirror." She repeatedly asks her reflection, "Who are you?" and thus the mirror helps her give grammatical (or at least semiotic) form to the psychic longing, to provide a structure, to literalize and objectify the puzzle of identity. It is a little easier for the adolescent girl to consider the query Who is that in the mirror? than Who am I? She can deal with the senses and her response to the world rather than with the more abstract and philosophical processes of introspection and self-analysis. Indeed, she has yet to develop an interior capable of inspection.

The girl moves back and forth very quickly within the oxymoronic spectrum of the mirror, but she still controls the image. From observing her own eyes in the glass and pretending (although a serious pretense) that those eyes are someone else's, she begins to learn how to look at men, as though the person in the mirror were her instructor. The mirror becomes an instrument for social and psychic development, for the girl's relationship with herself and with others.

The adolescent experience with the mirror is repeated (of course with variations) at other turning points in the woman's life. In the following passage, she is in her thirties and has just taken a new lover: ". . . in the falling lamplight I saw a heavy-breasted, forked creature caught in the shadows of the long oval mirror. I moved closer and stood, shocked, staring into the wild eyes, black, burning, which looked out from skin not just glowing, but incandescent, a white shape with a head surrounded by a wild bush of confused hair. So this is me, I thought. I have become a burning torch" (55–56). The young girl saw in the mirror what she would become. Now the woman sees what she has become, but once again with an underlying sense of the alterity of the image which shifts toward identification with that gleaming otherness.

As the woman ages and as time is no longer on her side, the author continues to play on the "not me" half of the oxymoron. What made for fruitful mirrors in adolescence, however, can lead to disturbing ones in maturity. When the woman starts to feel old, the otherness in the mirror becomes frightening because, in spite of the consciousness of difference, she senses it is also herself: "I do not wish to get up and confront the hollow, even slightly horrific face which will look back at me from the glass. Self-hatred. She looks at me with loathing and disgust, the sick face which resembles my mother. No, I wish to say, it is not true, . . . but nothing will belie the fact. Flat, lacking in depth, dull and tired, the eyes of a woman who has given up the ghost, but who is ashamed of defeat" (62). In youth, the other person in the mirror was an object of desire. Now that image is an object of hatred, and the woman resists the notion it is she and tries, with little success, to deny half the oxymoron. A character in Doris Lessing's *The Summer before the Dark* refers to "sweet-sour mirror encounters" (103). She realizes, as does Figes's speaker, that not only is the mirror oxymoronic, but the kinds of responses that women have to the image in the mirror are also multiple and contradictory within a single glance.

In *Waking*, the woman's grown son tells her that she is ugly and hideous. Like so many women who hear such words from a male, she turns to her mirror to test their validity. She both knows and dreads that "the long glass" will "confirm what he sees" (65). The son might be lying, but the mirror will not. The woman doesn't want to look at herself, yet she does not smash the glass. If hers is a revolt against the mirror, it is a pitiful one, an attempted rejection that will never be accomplished. She recalls the person she used to be "who smiled at herself in the glass". "What happened to her? I do not know, only that she slipped away one night, will not come back, that I am doomed to drag about this other body who fills me with disgust, whom I do not like, nobody could. Eyes in the street . . . slide away, glance past or look straight through me as though I did not exist, that was when I first knew something had happened, that the person I had always been was dead" (70). As psychologist Elissa Melamed explains in *Mirror Mirror: The Terror of Not Being Young* (1983), "we [women] usually don't discover that we are getting old from internal cues; our first messages are liable to come from the outside. We feel no real diminution of capability, strength, or sexuality, but we are simply put into another category by the eyes of others. What these eyes tell us is that they will no longer mirror us. The eyes make no contact; they glance and slide off as if they had seen an inanimate object" (75). The first of these messages "from the outside," or at least their continual validation, comes not from other people but from that self / other image in the glass.

The aged woman has been trying to deny that the image in the glass is she. Now she carries her refusal as far as she can: she flees from the reflection. The rhetoric is also deflected away from the mirror and emphasizes the sense of distance and difference. The otherness of the mirror, a route to the self in adolescence,[2] now gives her a way to dismember the equation of self and image: "Outside I have become invisible in the dull stone light of winter, until I suddenly catch a glimpse . . . of a woman wrapped up against the cold. Her eyes light up, hurt and twisted, seeing them peer helplessly through two holes of pinched wintry flesh in the vivid patch of mottled mirror" (73). This woman, trying to define who she is, has spent almost every stage of her life "in a double complicity" (70), suspended between the two polarities of the oxymoronic "mottled mirror."

"Who are you?" the young woman in Figes's *Waking* whispers to the shadow looking out at her from the oval glass. As Laura Mullen's poem "Mirror, Mirror" demonstrates, the answers given by the mirror are always inquiries—because the image is both a true reflection and a mere reflection, both yourself and not yourself:

> Any answer you give me,
> Any answer is only another
> Question. The thin return,
> (Like a dime from a phone unanswered)
> Of myself. Doesn't the light ring?
> I say hello, but it is my mother's, my father's
> Face, or the face someone said
> Was beautiful. Beautiful.
> Maybe. Turn that way again. Smile.
> Smile, like a hook dragged over flat water, . . .

2. The fact that both adolescents and aging women make use of the alterity of the mirror may be symptomatic of more general similarities between the two. See, for example, Scarf's comment in *Unfinished Business* on "these two particularly critical periods of female existence": "The menarchal girl and the menopausal woman invite comparison. Both are dealing with major biological discontinuities, which create important new pressures in the person's life" (450). Melamed also compares the pubescent girl and the climacteric woman: "Much as in adolescence, [in aging] one loses track of who one is. But with the difference that the adolescent is motivated to claim her new identity and is rewarded for doing so. The older woman, on the other hand, is penalized. Like the teenager's, her image wavers in the glass—but it is further obscured by the shadows of her own dread" (111).

I watch for the flash in the shallows.
I wait for that woman to surface,
My smile breaking her jaws.
Isn't she all I have?
Isn't she all I ever have?
That woman turning the soap in her hands,
Over and over. (8)

The speaker looks into a mirror for a statement and the beginnings of a dialogue, but she gets none back. The poem stresses the otherness of the image: it is related to her, but no more so than her mother's face, her father's face. The speaker is trying to catch something, to hook her self in the mirror. What she captures is a fleeting image of her parents or a cultural ideal of beauty, but not her own presence. The reflection of her jaws is broken open when she smiles, but there is also a sense of opposition between "my smile" and "her jaws." We see again in this double-directed statement the necessary paradox of ego and other. The speaker looks for her self and finds "that woman." She asks, Am I not what I see in the mirror? What is there besides that? Yet there is someone else—the consciousness who asks these questions and can at least entertain the idea that she is not the specular image. The poem plays tantalizingly with the oxymoronic glass, with the forever doubled and doubling "Mirror, Mirror."

The complex interchanges between the self and its mirror images raise more general concerns about the relationship between the self as subject and the self as its own object. Self-consciousness has often been thought to depend on this very phenomenon, one in which the self is both that which knows and that which is known. Plotinus (ca. 205–270 A.D.) was one of the earliest writers to wrestle with the problem of how the "I" comes to know itself as a process of division into subject and object. In the Third Tractate of *The Enneads*, "On Gnostic Hypostases, and that which is beyond them," Plotinus indicates that the ego cannot be "entirely simple" (i.e., unitary) but "composite, to have the intellection of itself" (257). As we have already seen, this sense of a double or complex self, one that is both subject and object, is intrinsic to the mirror experience. By the late eighteenth century, particularly in German romantic thought, this objectification of the subject became a key element in theories of self-consciousness. As is so often the case, Samuel Taylor Coleridge nicely summed up this position and presented it to an English speaking audience. In his *Biographia Literaria* (1817), he writes of "a subject which becomes a subject by the act of constructing itself objectively to itself" (1:273). This act of reflection is a kind of mirroring (metaphorically speaking) in which the self projects itself as an otherness so that the self as subject can observe itself—and by that very act constitute itself as a subject. Hegel further develops this idea, as well as the implicit mirror metaphors, in the preface to *The Phenomenology of Mind* (1807). The development of Hegelian "knowledge of spirit" must proceed through a stage in which spirit "must be presented to itself as an object, but at the same time straightway annul and transcend this objective form; it must be its own object in which it finds itself reflected" (86).

In our own century, the phenomenologist Maurice Merleau-Ponty continued to situate the objectification of self as a basic component of consciousness, but always as a purely mental, even transcendentalizing, experience. In the work of the American psychologist George Herbert Mead, a similarly conceived phenomenology of self-consciousness is set within a social and behaviorist context. The metaphor of mirroring haunts his texts, but the experience of objectification is situated only in language. He writes: "That the person should be responding to himself is necessary to the self, and it is this sort of social conduct which provides behavior within which that self appears. I know of no other form of behavior than the linguistic in which the individual is an object to himself" (219). All these philosophers (need I point out, male philosophers?) view self-realization through objectification as a mental act not necessarily or directly related to a physical correlative. Looking at one's face or body in a mirror offers just such a correlative, a profoundly literal projection of an image of self as an object capable of observation by the self. Further, the oxymoronic nature of the mirror experience, the sense of the image as simultaneously subject and object, embodies the reflexivity of Coleridge's grammar of self-creation.[3]

3. The objectification of the subjective described here bears some obvious parallels with the distinction between *en-soi* and *pour-soi* used by de Beauvoir in *The*

Many of the mirror scenes already discussed imply a close relation among mirroring, self-consciousness, and self-creation. In some of Anaïs Nin's writings, however, this relation becomes a dominant motif that dramatizes, literalizes, and virtually replaces the cognitive objectifications of the masculine philosophers. Nin reveals in her diary (March 1937) that she cannot remember what she saw in the mirror as a child:

> Perhaps a child never looks at a mirror. Perhaps a child, like a cat, is so much inside of himself that he does not see himself in the mirror. He sees a child. The child does not remember what he looks like. Later I remembered what I looked like. But when I look at photographs of myself one, two, three, four, five years old, I do not recognize myself. The child is *one*. At one with himself. Never outside of himself. I can remember what I did but not the reflection of what I did. No reflections. Six years old. Seven years old. Eight years old. Nine. Ten. Eleven. No images. No reflections. . . . Yet at the age of six the perfection of the blue bow on my hair, shaped like a butterfly, preoccupied me, since I insisted that my godmother tie it because she tied it better than anyone else. I must have seen this bow in the mirror then. I do not remember whether I saw this bow, the little girl in the very short white lace edged dress, or again a photograph taken in Havana where all my cousins and I stood in a row according to our heights, all wearing enormous ribbons and short white dresses. In the mirror there never was a child. (2:180–81)

Nin is suggesting that the reason the child does not recognize herself in the mirror is that she does not know what she looks like. How do human beings learn what they look like? It is a rather strange process in which mirrors play a significant part. At some point a child comes to realize, through her own experiments or

---

Second Sex. I have chosen, however, not to adopt her terminology because of the existentialist—one might almost say neo-Platonic—emphasis on the *en-soi* as a changeless essence (see the translator's footnote on p. 702 of *The Second Sex*). My own understanding of the strategies of objectification before the mirror does not require a self pre-existing the phenomenon of reflection, except in the most elementary, purely perceptual sense. For me, the *en-soi* may be a product of the *pour-soi*. For a discussion of Lacan's formulation of mirroring and the genesis of the divided self of consciousness, see my "Introductory Reflections."

adult demonstrations, that what she perceives in the glass is herself.

Nin's comparison of a child to a cat suggests that they share a similar level of awareness—that is, a stage before *self*-consciousness. Nin can remember doing things, but she can't look at herself as an object doing them. "No images. No reflections." In the context of the whole passage, these terms assume both cognitive and physical meanings, and thus establish an intimate relationship between mental imaging and body imaging in a mirror. Nin is conscious of numerous sense impressions, but she is not seeing herself as an object because she has yet to see her *self* in the mirror. With some remembrances, such as the blue hair ribbon, she doesn't know if the memory is from personal recollection or from photographic objectifications of that experience which are subject to re-experience at a later stage of consciousness. "The child is *one*" because she is incapable of dividing herself between a subject who perceives and the object perceived. Yet this very fall into division, this birth of self-consciousness, is what literally happens when a girl looks into the glass and sees *her* self (not just "a child"). Such an experience is the end of childhood. The mirror destroys the Edenic absence of self-cognizance.

For Nin, "there never was a child" in the mirror because a child has not yet learned a system in which one projects a self-image, in which one says, "That is I over there." The process of becoming yourself by being outside yourself is at the very heart of human consciousness as defined in the West since at least the late eighteenth century, and Nin associates this basic phenomenon with mirrors. But when she looks into her "first mirror," she finds "no Anaïs Nin, but Marie Antoinette." The child becomes "an actress playing all the parts of characters in French history" (2:181). At this stage, the mirror's power resides in its ability to reveal alternative selves out of which the girl can mold the self. Before she can have any control over what she is, she has to be able to conceive what she can be. The mirror allows her to do that.

Nin's portrayal of the formation of the *I* has a superficial similarity to Jacques Lacan's conception of the mirror stage, including the fall from unitary unselfconsciousness into the doubled—and hence split—ego. But, according to Nin, the primal confrontation, what Nin calls "the first mirror in which the self appears," comes for the female in puberty, not in infancy, and thus unfolds within a social environment already established within the girl's acculturated psyche. This moment of self-confrontation comes not spontaneously, but only after the childhood stages of nonrecognition and role playing, a testing of alternative "selves" that always remain "others." In describing the mirror in which she first sees her "self," Nin speaks in the third person, stressing the way the mirror objectifies ego:

> The first mirror in which the self appears is very large. . . . The image of the girl who approaches it is brought into luminous relief. Against a foggy darkness, the girl of fifteen stands with frightened eyes. She is looking at her dress, . . . It does not fit her. It is meager. It looks poor. The girl is looking at the worn shiny dark-blue serge dress with shame. It is the day she has been told in school that she is gifted for writing. . . . she had written the best essay in the class. She who was always quiet and who did not wish to be noticed, was told to come up the aisle and speak to the English teacher before everyone, to hear the compliment. And the joy, the dazzling joy which had first struck her was instantly killed by the awareness of the dress. I did not want to get up, to be noticed. I was ashamed of this meager dress. (2:181)

Nin's sense of herself comes through language, as Mead asserted it must, but also through mirroring. The self-definition through the mirror leads in one direction, and the self-definition through the writing in another. The mirror reveals the ugly dress of which she is ashamed; the writing permits her to live in a world in which she is honored. A sense of doubleness, necessary for self-consciousness and intrinsic to mirroring, now infects her identity and creates conflicts. At the very end of the passage, Nin switches to the first person, but almost immediately she moves back to third when she looks into yet "another mirror" that invites a complex series of alternations between the poles of oxymoronic identity:

> The girl is looking at the new dress which transfigures her. What an extraordinary change. She leans over very close to look at the humid eyes, the humid mouth, the moisture and luminousness brought about by the change of dress. She walks up very slowly to the mirror, very slowly, as if she did not want to frighten reflections

> away. Several times, at fifteen, she walks very slowly towards the mirror. Every girl of fifteen has put the same question to a mirror: "Am I beautiful?" The face is masklike. It does not smile. It does not want to charm the mirror, or deceive the mirror, or flirt with it and gain a false answer. The girl is in a trance. . . . She approaches the mirror and stands very still like a statue. . . . She only moves to become someone else, impersonating Sarah Bernhardt, Mélisande, *La Dame aux Camélias*, Madame Bovary, Thaïs. She is never Anaïs Nin who goes to school, and grows vegetables and flowers in her backyard. . . . She is decomposed before the mirror into a hundred personages, recomposed into paleness and immobility. (2:182)

The pun on "transfigures" in the first sentence underscores the significance of Nin's intimacy with the glass. The dress modifies her figure in a literal sense, but also, spiritually and psychologically, the self is changed, elevated. Nin's complicated relationship with the mirror includes a recognition of its power; yet she is also conscious of alternatives to self-definition through the mirror. It is highly unlikely for a man in Western culture to have this kind of experience, for the depth of the sense of transfiguration, of "extraordinary change," goes beyond what males in our culture have historically experienced in front of a glass. The new dress alters her body chemistry. Further, there is a sense of the otherness of the reflection, the paradox of knowing the image in the mirror is and is not herself. "Am I beautiful?" she asks, which is also a version of "Who am I?" The girl is in a trance created by the mirror—itself a male, standing *in loco homino*. The mirror creates the self, that psychic and social construct, as the sense of a unitary (or at least not radically fragmented) identity slowly comes into being through processes of literal objectification and the testing of alternative modes of self-conception. "She is never Anaïs Nin" at the beginning, but it is only through that sense of the otherness of the reflected image that the mirror can serve as an instrument of self-objectification and hence take on an essential role in the production of "Anaïs Nin" to herself. The process of taking on a new self is also a deconstructing of the previous person as she grows into this new persona. With Nin and her extreme self-involvement, this act is willful. With some other young women before other mirrors, the drama may be less intense and less conscious, but no less important.

The central figure in Jessamyn West's *Cress Delahanty* (1945) is only twelve years old when she, like Nin, decomposes and recomposes her presence before the glass, when she asks (and answers) the question, "Am I beautiful?" Unlike Nin, Cress does want to charm the mirror, to flirt with it, even to deceive it. For her, the mirror is the man before the real man appears. Cress is looking at herself in the mirror but thinking of "him":

> She stepped out of her skirt and threw her jacket and sweater across the room and sent her panties in a flying arc. She knew what she wanted. She had used it before—Mother's long, black lace shawl. She wound it tightly about herself from armpits to thighs. She unbraided her hair and let it hang across her shoulders. Then she turned to the mirror. "I have a beautiful body," she breathed, "a beautiful, beautiful body."
>
> And because she regarded herself, thinking of him, he who was yet to come, it was as if he too, saw her. She loaned him her eyes so that he might see her, and to her flesh she gave this gift of his seeing. She raised her arms and slowly turned and her flesh was warm with his seeing. Somberly and quietly she turned and swayed and gravely touched now thigh, now breast, now cheek, and looked and looked with the eyes she had given him. (24–25)

Cress is seducing herself and, by seducing herself before a mirror, she is also seducing a man. When she lends him her eyes so that he might see her, she is objectifying herself into another whose very sex underscores that otherness. In so doing, she is giving herself to a man. Yet this whole performance is a part of the dialectic of self-conception, of developing a sense of what she is. A serious sexual education is unfolding and a profound process of negation as a means of creation. The subject (that which perceives) becomes the fictive male, and the girl's image in the mirror becomes the female object he perceives. The subject / object reversal, plus the fact that the "real" person here becomes in the mirror the object of an imaginary subject, creates a psychological situation more complex than the Coleridgean formula of self-objectification. This is a particularly feminine gesture, this transformation of the self into an object perceived by another, for in our culture it is preeminently men (as subjects) who observe women (as objects).[4] It is within

4. John Berger makes much the same basic point: "Men look at women. Women watch themselves being looked at. This determines not only most relations be-

that social / perceptual paradigm that females take on their cultural roles, just as Cress assumes the role of female object, defined by a male presence, before the glass. Yet out of this apparent draining of self before the male mirror and turning the self into an object comes a very strong sense of identity:

> She moved through the gray dust-filled room weaving an ivory pattern. Not any of the dust or disorder of her mother's room fazed her. . . . She made, in her mind, a heap of all that was ugly and disordered. She made a dunghill of them and from its top she crowed.
>
> "The curtains, green as vomit, and hanging crooked, the gray neckband on the white flannel nightgown, the dust on the patent leather shoes," she said, providing her imaginary stage with imaginary props, "I hate them and dance them down. Nothing can touch me. I am Cress. Or I can dance *with* them," she said and she clasped the nightgown to her and leaped and bent. (25)

Cress defines herself independent of her mother (she denies any connection with the clutter that represents the parent) and free of her environment. Instead, she uses the disorder as a stage for creating herself through the mirror. As she dances barefoot on the gritty dust and before the glass, she dramatizes and feminizes Merleau-Ponty's environmental definition of ego as center: "Visible and mobile, my body is a thing among things; it is caught in the fabric of the world, and its cohesion is that of a thing. But because it moves itself and sees, it holds things in a circle around itself. Things are an annex or prolongation of itself; they are incrusted into its flesh, they are part of its full definition" (284).

Because Cress has started to define herself through the eyes of a man, she will become what the mirror shows her, and hence what

---

tween men and women but also the relation of women to themselves. The surveyor of woman in herself is male: the surveyed female. Thus she turns herself into an object—and most particularly an object of vision: a sight" (47). This same transformation unfolds in Elizabeth Tallent's short story "Asteroids" when an eleven-year-old girl looks in the mirror, cocks her head slightly, and whistles at herself—"a brief, two-note wolf whistle" (19). For a radical literalizing of this type of psychological transference, see Angela Carter's apocalyptic fantasy *The Passion of New Eve* (1977). After a sex-change operation and plastic surgery, a man sees his new female image in a mirror as the object of his still male desires (74–75).

men will think of her: "She regarded her face more closely in the spattered mirror. 'There is something wanton and evil there,' she thought, 'something not good. Perhaps I shall be faithless,' and she trembled with pity for that dark one who loved her so dearly. . . . She . . . looked deep into the mirror and said, 'There is nothing I will not touch. I am Cress. I will know everything'" (25–26). This is not just a process of ego definition, but almost a creation of a Satanic or Promethean self. What we are left with is "I am Cress," a proclamation of self-instituted being. Her ultimate thrill is gaining this invincible sense of identity produced by projecting her presence as an object seen by a man. Her sudden vision of faithlessness followed by pity indicates how the power of the female comes into being in its social context. By becoming an object of desire, she can gain presence as a subject that can then convert the male into an object (of pity). Cress dreams with her mirror of the traditional route to self-definition and power for women in our culture.

A scene in Jean Rhys's *Wide Sargasso Sea* (1966) presents an extreme exaggeration of objectification. While a child living in Jamaica, Antoinette Cosway awakens one night to find "two enormous rats" staring at her (69). Yet she is not frightened, for she can see herself staring at the rats and the rats, quite still, staring back at her "in the looking-glass the other side of the room." She turns over and instantly falls asleep. The mirror and its power of ocular projection provide Antoinette with a means for emotional detachment from immediate experience. She is not a little girl who is face to face with rats, but a person watching a little girl faced with rats. "I could see myself [as an other] . . . staring at those rats." If she remained within the unitary ego, a "one" like Nin's child, she could only see the rats staring at her. She is acting out what Merleau-Ponty says about the interchange of intentionality and its object: "The scene invites me to become its adequate viewer, as if a different mind than my own suddenly came to dwell in my body, or rather as if my mind were drawn out there and emigrated into the scene it was in the process of setting for itself. I am snapped up by a second myself outside me; I perceive an other" (91). In Rhys's story, the mirror once again plays a crucial role in a scene of feminine consciousness that embodies, in a real bodily action, the phenomenology of self-objectification and self-presence. The abstract figurations of epistemology are literalized and corporealized through the figure in the glass.

3.

The Doubled I

Anyone that leans to look into a pool
is the woman in the pool.
Marilynne Robinson

In the previous chapter, we explored the copular mirror, the way in which women's experiences before the glass contain both identity and difference. But there are, of course, other varieties of such confrontations in which the oxymoron is bifurcated, and the emphasis falls heavily on just one aspect of the mirror's doubleness. As we shall see in Chapter 6, an exaggeration of difference can signal psychic dislocations. In contrast, the condition in which the woman strongly identifies with her mirror image has generally been taken as normative in our culture. This configuration of the woman / image relationship is assumed by many of the characters we encountered in the first chapter, but we must now look more closely at extreme cases of identification.

Valerie Marneffe, in Balzac's *Cousin Bette* (1847), is a fine example of those French ladies who make their way through the world of the nineteenth-century novel on the basis of their looks. Before attending a dinner party, Valerie must first create her appearance in front of the mirror. She arranges her hair (dyed to an ashen fairness), ties a wide black velvet ribbon around her neck, and, as the final "man-slayer" (as Balzac calls it), sets "a darling little rosebud in the stiffened top of her bodice, just in the centre, in the sweetest hollow. It was calculated to draw the eyes of all men under thirty downwards" (226). Balzac describes this scene of Valerie in front of the glass in terms that suggest both an artist at work and a soldier preparing for battle—activities representative of the way men create who and what they are. Valerie becomes herself through what she does before the mirror. Within the context of the novel she can be assumed to have a physical existence outside the glass, but such women have no social and psychological presence outside modes of being established by the mirror. Valerie's role as a courtesan depends wholly on the way in which she is perceived by men as an image of desire. That is both her role in the society of Balzac's novel and the way in which she conceives of herself. She is, in effect, a reflection in a man's eye, and the first male against which she tests her coming into being is the mirror. Balzac is describing more than the cosmetic arts: Valerie, before her glass, is involved in an act not just of self-presentation but of self-conception. The process is intimate and artificial but also deeply embedded in social structures. The phenomena in which she is engaged (and entrapped) break down the usual and useful differences between self and context—whether the latter is defined as the body or the cultural environment. Valerie can have a private relationship with the mirror, but that relationship becomes important (indeed, essential) only because the mirror is a convenient and objective substitute for the men who establish the rationale for her being, and that raison d'être is ultimately to be a consumer item. As Valerie says to her mirror, "I look delicious, good enough to eat!"

Valerie is a representative type that appears in a good many nineteenth-century French novels.[1] Perhaps her best-known cousin is Flaubert's Emma Bovary (*Madame Bovary*, 1857). Madame Bovary's preparation for death includes an act of self-possession and self-realization, and this final communion with the self (just after the priest has administered extreme unction) is performed with a looking glass in her hand. "And indeed, she looked all about her, slowly, like someone waking from a dream; then, in a distinct voice, she asked for her mirror, and she remained bowed over it for some time, until great tears flowed from her eyes" (369). The last rites are not those administered by the priest. The communion between Emma and her mirror, between a high priestess and the image she has worshiped throughout her life, constitutes the final ceremony of reflection and farewell.

1. For one of the more erotic developments of this character type and her depraved self-indulgences before the mirror, see Emile Zola's *Nana* (220, 222–23). Nana even uses the mirror in an attempt to discover what she would look like as a corpse (384).

Rosanette Bron in *Sentimental Education* (1869) is another of Flaubert's female characters who accepts the unquestioned authority of what she can see in the glass. Her lover Frederic always has to wait for her when they are going out because she spends ages arranging the ribbons on her bonnet and smiling at herself in the wardrobe mirror: "Then she would tuck her arm in his and make him stand beside her in front of the glass. 'We look nice like that, the two of us side by side! Poor darling, I could eat you!'" (350). The depth of concern with her outer appearance indicates that Rosanette's self-conception *is* that outer appearance. Since she conceives of herself in terms of the mirror image, she judges others in those terms. Rosanette is concerned not with her personal relationship with Frederic and the quality of their love, but with how they look together. The man's value and his significance to Rosanette's life depend upon his purely visual companionship with her image in the mirror. Since Rosanette reduces herself to that reflected presence, it is only consistent for her to do likewise to those around her.

The woman who conceives of herself as a mirror image is of course not exclusively French. There are great Russian examples, such as Anna Karenina's consulting her cheval glass just before her suicide. There is a South African heroine whose "dying eyes on the pillow looked into the dying eyes in the glass" in Olive Schreiner's *The Story of an African Farm* (284). A young German woman in Gisela Elsner's *Offside* (1982) wants to be "beautiful for her death" and carefully inspects herself in "a large mirror" just moments before lifing a jar of cyanide to her lips (199–200). In an American short story, Dorothy Parker's "Big Blonde," Hazel Morse bows graciously to her image in the glass and then swallows twenty sleeping tablets—all the while "watching her reflection with deep, impersonal interest, studying the movements of the gulping throat" (298). These last rites of the mirror are the conclusions to lives lived, in large measure, in terms ordained by the mirror.[2] Doris Lessing comments tellingly on this type of woman when she

2. Perhaps the most telling background for these modern rites is the practice of ancient Etruscans of burying women with their mirrors. These artifacts generally were inscribed with their owner's name; indeed, the names on all extant Etruscan mirrors are female. For a discussion, see de Grummond, "The Bronze Mirrors of the Etruscans."

asks of her character Kate Brown in *The Summer before the Dark* (1974), "Had she really spent so many years of her life—it would almost certainly add up to years!—in front of a looking glass? Just like all women" (161).

In *Daniel Deronda*, Gwendolen Harleth's daily rites include sessions of self-creation before her mirror. In an early scene in George Eliot's novel, beautiful Gwendolen gazes at her image until at last she leans forward and kisses the cold glass. In a different context we might take this performance as an indication that the subject sees her mirror image as another person whom she kisses. With Gwendolen, however, we are prepared for something far more narcissistic. Eliot implies that Gwendolen simply cannot resist kissing herself because she is so lovely. Like Pope's Belinda in *The Rape of the Lock* ("A heav'nly Image in the Glass appears, / To that she bends, to that her Eyes she rears" [155]), Gwendolen before her mirror—and *only* before her mirror—can be both goddess and priestess, both the object of worship and the subject who worships. In Eliot's version of the oxymoronic mirror, Gwendolen's identification of herself with the fair image is so extreme that, in her little drama with the glass, the Gwendolen outside the mirror plays the role of someone other than herself. The female self who is beautiful, who instills passion, and who receives a kiss—that is to say, the woman who functions in this scene as does Gwendolen in her society—is the image in the mirror.

Valerie, Emma, Anna, Gwendolen, and their many sisters grant enormous power to their mirrors. The basis of this power is the practical utility of the mirror (for both sexes) as a tool for seeing how one appears to others. For the legions of Valeries, Emmas, Annas, and Gwendolens of the world, physical appearance and the reactions of men to it constitute social destiny. Hence the objective reflectivity of the mirror allows them to see that destiny and transform it into the foundation of their self-conception in the context of social realities.

Edith Wharton is the most significant American novelist to continue and extend the French tradition—at least as far as mirror scenes are concerned. For her female characters, there is no questioning of the fate determined by the glass. Wharton's women accept that their selves and their lives are decided in large measure by what they look like in the mirror. Lily Bart, the lovely heroine of *The House of Mirth* (1905), often studies herself in the glass. When she discovers there some "faint flaws" in her considerable beauty, she decides that they are only the marks left by "petty cares" (32). In contrast, Lily's friend Gerty Farish finds something of more permanence when she confronts the mirror: "In the little glass above her dressing-table she saw her face reflected against the shadows of the room, and tears blotted the reflection. What right had she to dream the dreams of loveliness? A dull face invited a dull fate. She cried quietly as she undressed" (171). These women recognize a disparity between what one desires and what one sees, but neither questions the inevitable power of the mirror. The difference between Lily Bart and Gerty Farish is a difference in degree, not kind. In both passages a woman looks into a glass and sees a flaw. Lily, a woman of undeniable beauty, hopes that the flaw is minor and will disappear after a good night's sleep. For Gerty, burdened with plainness, the defect is major and she cries. In neither case does the woman think to challenge the efficacy of the mirror as a presenter of self.

A subtle change occurs in the quality of Lily's beauty in the course of the novel. At first it has "a transparency through which the fluctuations of the spirit were sometimes tragically visible." Later, "its impenetrable surface" suggests "a process of crystallization which had fused her whole being into one hard, brilliant substance" (198). What began as a windowlike beauty through which one could see to her personality becomes, like the surface of a mirror, an image with nothing behind it. What had been only a tool for creating the self has become the self—a moment of triumph for the mirror and total effacement for any part of Lily's being not defined by the mirror.

Sophy Viner in *The Reef* (1912) is another one of Wharton's female characters who identifies with the mirror and even builds a principle of justice on the basis of the image in the glass. Sophy wonders why some other women have fine things "all tumbled into their laps" and she does not, even though her mirror tells her she is just as pretty as they are. Wharton makes it clear that this is not merely "the petulance of vanity," but a touchstone of how Sophy measures right and wrong (19). Justice—that is, male justice—is supposed to look into the radical nature of things, and is concerned with the true self, with guilt and innocence. But here a principle of justice is founded on an outer presence revealed by the mirror, the final arbiter of the only virtue Sophy recognizes.

In this same novel, George Darrow says of Anna Leath, "nothing short of hairpins and a glass would have restored her self-possession" (29). This could serve as an epigram for all women who do not rebel against the mirror, for such women can compose themselves, know themselves, create themselves only through the mirror. A kind of Blakean point is being made here: "She became what she beheld" is all too true psychologically of a woman who continues through the novel as a paradigm of almost complete mirror-mindedness.[3] When Anna (with her appropriately palindromic name) says that she wants her lover to see her as she is, she means that she wants him to see her as she appears at this moment in the mirror and not as something other than a visual image. For Anna, while looking into her glass, even love becomes "a luminous medium into which she had been bodily plunged" (124). This union of the mirror's reflective surface and the most profound emotions of which Anna is capable reduces love to the exteriority of her own self-conception.

The heroine of Wharton's *The Custom of the Country* (1913), the beautiful and ruthless Undine Spragg, is described early in the novel as a creature who exists totally within the mirror. More specifically, Wharton's imagery of a suffusing brightness transforms Undine before her glass into "some fabled creature whose home was in a beam of light" (21). A mirror image is nothing but reflected light, and Undine similarly exists only as a catoptric presence. Such a metamorphosis into pure brightness might suggest an elevation to a higher plane of being, but for this woman it is a diminution of her humanity to the visual and the evanescent. Although she seems to defy what Wharton calls a "decomposing radiance," a decomposition unfolds when Undine becomes a creature of that incandescence.

Even as a child, Undine defined herself not through active engagement with the people around her, but through the looking glass: she "had taken but a lukewarm interest in the diversions of

3. I paraphrase Blake's line from *The Four Zoas* and extrapolate the useful term "mirror-mindedness" from Joyce's *Finnegans Wake* where he refers to "mirror-minded curiositease" (576).

her playmates. . . . Already Undine's chief delight was to 'dress up' in her mother's Sunday skirt and 'play lady' before the wardrobe mirror." Undine's taste for mirrors outlasts childhood and "she still practised the same secret pantomime":

> Within a few days she would be enacting the scene she was now mimicking; and it amused her to see in advance just what impression she would produce on Mrs. Fairford's guests.
>
> For a while she carried on her chat with an imaginary circle of admirers, twisting this way and that, fanning, fidgeting, twitching at her draperies, as she did in real life when people were noticing her. . . . She therefore watched herself approvingly, admiring the light on her hair, the flash of teeth between her smiling lips, the pure shadows of her throat and shoulders as she passed from one attitude to another. . . .
>
> Presently she ceased to twist and sparkle at her image, and sinking into her chair gave herself up to retrospection. (22–23)

The mirror is both herself (her definition of what she is) and also the other (the audience). This paradoxical doubleness of the mirror is essential to its power. Further, it permits Undine to be an audience to her self, judging the image in the mirror as others will judge her. There is as well a social, sexual, political point in this passage. In male-dominated societies (in this case, New York and Paris at the turn of the century), men use conversation as a means of self-definition and self-projection. Women use mirrors. For Undine, even the basic act of speaking is reduced to a purely visual effect of lips moving in "soundless talk" (22). What is said is inconsequential to her self-representations. This same point is made later in the novel in a discussion among Undine, her mother, and Mrs. Heeny (the masseuse):

> "So you're to see the old gentleman for the first time at this dinner?" Mrs. Heeny pursued. . . .
>
> "Yes, I'm frightened to death!" Undine, laughing confidently, took up a hand-glass and scrutinized the small brown mole above the curve of her upper lip.
>
> "I guess she'll know how to talk to him," Mrs. Spragg averred with a kind of quavering triumph.
>
> "She'll know how to *look* at him, anyhow," said Mrs. Heeny; and Undine smiled at her own image. (86)

Whenever Undine feels threatened, she goes through the ritual of the mirror to regain her power—both her power of self-definition and her power over men. When the wealthy Peter Van Degen tries to escape from Undine's spell, she stands in front of her mirror to gather energy from her reflection that "bloomed out like a flower" (300). This means of charging her self-presence is extended into control over others. Van Degen returns, defeated, as Undine turns from the mirror to gaze with a conqueror's potency at the trembling man.

It is only near the end of the novel when Undine is married to a billionaire Railroad King that she has even an inkling that there is a self beyond the glass: "She had everything she wanted, but she still felt, at times, that there were other things she might want if she knew about them" (591). This statement subtly suggests that self-definition through mirrors is a self-limitation, an imprisonment within the economy of the mirroring process. Some women don't chafe against this; others do. Undine is beginning to chafe. On the very last page of the novel she discovers she wants something the mirror can't provide. She wants to be an ambassador's wife, but her divorces bar her from that station. As she prepares for a party,

> she turned to give herself a last look in the glass, saw the blaze of her rubies, the glitter of her hair, and remembered the brilliant names on her list.
>
> But under all the dazzle a tiny black cloud remained. She had learned that there was something she could never get, something that neither beauty nor influence nor millions could ever buy for her. She could never be an Ambassador's wife; and as she advanced to welcome her first guests she said to herself that it was the one part she was really made for. (594)

"Glass," "blaze," "glitter," "brilliant," "dazzle"—all these words associate her with the mirror. Before, everything could be provided by the ideology—indeed, the theology—of mirrorness. The divorces in her past are something that can't be seen in the mirror; yet they have become part of how people define her. Wharton's extensive dramatization of women who are their images in the glass finally leads to some disturbing questions about that method of becoming one's self.

Female children learn very early in life that the creation of the self and seeing oneself in the mirror are intimately intertwined. For instance, in Margaret Atwood's *Lady Oracle* (1976), a little girl learns this notion by participating in the initiation ritual to become a Brownie:

> . . . you were led across cardboard stepping stones that read CHEERFULNESS, OBEDIENCE, GOOD TURNS and SMILES. You then had to close your eyes and be turned around three times, while the pack chanted,
>
> Twist me and turn me and show me the elf,
> I looked in the water and there saw . . .
>
> Here you were supposed to open your eyes, look into the enchanted pool, which was a hand-mirror surrounded by plastic flowers and ceramic bunnies, and say, "Myself." (61)

This playful ceremony embodies an important phenomenon in a child's development. Atwood calls "Myself" the "magic word," and the mirror is the magic instrument that reveals the self. This same little girl is also fascinated by her mother's daily rite of transformation and self-creation. "Sit there quietly, Joan," the mother says to the daughter. And then, because the rituals at the glass are indeed her profession, the mother tucks a towel around her neck and goes "to work." Joan sometimes dreams she is sitting in a corner of her mother's bedroom, watching her put on her makeup:

> Although her vanity tables became more grandiose as my father got richer, my mother always had a triple mirror, so she could see both sides as well as the front of her head. In the dream, as I watched, I suddenly realized that instead of three reflections she had three actual heads, which rose from her toweled shoulders on three separate necks. This didn't frighten me, as it seemed merely a confirmation of something I'd always known; but outside the door there was a man, a man who was about to open the door and come in. If he saw, if he found out the truth about my mother, something terrible would happen, not only to my mother but to me. . . .
>
> As I grew older, this dream changed. Instead of wanting to stop the mysterious man, I would sit there wishing for him to enter. I wanted him to find out her secret, the secret that I alone knew: my mother was a monster. (66–67)

Joan's dream reveals a psychological truth she is gradually becoming aware of—that women have alternative faces and alternative selves and that it is before the mirror that these different faces are created. The motivation for these acts of self-creation is to construct a face the world, the male, will accept, even desire. Joan realizes that to reveal this transformational magic to men would destroy the feminine illusion. As she grows older and dissociates her own sense of self from her mother's, Joan hopes this "terrible" revelation will occur as a final step toward freedom from the mysterious and Cerberean rites of the mother and of the mirror.

The monstrous implications, and the sense that a woman is changing "actual heads" in Atwood's story, are literalized in a fantasy tale by L. Frank Baum. His *Ozma of Oz* (1907) contains an ultimate, fantastic, hyperbolic dramatization of the woman who becomes a mirror image, a woman in whom there is the total absence of any single, continuous self beyond the various selves revealed by the glass. The route to exaggeration begins with the multiplication of mirrors. Princess Langwidere's rooms are paneled with polished silver so that "her form was mirrored hundreds of times, in walls and ceiling and floor, and whichever way the lady turned her head she could see and admire her own features" (75). The Princess has a collection of thirty heads; but, because she has only one neck, she can wear just one of the heads at a time. She keeps them in separate cupboards with jeweled-framed mirrors on the inside.

> When the Princess got out of her crystal bed in the morning she went to her cabinet, opened one of the velvet-lined cupboards, and took the head it contained from its golden shelf. Then, by the aid of the mirror inside the open door, she put on the head—as neat and straight as could be—and afterwards called her maids to robe her for the day. She always wore a simple white costume, that suited all the heads. For, being able to change her face whenever she liked, the Princess had no interest in wearing a variety of gowns, as have other ladies who are compelled to wear the same face constantly. (77)

This enormously magnified acceptance of the mirror results in self-fragmentation. Since Princess Langwidere can conceive of no personal presence outside the glass, she has all these various selves she can put on. These multiple heads are a spatial equivalent of the temporal change to which any single head of a real person is vulnerable. The fable points to a very real psychological peril. This woman is involved in a wildly exaggerated process of changing appearances, completely undermining the usual desire for continuity of self-presence. The danger is that there is no single, unitary conception of self which at least seems to transcend time and change. Princess Langwidere is totally and comically embedded in the nontranscendent. She has lost her head in mirrors. The only place she finds herself is in the selection of all these images.

Baum presents a kind of horrific wish-fulfillment of women who believe that they are what is in the mirror.[4] It is also a fulfillment of a common male fantasy: every night of the month the lover of Princess Langwidere could go to bed with a different woman. For Baum makes it clear that the Princess is not just putting on different masks and retaining an unchanging self beneath. She is putting on separate selves: "There was only one trouble with [head] No. 17; the temper that went with it (and which was hidden somewhere under the glossy black hair) was fiery, harsh and haughty in the extreme, and it often led the Princess to do unpleasant things which she regretted when she came to wear her other heads" (79). Baum has radically literalized what we have found in so many women in and out of the glass—the constant communion between outer appearance and psychological state.

Just as many women identify themselves with their mirror reflections, so too many men conceive of women in terms provided by those images. Hardy even writes a brief story-poem, "The Cheval-Glass," about a man who thinks that the mirror captures the woman he loves. The glass possesses what is for him the essential presence of the woman. Thus when the beloved dies and all her

4. See Erica Jong's "The Girl in the Mirror":

> Remember how we both loved
> that girl from the Kingdom of Oz?
>
> She had thirty heads—all beautiful—
> but just one dress.
> She kept her heads in a mirrored cupboard
> opened with a ruby key.
> It was chained to her wrist.
>
> She had my heart chained to her wrist!
> I wanted to *be* her. (162–63)

belongings are to be auctioned, the man buys the looking glass that stood in her former chamber and places it next to his bed. For this man, the woman's association with her mirror is so strong that the mirror itself becomes, after her death, a talismanic substitution for the woman.[5] He even intends to break the glass "and bury its fragments" where his grave is to be (339).

Since the mirror image is both self and other, it becomes possible to conceive of a relationship with the glass having a degree of intimacy more intense than any relationship a woman can have with a lover. The most confidential and intrinsic connection a woman can experience is with another who is also herself. The man in W. M. Spackman's *A Presence with Secrets* (1980) sees that this is true about the woman he loves: "Again he saw in his mind the tall cool room that for this whole year now the faint scent of her presence had made her own, and the scrolled and gilded pier glass that a thousand times must have held her image in its blackening depths; and from *it*, he thought despondently, her eyes would have looked out at her open and undissembling, as at no lover ever, but unguarded, primeval, solitary, all-knowing, and serene" (47). For this male speaker, the realm of greatest intimacy is not the bed, but the mirror. When he is thinking about the beloved at her most essential moments, he realizes that these moments are not with him but with an ocular projection of herself. If he wants to see her in a particularly intimate way, he stands in front of the pier glass and imagines her reflection looking back at her. The literal impossibility of seeing her when he stands in front of the mirror indicates the barriers to complete closeness which stand between this man and woman.

Hardy and Spackman create male characters who believe that the image in the mirror represents the totality of the woman as an object of male desire. The woman may function in other ways outside that relationship, but within it she is, for the man, essentially a visual image.[6] Both writers recognize the destructive lim-

5. For a similar keepsake but on a smaller scale and in a lighter vein, see Alison Lurie's *Foreign Affairs* (1984). The man (a professor of English) preserves "a square of pocket mirror with the mauve-pink imprint" of his beloved's lipsticked mouth on it (227).

6. It is almost as though such men were unconscious believers in the Japanese myth (cited by Pounds and Salus) of the sun goddess who, when she "handed her

itations of the masculine tendency to create this substitution. They differ from most other male writers who also identify the woman with the mirror but then proceed to criticize the woman for what they take to be her self-absorption. Traditionally, the mirror is employed as an attribute of the vain woman—whether she be Guillaume de Lorris's Idleness in the thirteenth century, Spenser's Duessa (daughter of Deceit and Shame) in the sixteenth century, or Superbia from any of a dozen Renaissance emblem books.[7] One of the clearest examples of the male critique of the woman / mirror relationship is the fear by the first male that the first female will prefer self-love to other-love. Adam, in Milton's *Paradise Lost*, must cry out, "Return fair *Eve*," as he sees her running away from him and back to "that smooth wat'ry image" of herself she saw reflected in the lake (4.480–81). The scene with Adam and Eve is an apt epitome of many standard emblems about the mirror of vanity and suggests why men find it so threatening.

Milton sees Eve's "fall" for her self-image in the water as a typological harbinger of the Fall itself. In our own century, D. H. Lawrence has suggested that the human propensity for immorality is the product of self-consciousness established through mirroring, literal or metaphoric. From the recognition of an otherness as a projection of the self come the categories of good and evil:

> Man alone is immoral
> Neither beasts nor flowers are.
>
> Because man, poor beast, can look at himself
> And know himself in the glass.
>
> He doesn't bark at himself, as a dog does
> When he looks at himself in the glass.
> He takes himself seriously. (836)

---

grandson Nini-gi no mikoto the first mirror, told him, 'Look upon this mirror as my spirit: keep it in the same house and on the same floor with yourself, and worship it as if you were worshipping my actual presence'" (157).

7. See de Lorris, "The Dreamer Enters the Garden of Mirth," *The Romance of the Rose*, where Idleness holds a mirror in her hand; Spenser, *Faerie Queene*, book 1, canto 4, stanza 10, in which Duessa holds "a mirrhour bright, / Wherein her face she often vewed fayne" (1:44). For the standard Renaissance emblem of Superbia or Pride, see illustrated editions of Cesare Ripa's *Iconologia*, first published in 1593.

Although in this poem it is human beings, whether male or female, who take themselves "seriously" in the glass and thus create self-consciousness, in much of Lawrence's writing it is the woman's toxic relationship with her mirror that comes under attack. One of his short stories, "The White Stocking," traces just how the male / female bond breaks down as the mirror / female bond becomes stronger. The young wife is initially described as an untamed natural creature; and, even when she is before the mirror, her activities are merely functional, like a man's, and indulge in nothing resembling vanity or meditation. But after an ex-lover sends her some earrings, she becomes a far more self-conscious personality: "With a little flash of triumph, she lifted a pair of pearl ear-rings from the small box, and she went to the mirror. There, earnestly, she began to hook them through her ears, looking at herself sideways in the glass. Curiously concentrated and intent she seemed as she fingered the lobes of her ears, her head bent on one side. . . . She turned to look at the box. . . . But she was drawn to the mirror again, to look at her ear-rings" (245–46). The young woman has changed. Before, she was careless and active; now she is beginning "earnestly" to construct herself as an independent female will directed toward self-involvement. Her action is turning deliberate and inward. She is becoming more interested in herself than in the men (either husband or ex-lover) as her acts all become projections of mental attitudes: "She examined [the ear-rings] with voluptuous pleasure, she threaded them in her ears, she looked at herself, she posed and postured and smiled and looked sad and tragic and winning and appealing, all in turn before the mirror" (250). Her poses are self-consciously constructed, and it is the mirror that assists her in this artifice.

Lawrence's poem "Intimates" is a little parable that he offers to the self-involved woman:

> Don't you care for my love? she said bitterly.
>
> I handed her the mirror, and said:
> Please address these questions to the proper person!
> Please make all requests to head-quarters!
> In all matters of emotional importance
> please approach the supreme authority direct!
> So I handed her the mirror.

> And she would have broken it over my head,
> but she caught sight of her own reflection
> and that held her spellbound for two seconds
> while I fled. (604)

According to the male speaker, the woman should not be worrying about the exact degree of appreciation of her love. The man realizes that the mirror is the center of control and command for this woman—a mirror connected with the mind ("head-quarters"), not with the vital body (with an implied pun on "hindquarters"). Again, Lawrence implicitly but bitterly criticizes self-objectification and contemplation of the projected image as a form of vanity.

Lawrence wants men and women to love and to give themselves up to each other. The mirror irritates him so thoroughly because he sees a fascination with the image in the glass as a form of unfruitful, solipsistic love since the beloved is only the self. This formulation of mirroring matches Lawrence's description of the result of masturbation: all that remains afterward is "a half-empty creature fatally self-preoccupied and incapable of either giving or taking" ("Pornography and Obscenity," 43). For so many of the writers we have considered, the mirror is a social instrument, one that assists in the formation of the self according to cultural norms. But for Lawrence, a woman's relationship with the glass thwarts that basic process of surrendering to the other. The power of the male, through which the woman is supposed to define herself, is broken when she becomes involved with the substitute male, the mirror. Thus the woman in Lawrence's short story "The Border Line" avoids "the sight of her own face in the mirror" as she undresses because "she must not rupture the spell of [the man's] presence" (597). Lawrence seems perfectly willing to define women as objects to men but not to themselves.

The woman, as Lawrence suggests in his poem "Know Deeply, Know Thyself More Deeply," should lose herself in the man, not in the mirror:

> . . . Go down to your deep old heart, woman, and lose sight of
> yourself.
> And lose sight of me, the me whom you turbulently loved.

> Let us lose sight of ourselves, and break the mirrors. . . .
>
> If you can only sit with a mirror in your hand,
> an ageing woman
> posing on and on as a lover,
> in love with a self that now is shallow and withered,
> your own self—that has passed like a last summer's flower—
> then go away— (477–78)

Because Lawrence so identifies the act of looking in a mirror with the act of individuating self-conception, the breaking of the mirrors is a physical symbol of the process of losing one's self. The self-love promoted by the glass is vain and "shallow"—literally, because its object is on the silvered surface, and psychologically, because the feelings it stimulates do not penetrate to "the deep dark living heart" (478) of Lawrentian blood-consciousness. The woman must forget the ego and dissolve into the greater male / female unity.

Hermione Roddice is described in Lawrence's *Women in Love* (1920) as "a woman of the new school, full of intellectuality and . . . nerve-worn with consciousness" (17). In one of his verbal attacks on Hermione, Rupert Birkin intimates an important truth about the centrality of the mirror in female identity: "'It's all that Lady of Shalott business,' [Birkin] said, in his strong abstract voice. . . . 'You've got that mirror, your own fixed will, your immortal understanding, your own tight conscious world, and there is nothing beyond it. There, in the mirror, you must have everything'" (45–46). As a Lawrentian male, Birkin is against those actions, mental and physical, whereby the female creates her conscious will in private in front of a glass. That process of composition has many different facets, but here Birkin is seeing the mirror as a substitute for a man. The four words, "your own fixed will," describe a state of female consciousness that it is Lawrence's whole business to destroy. Birkin and Lawrence want the woman to be created as a reflection of masculine desires rather than through acts of self-reflection. In Lawrence's paradigms of sexual psychology, the man and the mirror struggle for mastery over female consciousness.

Birkin's attack on the mirror is an integral part of his attack on self-consciousness. Lawrence, speaking through Birkin, senses that within the mirror, that self-enclosure, the woman develops her conscious will: "What you want is pornography—looking at yourself in mirrors, watching your naked animal actions in mirrors, so that you can have it all in your consciousness, make it all mental" (46). Most authors who criticize the glass do so because it is a sign of a woman's submission to masculine values. Lawrence presents just the reverse: the mirror does not make the woman a slave to the male world, but stimulates a woman's self-consciousness that inhibits her merging into the male. In some ways the authors closest to Lawrence's critique of the mirror are women writers, beginning with the Brontës and George Eliot, who see that the mirror is intimately connected with self-realization and self-creation. Beyond that initial connection, however, they valorize the processes and products of mirroring in very different ways. For Lawrence, the result is only a form of "pornography" and the willful search for self-stimulation.

For Theodore Roethke, a woman can become stuck in the mirror stage of development, a self-absorption that inhibits the male / female union much as it does in the Lawrentian view.[8] The speaker in Roethke's "Fourth Meditation" from *Meditations of an Old Woman* (1958) asks:

> What is it to be a woman?
> To be contained, to be a vessel?
> To prefer a window to a door?
> A pool to a river? . . . (169)

A man walks through the "door" into the world, but a woman can be reflected in a "window." The "river" suggests the passage of time as men define themselves through past and future; women define themselves through looking in the still "pool." As the poet states a few lines later, women are "ritualists of the mirror" who become "self-involved." Roethke's moral objection to this condition is registered in one of his unpublished notebooks where he

8. Richard Blessing is another modern American poet who senses that the mirror is powerful and can take the woman away from the man. As he writes in "What I Know by Heart," "You said one day you'd walk into a mirror / until it pulled out like a train" (65).

describes a woman "who expends herself in mirrors, like a whore."[9]

Doris Lessing's *Martha Quest* (1952) illustrates the kind of situation that Lawrence and Roethke begin with and attack. The eponymous heroine of the novel is an adolescent girl living with her provincial parents in a town in central Africa: "She spent much time, at night, examining herself with a hand mirror; she sometimes propped the mirror by her pillow, and, lying beside it, would murmur like a lover, 'Beautiful, you are so beautiful'" (16). We again confront some of the basic features of the mirror image and its capabilities to be both self and other. The mirror facilitates the pretense, the psychic fiction, that there is someone else crooning, "You are so beautiful." The mirror is a male who will compliment, rather than a female, like Martha's mother, who frequently criticizes. The mirror allows Martha to establish an identity outside of the only social context available, her family, which Lessing characterizes as disparaging. Through the glass Martha can escape into a world where there is a voice softly reiterating her own desires.

Martha sometimes uses two mirrors to study herself: "She would take the mirror to her parents' bedroom, and hold it at an angle to the one at the window, and examine herself, at this double remove, in profile; for this view of herself had a delicacy her full face lacked" (16). Her "double remove" is also a double projection so that she can see herself in profile, a way in which others can normally perceive her but she cannot. This additional step shows how important the mirror is—almost as though the further she removes the mirror image from herself, the more beautiful she can seem to be to herself. She is searching for an image others can see which will fulfill her own ideal of beauty. Sensing that her parents still want her to be a little girl, she uses the mirror as a way of creating another self, not as a child but as a woman visible to men.

In a much later scene with Douglas, the man she eventually marries, Martha internalizes the mirror. Even in its absence, she can see herself as an object of her own concentrated gaze. In Douglas's room, they lie together on the bed, and he begins to caress

9. Theodore Roethke Collection, University of Washington, Seattle (Notebooks, Box 44, No. 218 [1958]).

her. She is ready "to abandon herself," but the man keeps murmuring how beautiful she is (220). The detachment that comes with self-consciousness forces Martha into the role of an observer—not of the man but "of her own body, as if she were scrutinizing it with his eyes."[10] Douglas's "fervent rite of adoration" continues for what seems like hours. Unsatisfied, and with "her spirit cold and hostile," Martha leaves the bed, dresses herself, and crosses "in front of a mirror" to see "if the lines of her body . . . approximate . . . those laid down by the idea of what is desirable" (220–21). Martha receives nothing from Douglas she has not already acquired from the looking glass. This young woman, when she is with a man, repeats her experiences with a mirror, as though she were imprisoned in the mirror stage of self-conception and fantasy. She waits for the man to do something that will stop her from identifying her vision with his and will submerge the detached self in the active body, but this experience merely reinforces the division. Instead of going beyond the glass, Martha is going back into it, back into an idea of the desirable established by those private rites of self-scrutiny before her mirror.

In his poem "Know Deeply," Lawrence says to the woman, "Lose sight of yourself" (477). This is precisely what Martha cannot do. The mirror won't let her, and the man's actions only increase the mirror's dominion over her mind. Douglas says, "Look at yourself," as he insistently forces her "back to consciousness" (220). At first, Martha substituted the mirror for the man. Now, in another act of displacement, she has chosen a man who is a substitute for the mirror. She is, to borrow Lawrence's vocabulary, "enclosed within the vicious circle of the self" ("Pornography and Obscenity," 43). She is not released from the glass, neither has she found the kind of man who might be able to rescue her. We need not accept Lawrence's vision of female self-abnegation to appreciate his insights into women who cannot conceive of alternatives to an identity wholly dependent on the mirror. Beyond the emblems of vanity lie very real predicaments for the woman ab-

10. In her discussion of Lessing's *Martha Quest*, Spacks notes that "Douglas deprives her [Martha] of reality in the act of worshipping her body" by "participating in that aspect of her fantasy that makes her beauty something external to her self" (154).

sorbed in and by the looking glass. Her self-image is quite literally external, visual, and physical. Incorporated and incarcerated, her self-conception is subject to the same acts of time and chance that flesh is heir to. As we shall see in the following chapter, it is again the mirror that can privately and minutely register these material changes, predict their social consequences, and translate them into psychological conditions.

4.

The Glass of Time

All the future is concentrated in that sheet of light,
a universe within the mirror's frame.
Simone de Beauvoir

The experiences provided by the mirror are so obviously ocular and spatial that it is easy to overlook the ways in which repeated acts of mirroring give the glass a temporal dimension. When a woman looks at her reflected image, it is often difficult for her to avoid two other faces besides the one existing in the present tense: what she has seen before in the mirror, and what she hopes or fears she will see in the future. These tenses of the mirror multiply the possibilities for differences among a variety of self-conceptions. In turn, these centripetal movements will lead us to more entangled dramas of identification and alienation operating along both the spatial and temporal axes of the glass.

Literature, especially from the medieval period through the Renaissance, has many fantastic mirrors that reveal future evils and catastrophes. In "The Squire's Tale" from Chaucer's *The Canterbury Tales*, for instance, he who looks in the magic mirror "may see / The coming shadow of adversity" upon himself and his kingdom (408). The Witches present a Show of Kings who "come like shadows" to Macbeth, and the last king bears a "glass" that shows the Stuart line stretching out "to the crack of doom" (*Macbeth*,4.1.117). For women, the mirror need not be supernatural to be prophetic. Every mirror can indicate a future.[1] For the most

1. This is the message that a woman finds written in crimson lipstick on a mirror in a ladies' room: "If you're looking for the future, you're looking in the right place" (31). See Mary Robison's short story "Mirror" (1985).

part, the coming shadows are under the eyes, and what the mirror indicates to women is aging.

Hsüeh T'ao (768–831), one of the leading women poets of the T'ang dynasty, shows that the belief in the mirror's mantic powers is centuries old:

> Blossoms crowd the branches: too beautiful to endure.
> Thinking of you, I break into bloom again.
> One morning soon, my tears will mist the mirror.
> I see the future, and I will not see. (123)

Even in their fruitfulness, both the branches and the woman bespeak decay. The woman is beautiful now, but she knows she will presently look in the glass and weep. What the human being brings to the blossoms, to the mirror, to everything is the knowledge of *tempus edax*.

There are numerous lyrics by Hsüeh T'ao, Yü Hsüan-chi (ca. 843–868), Li Ch'ing-chao (1084?–ca. 1151), Chu Shu-chen (ca. 1200), and many other Chinese women poets in which a woman watches her face in her jade mirror and sees herself as a symbol of time. As Lady Ise of tenth-century Japan writes, "Each day more clearly / my mirror offers / a face I am ashamed to show" (164). Or as Tada Chimako of twentieth-century Japan concludes her brief poem "Mirror":

> My mirror is the cemetery of smiles.
> Traveler, when you come to Lakaidaimon,
> tell them that there stands here a grave,
> painted white with heavy makeup,
> with only wind blowing in the mirror. (176–77)

All these are spatial poems in the sense that we see their brief form and seize their meaning as a single image. Yet the whole force of them is toward time. This is the same quality we find in mirrors: the reflection is nontemporal and exists only in the moment of perception; still, it can be used as a stimulus to thoughts of temporality. Perhaps the mirror appears so often in these Asian verses because the poems themselves are spatial forms with the potential for temporal extension.

In Virginia Woolf's *Mrs. Dalloway* (1925), Clarissa is deeply worried about her age, having "just broken into her fifty-second year." She tries "to catch the falling drop" of the passing months and hold back their "icy claws" in an instant of self-possession outside time. She "plunged into the very heart of the moment, transfixed it, there—the moment of this June morning on which was the pressure of all the other mornings, seeing the glass, the dressing-table, and all the bottles afresh, collecting the whole of her at one point (as she looked into the glass), seeing the delicate pink face of the woman who was that very night to give a party; of Clarissa Dalloway; of herself" (54). Clarissa looks into the mirror as if it were a camera taking a snapshot of her permanent identity that will not grow older. The experience reveals its conceptual kinship with Joyce's epiphanies and T. S. Eliot's "still point of the turning world" (180). So often the mirror is used as a clock, as a record of duration, but here it is used as a way of suspending time for a moment. Perhaps this may help explain why a character in Ann Beattie's short story "Shifting" goes to the glass in the bedroom, holds her Instamatic camera above her head, and photographs her image in the mirror to create a lasting record of a frozen instant (67). The same process occurs in Betty Smith's *A Tree Grows in Brooklyn* (1943) when a young girl takes out her compact and looks at herself in the mirror after she reads in a newspaper (dated 6 April 1917) that war has been declared. "If I can fix every detail of this time in my mind, I can keep this moment always," she states (370).

In some contexts, the dominance of the mirror is so great that time itself is measured by the glass. In Wharton's *The Mother's Recompense* (1925), Kate Clephane is trying to figure out the age of her daughter Anne whom she deserted years ago: "But if Chris [her ex-lover] were thirty-one, and she forty-five, then how old *was* Anne? With impatient fingers she began all over again. . . . Mrs. Clephane roused herself, looked about the room, and exclaimed: 'My looking-glass, please.' She wanted to settle that question of ages" (11). The mirror that reflects space (not time) becomes the decider of temporal issues. Since a woman is, in this masculine world, as old as she looks, time is defined by, almost created by, men. Age is less a matter of chronology in an objective sense than of how males react to her and thereby begin or end the stages of her life. That other self cast in a mirror is a way of seeing what men see, and then the woman can determine at a glance how old she is in this social sense. From that information, Kate believes she can extrapolate the age of someone else. The reasoning here is extremely weak, perhaps nonsensical, but its emotional and cultural underpinnings are real enough.

Some women can even measure time by their physical location relative to a mirror. Lydia in Godwin's *A Mother and Two Daughters* has returned to the house where she grew up. She admires herself in an oval mirror that hangs above a table in the hall: "When they had first moved into the house, she could see only the top of her curly head in this glass, but now she was completely centered in it. She had to admit she was better-looking now than at any previous time in her life" (86). It was in this home and in the mirror that Lydia first developed a concept of selfhood, now fully "centered," psychically as much as spatially, in the mirror and in those confident good-looks she confirms by gazing in the glass.

One way a woman knows she is growing older is by looking in the mirror and meeting her mother's face. In *Beauty Bound*, psychologist Rita Freedman cites a forty-two-year-old woman who confides, "I see myself shriveling up with age, just like my mother. Every morning when I put on my makeup, I see her face staring up at me" (33). The daughter's experience of finding out what she has always known—that she is her mother's reflection—does not necessarily have to be distressing. The woman in Alice Walker's short story "Coming Apart" (1980) looks in a mirror "at her plump brown and black body, crinkly hair and black eyes" and realizes that she is turning into her mother. "But, surprisingly, while watching herself become her mother in the mirror, she discovers that *she* considers her mother . . . *very* sexy. At once she feels restored" (45). When Eugenia Ginzburg (1906–1977), confined for years in various Russian prisons, finally had the chance to look into a mirror, it was *only* through her resemblance to her mother that she was able even to recognize herself (315). In this case, similitude became the ground of identity.

Many authors even make a point of having their characters look into mirrors that actually belong, or formerly belonged, to their mothers.[2] What a woman sees in such a mirror is, of course, her mother. Dorinda Oakley in Ellen Glasgow's *Barren Ground* (1925) has been toiling arduously on an impoverished farm. When she stares at herself in her mother's mirror, "it seemed to her that another face was watching her beyond her reflection, a face that was drawn and pallid, with a corded neck and the famished eyes of a disappointed dreamer" (276). The daughter is in part a genetic replication of the mother, a biological mirroring that can be signified by the image in the glass as the girl becomes what her mother became—old. The basic self / other paradox (both me and not me) of the mirror image is analogous to the self / other interrelationship of mother and daughter. In one's mother's mirror, there is a double image, the echo and re-echo, the reflection of the self and the ghostly unseen presence of the parent. The woman undergoes a twofold testing of identity, proved both by that cold objective glass and by the overlay of the image of the mother. And that real reflection can make adjustments both in the woman's self-conception and in her conception of her mother. The daughter is the mother in some biological and even sociological ways; and, the more rigid the society, the more literally this is true. Even in the most advanced Western cultures, there is a sense in which daughters recapitulate the lives of their mothers. These authentic yet prophetic mirrors, like the ones in the stories by Walker and Glasgow, reveal such truths whether hopeful or bitter.[3]

Sometimes a daughter looks in her mother's mirror because she is looking *for* her mother. Clara Maugham's mother is in the hospital dying of cancer (Margaret Drabble, *Jerusalem the Golden*, 1967). Although Clara does not love her mother, she returns home to see her. She spends the night in her old house filled "with so many recollections of the suffering of her childhood." Because she wants

2. I have found very few examples in which a son looks into his mother's mirror, but one such instance does occur in Joyce's *A Portrait of the Artist as a Young Man* (1916). Stephen Dedalus, after writing a love poem, "went into his mother's bedroom and gazed at his face for a long time in the mirror of her dressing table" (71).

3. For a detailed study of mother-daughter interrelationships, but without specific reference to scenes of actual mirroring, see Chodorow, *The Reproduction of Mothering*. Chodorow's sense of a daughter / mother "dual unity" as a satisfying but potentially dangerous dependency (109, 166, 199, 200) parallels the woman / mirror relationship for those whose identity is heavily dependent on their reflected image.

to try to understand her mother and her connection with her, Clara rummages through various drawers and comes upon some old notebooks and photographs (lasting mirror images) which finally give her some insight into her mother's life. But the quest starts with an inquiring look in the mother's mirror (239). Joanna Bannerman in Catherine Carswell's *Open the Door!* (1920) also searches through her mother's wardrobe and finds packets of letters, faded photographs, and old journals. She finds a box full of plaits of hair, each "lovingly labelled." She draws out a lock of her mother's hair: "And there before the dressing-table mirror which had so often reflected her mother's painful toilets, she laid it against her own light brown head. As she had thought, it was of the very same texture and colour as her own hair" (242). It is a tender moment for this somewhat rebellious daughter to feel, and see in the glass, her connection with her mother.

In addition to scenes of a daughter seeing herself becoming her mother in the mirror, a mother can see in her reflection a prophecy of what her child will become. Harriet in Elizabeth Taylor's *A Game of Hide-and-Seek* (1951) catches her own face faintly reflected in the glass over her daughter's photograph. She notices that in some respects the two faces are the same; "yet, physically, the reflection was something in the future, a forward-going ghost, awaiting the child. The faint lines on the forehead and the less clear outline of the jaw were in the nature of a premonition" (159). In another of her novels, *Palladian* (1969), Taylor presents the reverse of this scene, a little girl observing her own reflection above a photograph of her mother. The same question about the daughter's future arises, for the child tries as best she can to imitate her mother's provocative expression (77).

Women, when they look in mirrors, apprehend things that are not literally present. They can see a future (what Taylor calls a "forward-going ghost") or a past. In Lessing's *Martha Quest*, Martha sees both. While attending her first dance, she wanders into a bedroom. Coming upon a large mirror, she strips off her clothes and confronts her first full-length image of herself: "It was as if she saw a vision of someone not herself; or rather, herself transfigured to the measure of a burningly insistent future. The white naked girl with high small breasts that leaned forward out of the mirror was like a girl from a legend; she put forward her hands to touch, then as they encountered the cold glass, she saw the naked arms of the girl slowly rise to fold defensively across those breasts. She did not know herself" (78). Martha beholds herself "transfigured" in a mirror—literally seeing her whole figure and psychically moving toward a more complete concept of identity. Paradoxically, that "quest" begins with an alienation from her own bodily presence, now projected as "someone not herself." But this sense of spatial difference is immediately transformed into a temporal doubleness: the self Martha sees is both a harbinger of a "burningly insistent future" and a recollection of something from the mythic past of "legend," a term that further complicates the distinction between the real and the imagined. The glass has assisted Martha in a process of diffusion and fragmentation necessary to retrieve her past and gain a sense of destiny. Like the psychoanalytic methods this mirror scene replicates structurally, the experience is not without danger to the present self. Given these manifold complexities, it is not surprising that the encounter ends with an act of nonrecognition.

Belying the title of the novel in which she appears, when Joan Foster gazes into the glass in Atwood's *Lady Oracle*, she sees only the time gone by. Even as a child Joan was fat. She finally manages, when she is a teen-ager, to lose one hundred pounds, and she eventually marries Arthur, who knows nothing about her earlier problem. But that other male, the mirror, remembers Joan's past: "When I looked at myself in the mirror, I didn't see what Arthur saw. The outline of my former body still surrounded me, like a mist, like a phantom moon, like the image of Dumbo the Flying Elephant superimposed on my own. I wanted to forget the past, but it refused to forget me" (214). The temporal dimension of the mirror is again revealed. Since Joan first saw herself and thus conceived of herself as a fat girl, the residual outline is still present around the thin self. When Joan looks at herself in the glass, there are three forms in attendance: the woman, the image in the mirror, and the "former body." This third image can have a profound influence on behavior because it is part of her psychological being. The past and one's ideas about the future are part of the self shaped by those repeated experiences, from childhood to old age, before the mirror.

As I noted in the introduction, Lacan has alerted us to the importance of first encounters with mirrors. For most females, at least those created in fiction, the memorable scene is not in infancy as Lacan indicates. Neither is it necessarily a singular incident; indeed, many characters experience a succession of "primal" confrontations with the mirror at various stages in their development, from childhood through adolescence.[4] These moments of self-discovery and self-creation often adumbrate much in a woman's later life. A consideration of some important acts of mirroring early in a female character's history will extend our understanding of the temporality of the glass.

In *The Scarlet Letter*, Hester Prynne tells her six-year-old daughter Pearl to run down to the edge of the water and play with the shells and seaweed. There the child looks into a tide pool but, instead of seeing herself, believes she is seeing "the image of a little maid" who invites her into the water. When Pearl steps in, she beholds "her own white feet," and all that remains of "the visionary little maid" is "the gleam of a kind of fragmentary smile, floating to and fro in the agitated water" (160). By stepping into the pool and physically joining with the mirror, Pearl begins to undermine the fantasy of the absolute otherness of the image. By the end of the passage, she is just starting to realize that the reflection is she, although she is still not able to integrate all the parts of herself into a unified self-conception.

Later, we learn that Pearl's experience at the pool has created an indeterminacy, for she does not know whether "she or the image was unreal" (168). As we have seen, Balzac's Valerie, whose self is submerged in a masculine, social conception of the female as object, decides that she is not real, but that the image is. As we shall see, for a child like Charlotte Brontë's Jane Eyre, the otherness of the phantom prophesies a revolt against the mirror. At this point for Little Pearl, we are as uncertain as she is which route will be followed—whether she will be completely absorbed by the *alter*

4. Girls look into the mirror after experiencing their first menstrual cramps in Betty Smith's *A Tree Grows in Brooklyn* and in Lillian Hellman's *An Unfinished Woman*; a thirteen-year-old takes the first puff of her first cigarette in front of the mirror in Jessamyn West's *Cress Delahanty*; a nineteen-year-old looks deep into her eyes in the mirror just before attempting her first liquor store robbery in an Ellen Gilchrist story. Each of these acts takes on something of the importance of a primal scene in the lives of these characters.

idem in the mirror or will mature into a heroine who has a strong conception of self and refuses to identify self-presence with the image in the pool. Because she smiles at and flirts with her reflection, however, we might suspect a Valerie in the making, not a Jane.

Since she is only a child, albeit a precocious one, Pearl soon loses interest in the watery image and turns elsewhere for amusement. But for the adolescent girl, there is often no better pastime than gazing in the looking glass. As Kim Chernin writes in *The Obsession*, "Adolescent girls are drawn to study their own reflection in the mirror. This musing observation of self becomes for them a ritual activity, performed in private, away from the judgmental, censorious, often punitive attitudes of their culture. It is a tender activity, having less to do with vanity, more to do with introspection and the acquisition of self-knowledge" (157–58).

A girl in preadolescence frequently has a fragmented sense of self. This problem is dramatized and elevated above the threshold of self-consciousness through her attempts to perceive, and establish a balanced relationship with, her image (or images) in the mirror. Frankie Addams in Carson McCullers's *The Member of the Wedding* (1946) is a gawky, lonely twelve-year-old suspended between being a child and an adult. Being motherless, Frankie feels cut off from the past; and she is frightened of the future because she is taller than other girls her age and fears she will grow even more. Again and again she stares at her reflection in the "watery mirror" above the kitchen sink. With her painfully short hair, Frankie seems to herself half-girl, half-boy, like the "morphodite" she saw in the Freak House: "She stood before the mirror and she was afraid" (16). Her indeterminacy in conceiving of herself and even of her gender is suggested by her multiple names (Frankie, F. Jasmine, Frances). And her lack of a single self-conception is acted out when she tries on an overly sophisticated orange satin evening gown that she has purchased to wear at her brother's wedding: "F. Jasmine looked in the mirror over the sink. She could only see herself from the chest up, so after admiring this top part of herself, she stood on a chair and looked at the middle section. Then she began to clear away a corner of the table so she could climb up and see in the mirror the silver shoes" (86). Frankie has yet to put all her "sections" together into a unified identity. These passages stress the ways looking in the glass can be a profound psychological confrontation. The fragmented mirror suggests a fragmented self. The "warped and crooked" (2) reflection in the glass overstates only slightly Frankie's (and most pre-teenage girls') capacity to distort body image.

The fact that an adolescent girl has not established a stable relationship with her mirror image is part and parcel of her inability to establish relationships with other people, particularly with young men. In Joyce Carol Oates's novella "A Sentimental Education" (1979), for instance, fourteen-year-old Antoinette is in love with Duncan, her older and "frequently critical" cousin. In his presence, she finds it difficult "to keep her rapt worshipful gaze from him." When alone, she spends hours gazing at the mirror, "as if seeking confirmation of her love" from that image which "shared her secret":

> She studied her mirror image with care and knew that she was pretty. She was very pretty. . . . And then again she saw with a sickening dismay that she was not pretty at all: she was quite plain, even homely. . . .
>
> "Does he love me?" she said aloud. "Does he think about me . . . . What does he think about me . . . ?"
>
> It was a riddle so perplexing, so exhilarating, that she sometimes burst into laughter. . . . And sometimes into tears. (149)

As she awakens to her sense of self and of sexual longing, Antoinette cannot withhold her gaze from the mirror or from the man. But because she is so ill-defined, she has trouble making use of the glass and reading its images as anything other than multiple and contradictory. In response to her implicit questions, it alternatively replies "pretty" and "homely." She can "read" the mirror no better than she can interpret the man. The instability of this situation is registered in her emotional response—alternating smiles and tears. Neither society (her cousin) nor its substitute (the mirror) is offering the sorts of reflections that can aid in constructing a stable self-image.

The more unsure of herself the adolescent girl is, the more frequently and frantically she looks into the glass. In another of Oates's stories, "Honeybit" (1966), Honeybit Mason's father is gone and her alcoholic mother provides no mirroring, no nurturing presence to help the daughter develop her own sense of self. Thus Oates hints at a slight disparity between Honeybit's self and her mirror image: "Honeybit lifted her eyes against her will and looked into the room, but she was safe from having to see her mother because the bed was off to the right, out of sight. Instead Honeybit noticed her own pale blue reflection, across the way, in the mirrored door of her mother's closet. The door was ajar just a little, an inch or so, and Honeybit's image was subtly slanted. She looked even thinner than she was. She looked frightened. To bring the image to life, Honeybit raised one hand to her hair, quickly . . . brushed it back behind her ear and lifted her chin . . . and the girl in the mirror did the same" (420). Lacking parents, Honeybit turns to something else—the glass. There she finds a second, perceived self, similar but not identical to the perceiving self. In *The Second Sex*, Simone de Beauvoir has described such an experience as one in which the girl "becomes as object, and she sees herself as object; she discovers this new aspect of her being with surprise: it seems to her that she has been doubled; instead of coinciding exactly with herself, she now begins to exist *outside*" (378). Honeybit attempts, however tentatively, to go beyond this disturbing doubleness and assert identity by controlling the mirror image, making it one with her self. Both images—psychological and visual—will thereby be brought "to life."

Honeybit's sense of self is awry:

> . . . she stood motionless in the doorway, looking across at the girl in the mirror who was slanted from her, a little distorted. The girl in the mirror could probably see her mother's bed. In fact she seemed to be staring at it. . . . The girl in the mirror blandly faced the thickset body there in the bed . . . face sagging, dead white, old lipstick from the day before outlandishly bright against the skin. . . .
>
> Honeybit whispered, "Mother . . . ?"
>
> But no reply. Her image across the way seemed to be gazing indifferently at the body on the bed. . . . But Honeybit could not see around the corner and she did not know. She was not going to look. (421–22)

There is something self-protective in *not* looking at the mother—except through this fiction of the glass. Honeybit does not want to become what the mother is. She desperately wants to control the image in the mirror, to have control over herself—the one thing that she can regulate in her disordered life. The otherness, the apparent detachment, of the mirror image serves as a buffer between the girl and the squalid parental environment that threatens to mold her in its own image.

Honeybit feels unsafe when she doesn't have a firm grasp on herself. The mirror tells her that she exists as an object she can perceive, and thus it confirms an "I" that must also exist as a subject. At school, the girl gets excused during study hall to go to the lavatory, where she can gaze at her reflection and thus validate herself. Even though the bathroom is dirty, "Honeybit always felt safe in it" because of the mirror (427). For this mirroraholic daughter, as for her alcoholic mother, one glass is never enough. Even during class, she nervously and addictively sneaks a quick "fix" by surreptitiously opening her compact (428). There she is relieved to find herself "looking the same as usual." Except for the mirror, Honeybit has no resource for asserting her fragile and anguished self-presence or for calming her excessive anxiety. An absent or threatening or sick mother forces on a young woman a special need for the looking glass.

For some adolescent girls, almost every significant episode in their lives is connected with the mirror. At seventeen, Charity Royall (*Summer*, 1917) is one of Edith Wharton's youngest heroines. Charity's mother gave her away when she was an infant, and thus, like Frankie and Honeybit, Charity has had no mother to help her struggle through the problems of female development. As the novel begins, she is about to step out of the house where she lives with her guardian, but the sight of a young man, a stranger, causes her to draw back. Once inside, she immediately turns to "a narrow greenish mirror with a gilt eagle over it" and examines her image critically. When Charity murmurs to her reflection, "How I hate everything!" (4), she means that she hates what she thinks must be every man's evaluation of her. She has seen in the mirror—with its hovering, masculine bird of prey—what she believes to be the verdict of the male world: she is young, poorly dressed, swarthy.

The night after she has actually met the young stranger, Lucius Harney, Charity performs a basic ritual for the adolescent girl whose sense of self-presence has not been formed: having been seen by the male, she hurries to the mirror to see what he saw. Her primary concern is not with what the man looks like or how he may have impressed her, but with how *she* looked to him. The man is the one who must be pleased with what he sees. Alone in her room, Charity remembers the change in Lucius's expression when he first noticed her: "She ran over the bare boards to her washstand, found the matches, lit a candle, and lifted it to the square of looking-glass on the whitewashed wall. . . . A clumsy band and button fastened her unbleached night-gown about the throat. She undid it, freed her thin shoulders, and saw herself a bride in low-necked satin, walking down an aisle with Lucius Harney. He would kiss her as they left the church. . . . She put down the candle and covered her face with her hands as if to imprison the kiss" (27–28). Charity is trying to create herself according to her own fantasies. The relations among the mirror, the male, and the process of self-definition are clear: "he" is the active principle here; the girl sees herself as object—to be looked at, chosen, kissed, undressed. The girl conceives of herself wholly as a perceived object and invests in the male all the powers of the perceiving subject. Her own subjectivity is under the control of the man, the mirror, and the private narratives they stimulate.

As Charity falls more in love (and into sexuality) with Lucius, she falls more in love with her own reflection. When fashionably attired and in the right light, her small face glows in the mirror. To study herself closely, Charity props "the square of looking-glass against Mr. Royall's black leather Bible" (91). The mirror becomes her Gospel, the book wherein the truth is revealed for her, for the only truth she is interested in at this point in her life is how she looks to a man.

When Lucius takes Charity into town for a day, Wharton opens up the mirror process to a wider social environment: "Charity found herself in a dressing-room all looking-glass and lustrous surfaces, where a party of showy-looking girls were dabbing on powder and straightening immense plumed hats" (99). There are whole communities of women preparing their faces to please men. The mirror is thus connected with Charity's introduction to the greater world—she learns she must compete with all the other creatures who create themselves in mirrors. Charity ultimately fails in this competition, for her affair with Lucius ends when he leaves her for another woman. After she finds out she is going to have a baby, Charity again consults the mirror: "The coming of a new day brought a sharper consciousness of ineluctable reality, and with it a sense of the need of action. She looked at herself in the glass, and saw her face, white in the autumn dawn, with pinched cheeks and dark-ringed eyes, and all the marks of her state that she herself would never have noticed, but that Dr. Merkle's diagnosis had made plain to her. She could not hope that those signs would escape the watchful village; even before her figure lost its shape she knew her face would betray her" (174). When the consciousness of "ineluctable reality" strikes her, she looks at her glass, because for her the glass is the touchstone of the real. It is almost as if the pregnancy doesn't exist for her unless it is indicated in the mirror, for she is enslaved by what others see. Dr. Merkle has made the diagnosis, but finally it is what she sees in the glass that confirms it.[5] What the doctor has said may be kept private; what the mirror says is ipso facto in the public domain. Because the self is essentially defined in exterior terms, the devastating reality is not the inner pregnancy but the outer manifestation of that condition.

Even though Lucius marries someone else, Charity decides not to terminate her pregnancy. Instead she agrees to wed her guardian, Lawyer Royall. He had asked her to marry him earlier, but then she was falling in love with Lucius and was just becoming conscious of her youth and strength, and she had nothing but contempt for this "old" man in his forties. She asked him scornfully, "How long is it since you looked at yourself in the glass?" (23), for that instrument is the universal arbiter of all her questions. Now Charity waits for the clergyman to unite them. Even at the humble ceremony, there is "a looking-glass in a carved frame on the wall," but she is "ashamed to look at herself in it" (206). Marrying this man violates her sense of self-definition based on the mirror, for that process is connected with a young man like Lucius. Months before, in her candlelit mirror and in her dreamy imagination, she "saw herself a bride in low-necked satin, walking

5. It is an interesting coincidence that the new at-home pregnancy testing kits are equipped with small mirrors. The instructions for the "Fact Pregnancy Test" warn as follows: "Read the result of the test in the mirror only. What you see in the mirror is the only reading that counts."

down an aisle with Lucius" (28). By marrying Lawyer Royall, she has tentatively moved toward another method of self-realization. Put to the test of a reality beyond the looking glass, she is about to start defining herself as a wife and mother, still in relation to men, but not through the adolescent image presented by the mirror. At this moment she is reluctant to look in the glass, but she has yet to develop a new system of self-determination to replace it.

Even in works of literature in which the adolescent girl is situated in a safe home and a happy family, the mirror remains the scene of self-scrutiny and the medium of identity. The confrontations with the glass are just as intense but are somehow more leisured and less fraught with threatening distortions than in the texts discussed so far. In her *Invitation to the Waltz* (1932), Rosamond Lehmann very clearly demonstrates that looking into a mirror is intimately connected with the creative discovery of the self. The adolescent (here, Olivia Curtis, age seventeen) keeps restlessly scanning the mirror for a sign of an emerging self that she believes is hidden just beneath its silvered surface.

> She cast a glance at her figure in the long glass; but the image failed her, remained unequivocally familiar and utilitarian.
>
> Nowadays a peculiar emotion accompanied the moment of looking in the mirror: fitfully, rarely a stranger might emerge: a new self.
>
> It had happened two or three times already. . . . She looked in the glass and saw herself. . . . Well, what was it? She knew what she looked like, had for some years thought the reflection interesting, because it was her own; though disappointing, unreliable, subject twenty times a day to blottings-out and blurrings. . . . But this was something else. This was a mysterious face; both dark and glowing; hair tumbling down, pushed back and upwards, as if in currents of fierce energy. Was it the frock that did it? Her body seemed to assemble itself harmoniously within it, to become centralised, to expand, both static and fluid; alive. It was the portrait of a young girl in pink. All the room's reflected objects seemed to frame, to present her, whispering: Here are You. (13–14)

Lehmann shows the developmental processes in the adolescent and their underlying dialectic of identity and difference. Olivia starts out with an identity that, with minor fluctuations, is registered by the mirror, and that reflection is a reasonably accurate indication of what the self is to her. But sometimes she looks in the glass and strangeness appears, and with it a shock of nonrecognition. Something comes into focus which she had not previously seen as part of herself. The contradictory images ("both dark and glowing," hair "down" and "upwards," "static and fluid") indicate the binary dynamic of this experience as a new self just begins to come forth, like a butterfly from a chrysalis, out of the old.

The phrase "Here are You" suggests a speaking mirror, like the one in "Snow White." The words emphasize and crystallize the fact that the self is defined by and through the glass. There is a significant distinction between saying "Here is a reflection of you" and "Here are You." The mirror image is not a metaphor of self or a presentation of part of the self; it is the self. Nothing is left out. "Here are You" is not an expression of place as in "you are here," but an expression of being. Where is "Here"? "Here" is in the mirror, not in the body. The reflection goes beyond sign or metaphor and becomes the self itself; the reflection becomes the predicate of existence.

The merging of inner and outer which occurs when looking in a glass is at the center of Olivia's sense of harmonious communication between ego and other. Yet the pleasures and sense of hope engendered by this synthesis are subject to doubt at the hands of the same instrument that prompted them: "She went on staring [in the mirror]; but soon the impression collapsed; the urgent expectation diminished flatly. After all, the veil was not rent. It had been a false crisis. Nothing exciting was going to happen. There was nowhere to go: nothing to do. In the glass was a rather plain girl with brown hair and eyes, and a figure well grown but neither particularly graceful nor compact. . . . But hope had sprung up, half-suppressed, dubious, irrational, as if a dream had left a sense of prophecy. . . . Am I not to be ugly after all?" (14). The words "collapsed" and "flatly" suggest that the glass and the girl are shrinking back into ordinariness. Olivia hasn't become another person. The self that was dawning is a self completely determined by whether or not it is beautiful, and the kind of beauty is that which can be reflected in a mirror. The adolescent girl has at most only fleeting inklings of a lovely adult presence about to become visible.

In Katherine Mansfield's "Prelude" (1918), Beryl Fairfield conceives of herself as an object perceived by someone else. For instance, while playing the guitar, she is "watching herself playing": "'If I were outside the window and looked in and saw myself I really would be rather struck,' thought she" (79). Because of this emphasis on self-objectification, Beryl will naturally end up looking into a mirror to literalize the conceptual process. Although she is enchanted by what she sees, the young woman doesn't know whether she wants to define herself in and through the psychology of the mirror or whether there is some other way (she doesn't know quite what) not captured by the glass. While musing upon her reflection, she initiates a dialogue with it: "Yes, my dear, there is no doubt about it, you really are a lovely little thing" (97). But almost immediately Beryl doubts the truthfulness of this "old game" before the mirror and senses a widening gap between self and image: "What had that creature in the glass to do with her, and why was she staring?" The dichotomy resolves itself in Beryl's mind into the difference between a "false self"—the one associated with social role-playing and observable in the mirror—and a "real self" that Beryl conceives of as a source of fulfillment. Unfortunately, this "real" and somehow better identity remains for Beryl only a faint and unsubstantial "shadow." After this hesitant and somewhat confused meditation before the mirror, the child Kezia enters and tells Beryl that two men are waiting downstairs. The first step toward self-definition through some means other than the mirror is disrupted by this announcement. Beryl immediately goes back to the glass, returning to a sense of herself as an object seen by others—the very process she had just begun to question. Her concern is no longer with definitions of identity, but with her clothes and makeup.

When Kezia enters with her announcement, she also brings with her a calico cat: "When Beryl ran out of the room [Kezia] sat the cat up on the dressing table and stuck the top of the cream jar over its ear. 'Now look at yourself,' said she sternly. The calico cat was so overcome by the sight that it toppled over backwards and bumped and bumped on to the floor" (98–99). The little girl puts the very opposite of a socialized, self-conscious creature (like Beryl) before the mirror, and instructs it to look at itself. The cat is frightened and flees from the glass. Why? Because a cat does not see itself, but sees another cat. This is the ultimate form of a rejection of the similitude between self and visual image. It is the primitive analogue of the revolt against the mirror which we saw just developing, in a more sophisticated fashion, earlier in the story. The brief episode with the animal indicates symbolically (and comically), "That's not I." Previously, we saw Beryl taking the initial step on a journey to the same recognition. But at the end, Beryl is still caught by the mirror and what it represents. Only the calico cat, never having fallen into self-consciousness, is free. Mansfield's "cat" / "top" trick delineates the difference between cat and catoptric consciousness.

Women who become bound to the mirror in adolescence often maintain that self-sustaining relationship throughout their lives. When the inevitable processes of aging make their visible appearance, the mirror again plays a crucial role. Alison Lurie's *The War between the Tates* (1974) offers a typical yet particularly intense version of a woman confronting age in the mirror. Erica Tate is forty. She and her husband, a political science professor, separated a few months after she found out that he had been sleeping with one of his students. Erica is preparing to attend a party, her first since the separation:

> Erica crosses the room to her dressing table, sits down, and looks into the glass, smiling slightly. For forty years she has had a happy relationship with mirrors. She regarded them with delight from the very beginning; the walnut-framed oval mirror in the front hall, to which her father held her up as a laughing baby; the long narrow mirror fastened to the back of her mother's closet door by metal clips which rattled as if with applause as, aged seven or eight, she paraded before it in [her mother's] late 1930's fashions and wedgies. She liked the heavy triple-plate glass of stores; the neon-bright mirrors of bathrooms; the round and square and oval bits of glass dimmed with powder in a long series of compacts. All these, and many, many more, reflected Erica flatteringly, for she had from babyhood the sort of smooth beauty which adjusts effortlessly to its frame. Brushing her teeth in the dorm bathroom at college, she was all pink innocence; in the smoked glass of a Greenwich Village boutique, draped in a fringed shawl, she became dark and mysterious. She felt at ease even with the mirrors most women avoid. In the harsh light of public washrooms she was merely interestingly pale. (250)

We usually think of relationships as something we have with other people. But, for forty years, Erica has had "a happy relationship" with mirrors, each of which has an animate presence and is therefore capable of interacting with the self and assuming a crucial role in its life history. The "father" mirror and the "mother" mirror are both important—telling her what men think of her and how one becomes a woman like one's mother. The process of learning how to be a woman begins, in a sense, by seeing how you are supposed to act in front of mirrors. The mirror seemed to applaud her when, as a child, Erica showed off before it. Mirroring is presented here as a significant process of socialization.

Erica recounts a long series of mirrors, as another woman might list all the men she has known. She is the kind of woman who does not resist the power of the looking glass. She "adjusts effortlessly" to the mirror and to everything it represents. She is willing to give up herself to the mirror and become whatever the mirror tells her she is. Lurie uses varieties of mirrors to indicate the varieties of selves that constitute Erica. These "selves" are part of both a diachronic development and a synchronic structure made up of the different personalities she assumes in various relationships. The equivalent for a man might be a listing of the many jobs he has had over the years or the different roles he must play in any one job.

Erica has had a history of identifying with the image in the mirror and creating her own self-images in part through that involvement. But on this cold March night, when she looks closely into "the mirror she knows best,"

> a woman whom she scarcely recognizes looks back at her, first with a blank, then with an injured and startled expression. This person is whey-faced, middle-aged and skinny. . . . The stranger's nose is pinched, her mouth tight. Only the eyes are familiar to Erica, and now they blink and turn in nets of tiny wrinkles, like caught fish.
>
> With a fishlike gasp, Erica rises and backs off from the dressing table; and as she moves away the image she knows reappears: the familiar tall, elegant, pretty young woman. . . . It diminishes, leaves the glass, and reappears across the hall in the bathroom mirror, smiling with relief, drawing nearer, larger, leaning into the hard neon light over the sink, staring; then putting up both hands to shield its face, which has become, and remains, white, thin, creased. (251)

There is a sense, in the grammar of the passage, that Erica no longer has control over the image in the mirror. It is as if the reflection has an independent will. The old tool for ego-formation is returned to and is not working as it used to. Like her happy relationship with her husband, her happy marriage with mirrors is over. She no longer identifies with the image—now, a "stranger"—in the glass. This miniature but significant drama is not resolved, and we are left with questions of will, desire, and identification. Will Erica assimilate her self-conception to the aging presence in the glass, or will she undergo a second divorce, this time from her mirror? If the latter, what substitute resources could possibly provide its self-sustaining, self-generating powers?

Lurie presents a fundamental crisis here, and it is worked out in front of the mirror. When Erica's eyes "blink and turn in nets of tiny wrinkles, like caught fish" and she gives "a fishlike gasp" and "rises," we are reminded of Plath's poem "Mirror," in which "an old woman / Rises" to the surface of the mirror-lake "like a terrible fish" (174). In both texts, the unsettling image of a rising fish suggests the eruption of subconscious forces into the surface consciousness. C. G. Jung employs this same symbolic pattern when he discusses the psychological presences hidden in the depths of the mirror experience: "Whoever looks into the water sees his own image, but behind it living creatures soon loom up; fishes, presumably, harmless dwellers of the deep—harmless, if only the lake were not haunted" (24).[6]

There is for Erica a constant reciprocity between the psychological event and the physical actions. Even making an adjustment in the distance to and from the glass causes an adjustment in the emotional state. A relatively trivial physical event (moving closer to or farther from the mirror) changes Erica's conception of self. This process is grounded in ocular perspective and point of view, but it creates shifts in psychological perspective, as if Erica is walking into and out of herself by moving away from or closer to the glass. When she is far from the mirror, she can still assert an

6. John H. Timmerman has suggested in *The Explicator* that this passage is a source for Plath's "Mirror." In addition, it seems possible that Jung's description influenced Plath's "All the Dead Dears" where "an image looms under the fishpond surface" (71). See also the implicit fish image in Laura Mullen's poem "Mirror, Mirror," discussed earlier.

identity between herself and the image. When she gets close, there is a disturbing fragmentation and the self breaks down. The movement is between unity and perilous division—and, paradoxically, it is distance that creates the former, intimacy the latter.

There is an important difference between a woman who looks in the glass and says, "I'm getting old, pale, and gray" (which need not affect her basic conception of self), and one who looks in and says, "there is a creature there that is not I." Women can garner much information from mirrors, but that productivity can lead to a dependency. As the self / image bond begins to dissolve, the glass brings to the fore both the inherent doubleness of self-consciousness and the woman's increasing distance from culturally established norms. Erica is particularly burdened by the latter, for the mirror reveals her inevitable fall from "the pretty young woman" who, according to a male friend, is the central icon of an American "religion." "For over twenty years she, Erica, was one of the incarnations of the goddess," but "now the spirit has departed from her" (252). An ideal image in the mirror is built into our society as much as it is built into Erica's psyche. Erica does not think, Now my pretty face has departed, now my beauty has gone—but it is as if she has lost her "spirit," her soul. What might be considered, particularly from a masculine perspective, as only an exterior accident is for Erica the interior essence of her being.

The mirror has proved its destructive capacities, and now Erica wants to use it once more as a creative tool. She will try again to adjust herself to the glass, to bring back the old mirror, the perfect mirror where she will see herself rather than another creature. The only means she has for accomplishing this goal is to "camouflage the loss." Erica turns to an array of cosmetics supplied by her teenage daughter, but when she looks in the glass, "the total effect is somewhat masklike and artificial, and the pink paste [designed to cover adolescent acne] has turned her eye shadow an odd, bruised lavender" (252). Erica is still caught up in alternative selves, in masks, "but at least she does not look quite so old." By employing the tools of youth, she can force her external image a little closer to her psychic image of herself, itself the product of many earlier acts of mirroring.

Later the same evening, when Erica is at a party at her friend's house, she goes upstairs in search of the bathroom, where she carefully inspects herself in the small mirror over the sink, then in the long one on the door: "Up close under the light her face looks like a stone rubbed with pink chalk, powdery and worn. But as long as she keeps a certain distance from people—a bit over two feet—she will seem perfectly normal, though a little pale. . . . Erica looks for a last time into the two mirrors and, sighing, leaves the bathroom; she descends the stairs, fixing a social smile on her chalky face" (262–63). The presence of two mirrors is a rough equivalent to the two distances from the same mirror earlier in the chapter. Erica knows that when she is close up against the glass, she looks "as if she had walked into a spider's web" (257). She has learned from the mirror the idea of keeping a certain distance from people—and thus from her self in the mirror and in society.

Much later in the novel, Erica is introduced to drugs by her hippie-guru-astrologer friend Zed. Having already been prepared by these fairly lengthy scenes of confrontation with the glass, we are not surprised when, in the middle of the drug trip, Erica heads for the mirror in the bathroom:

> A face is looking at her through a peeling yellow window frame only a foot away: an old woman's face, blank, white, creased. Recognizing it, she groans. She tries to turn her head away. Cannot. Groans louder.
>
> "Erica?" Zed stands, with difficulty. "Are you all right in there?"
>
> "Yes. No." She laughs shudderingly. . . .
>
> "What I saw in the bathroom," she says abruptly. "In the mirror picture. It's not just the drug. I keep seeing her anyhow-where, this awful old woman. Only it's me. I'm turning into her. . . . I hate getting old and ugly. I hate it. I hate it!" The wailing turns to sobbing. "Somebody's crying," she remarks. "I think it's me." (336)

The influence of the drugs ("half an hour ago she swallowed a white powder mixed with ginger ale" [330]) heightens the sense of nonrecognition Erica feels when she looks at her reflection. She calls it "the mirror picture." She still realizes "it's me," but the drug makes her a little crazier, close to Esther Greenwood in Plath's *The Bell Jar,* who, when handed a mirror by a nurse, says, "At first I didn't see what the trouble was. It wasn't a mirror at all, but a picture" (142). Initially, Erica sees someone else in the glass. Then she realizes it is she, but she phrases the realization as "I'm turning into her." What does she mean? It seems contradictory. The mirror reflects what she looks like right now—so why does she use that expression? Erica knows that her face already belongs to that "awful old woman." What has not yet fully become the aged woman is her basic conception of identity. It is an undeniable physical fact that her face already is what she sees in the glass, but her method of self-definition has not caught up with that visible form. In a psychological sense, the mirror can be prophetic. Erica is pointing out to her friend how she hasn't, thus far, become to herself that image in the mirror, but she feels compelled to. There is no option for her of rejecting that reflection. For she does not conceive of the possibility of any alternative. The paradox of the mirror being both self and other, both "Yes" and "No," continues and is given a temporal dimension. "I hate getting old and ugly," Erica cries. One might argue that getting old is not necessarily becoming unattractive. But for females who establish a sense of their visual presence in youth, and identify that image as themselves, the process of aging can seem like a terrible peril, both physical and psychological.[7] Although the mirror established the youthful image, it will also register the descent into age. Thus the mirror seems to hold within it the menace of mutability—a combination that Christina Rossetti calls "passing and glassing" (410).

At the end of the novel, Erica feels that everything is disintegrating. She presents a catalogue of the changes in her life: her children have become strangers, the elm trees are dying, the old courthouse is being demolished, her responsible husband has turned into an adulterer. Her list culminates in a change in herself: "and she . . . has become the woman in the washroom mirror" (367). Mirrors play a central role in all this devastation, for it is in her relationship

7. An anecdote in de Beauvoir's *Force of Circumstance* asserts the equation in her life of age with ugliness: "One day, talking about the beginning of *Le Cheval roux*—in which the narrator has been so appallingly disfigured by an atomic explosion that she wears a stocking over her head to hide her face—Sartre had asked Elsa Triolet how she had had the courage to imagine herself with this scarecrow face. 'I only had to look in a mirror,' she replied. At the time, I said to myself: 'But she's wrong. An old woman isn't the same as an ugly woman. She's just an old woman.' In the eyes of others, yes; but for oneself, once past a certain stage, the looking glass reflects a disfigured face. Now I understand her" (492–93).

with them that the external ravages of time are ruthlessly brought home to her inner being. The core of the ruin is the woman in the glass.

The mirror reflects back to the woman what she is, but it also takes something away. For some women, the mirror is not just the recorder of the degradations of time, but is almost the cause of the aging process, or at least the place where it occurs. The mirror in Plath's poem, quoted in part above, is a lake where a young girl is drowned, where an old woman rises like a monstrous fish. The depth of the mirror is a fearful depth.[8] No one knows this better than the aging woman. "Deep in that looking glass," Simone de Beauvoir wrote when she was forty, "old age is watching and waiting for me" (*Force of Circumstance*, 672). Or as Plath writes in "All the Dead Dears," "From the mercury-backed glass / Mother, grandmother, greatgrandmother / Reach hag hands to haul me in" (70). A mirror is a pool with a threatening creature in it, and the creature is you. Once "the stained greenish glass of old bureaus, mercury-speckled like stagnant water" showed Erica as "a green nymph rising from a pond" (251). Now, day after day the ugly hagfish under the silver rises toward her. The inherent otherness of the mirror image has emerged into a powerful threat to the identity first established by means of the same phenomenon. In the next chapter, we will encounter further variations on this theme of difference and crisis as women look into the glass darkly.

8. See Arthur Symons's lines, "The mirror that has sucked your face / Into its secret deep of deeps" (1:123), and Plath's poem "Moonsong at Morning," which ends, "dive at your mirror / and drown within" (317). Angela Carter reverses the water imagery but makes the same point in her description of "that narcissic loss of being, when the face leaks into the looking-glass like water into sand" (*The Passion of New Eve*, 103).

5.

The Shock of Nonrecognition

O look, look in the mirror,
O look in your distress.
W. H. Auden

Almost any type of crisis, but particularly a personal loss or even fear of loss, seems to initiate in many female characters a powerful need for literal, as much as mental, reflection. When such women look into their mirrors, their psychological condition sometimes finds its visual correlative in at least a momentary inability to recognize themselves. Whatever blow they have suffered thereby becomes the harbinger of a failure in self-representation, a failure to maintain their former equation between identity and ocular presence.[1]

Near the end of *Anna Karenina*, Anna becomes terrified when her customary supports (her husband, her son, her place in respectable society) are gone and she suspects that Vronsky is falling out of love with her. She wants to look her best as she is frantically hoping that any minute Vronsky will return to the house; but, suddenly, she cannot remember whether or not she has arranged her hair:

> She felt her head with her hand. "Yes, I have, but I simply can't remember when." She did not even trust her hand and went up to the cheval glass to see whether she really had done her hair. She had, but she could not remember doing it. "Who's that?" she thought,

1. A disjuncture between self-conception and mirror image replicates what Gilligan (*In a Different Voice*, 8, 42) takes to be the most radical threat to female gender identity—that is, any act of separation.

> gazing in the looking glass at the feverish face with strangely glittering eyes looking at her with a frightened expression. "Why, it's me," she realized all at once and, examining herself from top to toe, she suddenly felt his kisses and, shuddering, moved her shoulders. Then she raised her hand to her lips and kissed it.
>
> "What's the matter with me? I'm going mad!" (746–47)

For Anna, what is real is what is in the mirror. Any other process of determining reality is not as definitive as consulting the glass. The body ("She did not even trust her hand") and the mind are subservient to the mirror. The self submits to the "other" in the looking glass, just as Anna depends on men for her position in the world and for her sense of self. Anna feels a disjunction between what she has become (what she can see in the mirror) and what she has conceived herself to be. She is deeply confused at this point. At first she does not recognize herself in the glass, for a small gap has opened up between her inner conception of self-presence and the way she looks to her own eyes. A similar alienation is repeated when a part of Anna's consciousness assumes the male role. Kissing her own hand is an acting out of what she wants her lover to do, a last effort to reassert her charm and beauty. This panicked passage is a prelude to her suicide. The initial sign of estrangement from herself manifests itself as a breakdown in her self-sustaining relationship with the mirror.

Very early in *Daniel Deronda*, Gwendolen Harleth receives a letter from her mother telling her that the family has been totally ruined financially. At first, the self-centered, self-confident girl is stupefied, unable to believe that her position has become one of poverty. After a few minutes, Gwendolen goes "automatically" to her glass, for this is both a constant and unconscious habit. Yet her concern at this moment, whether she realizes it or not, is not with a desire to look "lingeringly at herself for pleasure" and note her beauty, but with the far more subtle activity of finding out who she is. At this time of personal crisis, the mirror plays an important role. Gwendolen stares into the glass as though "waiting for any sign" to appear of what has so stunned her sense of identity (44).

Like Gwendolen, other female characters will turn to the glass even though their dilemmas have nothing to do, in any direct way, with physical appearance. When Olivia Curtis in Rosamond

Lehmann's *The Weather in the Streets* (1936) learns that her father is very ill, she says to herself, "He can't die," and then "she rummaged in her bag for mirror, powder, handkerchief, and attended minutely to her face" (10). The possibility of a parent's death shakes one's conception of self. The mirror and its auxiliary tools offer a ready means for trying to restore that concept. Similarly, in Alice Munro's short story "The Moons of Jupiter" (1978), a woman whose father is in the hospital for an operation suddenly becomes fanatically preoccupied with her appearance. She finds herself wandering through dress shops: "I shuffled clothes on the racks, pulled them on in hot little changing rooms in front of cruel mirrors. I was sweating; once or twice I thought I might faint" (229). Many women at transitional or transformational points in their lives use mirrors as tools for understanding the change, controlling the change, making the change. Sometimes the mirrors are "cruel" and the "changing rooms" extremely discomfiting, psychologically as well as physically.

In Marilynne Robinson's *Housekeeping* (1981), Ruth (the narrator) and her sister Lucille lost their mother when they were very young. They remember that the night before she committed suicide, their mother sat before her mirror. The two children now live with their mother's sister, Sylvie, who may also be suicidal. One evening as they walk past the door of Sylvie's room, they see her brushing her hair before the glass. The little girls watch Sylvie for a long time. They don't know how to decipher what they see, but they sense that the mirror is used when a confrontation with the self is necessary:

> She would brush her hair all to one side, and put down the brush and look at herself. Then she would brush it straight back . . . and look at herself. All this was startling in Sylvie, who seemed to give no thought to her looks at all. My mother, Helen, had hardly shown more interest in how she looked than Sylvie herself, and yet the night before she brought us to Fingerbone she had spent the evening just that way, brushing her hair before the mirror, changing and changing, and calmly appraising each change. What was to be made of this? Nothing at all. Why should two estranged sisters think the same thoughts before their mirrors? And how do we know what Helen's thoughts were? . . .

> Appearance paints itself on bright and sliding surfaces, for example, memory and dream. Sylvie's head falls to the side and we see the blades of my mother's shoulders. . . . Helen is the woman in the mirror, the woman in the dream, the woman remembered. . . . (131–32)

Robinson has given us yet another "changing" room, but one haunted by a ghost. Mother and aunt, past and present, merge at a common moment of threatened crisis, not only through "memory and dream" but also through the mirror, the literal "bright and sliding" surface in which Sylvie's complex emotions come into focus and pass into the narrator's consciousness.

For most of the women we have been considering, their distress comes after many years of familiarity with their own reflections. But what psychic shocks can occur when someone who is "born" an adult looks into a mirror for the first time? Two obvious instances are John Milton's fair Eve (*Paradise Lost*, 1667) and Mary Shelley's hideous monster (*Frankenstein*, 1818). Eve wakes into existence and wonders where and what she is. Not far from her, water has issued from a cave "and spread / Into a liquid Plain, then stood unmov'd" (4.454–55). The first woman approaches the first mirror and there sees "a Shape within the wat'ry gleam . . . / Bending to look" at her. Eve begins at a pre-Lacanian moment when the viewer doesn't recognize her reflection as her self. But Eve is "pleas'd" with what she sees, and "answering looks" suggest a dialogue between the self and the image (4.464).[2] God's voice breaks into Eve's private moment to reveal the truth—to tell her that the image in the water is she. The beginning of the history of being the mother of the human race starts with her learning self-recognition and evaluation in the mirror. For Milton, of course, Eve's sympathetic response to and fascination with her "shadow" in the water foreshadow the Fall itself as vain Eve falls for the illusion. A modern reader might interpret the passage differently.

2. In *Eve's Diary*, Mark Twain expands upon this relationship between Eve and the image in the pool: "It is where I go when I hunger for companionship. . . . It talks when I talk; it is sad when I am sad; it comforts me with its sympathy; it says, 'Do not be downhearted, you poor friendless girl; I will be your friend.' It *is* a good friend to me, and my only one; it is my sister" (43, 45).

Even though God tells Eve not to taste of the Tree of Knowledge, she eats. And even after He has "warn'd" her away from her reflection, back she turns. Although God forbids her the fruit and the mirror, she will not finally be denied the knowledge of good and evil or the knowledge of self through its objectification. From Milton's patriarchal point of view, this relationship between self and image threatens the divinely instituted relationship between Eve and Adam.

Scholars often compare Frankenstein's monster with Adam, but it is of Milton's Eve that we are reminded when this created being looks into a pool and, using Eve's exact words ("I started back," line 462), reacts to his first sight of his visage: "I had admired the perfect forms of my cottagers—their grace, beauty, and delicate complexions: but how was I terrified, when I viewed myself in a transparent pool! At first I started back, unable to believe that it was indeed I who was reflected in the mirror; and when I became fully convinced that I was in reality the monster that I am, I was filled with the bitterest sensations of despondence and mortification. Alas! I did not yet entirely know the fatal effects of this miserable deformity" (114). The monster is radically self-alienated. It initially responds to its own image in the water in the same way the cottagers will—with horror. We must remember that this is *not* a man looking in a mirror— it is a synthetic creation by a man, much as the self-conception of females and their role in society are in many ways male inventions. In this sense, the monster (like his actual creator, Mary Shelley) has a feminine, exterior notion of self in which mirroring can play a key role.

The creature's idea of himself is totally different from what he sees in the mirror, just as many women have a sense of that difference. But the grammar shows that he becomes convinced of the mirror's truthfulness ("the monster that I am"). He is coming to a realization of himself, a maturation, that is also a kind of fall. The passage presents stages in the response to the mirror image: first, otherness; then, self-recognition; and finally, and almost simultaneously with the second stage, a descent into a world where one does not have complete control of one's being. His sense of the way people will react to him modifies his self-conception—and not without good cause, since his destiny will be largely determined by that reaction. He has changed his consciousness of what he is in light of that impression all too accurately projected by the mirror.

Amnesia provides a convenient novelistic device for creating an adult character who must undergo primal acts of self-identification. Even before her memory loss, poor Dorothy Hare in George Orwell's *A Clergyman's Daughter* (1935) has almost no sense of a self at all—only of self-denial. Since her mother is dead and she is the sole child of the Reverend Charles Hare, Dorothy is expected to do all the dirty work of the parish plus run the household: "Dorothy hastened up to her room and dressed herself with the lightning speed which she found necessary six mornings out of seven. There was only a tiny square of mirror in the room, and even that she did not use. She simply hung her gold cross about her neck—plain gold cross; no crucifixes, please!—twisted her hair into a knot behind, stuck a number of hairpins rather sketchily into it, and threw her clothes . . . on to herself in the space of about three minutes" (9). This passage reveals an abnegation of self. Dorothy's haste is in response to an imposed regime. The "tiny square of mirror" that she does not use suggests an undernourished personality that has not been given the requisites for creating a female identity. Even if she looks into the glass, it is a meager mirror in which Dorothy is confined. The gold cross is an outward symbol of her own crucifixion, a sacrifice of the self. She twists her hair into a knot—enclosed, constricted, tight. She is not dressing up, but throwing her clothes on. Although she is only twenty-seven, everything about her is dull and worn out. Her duty is her outward world, dominated by her none too amiable father, the Rector.

Later in the novel, Dorothy totally loses her memory and has no "consciousness of time or place, or of her own body or even of her own existence" (80). Like Milton's Eve ("much wond'ring where / And what I was, whence thither brought, and how," lines 451–52) and Shelley's monster ("Who was I? What was I? Whence did I come?" [128]), Dorothy begins to speculate: "*Who was she*? She turned the question over in her mind, and found that she had not the dimmest notion of who she was" (81). She is even uncertain of her sex until she feels her breasts with her fingertips and concludes that she is indeed a woman. The question of identity is traditionally answered for many women by confronting the mirror. But Dorothy has always been prevented from developing a sense of self through literal self-reflection. Now it is as though she is in her infancy. She is undergoing the elemental experience of discovering the difference between the other and her own body. The first stage that Orwell shows here is the acknowledgement of a distinction between *me* and *not me*. Dorothy next grasps "that in order to identify herself she must examine her own body, beginning with her face; and for some moments she actually attempted to look at her own face, before realizing that this was impossible." Face and identity are so closely allied that knowledge of the self requires viewing the countenance. Without a mirror, one can see much of the body, but not the face. To have some sense of and control over her social presence, Dorothy has to behold her visage:

> After hesitating a few moments longer, she turned . . . and began to walk slowly along the pavement. A fragment of knowledge had come to her, mysteriously, out of the blank past: the existence of mirrors, their purpose, and the fact that there are often mirrors in shop windows. After a moment she came to a cheap little jeweller's shop in which a strip of mirror, set at an angle, reflected the faces of people passing. Dorothy picked her reflection out from among a dozen others, immediately realizing it to be her own. Yet it could not be said that she had recognized it; she had no memory of ever having seen it till this moment. . . . The face was quite unfamiliar to her, and yet not strange. She had not known till this moment what face to expect, but now that she had seen it she realized that it was the face she might have expected. It was appropriate. It corresponded to something within her. (82)

Dorothy's face is "unfamiliar to her" because she made such limited use of the mirror in her earlier life, and yet it is "not strange," for it quickly comes into correspondence with some internal sense of identity.[3] After her death and rebirth, she begins the essential coordination of self-conception and outer appearance by means of the glass. In this instance, the mirror assists the woman in resolv-

3. Compare Dorothy with a girl in Joyce Carol Oates's *Unholy Loves* (1979) who sees her image in a mirror coated with dust: "A face, vaporous and yet insistent, her own, not her own, familiar and unfamiliar at the same time" (231).

ing a critical disjunction within her enabling fiction of psychic / visual continuity.

Dorothy does not originally refuse to use the mirror, but an imposed series of constraints prohibits her from making use of it. Sometimes, however, a young woman voluntarily gives up the mirror, only to return to it later when she tries to regain a female self. In 1926, as the first female graduate student in mining engineering at the University of Wisconsin, Emily Hahn had various encounters with discrimination. But she usually managed to stay calm and unemotional and to follow the advice a well-meaning professor had given her in her freshman year: "Try to let them forget you're a woman" (63). When she was a senior, she made a determined effort to join the all-male Geology Club at the university. In her book, *Times and Places*, Hahn recalls that when Clyde, the club president, told her that she could not be a member, she burst into tears and ran down the hall. She had in short "been feminine." But by these very actions, Hahn gains entry into the club, for her tears have shocked the men into unanimous acceptance. Hahn now realizes that she had been following "a three-year program of mistaken strategy": "It was the friendly professor, I realized, who had started me off on the wrong foot. Well, it was all right now. I knew better now. Just in time, too. I blew my nose and started to search my briefcase, diving far down, trying to find a long-forgotten pocket mirror" (69). This brief tale offers nothing less than the sudden emergence of a socially feminine self within the life of a female individual. The audience for Emily Hahn's crying is clearly all male. What the men resisted was the attempt of the woman to establish her identity in ways that had been traditionally expropriated by males. They were not against women so long as these women allowed themselves to be defined—indeed, defined themselves—as women. From the point of view of the men who finally vote for her, what she has demonstrated is her humanity. For them, to be biologically female and to try to be sociologically male is to defy human nature. Hahn has suddenly come back to projecting herself as a woman through crying, and through that she has achieved a kind of social success. By the end of this incident, Hahn is a woman again. And the first thing she does when she is alone, after the crying, after the public reassertion of femininity, is to search for a mirror. The expression here is telling—"diving far down." She is literally digging into the bottom reaches of her briefcase, but also she is diving far down into the self to re-establish its femininity. The first willed act in that plunge is to find a tool that will assist in the discovery and creation of a woman as defined by her society. That instrument is, of course, the mirror. Hahn must now begin to recognize herself in the glass and through that recognition become to herself and to others what she beholds. The earlier difference between image and identity, to which the male world had so forcefully called her attention, requires Hahn to reinstitute the unity demanded by her culture.

Occasionally a woman quite unexpectedly discovers a new self in the looking glass and then immediately tries to summon up the old self. In Wolitzer's *Hearts*, at age twenty-six after a marriage of only six weeks, Linda Reismann is suddenly widowed. Although she doesn't realize it yet, she is also pregnant. Linda is traveling cross-country with her teen-age stepdaughter Robin, who spends most of her time being sullen and noisily munching rancid potato chips. "You'll get fat," Linda warns Robin (196). In response, the girl suggests that her stepmother is the one getting plump. To confirm this accusation, Linda consults the motel mirror distorted at the top so that "her forehead wavered and melted into her hairline." But the lower part of the glass gives a true image that signals Linda's increasing weight. Later, when alone, Linda pulls off her clothes to study her body: "Breathing heavily, she faced the mirror again, that new accuser. . . . This sleek fullness, this rosy roundness were surely new. She looked like a bowl of fruit. 'Oh, no,' she whispered. She went closer to the mirror, dissolving her forehead until she became a Neanderthal" (197). For this woman, the recognition of a significant *visual* change in her body directly alters her sense of self. As Wolitzer writes, Linda "knew immediately that [her reflection] was not her previously known self." Linda desires not to recognize what she so clearly is—pregnant. Thus she distorts the image in the glass, acting out a longing to look like, and thus be, someone else. The implicit need is to look as she looked before, a yearning to revert. Getting closer to the mirror fulfills the wish for regression in an extreme, almost anthropological manner: she has become a Neanderthal, an earlier species.

For a character in another modern novel, the desire to become a Neanderthal is transformed from the metaphoric to the literal. In Jean Auel's *The Clan of the Cave Bear* (1980), a Cro-Magnon baby is discovered and brought up by a Neanderthal medicine woman. At puberty, Ayla begins to think about attracting a mate. One morning she goes to fill a waterbag and discovers a "strange face looking at her out of the pool." Seeing herself for the first time, Ayla is devastated to find high cheekbones, a well-defined jaw, and "a smooth, straight forehead without the slightest hint of protruding brow ridges" (289). Since Ayla has seen no one other than Neanderthals, her "standard of measure" indicates that there is something wrong with her face. Like the monster in *Frankenstein*, Ayla sees in the pool a deformed creature, for both look abnormally different from everyone around them. "My person was hideous, and my stature gigantic," the monster says (128). "Look at me," Ayla sobs, "I'm too big, I'm taller than Broud and Goov. . . . And I'm ugly. I'm big and ugly and I'll never have a mate" (290). Once again, the mirror is the instrument of social self-consciousness. In this instance, the mirror offers the terrible truth that a purely visual difference will have profound interpersonal consequences for the individual reflected in the social glass.

The discovery of a new or even slightly altered reflection in the mirror can be particularly traumatic for the woman who completely accepts the mirror image as her true self. To understand the dynamics of this process, we again must look briefly at a woman confronting the glass of time and finding that degeneration can be even more frightening than nonexistence. In Margaret Drabble's *The Ice Age*, Alison Murray can face death. But she cannot face old age, "cannot face ugliness and decay":

> Slowly, Alison Murray . . . crossed to the wardrobe mirror. Slowly, she inclined her face toward her face. The harsh unshaded light fell without mercy. Yes, there were wrinkles. At last, after years of grace, there were wrinkles. There would be more. There was strain around the eye, the mouth, the nose. . . . Meditatively, she untied her wrap and stared at her body. There it was, source of so much

> pleasure, so much self-congratulation. And still lovely: hardly a mark upon it, hardly a sign of wear, the body of a young woman. But for how long, she said to herself, panic beating noisily in her ears; for how much longer? When will it collapse? . . . When will I cease to be able to look at myself naked in the mirror? And God, oh God, what then, what then will I do? What will I do, in five years, in ten?
>
> For Alison Murray, beauty had for years been identity. She had no other. (107–8)[4]

The author's analysis of this scene, embodied in the final sentences, prevents us from dismissing Alison Murray's anxiety as merely the product of excessive vanity. Aging, even when not perceived as the approach of ugliness, can still be threatening to a woman of the mirror because it inevitably brings change—not to her body alone, but to her "identity."

Any change, not just aging, is disruptive for these women, as Elizabeth Taylor's novel *The Sleeping Beauty* (1953) demonstrates. Taylor's character Emily has been in a serious car accident and, after many months and many operations in the hospital, she looks quite different—"very beautiful in a way, but not in the way in which she had been beautiful before" (46).[5] Yet this sideways change is as terrifying to her as is deterioration for Drabble's Alison: "The moment in my life when I felt really destroyed was the moment when everyone thought I was well again. For the first time, the doctor allowed me to have a looking-glass. He handed it to me with such a pleased smile and stood back to watch. . . . I stared and stared, but no words came. I knew I was lost. Until then, however in pain, bandaged, in darkness, despairing, I had

4. Jessie Stilwell, a woman in her late thirties, meditates on much the same fear in Nadine Gordimer's *Occasion for Loving* (1963): "She looked over her shoulder at her naked back and backside and legs in the mirror. How long? Five years? Six? (What did the bodies of women in their forties look like?) A few more years and she wouldn't be able to look at this any more" (193).

5. Truth follows fiction in the "real life" story of French test pilot Jacqueline Auriol—described in Nancy C. Baker's *The Beauty Trap*. When her plane crashed, Auriol was slammed, face first, into the instrument panel: "In 1949, regaining her beauty seemed beyond hope. Auriol became a beautiful woman again, but the face she acquired was not the one she had had before her accident. When she peered into the mirror after her series of reconstructive surgeries, she confronted an unfamiliar face. She would wear this 'manmade face' for the rest of her life" (208).

been myself. But in that looking-glass there was no vestige of me. . . . I dropped the mirror and was crying with rage and terror. I thought that I would never again have the courage to look at myself" (171). This passage forcefully dramatizes my contention that for many women there is a fundamental connection between mirror appearance and consciousness of self. What is implied in the male doctor's pleasure in handing Emily a looking glass is that identity is a transcendental category that is not revealed in the glass. He doesn't imagine the possibility of having one's self-conception changed by an auto accident; he believes that only one's appearance is altered. His concern is—does she look pretty? She does. Thus there should be no psychic disturbance. But, for a woman whose basic idea of self is intimately tied to the mirror, to have one's face changed, even if it is in effect a lateral movement with no loss of or addition in beauty, is to have the self changed. Emily feels "lost" because she feels alienated from herself. For her, she is no longer Emily, because one of the ways she constructed herself was to look in the mirror and see herself there. Now she gazes in the mirror and sees a lovely face, but it is not she. She thinks she will never again have the courage to look at her reflection. That repeatable act of confirmation by which she has constituted her identity is now denied to her.[6]

Western conceptions of self, at least during the last few centuries, always posit a phenomenon that is discrete—in the sense that it is not identical to any other ego—and relatively continuous in time. A being that merges into all others or that changes radically minute by minute is no self at all. Alison and Emily experience sudden displacements in self-continuity. Aging is a slow process, but the recognition of the inevitability of aging can come in a startling instant in front of the mirror. Alison and Emily are equally vulnerable to this elemental shock to their self-conceptions because neither woman considers the possibility of a gap between physical image and identity. But Drabble may be hinting at just such an opening when she writes that for Alison Murray, "beauty had for years been identity. She had no other." Once her beauty

6. Contrast the scene in chapter 36 of Charles Dickens's *Bleak House* (1853) when Esther Summerson, as defined by her male creator, accepts her altered appearance and easily becomes accustomed to it.

wanes, Alison has no alternative ways of conceiving of herself. But this limitation is the result of her failure to see (even in the height of her loveliness) a difference between her self and her mirror image. For her, the mirror has no otherness and she has no options.

Besides aging and accidents, various illnesses can bring about a change in the appearance and thus a problem in continuity. Just a few weeks before her fortieth birthday, Godwin's Cate in *A Mother and Two Daughters* comes down with Bell's palsy, a paralysis of the facial nerves. As she drives away from the doctor's office, Cate keeps "looking at herself in the rearview mirror" (506). When she moves her mouth, the effect is "grotesque." That evening, "for the first time in her life that she could recall, [Cate] went to bed without looking in the mirror first" (509). Looking at yourself before going to bed at night has a different motivation from the same act in the morning. At the beginning of the day, it might be a practical matter of creating a face for the world, but at night it is to reassure yourself of your own existence, to reaffirm the continuity of your self-image. A breakdown in that sense of continuum can be perilous to one's ego. Women may have other means for creating identity, but they also can use their semblance in the mirror to give reassurance that there is a self which, in spite of small or gradual changes, is still essentially the same. A very sudden shift has occurred in Cate's appearance, a disfigurement fraught with all kinds of fearful possibilities. It is a jolt to her sense of self.

Each morning Cate goes to the mirror to check her face. After a week there is dramatic improvement, although "she would always look slightly asymmetrical to herself in mirrors" (518). Finally, Cate is willing to adapt her personality to fit her afflicted face and accordingly tries out new expressions in front of the glass. She decides upon "a look of permanent wryness, a sort of chronic 'looking askance' at whatever was in front of her." Godwin comments that "some people earned such a look naturally; perhaps Cate also would have, in time" (537). It never occurs to Cate to dismiss the mirror entirely and break the bond between visual image and personality. For her, that social and psychological construct has the power and inevitability of nature. Yet this method of self-construction remains vulnerable to the contingencies inherent in the world of matter and time. These dangers lurking within the looking glass pose the constant threat of disjuncture, nonrecognition, and consequent destabilization of identity.

6.

Dangers of Dissociation

Take my looking glass and my wounds
and undo them.
Anne Sexton

We have traced so far a number of female / mirror relationships that, for all their intriguing differences, may be grouped within a broad spectrum of normative possibilities. While the nature of some of these relationships indicates a personality that is undergoing social disapproval or individual crisis, only a few can be defined as so disturbed as to be part of a pathological syndrome. We must now move beyond the limits of the acceptable and consider those confrontations with mirrors which are symptomatic of, and become synecdoches for, profoundly disorganized selves. Some of the most fascinating appearances of the mirror in fiction are to be found in this wilderness of disjointed relations among self, mirror, and world. As we have seen, women who totally identify with their reflections frequently find themselves endangered. The other extreme, a failure to recognize any similarity between self and visual image, often indicates a deep disturbance in a woman's self-conception.

A quartet of related novels by Antonia White permits us to trace the unfolding relationship between a woman and her mirror from childhood through her early twenties. *Frost in May* (1933) tells of a young girl's experiences in a Catholic boarding school. Nanda Grey is nine when she enters the Convent of the Five Wounds. She is assigned a tiny whitewashed room in the dormitory: "The possession of looking-glasses was forbidden. Instead, each cubicle contained a white china picture of the Immaculate Conception and a small red flannel badge of the Sacred Heart" (33–34). In this seminary, the prohibition of distinctive personalities is central.

Why are there no mirrors in such a world? The commonsensical response might be that the nuns do not want the girls to think about personal beauty, vanity, or the application of makeup—but there are deeper reasons. If, as I have tried to show, the mirror is a primal tool for forming a female presence, then there is an attempt at this school to prevent independent self-creation and a desire to have the students concentrate on the Immaculate Conception instead of on self-conception. Whether conscious or not on the part of the religious authorities, such an environment for a young girl sets up the possibility of arresting the phenomenon of self-reflection in later years. If the girl continues to live wholly within this community, she might be able to create a sense of being, even well-being, through an abnegation of ego. But if she goes out into the greater world, she will have a lot of catching-up to do, a lot of looking into mirrors to define her own identity within the range of female possibilities established by Western secular society since the Renaissance.

The absence of a mirror in the early years of a woman's existence may result in a magnificent flowering—such as a wonderful freedom from the social conditioning most young girls undergo. But this is not the usual process of self-development that many females experience. There is the groundwork in *Frost in May* for something abnormal to happen to Nanda. It might be good; it might be bad. It will not be typical.

In the cold, severe convent, Nanda finds it strange to live side by side with the nuns and yet know nothing of their lives: "Did they wear nightgowns? Did they have looking-glasses? It must be difficult to adjust those veils and wimples without them. Yet even to imagine such things seemed to Nanda blasphemous" (89). The looking glass goes hand in hand with a private secular self, and thus Nanda is asking if there is any human presence beyond the nun's vocation of being a nun. Does the faith, the ritual, so totally absorb the self that it is erased in the vocation? The young girl still suspects, or at least hopes, that a personal identity exists somewhere within the "habit."

In 1950, seventeen years after *Frost in May*, *The Lost Traveller* was published. In it White changed the name of her heroine Nanda Grey to Clara Batchelor. "Of course," White states, "Clara is a continuation of Nanda" ([iv]). The year is 1914. Clara, nearly fifteen, has left the harsh school of her childhood and is coming home to live with her father and mother (Claude and Isabel) and her father's mother. Claude's father has just died and his mother, much to the annoyance of his wife, has swathed all the household mirrors in black draperies. This "peasant superstition" (19) is not without psychological validity. Covering a mirror in a house where there is a corpse is a tradition perpetuated by women. Someone has died, male or female, and, for these women the household item most intimately associated with human self-presence is the mirror. Mirrors and eyes are of course closely connected, but the eyes are also a primary means of expression and self-discovery. We close someone's eyes when he or she dies. The exterior companion of the eyes, the mirror, is also covered.

Isabel is enraged, however, since her own sense of identity and daily reinstitution of that sense depend on looking in the mirror. While for the folk tradition an uncovered mirror desecrates the memory of the dead person, for Isabel the covered mirror violates the means by which she conceives of herself. Clara, just returned from the convent school, has been defining herself primarily through her relation to an institution without mirrors. In contrast, her mother Isabel is a conventional mirror-woman who spends much of her time studying her image in the looking glass "as if scanning the face of a beloved invalid" (31). Now the mother will try to impose on Clara a methodology of self-conception in which the mirror plays an important role. The daughter smiles "in spite of herself" when her mother forces her to observe herself in a new dress in front of the mirror (38). In spite of the identity that she has developed independent of the glass, Clara begins to consider the mirror's utility as a means of self-definition. A hidden other presence has shown itself—one that responds to the mother's blandishments and starts to respond to the mirror. A dichotomy emerges between a former and a potential personality. This crack can become a chasm.

The mother is introducing the daughter to the world of men and to a process of ego formation in terms of what men see. To Clara, "the flushed girl in the glass . . . was like a stranger," an unfamiliar self that she has yet to become (38). This new presence can only develop through a system of socialization and maturation prefigured by the mirror. "Thank goodness you're not *all* brains," the mother remarks. That is to say, "Thank goodness you have not become a person who totally defines herself without mirrors." At this point the daughter's self-conception is growing closer to the mother's sense of herself and of her daughter. But when Clara, a "daddy's girl" if there ever was one, hears her father come home, she says, "I couldn't possibly let him see me like this," and she flees the room and the long glass. The convention is that the daughter becomes like the mother in order to please the father, in order to please the mirror. But Clara has tried to create a self in the way the father creates himself. Thus she thinks she is doing something "disgraceful" and that her father would be disappointed to see her before the glass. Clara is, as her mother states, "out of [her] mind" to run from the mirror—if indeed the female mind is socially defined. When Clara leaves the room, her mother goes twice to stare at herself in the looking glass, for she must reassert that method of self-conception questioned by the uncertain girl's reluctance to accept the mirror.

I have found in literature many examples of adolescent girls who still conceive of themselves as children. Then they look in the mirror, see what they are becoming, and do not immediately identify with the image. This process happens to Clara when she attends a dinner with some members of her family whom she has not seen for a while. Seated at the table, she looks in "the dim greenish mirror of the sideboard" and "for a moment she did not recognize herself. All through the meal she had been so conscious of being the one child among the grown-ups that she was startled to find a reflection that did not look childish at all" (67). Clara next moves from nonrecognition of the mirror image to nonrecognition by a man. Again we have that close congruity between what is revealed by the mirror and what a male sees:

> "Blaze," she said petulantly, "why do you look as if you didn't recognize me?" She wanted to establish some connection between this brilliant person [her own reflection] in the mirror and the Clara Blaze knew, an untidy child in a crumpled holland frock, with a shiny nose and scratched knees.
>
> "I recognize you all right, Clara," he said with his Sussex drawl. "It's just, well, reckon you've grown a lot since last summer. You're quite a young lady."

> "I'm *not* different," she pleaded, half sincerely. . . . Suddenly she wanted to disown the girl in the glass. (67–68)

Clara's desire to establish some connection between the person in the glass and the Clara whom her relatives knew before distinguishes her as someone wrestling with self-identity and poised between denial and acceptance of the mirror. The wrinkled dress, shiny nose, and scraped knees are attributes not only of the child but of someone who has rejected the whole mirror-world. Clara is torn between accepting a new self registered by mirrors and men (and in a sense created by mirrors and men) and retaining a self independent of the mirror. The woman who continues to create herself free of the glass is often seen (by men) as childish, crazy, or unfeminine. The sanction of the mirror image offers an acceptable route to socialization. When the young man refers to Clara as a "lady," he indicates not biological gender, but the new cultural role that two of society's most powerful agents, males and mirrors, are forcing upon the girl.

Clara believes that the world of the mirror constricts her ability to define herself according to her own desires. She wants to "disown the girl in the glass" and thereby reject the new, imposed identity. "I still like the same things," she insists, as though some internal process of the will is the real self, rather than what mirrors and men see. She next converts her hope for freedom into quasi-revolutionary action by making a rude remark at the dinner table and running into the garden, "her hair blown into tangles, her eyes watering, and her nose turning blue with cold." She has become "just Clara again, an idiotic schoolgirl," and "the girl in the glass didn't exist any more" (72). Clara has at least temporarily halted her metamorphosis into the otherness in the mirror.

Two years later (1952), White continued Clara's story in *The Sugar House*. The narrative is set in 1920, and Clara, now an actress in a touring repertory company, has just turned twenty-one. In the opening scene of the novel, she sits in a restaurant waiting for her lover, Stephen. Glancing sideways at herself in a steamy mirror behind the counter, she sees "her own reflection," but it "looked like a stranger's" (11). We have seen a continual pattern in White's novels of a sense of estrangement from the mirror. No single example is significant, but the reiteration is important. This pattern of alienation from the reflected image is part of the foundation of Clara's subsequent history, a history dominated by difficulties in self-conception. There is also a fragmentation of the self in this scene, for Clara sees only her "anxious eyes" and "curls" in the glass, not the whole face. Clara next recalls the first time she saw Stephen. One evening in a rehearsal room, his image appeared in a "ballet practice mirror," and Clara was "half convinced she was seeing a ghost" (12). Stephen was wearing a black doublet and hose, and Clara could not resolve the clearly visible face and hands into a completed human form. Thus even when Clara sees someone else in the mirror, she perceives only a disjointed image and has trouble identifying who, or even what, it is. There is something frightening here, and it tells us that Clara has problems relating to and understanding the world, just as she has trouble understanding herself.

When Stephen marries another woman, Clara all too hastily weds Archie Hughes-Follett, the fiancé whom she discarded four years earlier. Clara and Archie move into a little box of a house, a doll's house. Because an ingenious arrangement of mirrors gives a deceptive sense of space, it takes Clara a few days to realize how very small the rooms actually are. In the sitting room, Clara is fearfully conscious "of the number of mirrors in the tiny space": "Three different angles of her head and shoulders and one full length figure sprang towards her. The little room . . . seemed to close in on her. For a moment, it was an effort to remember that this house was the symbol of her new-found freedom and not a room in a horrible story she had once heard where each day the walls of a prisoner's cell drew imperceptibly nearer together" (142). Multiple mirrors mean multiple perspectives on the self. That might be positive in some contexts, but here the multiplication of images is tantamount to a fragmenting of identity. There is no single, continuous conception of ego, but a breakdown of that unity. The reflections springing toward her suggest both an otherness and a sudden, malevolent power. Clara's adolescent dissociations of self from mirror image have grown into something far less natural and far more disturbing.

After Clara has been unhappily married for two months, she finds herself more alone than she has ever been. Archie is out a good deal, and Clara makes no effort to contact any of her old friends. She becomes isolated and begins to question her own existence: "Once this sense of non-existence was so acute that she ran up from the basement to the sitting-room full of mirrors almost expecting to find nothing reflected in them. But her face stared back at her anxiously from various angles and she was horrified to see how much she had changed in a few weeks. . . . there was a vacancy in her expression that frightened her. She found herself addressing her reflection as she used to do when she was a child. 'Really, my dear,' she said severely, 'You look as if you weren't in your right mind'" (154). Clara runs to the mirror to see if she exists, and what she finds there is a problematic answer. To exist in multiplicity is, in a sense, not to exist at all because self-conception requires some conviction in the singularity of one's being. There is, for Clara, a breakdown of basic ontological requirements for a self—and even doubt about its existence at all. The "vacancy" she finds is the chasm between identity and reflection into which she is about to tumble. In an attempt to fill the void, Clara starts to keep a diary as a substitute for the mirroring that has brought her to this terrible state. The writing "gave her the illusion that she was producing something"—at the very least, the sense of a subject who produces.

In 1954, in *Beyond the Glass*, White completed the story of Clara. At the beginning of this novel, Clara and Archie, married for only a few months, are thinking of separation. Their marriage has never been consummated, and both are miserably depressed. Archie, believing that if he goes away it will be easier for Clara to make her mind up about what she wants to do, has left her alone in their little house. Clara finds herself "suddenly confronted with her image in one of the mirrors" and is "as startled as if she had discovered a stranger spying on her" (30). The otherness in the glass has her hair and dress, but "its face" is "almost unrecognisable." The features are "rigid and distorted," and Clara forces herself "to smile, half-hoping the mask in the mirror would remain unchanged." Clara recalls that as a child she often "held long conversations" with her reflection. Usually this "other" was "friendly," but occasionally it "became mocking, even menacing." This "tyrant in the looking-glass" would take charge and hold her "hypnotized": "Now, staring at the other, she felt the old spell beginning to work. The dull stony eyes fixed her; the teeth bared slowly in a grin. In spite of herself, she felt the muscles of her own cheeks twitch and lift. As if something were pulling her over an invisible line, she took a reluctant step forward" (31).

As we shall see in certain other novels, nonrecognition of self in a mirror can be an act of heroism. But sometimes this failure signifies a weak conception of ego or no sense of ego at all. Here, Clara's sense of her own subjectivity is so limited that she cannot fully recognize its objective image. Instead of rejecting the glass, she, in a trance, rejects the self. In her adolescence (in *The Lost Traveller*), Clara's wrestling with the mirror image was fairly normal. Moving from nondependence on the mirror to dependence is a difficult journey, but a common one prompted by other facets of socialization. Yet Clara has been unable to complete the journey. Rather than losing the child and gaining the young woman, she has lost all sense of identity. Some authors criticize the mirror as a male imposition on women, but White has a positive attitude toward it. She accepts it as a normative device, and Clara's problems with the mirror are used as ways of indicating a severe psychological disturbance—alienation from self and from social norms. Clara is regressing to an earlier stage, yet she does so through a kind of hyper-reflexivity, a too intense magnification of self-consciousness that converts objectification into alienation.[1] Hers is a first feminine step toward schizophrenia. The pathology begins when two things happen: first, the nonrecognition of the reflection as the self, and second, the transference of will to the supposed otherness in the glass. Clara creates a sneering monster that then controls her. The horrid perversity here is that the tool (the mirror), so often used to create a psychologically and socially acceptable personality, is used for just the opposite process—the destruction of the self and estrangement from society. One sort of tyrant, the social institutions of femininity represented by the mirror, has been transformed into another, even more destructive, version of tyranny.

As in *The Sugar House*, Clara tries again to turn to writing as an alternative means of self-production. She begins to read the entries from the notebook she had begun in the first weeks of her doomed

1. For an interesting attempt to redefine schizophrenia as hyper-reflexivity, see Sass, "Introspection, Schizophrenia, and the Fragmentation of Self."

marriage. She has a great deal of trouble comprehending the "almost illegible" words, "so incoherent that they might have been written by a lunatic" (120). One page is "even written the wrong way round so that she had to hold it up to a looking-glass to read it." These confrontations with her written self parallel Clara's reactions to her mirror image. Both types of signs are difficult to decipher and show an unsettling dissonance between signifier and signified. These multiple confusions force on Clara the "charms" of "nullity," and she feels herself becoming "null and void." When she glances up at the mirror on her dressing table, "a face stared back at her, rigid and vacant" (121). Clara can barely remember or recognize her own handwriting or herself in a looking glass. In each case there is a visual reversal. With backward writing, right and left are reversed, exactly like an image in a mirror. These literal reversals parallel the earlier psychological reversal of Clara looking in a mirror and, instead of seeing herself, seeing someone else. As she repeats over and over the words "null and void," she is reversing previous decisions, canceling both the self and the world, and the two are becoming one as they both become nothing.

While she is waiting to have her brief marriage to Archie annulled, Clara falls suddenly and passionately in love with a young soldier, Richard Crayshaw. For a short time she is wildly happy, but the strain begins to overwhelm her already fragile sense of identity. When Clara sees their faces together in the mirror, hers looks "frightful" and his looks "almost sinister": "'Richard . . . do you think those two people in the glass really are us?' she asked anxiously. 'When I was little I used to think it was another *person* I saw there. She frightened me sometimes. I thought she wanted to pull me through into her world. Looking-glass Land, you know. Where everything's the wrong way round'" (168). Again Clara experiences a disturbing division between herself and her mirror image. The fundamental problem with this bifurcation is that it is based upon and increases her inability to conceive of herself at all. In this passage, the problem of self-conception is extended into a difficulty about the relationship with Richard. For a child, it is not necessarily a revelation of psychological disorientation to think that it is "another *person*" in the glass, but for Clara, growing into maturity, such a thought suggests just that.

"Looking-glass Land" is a world of madness, a world of reversal and alienation. The mirror image represents an otherness—an other-ing or splitting of self—that can become a form of insanity called, loosely speaking, schizophrenia. If there is anything a normal person feels close to by definition, it is herself. To say "I am not I" constitutes a psychological equivalent of the mirror's right / left reversal.

Clara suffers even more violent and obvious attacks of mental illness and is finally taken by her father to an insane asylum. She calls it "The House of Mirrors" even though she is placed, as in the convent of her childhood, in a small, bare, whitewashed cell where looking glasses are forbidden. She has forgotten her name. One day the nurses take her out of her cell and into an enormous room filled with baths where she sees on the wall a mirror, dim with steam: "'Look, Clara, look who's there,' said the nurses. She looked and saw a face in the glass, the face of a fairy horse or stag, sometimes with antlers, sometimes with a wild golden mane, but always with the same dark stony eyes and nostrils red as blood. She threw up her head and neighed and made a dash for the door. The nurses caught and dragged her along a passage" (212–13). In her earlier scenes of self / image dissociations, Clara still saw in the glass what was presumably a human visage with an imitative relation to her own. Now she fails to find anything human in the utter otherness of the glass. In a sense White is still using the mirror as a device to characterize Clara, or at least a certain part of Clara's terribly disturbed personality. We remain in the presence of a physiognomic mirror, an image of internal truths, even if it is devoid of external mimesis of the sort we customarily expect from mirrors. But the real horror here for the young woman is that she sees in the glass such a totally unhuman creature. The horse or stag, in its ability to force Clara to imitate it, draws her ever further from a conception of self recognizable to herself. The confrontation with the mirror has provided the novelist a way of dramatizing and literalizing a metaphor of alienation from self and society.

Later, after months in the asylum, Clara begins slowly to recover from madness and to build an identity. She becomes aware of temporal continuity and of an essential presence that is "always the same person" (229). Her next step is a primal act of denomination: "this person was called Clara." She acts like a new Adam naming the animals—or, in this case, Eve naming herself to assert coherence and order. Although she does not have a mirror, she begins to wish for one and to associate it with seeing the self.

One day Clara wakes up to find that she is no longer on a mattress in a cell but in entirely new surroundings:

> She stared about her in delight. It was almost like being in a tiny bedroom in the other world. The walls were painted blue and on them hung a small mirror. . . . Best of all, there was a handle on the door. . . . By the window . . . was a small low cupboard on which lay a brush and comb. . . . She had such a desire to make herself as neat as possible in honour of this wonderful room that she went to the mirror and began to brush and comb her hair. The face it reflected reminded her strongly of someone she knew, someone who might even once have been herself. The hair seemed more familiar than the face. She went on brushing it till it shone, trying to get used to this rather odd-looking face. . . . In spite of its haggardness the face seemed strangely young, almost like a child's. (239)

The new room offers the possibility of using the mirror as a device for ego formation. Clara is at a stage in her recovery when she can be permitted to have this dangerous but useful tool. The door and the looking glass are both passageways to new kinds of experiences as she awakens to outward definitions of self-presence. With the mirror and brush, she is ready for a twofold process—self-possession and socialization. She begins to think in ways consistent with those social tools, the mirror and the brush, and reacts to something outside herself. The perception of who she is now includes responses to a mirror image that holds out the possibilities for unifying a fragmented self into personal identity. Her reflection is still an otherness, but it is now a companionable form, not the mad creature it had become in the depths of Clara's alienation. The practical activity of using a mirror and brush to arrange her hair requires a new sense of identification of herself with her image. Just by this simple activity, preparatory for social engagement, she is evolving toward a normative relationship with the glass. It is still tentative, but her thought that the reflected face "reminded her strongly of someone she knew" signifies a movement toward a similitude that is reinforced by her actions in front of the mirror. There is a sense here that Clara's first attempt at maturation didn't work and she must now be reborn as a psychological self-presence and social presence to others.

Later, when Clara has been released from the hospital and is home, she wants to complete the emerging visual image of herself. The small mirror at the asylum allowed her to see only "her head and shoulders," but when she returns to her old bedroom, she goes "straight to the wardrobe glass" to study "her full-length reflection" (264). The earlier rupture of the self / image compound has been repaired. And now Clara begins to be concerned with clothing—the outward and profoundly social extension of ego. She feels a sudden "affection" even for the old navy dress that she wore in the mental institution and rummages through drawers "in search of a scarlet belt" (265). The belt will define her physical shape as she defines her psychic self. Both acts of reformation take place before the mirror.

At the asylum it is necessary to keep the looking glass from Clara because she misuses it—or, more to the point, the mirror misuses Clara. But the absence of the glass also inhibits the full process of healing. Thus, at a certain stage in her recovery, the glass must be reintroduced and used correctly. Although in her novel White questions the distinctions between sanity and insanity, she does not question the normative value of the glass for Clara. As we shall see in the next chapter, the Brontës criticize the mirror as a form of repression. But for White, the mirror is a powerful implement that can be used for good or ill. And thus this same object is both a measure of Clara's descent into madness and a central tool in her re-education to sanity. Clara has to see the mirror as an instrument for relating herself to others and as a device for self-definition. At the end of White's last novel, Clara knows that she no longer belongs "to the world beyond the glass" (271).

In Sylvia Plath's autobiographical novel, *The Bell Jar,* Esther Greenwood is placed in much the same social context and relation to mirrors as we have seen in White's novels.[2] Nineteen-year-old

2. The connection between the two authors is reinforced by White's anticipation of Plath's title. In *The Sugar House* Clara is described as "sometimes overwhelmed by that sense of being utterly cut off from life, gasping for air inside a bell-jar" (211). Perhaps the archetypal image for these metaphorical uses of the bell jar is the

Esther has won a writing contest sponsored by a fashion magazine. When she arrives in New York for her month as a guest editor, she feels that people are judging her by how she looks rather than by how she writes. The situation is epitomized by the gifts from the magazine (cosmetics and a mirrored compact) and by a luncheon at which the place cards are small, decorated mirrors. Esther is inundated by experiences that disrupt her delicate psychic balance, and one of the casualties is her ability to follow the social norm of conceiving of herself in terms of the glass. Very early in the novel she enters an elevator and there she notices "a big, smudgy-eyed Chinese woman staring idiotically into [her] face" (15). But it is her own image, as she soon realizes, reflected in a distorting surface. The same pattern is repeated later when Esther looks into a mirror and sees a face that looks "like a sick Indian" (92). Even when Esther comes to a mirror for the practical purpose of applying makeup, she says, "The face that peered back at me seemed to be peering from the grating of a prison cell after a prolonged beating. It looked bruised and puffy and all the wrong colors" (83–84). Esther's alienation from her reflection is, in this case, embodied in the grammar as much as in the imagery of her statement: not "my face" but "the face," and then not a "face" at all, but merely "it."[3] The mirror as a medium of intimate exchange has become "the grating of a prison cell."

Like Antonia White's Clara, Esther is eventually institutionalized. The hospital staff does not permit her to have a mirror,

---

glass casket in which Snow White is placed after the wicked stepmother learns from the magic mirror of her rival's superior beauty. In all these cases, the sense of a woman trapped by the mirror is literalized into a glass container.

3. Esther's mirror encounters are more lasting and disturbing versions of Freud's momentary failure to recognize his own reflection. In a footnote to his essay "The 'Uncanny,'" he describes the effect "of meeting one's own image unbidden and unexpected": "I was sitting alone in my *wagon-lit* compartment when a more than usually violent jolt of the train swung back the door of the adjoining washing-cabinet, and an elderly gentleman in a dressing-gown and a travelling cap came in. I assumed that in leaving the washing-cabinet, which lay between the two compartments, he had taken the wrong direction and come into my compartment by mistake. Jumping up with the intention of putting him right, I at once realized to my dismay that the intruder was nothing but my own reflection in the looking-glass on the open door" (17:248).

until finally one nurse complies with Esther's demand to see herself:

> "Why can't I see a mirror? . . . Why can't I?"
> "Because you better not." The nurse shut the lid of the overnight case with a little snap.
> "Why?"
> "Because you don't look very pretty."
> "Oh, just let me see."
> The nurse sighed and opened the top bureau drawer. She took out a large mirror . . . and handed it to me.
> At first I didn't see what the trouble was. It wasn't a mirror at all, but a picture.
> You couldn't tell whether the person in the picture was a man or a woman, because their hair was shaved off and sprouted in bristly chicken-feather tufts all over their head. One side of the person's face was purple, and bulged out in a shapeless way, shading to green along the edges, and then to a sallow yellow. . . .
> The most startling thing about the face was its supernatural conglomeration of bright colors.
> I smiled.
> The mouth in the mirror cracked into a grin.
> A minute after the crash another nurse ran in. She took one look at the broken mirror, and at me, standing over the blind, white pieces, and hustled the young nurse out of the room. . . . (142–43)

Not only does Esther deny the identity of self and image, but also, initially, she denies that she is looking into a mirror at all. The picture she sees has all the characteristics of a portrait by Picasso—distorted, dehumanized in shape and color, and fragmented.[4] But the fact that the image responds mimetically to her smile tells Esther that she is actually holding a mirror. As the scene unfolds, Plath, like Antonia White, literalizes psychological metaphors. The fragmentation of ego is acted out in the shattering of the mirror into "blind," non-reflecting shards. Like Shakespeare's Richard II, Esther converts the glass into an even more truthful reflection of her own shattered self.

In *The Bell Jar* and *Beyond the Glass*, mirrors are introduced into

4. Perhaps the most relevant example is Picasso's *Girl before a Mirror* (1932; Museum of Modern Art, New York).

mental hospitals. Their presence indicates the way in which a woman's response to her face in the glass represents both the structure of her self-conception and her relation to the norms by which her world will judge her. The mirror tests Clara and Esther. To look in and see something bestial or fragmented is to fail both a social and a psychic examination. In *The Book of Imaginary Beings*, Jorge Luis Borges has expanded just such a failure into an apocalyptic vision, an ultimate division between human beings and their self-representations. "Little by little" our reflections will cease to imitate us, and we will lose control over them. These aliens "will break through the barriers of glass or metal," but, even before that "invasion," we will hear "from the depths of mirrors the clatter of weapons" (106).

Anne Hébert's surreal poem "Life in the Castle" develops another schizophrenic, hallucinatory myth about what happens when someone like White's Clara or Plath's Esther looks in a mirror.

> It is an ancestral castle
> With no tables or fire
> With no dust or rug.
>
> The perverse spell of this place
> Is wholly in its shiny mirrors.
>
> The only possible thing to do here
> Is to look at oneself day and night. . . .
>
> See, these mirrors are deep
> Like closets
> Some corpse always lives there under the silver
> Immediately covers your image
> And sticks to you like seaweed.
>
> It adjusts to you, skinny and naked,
> And simulates love in a slow bitter shiver. (240)

For Hébert, mirrors have enormous power to absorb you, to take you over. They are not reflectors, but captors—as Julia Kristeva writes, "the shining mercury that founders me" (163). The mirror becomes, in Frazer's *The Golden Bough,* the dark pool that the Zulus will not look into "because they think there is a beast in it which will take away their reflections, so that they die" (222). The mirror is not a neutral presence over which you have control; indeed it can rule your very being. It is not a flat object: something exists behind the silver, another dimension that is frightening and uncanny and dangerous to the self. That something strange is death, a psychic killing threatened by the mirror.[5] The "corpse" pretends to be you. The otherness in the mirror joins you, simulates you, by merging with you in the embrace of a demon-lover. The "slow bitter shiver" is the physical response to these horrifying thoughts, like the shudder in a sexual act or the last unconscious twitch before death. Behind this mad myth is a psychological truth about the mirror—its otherness, its strangeness, and at the same time its similitude to yourself. The fables of Borges and Hébert can be read as exaggerated yet insightful commentaries on the psychology of mirror-madness presented step by step in the more realistic and extended narratives of White and Plath.

5. Grabes mentions "the existence in fifteenth-century Provence of *miroirs de mort*, real mirrors whose lining had a death's head painted on it" (119).

7.

Mutiny against the Mirror

Until in sudden ecstasy
They break the boundaries of that glass
Jean Garrigue

The failure to identify self with mirror image has dimensions besides the pathological. For some fictive women, the alienation of self from mirror is a desire (rather than a chasm) that takes the form of a longing for a means of self-definition substantially outside the visual world of the looking glass. The first step in the pursuit of this goal is to reject the mirror image. "What had that creature in the glass to do with her?" wonders the young woman in Katherine Mansfield's "Prelude" (97). Frequently, such women are unable to define any alternative to the mirror; the longing remains strongly felt but undirected. In the case of Mansfield's character and as her title suggests, the questioning of the reflection often remains prelusory and may not lead to a self beyond the mirror. A more complex version of this thwarted process unfolds in George Eliot's *Daniel Deronda.*

We have already seen that very early in Eliot's novel Gwendolen Harleth is presented as a woman whose sense of identity is profoundly controlled by her image in the mirror. Gwendolen has "a *naïve* delight in her fortunate self, which any but the harshest saintliness will have some indulgence for in a girl who had every day seen a pleasant reflection of that self in her friends' flattery as well as in the looking-glass" (47). When the smiling Gwendolen gazes at and then kisses the lovely image in the mirror, her self-love is given a very clear and literal dramatization. After her family has lost all its fortune, Gwendolen considers going on the stage to earn money. She consults the musician Herr Klesmer, who informs her that she has neither the talent nor the discipline to be an actress or singer. The sharpness of this blow to her ego is indicated by the fact that even the "reflection of herself in the glass" gives her no pleasure: "For the first time since her consciousness began, she was having a vision of herself on the common level" (306). Gwendolen learns from the uncompromising Klesmer that, to be a successful artist, more is required than the outer appearance. Once she has realized this painful truth, she starts making distinctions between her self and what she sees in the mirror. Before she talked with Klesmer, the image in the mirror was not merely important, it was her whole being. Now, seeing her reflection emphasizes the limitations of a self based on it. The word "consciousness" in this passage implies a significant progression into a fuller, more mature self-conception. Gwendolen is undergoing a process of maturation, but it is not a happy one. She begins to see herself from other points of view than that provided by the glass. Yet this new plurality is for Gwendolen a tragedy, and she throws herself "into the shadiest corner of a settee," pressing "her fingers over her burning eyelids" (306). Mirrors cannot function without light, however, and by retreating from the light and shutting her eyes, Gwendolen in fact closes out that now insufficient self based solely on the looking glass.

Gwendolen again turns to the mirror when she decides to allow Grandcourt to call on her and make an offer of marriage—even though she knows of the existence of another woman by whom Grandcourt has several children.

> While Grandcourt on his beautiful black Yarico . . . was taking the pleasant ride from Diplow to Offendene, Gwendolen was seated before the mirror while her mother gathered up the lengthy mass of light-brown hair which she had been carefully brushing. . . .
>
> "Let me bring you some ear-rings, Gwen," said Mrs Davilow, when the hair was adjusted, and they were both looking at the reflection in the glass. It was impossible for them not to notice that the eyes looked brighter than they had done of late, leaving all the lines once more in their placid youthfulness. . . .
>
> . . . "I shall put on my black silk. Black is the only wear when one is going to refuse an offer," said Gwendolen, with one of her old smiles. (340)

Although she rejected the mirror in the earlier scene, Gwendolen is now creating herself in black silk in front of the glass. Or, more exactly, she sits passively while her mother creates her. She and her mother both believe that the woman is essentially the image in the mirror. The return of Gwendolen's beauty and brightness goes hand in hand with a restoration of the significance of the glass. Gwendolen cannot escape the dominance of the reflection: her happiness depends on her relationship with the attractive image that, in the eyes of the world, constitutes her very being. Although Gwendolen pretends to herself that she will refuse the offer of marriage, she knows that she must accept it to save her family from poverty and to save herself from becoming only a governess. Grandcourt on his black horse, a symbol latent with power and masculine dominion over lesser creatures, represents the forces to which the woman in black has proleptically submitted herself in front of the mirror.

When Gwendolen marries the selfish, arrogant Grandcourt, she acquires the diamonds he had promised. She sits in her grand new house—in a room full of glass panels—and receives from the housekeeper the jewels sent to her by Lydia Glasher, the woman Grandcourt had betrayed. An enclosed letter tells Gwendolen, "You have chosen to injure me and my children. . . . He would have married me at last, if you had not broken your word. You will have your punishment" (406). Gwendolen, in terror lest other eyes should see the paper, throws it in the fireplace. Because of her trembling movements, the casket falls on the floor and the gems scatter around her. As the words of the letter echo through her thoughts, Gwendolen sinks into a chair, and the mirrored walls reflect her image "like so many women petrified white" (407). The multiple reflections, like the spilled and multifaceted diamonds, suggest a fragmentation of personality. Gwendolen's self-conception is cracked in a hundred shivers, and all these reflected and reflecting objects are the emblems of that shattering. Her constitution of self through ocular reflection is shaken by a new representation: what a woman thinks of her supplants a man's opinions. The phrasing is quite telling—"those written words kept repeating themselves in her" (407). Her former method of conceiving of herself as an external and visual image has been usurped by an internalized linguistic restructuring of ego. She is not repeating the words: the words reiterate themselves like the manifold reflections they replace. All the jewels strewn on the floor suggest the bad luck proverbially associated with a broken mirror. The scattering of diamonds is followed by an inner shattering as Gwendolen screams "again and again with hysterical violence" when her husband enters the room. Eliot dramatizes, with symbolic and psychological detail, a passage from one mode of ego formation to another as the destruction of the earlier form.

Other forces than the mirror have come into play in Gwendolen's self-definition (her husband, her husband's mistress), and she realizes a gap between the mirror image and herself, an ironic dissociation that had not existed for her in her adolescence: "This beautiful, healthy young creature, with her two and twenty years and her gratified ambition, no longer felt inclined to kiss her fortunate image in the glass; she looked at it with wonder that she could be so miserable" (477). Gwendolen ceases to invest power in her reflection and looks at it with questioning surprise because what she perceives does not embody the identity she conceives. Eliot traces in these scenes a tragedy of self-consciousness—how terribly difficult it is for such a woman as Gwendolen to break away from defining herself through the mirror. It is not an act of joyous liberation, but a wrenching process of separation and loss without recompense.

Before Gwendolen married Grandcourt, she was married to the mirror. But by controlling her, the glass also sustained her. Now there is an important substitution—it is no longer the mirror that dominates her and gives her the confident self-possession to use her exceptional physical beauty to dominate men. The cruel and imperious husband begins to take over. Proud Gwendolen resists this new mastery and starts to define herself in opposition to it. The power relationships always present in a process of self-definition have shifted radically, and Gwendolen reacts to her brutal husband with thoughts of revolt and revenge. In her anguish, she turns increasingly to the high-minded Daniel Deronda for support and guidance in her longing for what Eliot terms "a new consciousness": "'I wish he [Deronda] could know everything about me without my telling him,' was one of her thoughts, as she sat leaning over the end of a couch, supporting her head with her hand, and looking at herself in a mirror—not in admiration, but in a sad kind of companionship. 'I wish he knew that I am not so contemptible as he thinks me— that I am in deep trouble, and want to be something better if I could'" (485). Eliot is making explicit what is implicit in the earlier mirror scenes. We have seen the self-suspicion and self-blame, but we have yet to see any positive contributions from a reformed consciousness. Gwendolen used to have the companionship of the image in the glass, another self she could worship, but this special relationship was destroyed. Now, as Deronda begins to affect her sense of identity, she returns to the mirror, finding there a sadder (but not wiser) companion in her reflection. She yearns for directions in self-creation from Deronda which will replace the lost powers of the glass.

When Grandcourt tells Gwendolen that she is mistaken to put her faith in Deronda, she becomes distraught and decides to find out from a friend of Deronda if the cruel things her husband says are true. While waiting for her carriage to arrive, she walks around the drawing room "like an imprisoned dumb creature, not recognizing herself in the glass panels, not noticing any object around her in the painted gilded prison" (651). Gwendolen's state of mind has moved far from the personality that embraced—indeed kissed—the mirror image. The "painted gilded prison" reminds us that she was trapped in mirrors, then in marriage. Both are limiting and perilous—in one, vanity, isolation, solipsism; in the other, the danger of hysteria, captivity, and domination by someone else, a shattering of self-possession.

Gwendolen foresees the rest of her life as always ruled by the sadistic Grandcourt. In her helpless despair, she asks Deronda to come see her and tell her what she can do. Just before he arrives, she catches sight of herself in a "long mirror" and quickly notices that her black dress shows off her "white pillar of a neck . . . to advantage" (671). Suddenly conscious that the mirror is still shaping her presence and fearful that Deronda will think her beauty the product of studied artifice, she hurries to the glass in her bedroom and covers her hair and neck with a large piece of black lace. Eliot describes this act as symptomatic of Gwendolen's "manifest contempt of appearance" and of her attempt "to be freer from nervousness." But Gwendolen's actions also reveal her desire to be freer from the mirror and to search for some other means of self-creation. The failure of this desire is foreshadowed by her strategy, still framed within the world of visible appearance.

In the last quarter of the novel, there are no more mirror scenes. "I have not looked at myself," Gwendolen says (766). She has a desperate, but only partially conscious, need for some other means than the glass to define herself. Her tragedy is that she never knows even how to begin to construct an alternative. It is always some force from without, not her own will, that drives her beyond the definition of self by the mirror. She is a woman released from prison who doesn't know what to do with freedom; forced out of victimization, she doesn't know how to deal with deliverance. As Patricia Meyer Spacks writes in her brilliant chapter "Power and Passivity" in *The Female Imagination*, Gwendolen "has learned through suffering the inadequacy of self-absorption" (54). But, as Spacks asks, "Is Gwendolen with her enlarged vision better off than Gwendolen obsessed with her mirrors?" (55).

Eliot's novel offers a broad historical view of ego formation, in part through the story of Deronda's search for his parentage. His quest for self is necessitated by a social context—a Jew in a Christian culture—that severely restricts the usual means for developing a masculine presence. Thus Deronda's uncertain and ironic relation to his world parallels Gwendolen's situation: both have tightly circumscribed roles thrust upon them (as a Jew in the Christian world, as a woman in Victorian society); both have great difficulty in finding their own chosen paths to personal identity. The many scenes in which Gwendolen confronts her mirror underscore the same psychological relationships between self and self-image at the heart of the novel's main plot.

Like Gwendolen, the heroine of Sarah Grand's *The Beth Book* (1897) senses that there is a self beyond the looking glass. Beth Caldwell's circumstances are somewhat like Gwendolen's, but her attitude to the mirror is very different. As a little girl, she hears the instructive story of Miss Augusta Noble from the *Fairfield Family*: "Augusta Noble was very vain, and got burnt to death for standing on tiptoe before the fire to look at herself in a new frock in the mirror on the mantelpiece. Beth thought it a suitable end for her, and did not pity her at all" (22). Beth learns early that mirror-image vanity can lead to self-annihilation.[1] If we trace Beth's responses to mirrors throughout the novel, this otherwise insignificant passage takes on a prophetic dimension.

The first time we encounter Beth looking at her own reflection is when she is still a small child. One evening her father playfully sets her on the dining-room table, and Beth exclaims, "Look at us, papa!" when she sees their embracing images reflected in a window (65). The father scarcely has time to comment that they "make a pretty picture" before a bullet from outside transforms the window / mirror into "a shower of glass" and whizzes close to the child's head. This incident is not explained very well in the plot of the novel, but its symbolic import is clear: in the little girl's mind, the mirror is again allied to a violent destruction of the self. Further, the mirror is clearly the ally of the father in this scene of self-beholding, and thus, for Beth, the male is implicated in this dangerous form of self-definition.

Even as a child, Beth tries to create herself through thinking and writing, rather than through physical appearance:

> "What kind of things do you want to write down, Beth?" Aunt Grace Mary asked. . . .
>
> "Oh, you know—things like—well, the day we came here there were great grey clouds with crimson caps hanging over the sea, and you could see them in the water."
>
> "See their reflection, you mean, I suppose."
>
> Beth looked puzzled. "When you think of things, isn't that reflection?" she asked.
>
> "Yes; and when you see yourself in the looking-glass, that's your reflection too," Aunt Grace Mary answered.
>
> "Oh, then I suppose it was the sea's thought of the sky I saw in the water—that makes it nicer than I had it before," Beth said, trying to turn the phrase as a young bird practises to round its notes in the spring. (99)

The aunt, a conventional woman, thinks of "reflection" in terms of a mirror. Beth converts the outward creation of self, that investing

1. In Mary Gordon's *Men and Angels* (1985), Mrs. Davenport, an elderly babysitter, tells a six-year-old child that if she looks at herself in the mirror too long, "the Devil would appear" (14).

of an external image with enormous power, to an internal process of "reflection"—in the sense of thinking about something, a reflection that transcends the physical and does not have the danger of projecting the self into an otherness.

As it was for Gwendolen, marriage is the only "career" open to Beth. She marries Dan, a young doctor, who turns out to be a profligate.

> Dan went to the mantelpiece, and stood there, studying himself with interest in the glass. "A lady told me the other day I looked like a military man," he said, smoothing his glossy black hair and twisting the ends of his long moustache.
>
> "Well, I think you look much more military than medical," Beth replied, considering him.
>
> "I'm glad of that," he said, smiling at himself complacently.
>
> "Are you?" Beth exclaimed in surprise. "Why? A medical man has a finer career than a military man, and should have a finer presence if ability, purpose, and character count for anything towards appearance. Personally I think I should wish to look like what I am, if I could choose."
>
> "So you do," he rejoined, adjusting his hat with precision as he spoke, and craning his neck to see himself sideways in the glass. "You look like a silly little idiot. But never mind. That's all a girl need be if she's pretty; and if she isn't pretty, she's of no account, so it doesn't matter what she is."
>
> When he had gone, Beth sat for a long time thinking; but she did no more reading that day, nor did she ever again consult Dan about the choice of books, or expect him to sympathise with her in her work. (341–42)

We have here a reversal of traditional roles—the female emerges as an independent self and the male becomes the one defined by exterior images. Beth's real interest (her only interest) in appearance is as an expression of an already established internal character, but she knows that this ideal signifying relationship is not inevitably the case. Her husband, in contrast, sees the outer image as a useful mask for a man or, for a woman, the powerful presence that defines the parameters of her nature. Characters such as Balzac's Valerie and Flaubert's Emma become what they behold; Beth wants to behold in the glass what she already is. She has a conception of "what I am" that is independent of "what I look like." In the course of the novel, she manages to escape from her restrictive Victorian marriage and develop into a writer and a feminist orator. She becomes, to use the phrase coined by her author Sarah Grand, one of the "New Women."

There are women who, unlike Grand's heroine, have not been free from mirror-mindedness since their childhood and instead must struggle for their freedom. These are not lost women, like Eliot's Gwendolen, but revolutionaries who rebel against the mirror as a primary tool of female self-realization. Such a revolt can take a gloriously simple and healthy form—a refusal to look in the glass. Lady Mary Wortley Montagu offers a straightforward example in her letter of 8 October 1757, to her daughter Lady Bute: "I beleive Mr. Anderson talks partialy of me, as to my looks; I know nothing of the Matter. It is eleven Year since I have seen my Figure in a Glass. The last Refflection I saw there was so disagreable, I resolv'd to spare my selfe such mortifications for the Future, and shall continue that resolution to my Live's end" (3:135).[2] One cannot help suspecting that this is a lie and that Lady Mary did not abjure the mirror after the age of 57. What she wishes to avoid is the tyranny of the mirror, its power to identify her as aged, ugly, or simply mortal. She will define herself through other means—by what she does and writes, and not by how she appears. Lady Mary wills to be, for herself and for her world, a mind not a face. While the actions of Lady Mary may seem facile, they contain the essential feature that distinguishes such personalities from women whose relation to the mirror signals an intensely troubled sense of self. Both types become alienated from their mirror images, but one crucial distinction is always present: the pathological personalities remain under the power of the looking glass—all the more so as they are unable to see themselves in it—while the women in the tradition of Lady Mary refuse that very power.

The heroines of three great nineteenth-century novels, Charlotte Brontë's *Jane Eyre* (1847) and *Shirley* (1849) and Emily Brontë's *Wuthering Heights* (1847), continue Lady Mary's insurrection

2. For a twentieth-century equivalent, see Noel Coward's description of Mrs. Astley-Cooper, who "draped scarves over all mirrors because she said she could find no charm in her own appearance whatever" (50).

against the reflection. But the Brontës show far greater concern for the complex consequences of such an act. When the orphan Jane Eyre is ten years old, she is locked into a room as a punishment for her spirited self-defense against a bully. Her only companion in this "jail" is a looking glass: "My fascinated glance involuntarily explored the depth it revealed. All looked colder and darker in that visionary hollow than in reality; and the strange little figure there gazing at me, with a white face and arms specking the gloom, and glittering eyes of fear moving where all else was still, had the effect of a real spirit. I thought it like one of the tiny phantoms, half fairy, half imp, Bessie's evening stories represented as coming out of lone, ferny dells in moors, and appearing before the eyes of belated travelers" (8). This scene of nonrecognition is deeply disturbing, for it demonstrates a division, with potentially pathogenic dimensions, between self-conception and exterior presence. Jane is of course staring at her own image in the looking glass, but she finds only a radical otherness and grants the power of sight to the phantom gazing at her. Such an experience could be the sign of and preparation for a collapse of self-identity, as are similar scenes in the twentieth-century novels discussed earlier. For example, in Plath's *The Bell Jar* and White's *Beyond the Glass*, the heroine's lowest, most psychologically fragmented state is dramatized by the breakdown of the self / mirror relationship established as normative in both narratives. In the unfolding of Charlotte Brontë's novel, however, the dissociation of ego from reflected image becomes the prophecy of a revolt against the dominion of the mirror. The image of an otherworldly creature coming out of the moors and appearing before a belated traveler foreshadows the dramatic first meeting of Jane with Rochester. The entire incident before the mirror predicts a later scene in which Jane sees an image in the glass which is literally someone else—indeed, it is the lunatic first Mrs. Rochester. The initial encounter in the locked chamber presages these later crucial confrontations with other beings who will mold and test Jane's will. By her primitive, even animal-like, sense of the otherness of her own image, Jane has taken a step, however unconscious, toward a radical freedom.

There are echoes of the early scene in the red room at Gateshead Hall in a much later scene in Thornfield Hall where the crazed Mrs. Rochester escapes from *her* locked room, comes to Jane's room, and destroys Jane's wedding apparel. Jane does not see the "fearful and ghastly" visage until the woman stands before "the dark oblong glass" and throws Jane's veil over her own head (259). Jane sees not herself but the madwoman's face in the mirror, thereby literalizing the childhood scene of nonrecognition in an adult context. Yet the savage woman in some sense *is* an image of Jane and of the darkness within the Jane / Rochester relationship. The ancient mystery of the mirror of divination now becomes the inner mirror, revealing the subconscious self not recognized by the conscious mind. At the end of this nightmarish incident, Jane says that she lost consciousness "for the second time in her life" (260). The first time was when she was locked in the red room with the dimly gleaming mirror. In each case, a demonic self rises to the surface of the glass.

On what was meant to be Jane's marriage day, the otherness of the mirror image is again used to body forth the alienation of the character from a self constructed in conventional social terms. While dressing for the ceremony, Jane fails to take even "one peep" at herself in the mirror until a French servant reminds her to do so. When she does look, she says, "I saw a robed and veiled figure, so unlike my usual self that it seemed almost the image of a stranger" (262). On this day, when in traditional society a woman supposedly fulfills her self and her purpose, Jane is still at a stage where she makes a radical distinction between what she is and what she sees in a mirror. The experience of seeing the first Mrs. Rochester looking into the dark glass and Jane's looking into the mirror are almost the same—in both cases Jane sees another person, veiled and clothed in white. The madwoman scene serves as a transition between the childhood example and this parallel encounter on Jane's wedding day when we might expect self-realization. It is part of Jane's strangeness, part of her special education, that she does not recognize the mirror image. She persists as a kind of "primitive," retaining her freedom and remaining unacculturated to social conventions and unsubmissive to masculine conceptions of the feminine. But by refusing to see herself in the glass, she is judged by society, and even by herself, to be descending into the alienation and social unacceptability represented, in an extreme form, by the first Mrs. Rochester. It is as though, in the world of this novel, any woman's refusal to identify with her reflection indicates insanity. Thus Jane's revolt against the mirror unfolds within a structure, social and literary, that is just beginning to generate the means for desynonymizing female madness and female freedom. In the full course of Charlotte Brontë's novel, however, we see the gradual emergence of a heroine who shapes her life and her concept of herself outside of those social and psychological forces that define women as images in the glass. At the end of the novel, the blindness of Rochester is the final measure of Jane's release from definition as an object of masculine vision. On the wedding day that was not a wedding day, Rochester pronounced Jane "the desire of his eyes" (263). Later in the novel, not only does Jane triumph over her mirror image, but the man in her life must of necessity perceive and thus conceive of her in nonvisual terms.

Charlotte Brontë's novel concentrates on the life of Jane Eyre from childhood till just after her marriage to Rochester. In Jean Rhys's *Wide Sargasso Sea*, it is not Jane but the figure of the first Mrs. Rochester, cast as the sensual Creole heiress Antoinette Cosway, who is the center of the novel. As we read Rhys's story, we are never entirely certain if Antoinette is crazy because imprisoned or, as in *Jane Eyre*, imprisoned because she is crazy. As a child, Antoinette's sense of self was jeopardized because her mother did not look at her, did not mirror her. As a wife, she felt that her husband was trying to make her into someone else by calling her by another name. Near the end of *Wide Sargasso Sea*, Antoinette, confined in an attic room in Thornfield Hall, recalls these past pains and muses upon another absence: "There is no looking-glass here and I don't know what I am like now. I remember watching myself brush my hair and how my eyes looked back at me. The girl I saw was myself yet not quite myself. Long ago when I was a child and very lonely I tried to kiss her. But the glass was between us—hard, cold and misted over with my breath. Now they have taken everything away. What am I doing in this place and who am I?" (147). In her disturbed mind, Antoinette half senses a parallel between herself as a little girl (who thought the image in the glass was someone else) and her present inability to apprehend her own being. What in the child or in the animal is an undeveloped self-consciousness is, in the adult, an alienation.

In both this novel and *Jane Eyre*, the children treat the image in the mirror not as self but as other. Brontë's Jane grows toward a greater understanding of and confidence in herself. Rhys's Antoinette loses her adult personality and goes back to the primitive childhood state. In one novel we find expanding self-consciousness free from the mirror; in the other, contracting self-consciousness in the absence of the mirror. In *Jane Eyre* there is a continual process of integration and recovery of identity; with Antoinette, only estrangement and fragmentation. Antoinette never reintegrates the projected image of the self back into the ego. Jane finally triumphs over the experience in the red room, converting it from a sign of incipient madness into a prophecy of liberation. Antoinette dreams of "drifting out of the window with her scents, her pretty clothes and her looking-glass," but she escapes the desolate attic prison only through death.

When Jane Eyre is a child, her animal-like inability to recognize the image in the mirror as the self indicates the primitiveness and potential power of her character. The same is true of Catherine Earnshaw, the passionate adolescent heroine of Emily Brontë's *Wuthering Heights*. Still in love with Heathcliff yet having chosen to marry Edgar Linton, Catherine tries to starve herself until she finally lies in bed ill and confused. In her delirium, she sees a face in what she thinks is a cabinet but is actually a mirror. Nelly Dean, the voice of everyday, practical, adult common sense, tries to convince Catherine that it is her own face she sees, and, as a last resort, Nelly covers the glass with a shawl. "It's behind there still!" Catherine shrieks. Many animals act as though there is a real world within or behind the mirror, and Catherine's similar response signals not only social alienation but almost a descent below the human. "There's nobody here!" Nelly insists. "It was *yourself*" (148). Given her state of mind, Catherine is frightened to think that the image in the glass is another creature but even more terrified to be told that the otherness is herself. We are once again placed in a context in which the border between madness and freedom is not clearly delineated and alternatives to the mirror self are not readily available. Catherine, in her passionate struggle against convention, descends very close to a pathological alienation from *any* self-image. Yet in both *Wuthering Heights* and *Jane Eyre*, atavism is offered to us as a virtue. Catherine's inability to recognize her reflection grows from her refusal to identify herself as Mrs. Linton, just as

Jane Eyre insists that she is something other than she appears to be in the eyes of the world. Catherine sees her mirror image in the fiery, half-savage Heathcliff, not in an actual mirror.

The mirror scene in Charlotte Brontë's *Shirley* presents a phantasmagoric working-out of certain issues raised in *Jane Eyre* and *Wuthering Heights*. The protagonists are Shirley Keeldar (in whom Charlotte Brontë depicted the character of her sister Emily) and Caroline Helstone. The two friends are planning an excursion, and Shirley says she will take Caroline with her on a sea voyage. "I suppose," says Caroline, "you expect to see mermaids?" Shirley then conjures up a dream vision, notable for its intimations of a fully mirrored context. In the vision, the two women will be "watching and being watched by a full harvest-moon," and "something is to rise white on the surface of the sea." Finally, a glittering mermaid will emerge from the waves:

> "We both see the long hair, the lifted and foam-white arm, the oval mirror brilliant as a star. It glides nearer: a human face is plainly visible; a face in the style of yours. . . . It looks at us, but not with your eyes. I see a preternatural lure in its wily glance: it beckons. Were we men, we should spring at the sign, the cold billow would be dared for the sake of the colder enchantress; being women, we stand safe, though not dreadless. She comprehends our unmoved gaze; she feels herself powerless; anger crosses her front; she cannot charm, but she will appal us: she rises high, and glides all revealed, on the dark wave-ridge. Temptress-terror! monstrous likeness of ourselves! Are you not glad, Caroline, when at last, and with a wild shriek, she dives?"
>
> "But, Shirley, she is not like us: we are neither temptresses, nor terrors, nor monsters."
>
> "Some of our kind, it is said, are all three. There are men who ascribe to 'woman,' in general, such attributes." (249–50)

Traditionally, at least heraldically, the mermaid is depicted as holding in her right hand a comb and in her left a mirror, while the merman holds a trident and a conch-shell trumpet. The merman's attributes are outward and active, whereas the mermaid has instruments connected with the creation of a purely visual presence. The mermaid combs her hair to make herself even more lovely so that she can lure men to their death or, at least, to a state of nympholepsy. The importance of the mirror in mermaid mythology is its connection with a destructive illusion. And mermaids are themselves illusions—they are reflections of masculine desires.

Charlotte Brontë indicates the cultural origins of the mermaid myth by introducing the role of men in creating the identification of female self with image. The mermaid does not just hold a mirror, but is herself a mirror of the women beholding her. If we were men, explains the speaker, the mermaid would be a "sign" of our passions and an object to pursue. But the female experience depends on an "unmoved gaze"—as does looking in mirrors. Shirley conjures up a beautiful though terrifying figure of an enchantress who is ourselves but also a production of men and a frightening other. Some of the psychology is similar to what we found in *Jane Eyre* and *Wuthering Heights*, but it takes the rejection of the mirror self even further and with more knowledge. Brontë's character extrapolates the mirror image into a total otherness, yet with the realization that it remains a "monstrous likeness of ourselves."

Shirley delineates an essential step in the revolt against the glass. The heroines of *Jane Eyre* and *Wuthering Heights*, for all their energetic repudiation of the mirror, fail to realize fully its masculine nature—that is, the way in which the mirror is a substitute for men and how a woman's identification with her reflection produces a self in accord with male desires. In *Shirley*, just such knowledge rises to consciousness through metaphor and myth. And we are led to yet a further insight: the feminine selves produced as projections of male desires become objects of men's fears—as temptresses, terrors, monsters. This system of self-creation draws both parties into the whirlpool, the women who die into mirror images and the men who see their own deaths as the end of desire. With such awareness, we may discover alternatives to the mirror other than madness.[3]

It is instructive to compare Anthony Trollope's light treatment of the mermaid myth with what Charlotte Brontë takes seriously in the mermaid / mirror passage in *Shirley*. In Trollope's *Rachel Ray* (1863), a woman wonders how the idea of mermaids origi-

3. For a rather different analysis of the passage, which concentrates on the "desexed" lower body of the mermaid, see Sandra M. Gilbert and Susan Gubar, *The Madwoman in the Attic*, 386–87.

nated. "'Some one saw a crowd of young women bathing,'" the man answers. "'But then,'" the woman asks, "'how came they to have looking-glasses and fishes' tails?'" "'The fishes' tails were taken as granted because they were in the sea, and the looking-glasses because they were women,'" says the man (338–39). The man's immediate and almost syllogistic identification of women with mirrors is exactly the sort of formula Charlotte Brontë questions. Trollope's male speaker is one of those "men who ascribe to 'woman,' in general, such attributes" (*Shirley*, 250).

Like the Brontës, George Eliot shows in her novels that the mutiny against the mirror is not an easy one, for it is fraught with many dangers, not the least of which is failure. Nine-year-old Maggie Tulliver in *The Mill on the Floss* is one year younger than Jane Eyre when her revolt against social norms becomes intertwined with the mirror. Both her mother and her aunt have objected to her symbolically unruly hair. Rather than submitting, Maggie wishes to escape from the entire principle of defining someone in terms that she finds both superficial and repressive. She goes upstairs, cuts off part of her hair, and gets her brother Tom to help her finish the operation:

> One delicious grinding snip, and then another and another, and the hinder-locks fell heavily on the floor, and Maggie stood cropped in a jagged, uneven manner, but with a sense of clearness and freedom, as if she had emerged from a wood into the open plain.
>
> "O, Maggie," said Tom, jumping round her, and slapping his knees as he laughed, "O, my buttons, what a queer thing you look! Look at yourself in the glass—you look like the idiot we throw our nutshells to at school."
>
> Maggie felt an unexpected pang. She had thought beforehand chiefly of her own deliverance from her teasing hair and teasing remarks about it, and something also of the triumph she should have over her mother and her aunts by this very decided course of action: she didn't want her hair to look pretty—that was out of the question—she only wanted people to think her a clever little girl, and not to find fault with her. But now, when Tom began to laugh at her, and say she was like the idiot, the affair had quite a new aspect. She looked in the glass and still Tom laughed and clapped his hands, and Maggie's flushed cheeks began to pale, and her lips to tremble a little. (58)

We have, in brief compass, the failure of a revolution. At first, Maggie feels clear and free and hopes to be considered "clever." But immediately the male enlists the power of his ally, the mirror, to define the female as a visual image. Tom tells her, and the mirror shows her, that the world will continue to define her through her looks. What she has done *is* a kind of idiocy from the perspective of the glass. Her pale cheeks and trembling lips are the outward signs of her recognition of an inability to escape the world of the mirror. The very course that Maggie takes to free herself results in a reimposition of the social (preeminently masculine) tyranny. Yet the failure of the revolt has led to a growing consciousness of her place in society and the forces that keep her there.[4] Maggie recognizes the practical consequences of her deed, and Eliot gives to this moment of anagnorisis a mythic dimension. "Now the thing was done," Maggie knows she will "have to hear and think more about her hair than ever." The prophetic "glass" before which she weeps tells Maggie that she will be unable "to endure the severe eyes" of her family. She feels "as helpless and despairing among her black locks as Ajax among the slaughtered sheep" (58–59).

As we see in Eliot's *The Mill on the Floss*, Victorian culture tended to associate a woman's hair with her self-conception. In such a context, to change one's hair—a change usually created before and first registered in a mirror—is to alter the sense of one's identity. It is illuminating to contrast Maggie Tulliver with a character in Thomas Hardy's *The Woodlanders* (1887). Poor, plain, hard-working Marty South has "but little pretension to beauty, save in one prominent particular—her hair" (13). A wigmaker has offered her two sovereigns for her abundant chestnut curls, and she finally agrees because her father is ill and can't work. The barber has left the money as both payment and temptation, and Marty sees the sovereigns "staring at her from the looking-glass" (23).

4. A passage in Lessing's *A Proper Marriage* (22–23), in which nineteen-year-old Martha Quest cuts her hair in front of the mirror, seems to be a purposeful allusion (in broad outline and in individual images) to this scene in *The Mill on the Floss*. In Lessing's version, however, the girl attempts unsuccessfully to create a new image of herself and does not revolt against the very concept of visual self-definition. Martha, unlike Maggie, is not conscious of her motives and of the external structures of mirroring and socialization that shape her sense of identity.

With tears in her eyes, she begins "mercilessly cutting off the long locks of her hair." By substituting the gold in the mirror for Marty's visage, Hardy indicates how much this transaction is concerned with her self-conception. Instead of her own eyes, the two sovereigns gaze back at her—almost as if part of herself is being taken over by the money. In fact, the wigmaker probably stuck the coins edgewise into the frame of the looking glass so that they would already be part of her image, and thus, in a sense, the deal has already been made. After Marty cuts her hair, she refuses to look in the glass. Unlike Lady Mary or Maggie Tulliver, Marty is not revolting against the mirror. She doesn't look because she doesn't want to conceive of herself as someone with her hair chopped off: "She would not turn again to the little looking-glass out of humanity to herself, knowing what a deflowered visage would look back at her and almost break her heart; she dreaded it as much as did her own ancestral goddess the reflection in the pool after the rape of her locks by Loke the Malicious" (23). Marty sees her humanness as dependent on the looking-glass image; the money has been an inadequate substitute for what that image has lost. The "rape of her locks" is a violation that, in her unliberated eyes, has changed her very being.

In the tradition of Maggie Tulliver, certain women purposefully make themselves ugly in an attempt to rebel against the mirror image, to free themselves from it, so that they can define themselves by other means. Simone Weil was such a personality and understood that her liberation depended upon a reconception of the woman / reflection equation: "A beautiful woman," she writes, "looking at her image in the mirror may very well believe the image is herself. An ugly woman knows it is not" (16). The interesting and ambiguous word in this statement is "knows." An ugly woman does not "know" that the reflection is not the self: it takes resolution to create such knowledge. Weil went to considerable lengths to avoid self-identification through the mirror image and to construct an ego through other means, such as being a writer. As Leslie A. Fiedler points out in his introduction to *Waiting for God*, Weil "did her best to destroy what in her was 'beautiful,' . . . to turn herself into the antimask of the appealing young girl" (15). She demonstrated a "refusal to be charming," wore shapeless clothes that amounted almost to a disguise, and even emphasized a monotonous tone of voice. Ugliness was not Weil's natural condition, and her spurning of the glass did not follow as an unavoidable consequence of that ugliness. Like the Romantic heroines we have seen, Weil had to perform an act of the will, an act of the imagination, to find an alternative selfhood and reject the mirror. One might regret that Weil found no way to deny the power of the mirror other than through a conscious pursuit of what, in her own terms, was unattractive; but at least this identity was a creation of her own formidable volition.

In her *Diary* for 1929, Virginia Woolf revolts against the mirror by turning the conventional formula upside down: "Old age is withering us; Clive, Sibyl, Francis—all wrinkled & dusty. . . . Only in myself, I say, forever bubbles this impetuous torrent. So that even if I see ugliness in the glass, I think, very well, inwardly I am more full of shape & colour than ever" (3:219). The physiognomic mirror tells the woman, "you are what you look like." Woolf says, in effect, "you are the exact opposite of what you look like." This is not an utter rejection of the mirror, for the glass is used as an instrument to reveal an inverse proportion relating outer beauty and inner being. Further, Woolf's view contains a self-questioning irony: she continues to characterize the inner self in terms of shape and color. It is not easy to remove completely from a woman's self-conception the terminology established by the glass.

Most mutineers against the mirror have been actual women or heroines created by female writers. But, occasionally, a male writer creates such a character. In W. B. Yeats's "The Hero, the Girl, and the Fool," the girl rebels against the mirror (like Maggie Tulliver, like Jane Eyre) and claims that those who love her only on the basis of the "she" visible in the mirror are being deceived:

> I rage at my own image in the glass.
> That's so unlike myself that when you praise it
> It is as though you praised another, or even
> Mocked me with praise of my mere opposite;
> And when I wake towards morn I dread myself,
> For the heart cries that what deception wins
> Cruelty must keep; therefore be warned and go
> If you have seen that image and not the woman. (216)

The rejection of the mirror and everything it represents could not be stated more clearly and directly. Even the reversal of right and left inherent in "mere" / mirror imaging becomes here an implicit metaphor for the opposition and deception that the girl laments. Yeats does not, however, follow this bold speech with proposals for alternative means of self-creation. Perhaps because he, or at least his female persona, believes that a self is a natural possession of any human organism, existing prior to and essentially free from mirroring or any other act of consciousness. Revolutions based on such theories of what is "given" or "natural" contain the seeds of their own failure by not realizing that self-consciousness is a profoundly cultural phenomenon.

In Hardy's "The Beauty," a male author again dramatizes a woman who does not wish to accept either the image in the glass or a process of self-definition based on what men think of her. The speaker asks men not to praise her beauty because their words "harass" her:

> I hate my beauty in the glass:
> My beauty is not I:
> I wear it: none cares whether, alas,
> Its wearer live or die!
>
> The inner I O care for, then,
> Yea, me and what I am,
> And shall be at the gray hour when
> My cheek begins to clam. (583–84)

This woman's concept of a difference between self and image eventually leads to her death, as we learn from a "Note" Hardy appended to this poem: "'The Regent Street beauty, Miss Verrey, the Swiss confectioner's daughter, whose personal attractions have been so mischievously exaggerated, died of fever on Monday evening, brought on by the annoyance she had been for some time subject to.' London paper, October 1828."[5] The young woman is psychically troubled because she refuses to define herself as the world sees her. "I wear it," she says of her beauty. It is something outer, no more essential to her being than clothes are to the body.

5. History repeats itself in the story of Csilla Andrea Molnar, Miss Hungary of 1986, who "committed suicide after complaining of harassment over winning the national crown. . . . The girl complained in a recent Budapest radio interview of all the attention focused on her." *Los Angeles Times*, 13 July 1986.

She experiences a social and psychic death before biological death because others do not care about the life of the "I" that is not the beauty. She is trying to create, as are the Romantic heroines, a self that escapes the purely physical otherness of appearance.

Hardy often uses Romantic paradigms to reveal their failure. In "The Beauty" we are given a critique of heroines who refuse to identify themselves through the mirror. The woman's death, appended as a note from the newspaper, shows her inability to be successful in this revolt. The differences of genre between the poem and the newspaper clipping embody the gap between desire and reality. The woman is trying to create a self that will survive, but her attempt is highly qualified. The ironic poignancy in the poem is that the confectioner's daughter tries to have an identity that transcends the "gray hour" that will inevitably attack the presence in the glass. Yet she cannot overcome an environment that offers no alternative means of self-creation. Simple insistence that she is already something other than her outer beauty is not sufficient for survival, for that very proclamation cuts her off from the only available milieu capable of sustaining her self-image.

Sometimes a woman character rebels against the mirror not in order to preserve the self but to lose it. The heroine's revolt in Margaret Atwood's *Surfacing* (1972) takes on the nature of a mystical experience. The nameless narrator has returned to her childhood home after she receives, from one of her father's neighbors, a letter that states, "You're father is gone, nobody can't find him" (28). The young woman is accompanied by her lover and her married friends, Anna and David. They all lodge in her father's small cabin on an island in Canada, cut off from civilization. On the first morning of their stay, the narrator gets up early to start a fire and discovers Anna "standing in front of the wavery yellowish mirror . . . putting on makeup" (50). The speaker realizes that she has never seen Anna without her "artificial face," which to all who know Anna, including even her husband David, "is the natural one." Seeing Anna without her makeup is not seeing the real Anna: the real Anna is the surface. There is no need for cosmetics on the isolated island, the narrator says, because "there's no one to look at you" (51). But since Anna defines her being by what she sees in the mirror, she is the audience. Anna "blends and mutes herself" until there is no difference (for her or for David) between herself and her makeup. It takes another habit of mind, that of the narrator, to propose the distinction. Throughout the novel, Anna has no self separate from the mask: "From her handbag she takes a round gilt compact. . . . She opens it, unclosing her other self, and runs her fingertip around the corners of her mouth, left one, right one; then she unswivels a pink stick and dots her cheeks and blends them, changing her shape, performing the only magic left to her" (194). Anna blends herself into that "other self" and merges with the mirror.

In contrast, the woman who is the narrator wants to blend into nature and cease creating ego through artifice. If the mirror is the primary tool for a woman to use in defining an identity distinct from everything else in the unimproved "given" of the physical environment, then to unite with the forces of nature the narrator has to stop confronting the glass: "I turn to the mirror to brush my hair. But when I pick up the brush there is a surge of fear in my hand. . . . I know that the brush is forbidden, I must stop being in the mirror. I look for the last time at my distorted glass face: eyes light blue in dark-red skin, hair standing tangled out from my head, reflection intruding between my eyes and vision. Not to see myself but to see. I reverse the mirror so it's toward the wall, it no longer traps me, Anna's soul closed in the gold compact. . . . I unfasten the window and go out" (205). The narrator wants to focus her eyes on a vision of the natural world, and what stands between her and nature is the self-consciousness instituted by self-objectification. As long as she remains an independent ego, she cannot merge with the otherness of nature. The confining mirror is identified with an exclusionary form of selfhood. She wants "not to see myself but to see" because to see her image in the mirror is to create herself as a separate identity that will prevent her from seeing and being one with the other. These psychic readjustments are symbolized by her movement from the mirror to the window.

Just as the narrator must reject the mirror as part of her mystic quest, she must lose her socialized sense of self by escaping from people. She hides when her friends depart by boat, and she is left all alone on the island. She leaves the cabin and goes out into the woods where she removes her clothes, sleeps in a hollow lair, chews on roots. After this period of primal relationship with nature, she comes back to see if she has changed. She has.

> I turn the mirror around: in it there's a creature neither animal nor human, furless, only a dirty blanket, shoulders huddled over into a crouch, eyes staring blue as ice from the deep sockets; the lips move by themselves. . . .
>
> That is the real danger now, the hospital or the zoo, where we are put, species and individual, when we can no longer cope. They would never believe it's only a natural woman, state of nature, they think of that as a tanned body on a beach with washed hair waving like scarves; not this, face dirt-caked and streaked, skin grimed and scabby, hair like a frayed bathmat stuck with leaves and twigs. A new kind of centerfold. (222)

The narrator, whose very namelessness suggests an absence of specified identity, has lost the sense of identification with any socialized self-image. From the world's point of view she has gone mad. She's either crazy, or an animal, or some exotic compound of the two. But it is a new being that she is creating. There is something frightening and powerful about it—unaccommodated woman. The novel's title suggests the surfacing of this new, still indeterminate and liminal form of consciousness. For the speaker, the conventional matrices of self-definition established by the mirror must be rejected in order for the animal within to rise and reveal itself, physiognomically, in the silver surface of the glass.

As I discussed earlier, Coleridge defines (masculine) self-consciousness as "a subject which becomes a subject by the act of constructing itself objectively to itself." Historically, the mirror has been one of the few means always available to women for such objectification, which, as Coleridge points out, is necessary for developing a concept of ego. Self-imaging in a mirror is an almost too literal acting-out of Coleridge's definition and is of course not an explicit concern in his philosophical investigations. While the mirror has provided women with an essential means for the subject / object interchange, it has also been a trap and a tool for the imposition of social limitations. These are the very strictures from which the Brontës, Eliot, and Atwood needed to free not only their fictive self-projections but also their own conceptions of themselves as writers. Or, in the words of Mary Elizabeth Coleridge, as if in reply to her great-uncle, "O set the crystal surface free!" (9).

8.

The Semiotic Surface

I held my spirit to the Glass,
To prove it possibler—
Emily Dickinson

In the act of mirroring, a special kind of communication takes place between two presences. Thus I have on occasion in these chapters found it useful to take a broad semiotic perspective on the phenomenon. That point of view deserves more sustained consideration here, particularly since the mirror has, paradoxically enough, been both contrasted and intimately connected with another semiotic medium, language. The precise relation between the catoptric and the semiotic is a complex philosophical issue. Two basic positions have received most of the attention in recent discussions. Lacan's sense of "le stade du miroir" (noted earlier) maintains that the mirror is the threshold between the purely imaginary (i.e., a state of consciousness that does not rise above the apprehension of images) and what he calls the "symbolic." As Umberto Eco has pointed out, this latter term in Lacan's technical vocabulary seems to include all semiosis and not just a special motivated form of it. Thus, for Lacan, mirroring does participate in the movement of consciousness from the presemiotic toward prelinguistic semiosis and is a necessary stage in that evolutionary process. Eco, however, dissents in interesting ways from this view. He considers the mirror as merely a "catoptric prosthesis" (210) and its imaging capabilities as productive of only a "(pseudo-) semantics" (213). Mirroring provides Eco with a means of delimiting the lower margin of the semiotic, the kind of experience that most closely reaches toward but never achieves true semiosis. To state Eco's view in Lacan's terms, the mirror never moves beyond the imaginary into the symbolic.

Eco's conclusion is the unavoidable consequence of the limitations of his method. He considers mirroring as a perceptual medium, an extension of sight as a physical phenomenon, and never touches upon the psychology of mirroring which is at the heart of this book. His considerable intellect is focused somewhat narrowly on the relationship between the mirror and the eye—never on the interchanges between the mirror and the "I." However wrong women may be, from Eco's point of view, in treating the mirror as semiotic, they have done so in literature (and I suspect in life) countless times.

The general relationship between language and a nonlinguistic medium of semiosis is fraught with even greater complexities. It is possible to argue that language is the basis of all semiosis and that other sorts of experiences become semiotic only when captured by the linguistic. On the other hand, the sophistication of language suggests that it evolved (both for the species and the individual) out of some simpler form of semiosis, such as mirroring. I do not intend to argue on either side of this debate or to make any attempt to resolve it; but no matter which school of thought one holds to, inevitably the catoptric and the linguistic become intertwined not only when the experience of mirroring is communicated to us through a text, but even, I suspect, at a more fundamental level when one recognizes one's own reflection.

Perhaps the most basic distinction between the semiotic and the nonsemiotic is that the semiotic experience involves a difference between the thing perceived and the idea it brings to mind and the nonsemiotic does not. Eco's proposal (although it might be argued that he does not consistently hold to it) that there is no difference between the object and its reflection is central to his thesis about the nonsemiotic character of mirroring. Yet as soon as we shift toward the psychological perspective that I have been developing in this book, we almost immediately encounter just such a distinction defining signification. What I have called the oxymoronic mirror and have contended is fundamental to the whole psychology of female ocular reflection provides mirroring with the differential nature of the lingual sign. This similarity is the enabling substructure for the complex transactions between mirroring and writing we will consider in this chapter.

The disagreements with Eco I have registered here lead us to a controversial motif—the differences between masculine and feminine conceptions of the mirror experience. One of Jonathan Swift's couplets from "The Progress of Marriage" directly indicates that alternative ways of creating a self are historically divided along gender lines: "While He goes out to cheapen Books, / She at the Glass consults her Looks" (1:291). Part of Swift's point is to emphasize the disparity between male and female, but these lines also show Swift's sense of an implicit parallel: the female equivalent of man's confrontation with texts is the face-to-face meeting with the self in the glass. From reading books and criticizing them, we learn to become ourselves within a cultural continuity in large measure defined by those books. The woman "consulting" her looks in the mirror is also undergoing an educative experience. Confronting books supposedly improves one's position in the world; for a woman, confronting her looks is her route to improving that position. The essential place of light, or enlightenment, for the woman is the mirror. The old injunction "nosce teipsum" is literalized in the woman's encounter with herself in the glass.

The juxtaposition of man / book and woman / mirror continues through the centuries in the works of many writers. As Leonard Wolf writes in his 1963 short story "Fifty-Fifty," "her at her mirror, me at my book" (389). Sometimes it is not books but language itself that is seen as the male counterpart of female mirroring. In settling questions of extreme importance, the man often puts his trust, even his deepest religious convictions, in the word; the woman goes to her mirror as the infallible test. For instance, in David Lodge's comic novel *Changing Places* (1975), the man worries that his penis is rather small. The woman explains that "it looks smaller to you, because you're always looking down on it. It gets foreshortened." "That's a thought," the man replies. She says, "Go take a look in the mirror." He says, "No, I'll take your word for it" (167). Although the next morning he does stand on a chair in the bathroom to examine his torso in the mirror, in the initial dialogue on his fear the man finds the verbal explanation sufficient validation of his masculinity. Perhaps his hesitancy to consult the glass is due to the mirror's associations with the feminine. Its use would call into question the very maleness he wants to substantiate.

Some women writers, however, see a connection between reading and mirroring that hints at a shared semiotic ground. Louise Bogan's "Man Alone" (1933) suggests that books and mirrors are alternative activities that intertwine through the processes of self-becoming:

> It is yourself you seek
> In a long rage,
> Scanning through light and darkness
> Mirrors, the page,
>
> Where should reflected be
> Those eyes and that thick hair,
> That passionate look, that laughter.
> You should appear
>
> Within the book, or doubled,
> Freed, in the silvered glass;
> Into all other bodies
> Yourself should pass.
>
> The glass does not dissolve;
> Like walls the mirrors stand;
> The printed page gives back
> Words by another hand. . . . (75)

Both looking into mirrors and reading / writing are attempts to create the self without another person literally present. In the reflection or in the book, there is another presence. Once you objectify yourself into a mirror or onto a page, then that image has a separate reality. The poem suggests that there is a difficulty in finding one's identity in writing or in a mirror because the objectified self has an independence that is disturbing and is subject to multiple distortions. You do not become the image no matter how long you sit in front of the glass. Mirrors are "like walls" because there is no way actually to get into the mirror. And even if the book in question is one you have written yourself, the words have an otherness to them, both physical (the page is not part of your body) and linguistic (you did not invent the words). Through her evocative comparison, Bogan stresses the way in which both media participate in the differential structure of signs.

Even for Bogan, the interwoven alternatives of mirrors and texts can be placed in opposition to each other. In her autobiography, *Journey around My Room* (1980), she juxtaposes a woman who is defined by the mirror with a woman who wishes to be a writer: "Saw my real, half-withered, silly face in a shop mirror on the street, under the bald light of an evening shower, and shuddered. The woman who died without producing an *oeuvre*. The woman who ran away" (103). Bogan sees in the glass a particular definition of her self, but one that immediately suggests its contrary. If she did not produce texts containing her mental reflections, then she would be only the ocular reflection. She would be the woman who ran away from the difficult process of writing, of creating a self outside the mirror. The fear-ridden difference between the desire to create a linguistic presence and the sublinguistic but powerful sign of the mirror brings to Bogan's mind the greater rupture of death itself.

Virginia Woolf is another writer who wants to create herself as men do—not through what others see, not through what the glass sees. In "A Sketch of the Past" (1939–40), a memoir begun when she was nearly sixty, Woolf recollects her early sense of discomfort with mirrors. When she was six or seven, she "got into the habit" of looking at her face in the glass if she was sure she was alone (67). But this activity was accompanied by "a strong feeling of guilt" (68). In retrospect, Woolf believes that the fact that she and her sister "played cricket" and "climbed trees" contributed to her mixed feelings about mirrors. As a child she developed a personality through what were considered masculine pursuits—and thus to look into a mirror was to begin a different way, socially and sexually, of creating an identity. Woolf also suggests that looking into the mirror could become a trap. She might start defining herself through the glass rather than through being a tomboy or (as she later did) through writing. The reason this memory is still important to her is that it remains a threat and represents a road not taken. She confesses that "the looking-glass shame has lasted all [her] life"—not because she continued to be hoydenish, but because mirroring typified an alternative to the personality she constructed through language. When she writes that she cannot now powder her nose "in public," she is indicating that the self is an entity developed through relationships with other people, but she does not want to be seen by others as someone who indulges in archetypally feminine activities. Even "wearing a new dress" is menacing to her methods of self-realization.[1] She wants to dedicate herself to her work, not to the creation of an exterior self. Her at least partial denial of mirroring constitutes a covert revolt against the traditional way women define themselves.

Woolf reveals her tendency to identify with her father, whose "spartan, ascetic, [and] puritanical" character inhibited her "natural love for beauty": "Yet this did not prevent me from feeling ecstasies and raptures spontaneously and intensely and without any shame or the least sense of guilt, so long as they were disconnected with my own body. I thus detect another element in the shame which I had in being caught looking at myself in the glass in the hall. I must have been ashamed or afraid of my own body" (68). Woolf is afraid of being *only* a body, for herself and for others. Her description of the way she can accept beauty as an abstraction suggests a transcendental aesthetic defined in counterdistinction to physical presence, particularly one's own. Although the rhetoric may be foreign to Woolf's own sensibility, it is not too much of an exaggeration to characterize her as a female Prometheus who wants to steal language from the male gods. Like good children, women are permitted to be seen but not heard. Woolf's implicit revolt is to speak, to write, and to define herself through that medium.

Another of Woolf's haunting memories indicates not just the shades of shame, but the spectral dread of the mirror: "I dreamt that I was looking in a glass when a horrible face—the face of an animal—suddenly showed over my shoulder. I cannot be sure if this was a dream, or if it happened. Was I looking in the glass one day when something in the background moved, and seemed to me

1. See Woolf's short story "The New Dress," in which Mabel Waring spends all her time at a party glancing at herself in a mirror and worrying that people are thinking, "'What's Mabel wearing? What a fright she looks! What a hideous new dress!'" Mabel can see her dress "in the round looking-glass which made them all [the guests at the party] the size of boot-buttons or tadpoles; and it was amazing to think how much humiliation and agony and self-loathing and effort and passionate ups and downs of feeling were contained in a thing the size of a threepenny bit" (48).

alive? I cannot be sure. But I have always remembered the other face in the glass, whether it was a dream or a fact, and that it frightened me" (69). Woolf's dream is a foreboding of insanity. It is only a step away from looking in the mirror and, instead of seeing her own face, seeing something nonhuman. Some of Woolf's reasons for her difficulties with the mirror seem positive—there is more to her willed identity than the visual image. But her primal, instinctual relationship with the mirror also harbors a fear of the mirror, and hence of the self, a terror of what she will see in the glass. In this nightmare or vision, we witness the working-out of these negative, frightening implications. Woolf's "Sketch of the Past," in the several passages discussed here, touches upon both of the possible consequences of the rejection of, or inability to use, the mirror—freedom and madness. One result is to be independent of the process of self-definition through the glass (Lady Mary, Jane Eyre, Woolf herself); the other is to go crazy (Clara Batchelor, Esther Greenwood, Woolf herself).

As discussed in Chapter 6, Plath's adolescent heroine in *The Bell Jar* wins—on the strength of her poems and essays—a guest editorship at a women's magazine in Manhattan. Yet the world persists in judging Esther as an object of vision, a situation crystallized when the contest winners are photographed with props indicative of their professional goals. Asked what she wishes to be, Esther answers "a poet." When the photographer says, "'Show us how happy it makes you to write a poem,'" Esther starts to cry and later feels "limp and betrayed, like the skin shed by a terrible animal" (83). To revive her sense of self-possession, she turns to her "gilt compact," but finds in its mirror only a face that seems to be peering from the bars of "a prison cell." Esther reacts so emotionally to the photographer because his request tears something essential from her being—her ambition to be other than an object completely capturable in a photograph, that mirror with a memory. Even the concept of being a writer has been reduced to a visual image, to looking like a "happy" poet (perhaps a contradiction in terms for Plath).[2] Esther responds to this double trauma, both to

2. Plath's anonymous photographer repeats that reduction of writing to a visual image which was also promoted by eighteenth- and nineteenth-century mirrors made specifically for attachment to ladies' writing desks so that the women could gaze at their own images "gracefully writing letters." See Hollander, 405.

herself and to her ambition, by testing her sense of self-identity. But the single means for doing so immediately available to her is the glass, an instrument that demonstrates the way Esther is trapped in visual objectification not only by others but also by herself. The external incident with the photographer dramatizes an unresolved internal conflict between competing semiotic modes of self-realization: writing and mirroring.

Through writing, through a process of objectification of consciousness in which physical beauty plays no essential role, some women have found ways of escaping the mirror without losing the power to determine their identities. For a woman, to write, to create a persona, can be a substitution for looking in a mirror. Dorothy Parker's brief lyric, "Words of Comfort To Be Scratched on a Mirror," is an attempt to counteract the force of the glass:

> Helen of Troy had a wandering glance;
> Sappho's restriction was only the sky;
> Ninon was ever the chatter of France;
> But, oh, what a good girl am I! (173)

This is a light poem, yet it makes a serious point about the exchange of writing for mirroring. When the speaker of the poem looks in this mirror, she sees two images of the self—the visual reflection and, as an overlay or palimpsest, another sense of the self through writing. An irony arises out of the disparity between the mirror image and the letters incised in its surface. The speaker implies that she is not as beautiful as the other famous women she names but can take comfort in being more virtuous. But such a resolution is hardly to be taken at face value in a poem by Parker. Her triumph over the celebrated beauties is through writing itself, which quite literally defaces the mirror and replaces the visual reflection with the mental reflections of poetry. The real counter to the image in the glass is not goodness but language, for one powerful mode of semiosis (and its ability to produce self-presence) can only be challenged by another mode.

Although some women see writing as an escape from mirroring, others see it as an extension—a supplement rather than a substitution. This possibility is hinted at in Parker's inscribed mirror. Like the heroine of Jessamyn West's *Cress Delahanty*, such women want "to dance the word" in front of the looking glass. Anaïs Nin, for instance, doesn't see an opposition between mirroring and writing. She sees writing as a continuation of the mirror, "the diary as mirror" as she expresses it (2:86). There is a sense in which she perceives with considerable intelligence the power of the glass, but she never questions it. For a writer such as Nin, writing and mirroring are equivalent in their relation to ego.[3] Both allow for the exposition of her incredible vanity; both are forms of "publication."

Some female characters are so mirror dominated that they are interested in only the visual components of spoken language—the linguistic act that is one with the body. We recall Wharton's Undine Spragg in *The Custom of the Country*, who watches herself "chat" before the mirror as she moves "her lips in soundless talk" (22). What is said does not matter; what she looks like while saying it does. Similarly, a woman in Margaret Drabble's *The Garrick Year* (1964) uses the mirror to see what the man would see when she says his name: "I stared into the mirror . . . at my own chilly face and I said aloud 'Wyndham.'" She explains that she wants "to *see* [my emphasis] what the word would sound like" (162). A teenage girl in Joyce Carol Oates's short story "The Dying Child" (1966) is not quite prepared to say "bastard" to the boy she is with, but she shapes "the word 'bastard' to herself, watching her lips move in the mirror" (285). These female characters shift the emphasis away from the signifying capabilities of language itself to what is generally considered to be an inconsequential (albeit necessary) feature of speech. But for such women, the visual takes center stage as the most significant feature of language performance.[4]

Texts and mirrors can perform similar psychological functions for women, particularly during periods in their lives when objec-

3. See, for example, Nin's somewhat confused discussion of women, mirrors, nature, writing, and their equivalency (*Diary* 4:33–34).

4. This valorization of the visual over the verbal seems to stand behind Gloria Heidi's bizarre recommendation on how to improve your communication skills: "An easy way to study your facial mannerisms is to put a mirror by your telephone. Then study your facial expressions as you talk to your best friends. Are your expressions warm, friendly, responsive? Are they communicating the real you? The old mirror-by-the-telephone trick will also let you spot the tendency to allow your expressions to become exaggerated and over-active" (196).

tification and consciousness of self become necessary. Near the end of Alice Munro's novel *Lives of Girls and Women* (1971), Del Jordan, a senior in high school, breaks up with her boyfriend. Nonetheless she waits in the hope that he will return, and then begins to cry as that hope slips from her. She turns to look "in the dim mirror" at her "twisted wet face":

> Without diminishment of pain I observed myself; I was amazed to think that the person suffering was me, for it was not me at all; I was watching. I was watching, I was suffering. I said into the mirror a line from Tennyson, from my mother's *Complete Tennyson* that was a present from her old teacher, Miss Rush. I said it with absolute sincerity, absolute irony. *He cometh not, she said.*
>
> From "Mariana," one of the silliest poems I had ever read. It made my tears flow harder. Watching myself still, I went back to . . . the dining room where the city paper was still lying on the table. . . . I opened it up at the want ads, and got a pencil, so I could circle any job that seemed possible. I made myself understand what I was reading, and after some time I felt a mild, sensible gratitude for these printed words, these strange possibilities. (200)

When someone is suffering, physically or mentally, detachment comes as unbidden relief. The mind distances itself from the body because the body is making the person suffer. Del is experiencing that separation from self during this crisis, and the doubleness ("the person suffering was me," "it was not me at all") is reflected by the oxymoronic nature of the mirror. There is also a detachment that comes through literature, bringing a formal feeling to the moment of distress. The literary association gives the sorrow a frame, an objectified context or correlative. The fact that Del recognizes that she is quoting a bad line from what she considers a silly poem about a dejected and deserted woman contributes wonderfully to her sense of disconnection from her tears, even when they "flow harder." By becoming in effect a literary critic, she looks at the poem and herself objectively. Munro's passage interweaves three phenomena—the oxymoronic nature of the mirror, the sense of isolation from oneself which occurs as a response to pain, and the way literature (and the criticism of literature) can be a distancing and form-giving act. Del's initial act of disengagement is through the mirror in which she can literally watch herself.[5] Then that sense of remoteness and irony (a structural equivalent within rhetoric to the self / other duality of the glass) is continued in a literary context. Del starts with the mirror and then makes a very important move toward language—first by remembering the line from the poem, then through actually reading. Before there is a concern with content, there is an involvement with "these printed words" and the "possibilities" for another self they seem to offer. The referentiality of these words is less important than the process of reading, of engagement in textuality, which by itself draws the girl out of self-indulgent sorrow.

Munro's character starts with the mirror and moves toward language. Henry James's Kate Croy makes the same journey, but then returns to the mirror. *The Wings of the Dove* (1902) begins with Kate waiting for her father in his impoverished lodgings and looking into "the glass over the mantel." She scrutinizes her pale face for a moment, and then her thoughts turn inward to her deep awareness of "the whole history" of her family "that had the effect of some fine florid, voluminous phrase" (10). Her mind moves on to questions about accident and destiny: "The answer to these questions was not in Chirk Street, but the questions themselves bristled there, and the girl's repeated pause before the mirror and the chimney-place might have represented her nearest approach to an escape from them. Was it not in fact the partial escape from this 'worst' in which she was steeped to be able to make herself out again as agreeable to see? She stared into the tarnished glass too hard indeed to be staring at her beauty alone" (10). Kate's psychological pattern is almost an exact opposite of the Romantic heroine's: the latter, seeing in the mirror what the world thinks of her, wishes to avoid that exterior power and thus rejects the mirror image and plunges inward into forms of self-creation only possible in a state of consciousness not reflected in the glass. Kate is presented to us as a being defined through an internal monologue, as a

5. Compare Del watching herself crying in the mirror with a character in Storm Jameson's 1932 story "The Single Heart": "She calmed herself by looking in the glass at the tears trickling over her cheeks, and tasting one on the end of her tongue. There is no better way of checking a crying fit" (150). Like Del, this woman turns to the mirror to help her establish distance, objectification, and, finally, control.

woman who is burdened by a psychologically manipulative father and by a degree of language-centered self-consciousness equivalent almost to the author's. Kate's burden is not exteriority but interiority—the weight of her own feelings, perceptions, her own terribly complicated and ambiguous psyche and its bondage to a family "history," a patriarchal text inscribed in her mind. For her the outward world and the process of self-creation through the outer are "an escape." She revolts against a stultifyingly complex (and essentially linguistic) interiority rather than against a powerful exteriority. What has been for other women a trap is for Kate a release, a liberation, a casting outward from the unresolvable complexities on the inside.

The characters and episodes discussed above present a bewildering variety of mirror / language interactions that run the gamut between contrariety and near-identity. The general semiotic perspective introduced at the beginning of this chapter can help to sort out these complexities. In each instance, there is an interchange between a subject and an object that is taken to be more than what it is—in other words, the mirror image is taken to be a sign. Such a sign refers essentially to the perceiving subject of which it is a projection in the literal, ocular sense. This circularity shapes the circumference of the mirror's referentiality, but this limitation does not make the reflection any less functional within a structure of meanings. Indeed, for those seeking certain forms of feminine self-consciousness, this restriction makes the mirror image the most powerful sign of all. The special status of the reflection may be in part due to the nonarbitrary, or "motivated," relationship between the signifier (the mirror image in itself) and the signified (the human form presented in the mirror) which is established through detailed visual mimesis. The difference between the two is not absolute, at this basic level of semiotic functioning, but reemerges at the psychological level when the woman either accepts the shape in the mirror *as* the self or refuses that equation.

In some texts, the multiple passages between the catoptric and the linguistic constitute an almost seamless fabric. This heterogeneous condition is very probably normative for most women who, after all, think in language more often than they look in mirrors. But as we have seen, these two modes are sometimes placed in opposition as alternative possibilities, particularly when linguistic acts are held out as a replacement for the *public* image of the woman. That act of substitution or supplementation (the latter a compromise or attempt to have it both ways) becomes most significant when women move from speech to *writing*—the form of language capable of being published and distributed through the social matrix in ways clearly beyond the capabilities of the mirror. By writing texts (and thereby in a sense becoming a text in the eyes of the world), women find one of the few alternatives to becoming mirror images which have been historically permitted—if not always encouraged—by Western culture.

The relation between language and transcendence has become an important feature of modern meditations on signification, particularly in the works of Martin Heidegger and in Jacques Derrida's attacks on the phenomenology of Edmund Husserl. What role does the mirror play in these highly theoretical arguments? Do the semiotics of the glass lead us to another version of the transcendental signified or does the mirror hold us within the material signifier?

Anaïs Nin died in 1977, a few weeks before her seventy-fourth birthday. In the preface to the last volume of her intimate history, her editor Gunther Stuhlmann writes, "The diary still serves as a mirror of self-examination" (7:viii). In addition, Nin's mirror continued to serve as a diary of self-examination. Nin is the opposite of Lady Mary Wortley Montagu, who, after a certain age, refused to look in the glass. Even in her final years, Nin obviously devoted many hours to studying her reflection, as evinced by her long and lovingly detailed head-to-toe descriptions of what she believed to be her still youthful and beautiful body.[6] Nin tried to stay within the compass of the Western concept of the feminine physical self, yet still to triumph in time, not by going outside the mirror but by remaining immutably within its rim. Female and male have the same fate: they die. Masculine culture has, since time immemorial, devoted immense intellectual energy to developing ways for transcending this elemental fact. Most such strategies are based on a radical division between body and mind (or soul), the latter

6. Note also the kinship of Nin with a character in her sixties in Elizabeth Taylor's *A Game of Hide-and-Seek*: "She seemed to be lovely still to herself, as if no amount of looking into mirrors could ruin her illusion" (59).

category privileged over the former by virtue of its relatively greater freedom from the constraints of time and space. But when we are presented with Nin before her mirror, there is no hint of such transcendence. If she is to defeat time, it is only in and through the body. Her sense of feminine heroism unfolds completely within the arena of physical presence. In such circumstances, the masculine response, from Plato to Heidegger, has always been to develop categories of being which go beyond the mirror, beyond the body.

In Gail Godwin's short story "Some Side Effects of Time Travel" (1971), she presents a clear juxtaposition between those women who, like Nin, define themselves in the mirror and those who represent, however provisionally, attempts to rise above it. Virginia Woolf is offered up as a personification of such possibilities:

> "*Was your first lipstick Fire and Ice?*" A full-page color ad addresses itself to a reluctant Gretchen from the pages of *The New Yorker.*
> Yes, what about it?. . .
> "*Then* YOU *are ready for Eterna 27,*" the ad soberly reminds Gretchen. She runs to the mirror. Is it true? Does she need hormones to stir up blood in an aging face? Did Virginia Woolf use hormone cream? No, but her bones were better. (37–38)

The question about Virginia Woolf is a rhetorical one. Surely, Godwin implies, Woolf did not rush to the mirror in response to such an advertisement. But then this transcendental moment that suggests alternatives to the glass is suddenly undercut: the interior is not mind or soul but the physical frame supporting the external body. After the implication that Woolf is an exemplar of someone who stands outside the realm of visual reflections, we get a different answer from what we expect, an answer that drags Woolf back into mirrors, pulls her down from the position of a liberating alternative to just another woman who is still defined (at least by other people) in terms of appearance. From a semiotic perspective, we are offered "Woolf" as a sign whose signified is a general category—that which transcends the unavoidable physicality of the signifier. But we are almost immediately brought back to the level of the signifier, to the "bones" of the would-be symbol, a movement that unpacks the hypothetical sign and thereby questions the possibility of constructing any such signs, any such strategies of transcendence. In her own lighthearted way, Godwin performs a deconstructive turn, replicating, within the feminine culture of the mirror, Derrida's attacks on Western (masculine) metaphysics based on transcendental self-presence.[7]

Even women who desperately want *not* to be defined by the mirror realize that that is how they are defined. Lyndall, the beautiful restless heroine of Olive Schreiner's *The Story of an African Farm*, is profoundly aware of the ways in which men and women are shaped by the world: "To you [men] it says—*Work*! and to us [women] it says—*Seem*!" (188). The emphasis on visual appearance begins for women even "when we are tiny things" (189). Gender distinctions evolve as females cease to look longingly out "the window . . . at the boys in their happy play" and instead "go and stand before the glass." Then "the curse begins to act on us" and "finishes its work when we are grown women." Schreiner offers her critical evaluation of this process by comparing it to the way "a Chinese woman's foot fits her shoe." These and similar comments constitute a highly self-conscious analysis of the antitranscendentalism of the mirror and the women who, willing or not, are defined by it. According to Lyndall, the world of men and mirrors becomes a "curse" that inescapably forms her as an exterior presence in a way that deeply affects her inner being. Godwin's witty return to the body finds its tragic counterpart in Schreiner's vision of bondage. Lyndall, who must look in the mirror and not out of the window, resembles the Lady of Shalott. Both have to look in the glass to see the only world they are allowed. When Tennyson's Lady finally looks through the window, the mirror cracks from side to side and "The curse is come upon me," cries the Lady of Shalott (16). But, for Lyndall, it is when women stand before the glass that the curse begins to act on them.

Given Lyndall's critique, we might expect her to revolt against the mirror. But she does not. A later passage shows the irreplaceable intimacy of the relationship between this woman and her mirror image. Lyndall sits before the glass and speaks to her reflection: "'We are all alone, you and I,' she whispered; 'no one helps us, no one understands us; but we will help ourselves.' The eyes

7. See in particular Jacques Derrida's early work *Speech and Phenomena*.

looked back at her. There was a world of assurance in their still depths. So they had looked at her ever since she could remember, when it was but a small child's face above a blue pinafore. 'We shall never be quite alone, you and I,' she said; 'we shall always be together, as we were when we were little'" (242–43). When all else is lost, a man who wishes to reassert his own value traditionally returns to his soul, his mind, or the works that will outlive his body. What this representative woman has is an exterior self, her mirror image, as a female counterpart to the masculine, transcendental, interior concept of a self. And this remains true even for a woman conscious that her identity is socially determined by the fact of her femaleness. The grammar of such formulations, either masculine or feminine, unavoidably posits an ego other than the exterior image or the internal soul, but in both cases that grammatical "I" is defined—if defined at all—through its relation to the other-I. For the man, that otherness is within the I, protected, forever proclaiming the fiction of its power to rise above time, its own body, and the world. For the woman, the other-I is external, one with the body, and extraordinarily vulnerable to the ways of this world.

In the tragic denouement of the novel, Lyndall is dying after having given birth to an illegitimate child who lived only a few hours. While traveling in a closed wagon in a vain attempt to return to her home, she consults the mirror for the last time:

> She put the pillow on her breast, and stood the glass against it. Then the white face on the pillow looked into the white face in the glass. They had looked at each other often so before. . . . Now tonight it had come to this. The dying eyes on the pillow looked into the dying eyes in the glass; they knew that their hour had come. She raised one hand and pressed the stiff fingers against the glass. She tried to speak to it, but she would never speak again. Only, the wonderful yearning light was in the eyes still. The body was dead now, but the soul, clear and unclouded, looked forth.
>
> Then slowly, without a sound, the beautiful eyes closed. The dead face that the glass reflected was a thing of marvellous beauty and tranquillity. . . .
>
> Had she found what she sought for—something to worship? Had she ceased from being? Who shall tell us? There is a veil of terrible mist over the face of the Hereafter. (283–84)

Death, with peculiar force, always calls to mind the body / soul relationship and a concern with the nature of the soul and its destiny. As Lyndall gazes into the glass in her final moments, the soul is named in a context that intertwines this soon-to-be eternal self with the mirror. Schreiner's echoing repetitions in diction and syntax make reflectivity the pervasive structure of the whole passage. To confront her innermost being, Lyndall turns to her external image. That icon of worship becomes, in this traditional scene of parting, the portal through which the soul passes. But to what? The physicality of the mirror undercuts its role as a quasi-religious means of transcendence and thereby questions the very concepts of soul and its afterlife which the glass so tellingly fails to represent. The power of language to refer to the nonphysical has been marshaled for generations to support transcendence, but the semiotics of the glass force women back to earth—from the "face of the Hereafter" to their own faces.

Erica Jong offers a particularly interesting juxtaposition of masculine and feminine attitudes toward the relation between mirror imaging and the phenomenon of transcendence. In her *Fear of Flying* (1973), the heroine Isadora Wing stands naked in front of a "flaking full-length mirror":

> I had the oddest sunburn from our days of driving in the open car. My knees and thighs were red and peeling. My nose and cheeks were red. My shoulders and forearms were burnt to a crisp. But the rest of me was nearly white. A curious patchwork quilt.
>
> I stared into my eyes, white-circled from having worn sunglasses for weeks. Why was it I could never decide what color my eyes were? Was that significant? Was that somehow at the root of my problem? Grayish blue with yellow flecks. Not quite blue, not quite gray. Slate blue, Brian used to say. . . . Brian had the brownest eyes I'd ever seen—eyes like a Byzantine saint in a mosaic. When he was cracking up he used to stare at his eyes in the mirror for hours. . . . He spoke literally then of a looking-glass world, a world of antimatter into which he could pass. His eyes were the key to that world. He believed that his soul could be sucked out through his pupils like albumen being sucked from a pierced egg. (283–84)

We have seen other women who could not put their whole form together to constitute an identity. In this instance, however, this failure is contrasted with a man's use of a mirror. Although he too lacks a unified sense of self, he tries (however unsuccessfully) to repair internal dislocations by looking into a mirror. But unlike Isadora's, his mirror has depth; he moves beyond an external image of a "patchwork quilt" to imagine another world to which his "soul" can pass through his eyes and through the reversing portal of the glass. Even when crazy, and even when looking into a mirror, the man remains a transcendentalist. Jong underscores his otherworldliness through the Yeatsian reference to the "Byzantine saint" transported into the immutable realm of art. The juxtaposition of these two confrontations with the mirror, one typically feminine and the other typically masculine, implies that the woman's "problem" is here defined as an inability to deploy a transcendentalizing semiotic to overcome mere physicality. In short, she cannot create a soul. On the other hand, the man's pursuit of such fictions is represented as essentially crazy and not as a positive response to insanity.

Isadora's self-contemplation continues:

> Obviously it was dangerous to stare at your eyes in mirrors too long. I stood back to examine my body. Where did my body end and the air around it begin? Somewhere in an article on body image I had read that at times of stress—or ecstasy—we lose the boundaries of our bodies. . . .
>
> I tried to examine my physical self, to take stock so that I could remember who I was—if indeed my body could be said to be me. I remembered a story about Theodore Roethke alone in his big old house, dressing and undressing himself before the mirror, examining his nakedness in between bouts of composition. Perhaps the story was apocryphal, but it had the ring of truth for me. One's body is intimately related to one's writing, although the precise nature of the connection is subtle and may take years to understand. Some tall thin poets write short fat poems. But it's not a simple matter of the law of inversion. In a sense, every poem is an attempt to extend the boundaries of one's body. One's body becomes the landscape, the sky, and finally the cosmos. Perhaps that's why I often find myself writing in the nude. (285)

For many men, the mirror takes on significance beyond the merely utilitarian only when it becomes a magic glass, a sign of something beyond the visible world. But the essential mystery for the woman is in the visible. That is the I. That is the great enigma. What the woman is doing is not trivial compared with masculine activities, only different. Isadora uses the mirror as a nonmetaphoric representation of what others see and in that finds great power. The bodily self is viewed in direct relation to writing, an activity traditionally seen as an extension of soul or mind. The body, the self brought to consciousness by looking in a glass, here becomes the origin and constant companion of writing, that other "outering" of ego in an act of individual consciousness and social engagement. Those points of origin, soul and mind, so essential to male models of expression, become for Isadora unnecessary fictions. The difference between the traditional scene of writing the self and Jong's alternative is bridged through a necessary fable of androgynous autogenesis—a male precursor becoming himself through essentially feminine activities before the mirror.

Jong's antitranscendentalism is implicit in her heroine's question, "Where did my body end and the air around it begin?" The distinction between self and other, as an infantile psychic experience, may be much the same for both sexes, but for male-dominated philosophies this difference becomes a metaphysical issue having little to do with one's own physical body. Isadora's question before her mirror literalizes the distinction into a purely physical and personal matter. For male consciousness and its projections, the self is by definition that which is *not* revealed by a mirror. In *Phenomenology, Language, and Sociology*, Maurice Merleau-Ponty describes one such version of this masculine paradigm: "A Cartesian does not see *himself* in the mirror; he sees a dummy, an 'outside,' which, he has every reason to believe, other people see in the very same way but which, no more for himself than for others, is not a body in the flesh. His 'image' in the mirror is an effect of the mechanics of things. If he recognizes himself in it, if he thinks it 'looks like him,' it is his thought that weaves this connection. The mirror image is nothing that belongs to him" (291). Such philosophical statements find both analogues and alternatives in Jong's fiction.

Rebecca West, in *The Thinking Reed* (1936), provides a somewhat simpler but more direct juxtaposition of masculine and feminine approaches to the semiotics of the mirror and self-identity.

The husband says, "You see, none of us can see our own faces. The faces we see in mirrors are not our own, the left is turned to the right, and as soon as we know that we are regarding our own images we falsify our experiences" (414). For this representative male, a version of Merleau-Ponty's "thought" interjects itself between body and reflected image, and this seemingly disembodied act of consciousness becomes the center of self-conception. Again, the mirror becomes yet one more physical object available to the "higher" activities of mind, and through that availability validates yet again the existence of mind. But West describes the wife as looking "at herself in her long mirror" because she needs "to recognize herself as the person she knew, who she had been all her life" (39). For the woman, her visual image requires only interpretation, not displacement, to reveal the self.

A woman, particularly an old or ugly one, may desire to deny that the mirror reflection is she, but its acceptance can become a means of positive nontranscendence. Miss Despenser, a drunken old woman in Elizabeth Taylor's *Hester Lilly* (1969), initially tries to consider the specular I as a complete otherness rather than an essential identity: "I meet myself every so often. 'You hideous old baggage,' I say, and I nod. For years I thought it was someone else" (36). Next, however, she suggests that her optical counterpart is part of the self:

> "When I go into the town to get the cat's meat, the chances are that as I go round by the boot shop I see myself walking towards me—in a long panel of mirror at the side of the shop. 'Horrid old character,' I used to think. 'I must change my shopping morning.' So I changed to Fridays, but there she was on Fridays just the same. 'I can't seem to avoid her,' I told myself. And no one can. Go on your holidays. You take yourself along too. Go to the ends of the earth. No escape. And one gets so bored, bored. I've had nearly seventy years of it now. And I wonder if I'd been beautiful or clever I might have been less irritated. Perhaps I am difficult to please. My mother didn't care for *herself,* either. When she died, the Vicar said: 'It is only another life she has gone to, an *everlasting* life.' An extraordinarily trite little man. . . . I said to him: 'Oh dear, oh dear, for pity's sake, hasn't she had enough of herself?' He couldn't answer that one. 'I believe in personality,' I said. 'You believe in souls. That's the difference between us.'" (36–37)

This sibylline crone sees her inability to avoid her mirror image as a dramatic demonstration of that more general inability to escape the self. Like Yeats's Crazy Jane with her Bishop, she offers a direct rebuke to the masculine spirituality of the Vicar. In place of his concept of "soul," institutionalized by his very profession, the old woman hints at a theory of "personality," a term with no necessary trace of the transcendental and with clear allegiances to a social sense of being. Personalities are constructed through human interaction, human conversations, not the creative Word of an absent God. To get out of one's self means to join with others in a communal pursuit of transformed identity, not the Vicar's heavenly notion of the same old ego levitated to some other world. The old woman's theory of identity is less isolated, less alienated from the physical world, and more open to change than the Vicar's. Miss Despenser finds her freedom by dispensing with the whole, long, masculine history of transcendental rhetoric, metaphysics, and theology. Like Crazy Jane, Miss Despenser is an unsurpassed realist. Although the looking glass in her hall is "filmed with damp and dust," she can still see herself dimly in it: "Clutching the back of a chair she rocked to and fro, staring. 'It is what I am,' she told herself. 'It is what I live with'" (50). For a woman, what one *is* is what one is *with*. Community defines being, and the primary, most important, and unavoidable other-self with whom one forms a community is the presence in the mirror.

Seneca said, "No one is free who is a slave to the body." To a very large degree, Western religion and philosophy have depended upon this basic idea of the autonomous self, one that tends to exclude women who form identities in other ways. Perhaps the paucity of female contributions to transcendentalizing traditions has some basis in a woman's unwillingness to define self through its alienation from the body. The fact that God has been imaged as male in Western culture is but one indication of the sexism of transcendence. The exclusion of women from the institutions of intellect may appear to be only the imposition of an artificial barrier having little to do with the nature of the thought promoted by those institutions. But the roots of such prohibitions may go deeper. When women look at themselves in mirrors, they participate in a largely ignored panoply of body / self interactions programmatically excluded from the metaphysics of masculine self-presence.

9.

A Mirror of One's Own

I need a virgin mirror
no one's ever looked at,
that's never looked back at anyone.
Elizabeth Bishop

The mirror, I fear, has become something of a villain in this book. Those female characters for whom many of us would have most respect, given today's attitudes, are the least tied to mirrors and the varieties of social self-consciousness with which mirrors are intimately connected. Yet mirrors, simply as objects, are essentially neutral in value until they are used in particular ways within cultural contexts that they did not themselves create. It is, after all, the woman who does the looking and creating, not the glass. These simple facts, as well as Jong's Isadora and Taylor's Miss Despenser, suggest that mirrors may be valorized in alternative ways that aid rather than hinder the development of female identities freed from the trammels of traditional social conventions. We need to look more closely at these emerging feminist possibilities (and their roots in earlier literature) for reconstituting the psychology of the mirror experience.

Thomas Hardy's Bathsheba Everdene in *Far from the Madding Crowd* (1874) is in some respects the reverse of the heroines created by Emily and Charlotte Brontë. Instead of female authors creating heroines of freedom from the mirror, a male author creates a female character whose heroism is basically formed within the confines of a self-conception intimately associated with her reflected image. In the first few pages of the novel, we and Gabriel Oak are introduced to Bathsheba and her looking glass. Farmer Oak sees a wagon laden with household goods. When the tailboard falls off, the wagoner stops the horses and runs back to look for it. Oak watches the handsome young woman seated on the apex of the load. Thinking herself unobserved, Bathsheba unties the paper covering of "a small swing looking-glass," smiles at her reflection, and blushes (6). The male observer thinks that there is "no necessity whatever for her looking in the glass." But there is: she needs to unwrap the mirror to reassure herself that she exists, that she is lovely, that she is able to smile in a way that is pleasing to herself and to the world. Yet all of this is presented by Hardy as a natural process. Bathsheba can no more resist "survey[ing] herself attentively" in the glass than her cat (also female) can resist "affectionately survey[ing] the small birds." Further, Hardy goes to some lengths not to set up a dichotomy between the beauty of "Nature" and the artificial beauty of a woman, for Bathsheba is naturally beautiful. The privacy of her act and the lack of a utilitarian purpose indicate that it functions as an essential part of a process of self-creation.

With the Brontës, George Eliot, and Lady Mary (who is her own heroine), a woman's heroism is dependent on a rejection of the mirror. Bathsheba accepts the mirror image as an integral constituent of the self and knows that, before the world sees her as fair, she must see herself that way. "Vanity" may be Oak's word for Bathsheba (8), but it is not Hardy's final assessment of her. She is a self-willed, strong young woman, a tenant farmer who successfully directs her workmen, dismisses the bailiff of her estate, and manages everything with her own head and hands. Still, "'tis said here and there" among the peasants that Bathsheba "every night at going to bed . . . looks in the glass to put on her nightcap properly" (39). This gossip may indeed be right about Bathsheba's actions, but it is wrong in its implication that these activities bespeak nothing but vanity. Although Bathsheba continues to use the mirror as an intimate companion of self-definition, she is by no means wholly absorbed by the glass.

As Hardy very provisionally suggests in *Far from the Madding Crowd*, revolt is not the only pattern to be found in attempts at revisionary definitions of the female self. As we have seen in Chapter 3, D. H. Lawrence often attacks the narcissism he finds in a woman's relationship with her mirror. But in *Lady Chatterley's Lover* (1928) he presents a woman using her mirror as a valuable part of a process of personal realization: "When Connie went up to her bedroom she did what she had not done for a long time: took off all her clothes, and looked at herself naked in the huge mirror. She did not know what she was looking for, or at, very definitely, yet she moved the lamp till it shone full on her" (72). It is significant that Constance Chatterley looks at her entire body, not just her face, in the glass. The mirror as an onanistic replacement for a man is for Lawrence a false and destructive substitution. Looking at the whole figure can readjust that experience and begin a rediscovery of, or a readjustment in, the perceived relationship between mind and body. The entire novel explores the awakening of what is, from Lawrence's perspective, Connie's "true" self. She is here initiating the emergence of hitherto unrealized forces within the body of that self, and she does it before the glass.

When Connie looks at herself naked in the mirror, she realizes that her form lacks something—what Blake called "the lineaments of gratified desire." Her breasts are "unripe," her belly "slack," her thighs "flat" and "meaningless" (73). Then she begins to study her back in a second mirror's reflection, and the two mirrors offer an expansion of vision. She can now see "the most beautiful part of her . . . the long-sloping fall of the haunches from the socket of the back, and the slumberous, round stillness of the buttocks. . . . Here the life still lingered hoping" (73). Connie is starting to realize the existence of something that can be called "the whole being," and one step in getting away from the facial mirror is this opening up of the full potential of mirrors. The face is the physiognomic expression of mental life; the body, of emotional and biological life. The parts of this physical sign that most forcefully counter psychological abstraction and social generalization are farthest from those that are usually taken to express one's public personality. The "most beautiful part" of Connie is what she cannot see with a single mirror or a hand glass. A doubling of the mirror offers the woman an expanded field for the development of self—and body—consciousness. By heightening her awareness of her sheer material presence, Constance begins to integrate sexuality into her conception of what she is. Such a use of the mirror is neither a revolt against it, nor a submission to it. For Constance, mirroring is a phenomenon over which *she* has control. She has found a certain freedom within the glass to explore herself in terms given by her own body—rather than in terms established by the mirror as a representative of societal values. She comes to the mirror with the question, "What does my body look like and feel like to me?"—not "What does my body look like to the world?"

Lawrence is an unexpected celebrant of the liberated mirror, and, indeed, there is much in his writings antithetical to any form of female self-consciousness. Yet the presentation of Constance before the glass in *Lady Chatterley's Lover* is a precursor of an important motif in contemporary feminist literature. This approach to self-reflection as both a literal activity and a meditative exercise has been recommended to women in such recent guides as Susie Orbach's *Fat Is a Feminist Issue* (1978). Orbach strives to free women from the normative and judgmental dimensions of the mirror. Rather, it is to be used as a way of recognizing the body's (unidealized) existence and its connection to one's life. A psychotherapist specializing in the treatment of compulsive eating, Orbach suggests various strategies to help overweight women "in the very difficult task of self-acceptance and the preparation for a new slim body and new self-image":

> Bear in mind that you first have to own something before you can lose it. You must first accept your body in its largeness before you can give it up. A full-length undistorted mirror is the first place to start. Group members set aside time each day . . . to observe their bodies. We are using the mirror to see ourselves without judging the image it holds. This is both a frightening and difficult project for many women because one is so used to making a grimace and judgment on the few occasions we do see our whole bodies. We are so familiar with avoiding possibly unacceptable visions, keeping our heads down as we walk past shop windows lest we cast a glance at ourselves unaware and trigger negative feelings. So, in doing the exercise, a woman is asked initially to look at the reflected image of herself as she would a work of art, for example, a sculpture, getting to know its dimensions and textures. She is looking to find out where it begins and ends; where it curves or bumps in and out; what color changes there are. . . . Some people have a greater ease doing this exercise dressed; others find it more manageable nude.
>
> Many women experience their fat as something that surrounds them with their true selves inside or, alternatively, that their fat trails them, taking up more room than it really does. So when a woman is standing in front of the mirror the emphasis in this part of the exercise is to feel herself *throughout* her body. She follows her breath on its course from her lungs through her body. The large

> thighs she may wish to reject are as much a part of her body as the wrist that seems so much more acceptable. Try to see the various parts of your body as connected. Start with your toes and remind yourself of how your toes are connected to your feet and your feet are connected to your ankles and your ankles are connected to your lower legs, and so on. It will provide you with a holistic view of your body. You will begin to experience yourself as existing through the fat. (87–88)

Orbach is concerned with a process of transformation in which the mirror persists as a valuable tool. The nineteenth-century mirror scenes we have considered imply a clear distinction between women who accept the mirror and those who reject it. The latter group attempts to take hold of their lives by letting go of the glass. But, in a few telling works of this century, the mirror is used less as an instrument of fashion, of adornment, of preparation to be a commodity for the male world and more as a means of psychic assimilation. Some writers are starting to be quite conscious of the close relation that has always pertained for women in our culture between physical appearance and concept of self. The mirror is to be not rejected but reclaimed in order to be used in a new way—a way Maggie Tulliver didn't understand when she cut off her hair. Maggie wanted to define herself free of the mirror and what the mirror represented, but the world still judged her in the same terms. Hers was an unsuccessful revolt because she did not understand the power of the glass to establish the relationship between appearance and identity. Orbach's point in *Fat Is a Feminist Issue* is, in the largest sense, an existential one. Her interest is neither in judging the body in the mirror, nor in allowing the mirror to judge the body. Orbach is trying to increase awareness, to understand what the self is, not as a transcendental category opposed to the corporeal but as a phenomenal presence united with it. Seventeenth-century meditative exercises were meant to free religious devotees from their fleshy prisons. Orbach offers a meditative exercise for women with the consciousness of physicality as its *telos*. She does not rebel against the identification between mind and body but insists on it. Indeed, the therapy depends on an acceptance of that which most of us would want to deny. The "mirror exercise" is to give the woman a body, and then she can determine whether or not to change it. Let the female herself observe, decide, and take control.[1] This subtle revolution accepts the body, accepts the mirror, and proposes to lead the female self in new directions of its own making within a cultural context created by women, not imposed on them.

Orbach's book is only one among many recent studies that stress a woman's mind / body interactions. The titles of just a few indicate this emphasis: *Our Bodies, Ourselves* (1971), *The Mind / Body Effect* (1979), *Changing Bodies, Changing Lives* (1980). As Susan S. Lichtendorf explains in *Eve's Journey: The Physical Experience of Being Female* (1982), something "extraordinary" happened in the 1960s and 1970s when "women began to share knowledge about their bodies" and make "public the kind of information and insights hithertofore [*sic*] only the property of professionals": "And they did something else . . . they seized the speculum, that simple instrument that opens a woman's interior space for examination. In self-help centers and in some physician's offices, using the speculum and mirror women began to look within themselves. At last they could see the shape and color and characteristics of the vaginal wall and cervix, hidden features of their physical selves" (12). This passage shows how, for women, the psychological phenomena of self-presence have an objective correlative generally absent from male self-conceptions. For a man, to explore his "interior space" or "look within" himself means just what it meant for Socrates. It has nothing to do with mirrors or physical examinations of his anatomy. But for these women—I am tempted to say "for most women"—it does. To construct an interior sense of selfhood, women need to explore their bodies in this way.[2] Male concepts of human identity are founded on a radical division between mind and brain,

1. In her later study, *Fat Is a Feminist Issue II,* Orbach includes "Mirror Work" (149–51) as one of the recommended "Psychological Exercises."

2. For a kindred example, see Mary Kay Blakely's essay in which she remembers the birth of her son: "The nurse is holding a mirror between the stirrups. 'See! Can you see it! the head's crowning!' I see the swirling mass of hair, spinning strands, drawing me deeply into the mirror, into the rushed beginnings, the unstoppable contractions, the contradictions of motherhood" (187). In Lichtendorf's *Eve's Journey,* a sad instance is recounted by a woman who suffers a stillbirth: "I know it might seem disgusting or ghoulish but I was very interested in what was happening to my body. I used a bright metal bedpan as a mirror and I actually saw the sac emerge" (295).

soul and body, spiritualized self and physical container. For women, there is a continual two-way flowing back and forth of a very complex sort between their corporeal existence (how they look as physical objects to themselves and to others) and how they conceive of themselves as female human beings in a psychological or spiritual sense. The difference between these masculine and feminine perspectives was dramatized by Shakespeare almost four hundred years ago. Hamlet says to his mother, "You go not till I set you up a glass / Where you may see the inmost part of you" (*Hamlet*, 3.4.19–20). He is of course speaking metaphorically; he does not mean a real mirror and "the inmost part" is not something physical. But the Queen answers, "What wilt Thou do? thou wilt not murder me? / Help, ho!" (21–22). She takes what he says as a literal reference to a looking glass and to the insides of her body. This encounter between the transcendentalism of metaphor and the bodily presence of the literal demonstrates, within the arena of language, the fundamental contrarieties of male and female self-possession.

At a very different level of speculation, Luce Irigaray has touched upon some of these same themes central to women psychologists who aim their work at a large and general readership. In *Speculum of the Other Woman* she offers a wide-ranging critique of male-dominated structures (social, linguistic, epistemological) that forever posit the female as the object, sealing her off from access to full subjectivity and self-determined identity. The mirror, as a male-directed instrument of literal objectification, is part of this limiting syndrome. Yet Irigaray does not reject its possibilities: "And if it is indeed a question of breaking (with) a certain mode of specula(riza)tion, this does not imply renouncing all mirrors or refraining from analysis of the hold this plan/e of representation maintains. . . . But perhaps through this specular surface which sustains discourse is found not the void of nothingness but the dazzle of multifaceted speleology. A scintillating and incandescent concavity, of language also, that threatens to set fire to fetish-objects and gilded eyes" (143). Although the pressure of Irigaray's rhetoric tends to force all phenomena into polyvalent metaphor, we can perceive in her wordplay some important generalizations about the way mirroring can be used to burn away the fetishized woman-as-object seen in (and created by) the glass. Even the "gilded eyes" of mirror-mindedness can be replaced by eyes that search deeply into hidden caverns of female selfhood. Irigaray concludes that she is "seeking, in simplest terms, to be united with *an image in a mirror.* This is how I am. At last alone, copula. I-me, coupled together in an embrace that begins over and over again" (189–90). This feminist call to (nonmetaphoric) arms asks for nothing less than a state of consciousness defined through its constant commingling with corporeal being.

Instead of throwing the mirror away, women are making it a more flexible tool. By taking the mirror into their own hands, women are eliminating the mirror as tyrant, as dominant male. The alternative is to be like a man, to have an ego defined in counterdistinction to the body and thus not related to the mirror. But the objective of this liberation movement is not to turn women into men. The mirror and its representations are so related to feminine self-conception, in its distinctions from male identity, that the glass has to be saved and controlled. For women to liberate themselves as women is not to dismiss their bodies but to free them from male / mirror tyranny. To couch these desires in semiotic terms, the goal is not to erase the signifier, as in a transcendentalizing program, but to incorporate the signifier and the signified within a totalizing phenomenology of self-consciousness. In this process, the mirror serves as a useful but finally subordinate instrument for the assimilation of physicality into thought.

Using the mirror to transform a woman's sense of the relation between the physiological and the psychological has been dramatized in recent novels. Occasionally, a female character even refers directly to the very sort of self-help books that I have been discussing. In Godwin's *A Mother and Two Daughters*, Lydia Mansfield, a thirty-six-year-old mother recently separated from her husband, looks into a mirror and then immediately recalls a passage from *Life Crises of the Modern American Woman*:

> "If you are in your mid-thirties and put your mind in mothballs during those busy years when you were nurturing your children, now is the time when you may find yourself sneaking trips to the attic to take it out again and try it on for size. Have you become too small for your old ambitions? Too flabby for your former capacity for rigorous thought? And what about those secret dreams of ad-

> venture and romance? If there is a dusty old mirror, you clean it with the corner of your apron and look in. Why, you're still there. You look pretty good! It's now or never, you think." (86)

The book Lydia has been reading associates mirrors with a concern for one's own self-development. It calls for a positive return to the mirror experience. Earlier in the novel, Lydia said to herself that she despised this inane book, that she would find her own way and "not be regimented into . . . popular-psychology categories." Yet she does go back to both the glass and the text. The effect is humorous, but the language of the passage quoted above actualizes the very interplay between self and body at the heart of new feminist values: the "mind" is "too small . . . too flabby," as though it were a physical organ. The mind / body dichotomy, like the distinctions between subject and object, male and female, is embedded in the grammar of propositions and the metaphysics they enable. Here, however, Godwin uses a pattern of adjectives which suggests a deeper structure of essential unities.

In Alice Walker's *The Color Purple* (1982), a young black woman named Celie, who has been told all her life that she is ugly and dumb, marries a widower who doesn't care for her, beats her, and only wants someone to take care of his four children. Celie admits to her friend Shug Avery that she has never experienced any pleasure in sex. The sensual Shug is puzzled:

> You never enjoy it at all?. . .
>
> Never, I say.
>
> Why Miss Celie, she say, you still a virgin.
>
> What? I ast.
>
> Listen, she say, right down there in your pussy is a little button that gits real hot when you do you know what with somebody. . . . Lot of sucking go on, here and there, she say. Lot of finger and tongue work.
>
> Button? Finger and *tongue*? My face hot enough to melt itself.
>
> She say, Here, take this mirror and go look at yourself down there, I bet you never seen it, have you?
>
> Naw. . . .
>
> I stand there with the mirror.
>
> She say, What, too shame even to go off and look at yourself? . . .

> You come with me while I look, I say.
> And us run off to my room like two little prankish girls. . . .
> I lie back on the bed and haul up my dress. Yank down my bloomers. Stick the looking glass tween my legs. Ugh. All that hair. Then my pussy lips be black. Then inside look like a wet rose.
> It a lot prettier than you thought, ain't it? she say from the door.
> It mine, I say. Where the button?
> Right up near the top, she say. The part that stick out a little.
> I look at her and touch it with my finger. A little shiver go through me. (79–80)

The passage dramatizes and literalizes Irigaray's proposal for a female "speleology." With the support of her frank friend and of the mirror, Celie begins to get over her embarrassment and to allow herself the possibility of enjoying her body with physical and psychic intimacy. Her realization, via the looking glass, that a part of her body she thought repulsive is both pretty and pleasurable aids in the gradual growth of her self-esteem. This private act of self-revelation is a necessary prelude to her social liberation.[3]

Sometimes when a woman has relied all her life on her youthful looks but is now starting to grow old and is no longer the center of attention, it is hard for her to begin using the mirror not as a beauty aid but as an instrument of self-creation. Kate Brown, the central character of Doris Lessing's *The Summer before the Dark,* is, at forty-five, on the verge of middle age: "Still on the verge—she had not chosen to enter the state" (34). But after becoming sick while traveling, Kate looks nothing like the pretty, privileged, cared-for wife and mother she has been for so many years. Her several confrontations with the mirror all stress the otherness of the image that is becoming ever less recognizable to her as her beauty fades. She sees in the glass "a greenish-white face that had flaring scarlet on the cheekbones" (138); she sees "a white sagging face around which was a rough mat of brassy hair" (141). Finally, during the intermission of a play she has attended even though she

3. A related motif is scenes in which young women masturbate before the glass. For a particularly intriguing example, see Lois Gould, *A Sea-Change.* An adolescent, naked except for a pair of shiny silver high heels, watches herself in "a long mirror" as she masturbates, "studying her own climax" (61). In Gould's novel, this activity is part of the girl's awakening to her sexuality—the contrary of Lawrence's denunciation of mirroring as obscenely onanistic (see Chapter 3).

is still quite ill, Kate sees her image as not herself—as not even human: "Kate went to the cloakroom, where she was not surprised to see that a monkey looked back at her from the mirror" (157). When Kate returns from the theater, she goes to her room, "took up her hand mirror—she certainly could not have found the energy to sit upright a moment longer—and fell into bed and looked at her face" (160). Taking the mirror to bed suggests an extra intimacy, and Kate begins to relate a mini-history of what it has meant for her to look into mirrors, a background for all the other examples in the novel:

> Long ago, a young girl lay on her back in a bed, with a hand mirror held close to her face, and she was thinking: That is what *he* is going to see. . . .
>
> For years Kate, who spent the requisite amount of time in front of many different mirrors, had been able to see exactly what *he* was seeing, when his face was close above hers. . . . Had she really spent so many years of her life—it would almost certainly add up to years!—in front of a looking glass? Just like all women. Years spent asleep, or tranced. Did a woman choose *him*, or allow herself to be chosen by *him*, because he admired that face she had so much attended to, and touched, and turned this way and that—she wouldn't be surprised, she wouldn't be surprised at all! For the whole of her life, or since she was sixteen—yes, the girl making love to her own face had been that age—she had looked into mirrors and seen what other people would judge her by. And now the image had rolled itself up and thrown itself into a corner, leaving behind the face of a sick monkey. (160–61)

The passage almost too neatly summarizes some of the chief themes I have emphasized in this book: the masculine and social dimensions of the glass, the development of female identity through communication with the specular image, a sense of the trancelike limitations of that process, and even the insanity incipient in the collapse of the self / mirror equation. Yet after she looks in the mirror and sees the face of an animal—reminiscent of Clara's mad encounter with the otherness of her self-image in Antonia White's *Beyond the Glass*—Kate's reaction is not to leave the mirror altogether but to return to it in search of new dimensions. She learns that the mirror does not necessarily lock the woman into one "set of features" or one mode of being: "Kate was now grimacing into the hand glass, trying on different expressions, like an actress—there were hundreds she had never thought of using! She had been limiting herself to a frightfully small range, most of them, of course, creditable to her, and pleasing, or non-abrasive to others" (161). Kate tests alternative possibilities (or at least expressions) before the mirror, using it to help create other selves—although the maneuver is tentative and superficial at this point. By the end of the novel, Kate has chosen to let her attractive appearance lapse. Sometimes, when she looks in the glass, she is able to laugh at what she sees. "The light that is the desire to please had gone out. And about time too. . . ." (243) No longer caring to please the mirror, the world, she can begin to use the glass as a means of expanding, and thereby pleasing, herself. Once again we see an aging woman avoiding pathological dissociation from the catroptric sign of herself by transforming its otherness into a resource.

Lessing's Kate moves toward, but has not yet reached, the level of self-knowledge, acceptance, and ease attained by May Sarton's Hilary Stevens. In Sarton's *Mrs. Stevens Hears the Mermaids Singing* (1965), the heroine, a poet approaching seventy, confronts the glass and its cold objectivity with a strength of will fully capable of liberating the mirror from being only a recorder of decay:

> "God, you look awful," she told herself. "Old crone, with hardly a wisp of hair left, and those dewlaps, and those wrinkles." Merciless she was. But there was also the pleasure of recognition. In the mirror she recognized her *self,* her life companion, for better or worse. She looked at this self with compassion this morning. . . . The sense of who she was and what she meant about her own personage began to flow back as she ran a comb through the fine childlike hair, hardly gray, and brushed her teeth—her own, and those the dentists had had to provide over the years.
>
> "Damn it!" she said aloud. It meant, in spite of it all, false teeth, falling hair, wrinkles, I am still myself. They haven't got me yet. (13)

To look at one's image "with compassion" makes it clear that this engagement with the mirror is not just an external process (it seldom is—for a woman), but has an internal, psychic significance.

There is a constant affirmation of personal presence through the division of self into both subject and object. By objectifying the ego, in the grammar of the prose and literally in the mirror, Hilary can perceive herself, generate and assert that self, and thus validate that she does indeed exist as a human being. This act of objective self-recognition institutes a bifurcation, but at the same time can be used by women to break down the conceptual barriers between mind and body. Such experiences strive for Irigaray's "copula" of "I-me"—a recognition of a structure of difference to be re-configured through the oxymoronic doubleness of the reflection. Clearly, by its very nature, this process cannot overcome the inherent divisions of the lingual sign and of the self-consciousness with which it is so intimately allied. Yet it is a heroic act for a woman of Hilary's age to look in the glass with her still keen eyes, see ugliness, and declare that "they"—decay, death, all those enemies that lead to nonexistence—"haven't got me yet."[4] With such honesty comes knowledge—both about the self as a phenomenon of continual creation and about the uses of the mirror in the interchanges between "I" and "me." The image in the glass is a "life companion," at once an otherness she can study and an intrinsic part of the ego as it comes into being. This wise woman—without lies, without vanity—can use the alterity of the mirror image as a constituent of identity.

Characters like Hilary, real or fictive, show us how the mirror can become a tool of self-exploration and self-discovery. To say this is not to claim that all problems with identity are solved, but at least the mirror need no longer be a distorting imposition. Women are not obliged to reject the mirror or see it only as a prison in a patriarchal cultural tradition. We can be, to borrow a line from Louise Bogan, "freed, in the silvered glass." What women want is not the world's mirror, but a mirror of their own.

4. The actions and thoughts of Sarton's Mrs. Stevens are substantially repeated by Nora Porteous, a woman in her seventies, in Australian novelist Jessica Anderson's *Tirra Lirra by the River* (1978): "In the bathroom mirror I look with equanimity at an old woman with a dew-lapped face and hands like bunches of knotted sticks. . . . Well, I am what I am. . . . I forgive myself everything" (99).

Works Cited

Adam, Ruth. *I'm Not Complaining*. Garden City, N.Y.: Dial Press, 1984. First published 1938.

Adams, Alice. *Rich Rewards*. New York: Alfred A. Knopf, 1980.

Aleramo, Sibilla. *A Woman*. Trans. Rosalind Delmar. Berkeley: University of California Press, 1980. First published 1906.

Andersen, Hans Christian. "The Snow Queen." *Fairy Tales*. New York: Viking, 1981. First published in English 1846.

Anderson, Jessica. *Tirra Lirra by the River*. Harmondsworth: Penguin, 1984. First published 1978.

Ashbery, John. "Self-Portrait in a Convex Mirror." *Self-Portrait in a Convex Mirror*. Harmondsworth: Penguin, 1976.

Atwood, Margaret. *The Handmaid's Tale*. Boston: Houghton Mifflin, 1986.

———. *Lady Oracle*. New York: Simon and Schuster, 1976.

———. "Marrying the Hangman." *Two-Headed Poems*. New York: Simon and Schuster, 1978.

———. *Surfacing*. New York: Fawcett Popular Library, 1972.

Auden, W. H. "As I walked out one evening." *The Collected Poems of W. H. Auden*. New York: Random House, 1945.

Auel, Jean. *The Clan of the Cave Bear*. New York: Crown, 1980.

Baker, Nancy C. *The Beauty Trap: Exploring Woman's Greatest Obsession*. New York: Franklin Watts, 1984.

Balzac, Honoré de. *Cousin Bette*. Trans. Marion Ayton Crawford. Harmondsworth: Penguin, 1965. First published 1847.

Barnstone, Aliki, and Willis Barnstone, eds. *A Book of Women Poets from Antiquity to Now*. New York: Schocken Books, 1980.

Baum, L. Frank. *Ozma of Oz*. New York: Ballantine, 1979. First published 1907.

Beattie, Ann. *Falling in Place*. New York: Fawcett Popular Library, 1981. First published 1980.

——. "Shifting." *Secrets and Surprises*. New York: Warner Books, 1983. First published 1976.

Beckett, Samuel. *Happy Days*. New York: Grove Press, 1961.

Berger, John. *Ways of Seeing*. Harmondsworth: Penguin, 1972. New York: Viking Press, 1973.

Bierce, Ambrose. *The Devil's Dictionary*. Cleveland: World Publishing, 1911.

Bishop, Elizabeth. "The Riverman." *The Complete Poems*. New York: Farrar, Straus and Giroux, 1969.

Blakely, Mary Kay. Untitled essay in *Hers: Through Women's Eyes*. Ed. Nancy R. Newhouse. New York: Harper and Row, 1986. First published 1977.

Blessing, Richard. "What I Know by Heart." *A Closed Book*. Seattle: University of Washington Press, 1981.

Bogan, Louise. *Journey around My Room: The Autobiography*. Ed. Ruth Limmer. New York: Viking Press, 1980.

——. "Man Alone." *The Blue Estuaries: Poems: 1923–1968*. New York: Ecco Press, 1977.

Borges, Jorge Luis, with Margarita Guerrero. *The Book of Imaginary Beings*. Trans. Norman Thomas di Giovanni. New York: E. P. Dutton, 1978. First published 1967.

Brontë, Anne. *Agnes Grey*. London: Everyman's Library, 1958. First published 1847.

Brontë, Charlotte. *Jane Eyre*. Intro. Phyllis Bentley, Boston: Houghton Mifflin, 1965. First published 1847.

——. *Shirley*. Harmondsworth: Penguin, 1947. First published 1849.

Brontë, Emily. *Wuthering Heights*. New York: Washington Square Press, 1960. First published 1847.

Brookner, Anita. *Hotel du Lac*. New York: Pantheon Books, 1984.

Carswell, Catherine. *Open the Door!* New York: Penguin, 1986. First published 1920.

Carter, Angela. *The Magic Toyshop*. London: Virago, 1981. First published 1967.

——. *The Passion of New Eve*. London: Virago, 1985. First published 1977.

Chaucer, Geoffrey. *The Canterbury Tales*. Trans. Nevill Coghill. Baltimore: Penguin, 1952.

Chernin, Kim. *The Obsession: Reflections on the Tyranny of Slenderness.* New York: Harper and Row, 1981.

Chodorow, Nancy. *The Reproduction of Mothering: Psychoanalysis and the Sociology of Gender.* Berkeley: University of California Press, 1978.

Coleridge, Mary Elizabeth. "The Other Side of a Mirror." *Poems by Mary E. Coleridge.* London: Elkin Mathews, 1908.

Coleridge, Samuel Taylor. *Biographia Literaria.* Eds. James Engell and W. Jackson Bate. Princeton: Princeton University Press, 1983. First published 1817.

Colette. *Chéri.* Trans. Roger Senhouse. Baltimore: Penguin, 1974. First published 1920.

———. "The Judge." *The Other Woman.* Trans. Margaret Crosland. New York: Signet, 1975. First published 1951.

Coward, Noel. *Present Indicative.* Garden City, N.Y.: Doubleday, 1937.

Cravens, Gwyneth. "Vision." *Bitches and Sad Ladies: An Anthology of Fiction by and about Women.* Ed. Pat Rotter. New York: Dell, 1975.

Dalsimer, Katherine. *Female Adolescence: Psychoanalytic Reflections on Literature.* New Haven: Yale University Press, 1986.

de Beauvoir, Simone. *Force of Circumstance.* Trans. Richard Howard. New York: Penguin, 1968. First published 1963.

———. *The Second Sex.* Trans. H. M. Parshley. New York: Vintage Books, 1974. First published 1949.

de Grummond, Nancy Thomson. "The Bronze Mirrors of the Etruscans." *FMR* 15 (October 1985): 102–13.

de la Mare, Walter. *Memoirs of a Midget.* Oxford: Oxford University Press, 1982. First published 1921.

Derrida, Jacques. *Speech and Phenomena and Other Essays on Husserl's Theory of Signs.* Trans. David B. Allison. Evanston: Northwestern University Press, 1973. First published 1967.

Dickinson, Emily. "I felt my life with both my hands." *The Complete Poems.* Ed. Thomas H. Johnson. Boston: Little, Brown, 1957. First published 1945.

Drabble, Margaret. *The Garrick Year.* New York: Popular Library, 1977. First published 1964.

———. *The Ice Age.* New York: Popular Library, 1977.

———. *Jerusalem the Golden.* New York: Popular Library, 1967.

Dreiser, Theodore. *Sister Carrie.* Ed. Donald Pizer. New York: W. W. Norton, 1970. First published 1900.

Dugan, Alan. "The Mirror Perilous." *Collected Poems.* New Haven: Yale University Press, 1969.

Eco, Umberto. *Semiotics and the Philosophy of Language.* Bloomington: Indiana University Press, 1984.

Eliot, George. *Daniel Deronda.* Ed. Barbara Hardy. Harmondsworth: Penguin, 1967. First published 1876.

——. *The Mill on the Floss.* Ed. Gordon S. Haight. Boston: Houghton Mifflin, 1961. First published 1860.

Eliot, T. S. "Burnt Norton." *Collected Poems 1909–1962.* New York: Harcourt, Brace and World, 1963. First published 1936.

Elsner, Gisela. *Offside.* Trans. Anthea Bell. London: Virago, 1985. First published 1982.

Farrell, M. J. (pseudonym for Molly Keane). *Mad Puppetstown.* New York: Penguin, 1986. First published 1931.

Fiedler, Leslie A. See Weil, Simone.

Figes, Eva. *Waking.* New York: Pantheon, 1981.

Flaubert, Gustave. *Madame Bovary.* Trans. Francis Steegmuller. New York: Modern Library, 1957. First published 1857.

——. *Sentimental Education.* Trans. Robert Baldick. Harmondsworth: Penguin, 1964. First published 1869.

Frazer, Sir James George. *The Golden Bough: A Study in Magic and Religion.* New York: Macmillan, 1963. First published 1922.

Freedman, Rita. *Beauty Bound.* Massachusetts: D. C. Heath, 1986.

French, Marilyn. *The Women's Room.* New York: Summit Books, 1977.

Freud, Sigmund, "The 'Uncanny.'" *The Standard Edition of the Complete Psychological Works of Sigmund Freud.* Ed. James Strachey. London: Hogarth Press, 1955.

Garrigue, Jean. "Primer of Plato." *The Ego and the Centaur.* New York: New Directions, 1947.

Gilbert, Sandra M., and Susan Gubar. *The Madwoman in the Attic.* New Haven: Yale University Press, 1979.

Gilchrist, Ellen. "The Famous Poll at Jody's Bar." *In the Land of Dreamy Dreams: Short Fiction.* Boston: Little, Brown, 1981.

Gilligan, Carol. *In a Different Voice: Psychological Theory and Women's Development.* Cambridge, Massachusetts: Harvard University Press, 1982.

Ginzburg, Eugenia Semyonova. *Journey into the Whirlwind.* Trans. Paul Stevenson and Max Hayward. New York: Harcourt, Brace and World, 1967.

Glasgow, Ellen. *Barren Ground.* New York: Hill and Wang, 1957. First published 1925.

——. *Vein of Iron.* New York: Harcourt, Brace and World, 1963. First published 1935.

Godwin, Gail. "Death in Puerto Vallarta" and "Some Side Effects of Time Travel." *Dream Children*. New York: Avon, 1983. First published 1971.

———. *A Mother and Two Daughters*. New York: Avon, 1983. First published 1982.

Goldin, Frederick. *The Mirror of Narcissus in the Courtly Love Lyric*. Ithaca: Cornell University Press, 1967.

Gordimer, Nadine. *Occasion for Loving*. London: Victor Gollancz, 1963.

Gordon, Mary. *Men and Angels*. New York: Random House, 1985.

Gould, Lois. *A Sea-Change*. New York: Simon and Schuster, 1976.

Grabes, Herbert. *The Mutable Glass: Mirror Imagery in Titles and Texts of the Middle Ages and English Renaissance*. Trans. Gordon Collier. Cambridge: Cambridge University Press, 1982.

Grand, Sarah. *The Beth Book: Being a Study of the Life of Elizabeth Caldwell Maclure, A Woman of Genius*. Intro. Elaine Showalter. New York: Dial Press, 1980. First published 1897.

Graves, Robert. "The Face in the Mirror." *Five Pens in Hand*. Garden City, N.Y.: Doubleday, 1958.

Gregory, Horace. "The Postman's Bell Is Answered Everywhere." *Collected Poems*. New York: Holt, Rinehart and Winston, 1964.

Grimm, Jacob and Wilhelm. "Snow White." *The Twelve Dancing Princesses and Other Fairy Tales*. Bloomington: Indiana University Press, 1974. First published 1812.

Hahn, Emily. *Times and Places*. New York: Thomas Y. Crowell, 1970. Parts of this book originally published between 1937 and 1969.

Hardy, Thomas. *The Collected Poems of Thomas Hardy*. London: Macmillan, 1965. First published 1919.

———. *Far from the Madding Crowd*. Ed. Richard L. Purdy. Boston: Houghton Mifflin, 1957. First published 1874.

———. *Tess of the d'Urbervilles*. Ed. Scott Elledge. New York: W. W. Norton, 1965. First published 1891.

———. *The Woodlanders*. London: Macmillan, 1973. First published 1887.

Hartley, L. P. *A Perfect Woman*. New York: Alfred A. Knopf, 1956. First published 1955.

Hawthorne, Nathaniel. *The Scarlet Letter*. Ed. Larzer Ziff. Indianapolis: Bobbs-Merrill, 1963. First published 1850.

Hébert, Anne. *Kamouraska*. Trans. Norman Shapiro. Don Mills, Ontario: General Publishing, 1974. First published 1970.

———. "Life in the Castle." Trans. A. Barnstone and W. Barnstone. See Barnstone, Aliki.

Hegel, G. W. F. *The Phenomenology of Mind*. Trans. J. B. Baillie. New York: Harper and Row, 1967. First published 1807.

Heidi, Gloria. *Winning the Age Game*. Garden City, New York: Doubleday, 1976.

Hellman, Lillian. *An Unfinished Woman: A Memoir*. New York: Bantam, 1970. First published 1969.

Hollander, Anne. *Seeing through Clothes*. New York: Avon, 1980. First published 1975.

Hsüeh T'ao. "Spring-Gazing Song." Trans. Carolyn Kizer. See Barnstone, Aliki.

Humphreys, Josephine. *Dreams of Sleep*. New York: Viking, 1984.

Irigaray, Luce. *Speculum of the Other Woman*. Trans. Gillian C. Gill. Ithaca: Cornell University Press, 1985. First published 1974.

Ise, Lady. "Even in My Dreams." Trans. Etsuko Terasaki with Irma Brandeis. See Barnstone, Aliki.

Isherwood, Christopher. *A Single Man*. New York: Avon, 1978. First published 1964.

James, Henry. *The Wings of the Dove*. New York: New American Library, 1964. First published 1902.

Jameson, Storm. "The Single Heart." *Women against Men*. New York: Penguin, 1985. First published 1932.

Jarrell, Randall. "The End of the Rainbow." *The Complete Poems*. New York: Farrar, Straus and Giroux, 1969.

Jesse, F. Tennyson. *The Lacquer Lady*. New York: Dial Press, 1979. First published 1929.

Jewett, Sarah Orne. "The Flight of Betsey Lane." *A Native of Winby and Other Tales*. Boston: Houghton Mifflin, 1893.

Jolley, Elizabeth. *Foxybaby*. New York: Viking, 1985.

Jong, Erica. *Fear of Flying*. New York: New American Library, 1974. First published 1973.

———. "The Girl in the Mirror." *Here Comes and Other Poems*. New York: New American Library, 1975. First published under the titles *Fruits and Vegetables* (1968) and *Half-Lives* (1971).

Joyce, James. *Finnegans Wake*. London: Faber and Faber, 1939.

———. *A Portrait of the Artist as a Young Man*. New York: Viking, 1964. First published 1916.

Jullian, Philippe, and John Phillips. *Violet Trefusis: A Biography*. New York: Harcourt Brace Jovanovich, 1976.

Jung, C. G. *The Archetypes and the Collective Unconscious*. Trans. R. F. C. Hull. Volume 9 in *The Collected Works of C.G. Jung*. Second edition. Princeton: Princeton University Press, 1968.

Keane, Molly. See Farrell, M. J.

Kennedy, Margaret. *The Constant Nymph*. London: Heinemann, 1959. First published 1924.

Kenney, Susan. *In Another Country*. New York: Viking, 1984.
Kirkland, Gelsey, with Greg Lawrence. *Dancing on My Grave*. Garden City, N.Y.: Doubleday, 1986.
Klass, Perri. *Recombinations*. New York: G. P. Putnam's Sons, 1985.
Korda, Michael. *Queenie*. New York: Warner Books, 1985.
Kristeva, Julia. *Desire in Language: A Semiotic Approach to Literature and Art*. Ed. Leon S. Roudiez. Trans. Thomas Gora, Alice Jardine, Leon S. Roudiez. New York: Columbia University Press, 1980.
Lacan, Jacques. "The Mirror Stage as Formative of the Function of the I as Revealed in Psychoanalytic Experience." *Ecrits*. Trans. Alan Sheridan. New York: W. W. Norton, 1977. This version first published 1949.
Lawrence, D. H. *The Complete Poems of D. H. Lawrence*. Ed. Vivian de Sola Pinto and F. Warren Roberts. New York: Viking, 1964.
____. *The Complete Short Stories*. London: Heinemann, 1955. 3 vols.
____. *Lady Chatterley's Lover*. New York: Bantam Books, 1968. First published 1928.
____. "Pornography and Obscenity." *Selected Literary Criticism*. Ed. Anthony Beal. New York: Viking, 1956.
____. *Women in Love*. New York: Modern Library, 1948. First published 1920.
Lehmann, Rosamond. *Invitation to the Waltz*. New York: Harcourt Brace Jovanovich, 1975. First published 1932.
____. *The Weather in the Streets*. Garden City, N.Y.: Dial Press, 1983. First published 1936.
Lessing, Doris. *Martha Quest*. New York: New American Library, 1970. First published 1952.
____. *A Proper Marriage*. New York: New American Library, 1970. First published 1952.
____. *The Summer before the Dark*. New York: Bantam Books, 1974. First published 1973.
Levenson, Samuel. *Maud Gonne*. London: Cassell, 1977.
Leverson, Ada. "Love's Shadow." *The Little Ottleys*. New York: Dial Press, 1982. First published 1908.
Lichtendorf, Susan S. *Eve's Journey: The Physical Experience of Being Female*. New York: Berkley Books, 1983. First published 1982.
Lodge, David. *Changing Places*. Harmondsworth: Penguin, 1978. First published 1975.
Lurie, Alison. *Foreign Affairs*. New York: Random House, 1984.
____. *The War between the Tates*. New York: Random House, 1974.
McCourt, James. *Kaye Wayfaring in "Avenged"*. New York: Alfred A. Knopf, 1984.

McCullers, Carson. *The Member of the Wedding*. New York: Bantam Books, 1950. First published 1946.

Mansfield, Katherine. *Stories by Katherine Mansfield*. New York: Vintage Books, 1956. "Prelude" first published 1918.

Mead, George Herbert. *The Social Psychology of George Herbert Mead*. Ed. Anselm Strauss. Chicago: Chicago University Press, 1956. First published 1934.

Melamed, Elissa. *Mirror Mirror: The Terror of Not Being Young*. New York: Simon and Schuster, 1983.

Merleau-Ponty, Maurice. *Phenomenology, Language, and Sociology: Selected Essays of Maurice Merleau-Ponty*. Ed. John O'Neill. London: Heinemann, 1974.

Milton, John. *Complete Poems and Major Prose*. Ed. Merritt Y. Hughes. New York: Odyssey Press, 1957.

Mitford, Nancy. *The Pursuit of Love*. Harmondsworth: Penguin, 1949. First published 1945.

Montagu, Lady Mary Wortley. *Complete Letters*. Ed. Robert Halsband. Oxford: Clarendon Press, 1967.

Moreau, Jeanne. Quoted by Dale Pollock in "Gish—'Thank You for my Life.'" *Los Angeles Times* (3 March 1984): pt. 5, 5–6.

Mortimer, Penelope. *My Friend Says It's Bulletproof*. New York: Random House, 1967.

Mullen, Laura. "Mirror, Mirror." *Poetry Northwest* 23 (1982): 8.

Munro, Alice. *Lives of Girls and Women*. New York: New American Library, 1983. First published 1971.

——. "The Moons of Jupiter." *The Moons of Jupiter: Stories by Alice Munro*. New York: Knopf, 1983. First published 1978.

Nin, Anaïs. *The Diary of Anaïs Nin*. Ed. Gunther Stuhlmann. Vols. 2, 4, 7. New York: Harcourt Brace Jovanovich, 1967, 1971, 1980.

Oates, Joyce Carol. "Honeybit" and "The Dying Child." *The Goddess and Other Women*. Greenwich: Fawcett Publications, 1976. First published 1966.

——. "A Sentimental Education." *A Sentimental Education: Stories*. New York: E. P. Dutton, 1982. First published 1979.

——. *Unholy Loves*. New York: Vanguard, 1979.

O'Brien, Kate. *That Lady*. New York: Penguin, 1985. First published 1946.

Opie, Iona and Peter. *The Puffin Book of Nursery Rhymes*. Harmondsworth: Puffin Books, 1963.

Orbach, Susie. *Fat Is a Feminist Issue*. New York: Berkley Books, 1979. First published 1978.

——. *Fat Is a Feminist Issue II*. New York: Berkley Books, 1982.

Orwell, George *A Clergyman's Daughter.* Harmondsworth: Penguin, 1964. First published 1935.
Ovid. *The Metamorphoses.* Trans. Mary M. Innes. Baltimore: Penguin, 1955.
Parker, Dorothy. *The Viking Portable Library: Dorothy Parker.* New York: Viking, 1956. First published 1928.
Pausanias. *Descriptions of Greece.* Vol. 5. Trans. W. H. S. Jones. London: Heinemann, 1935.
Phillips, Jayne Anne. *Machine Dreams.* New York: E. P. Dutton, 1984.
Plath, Sylvia. *The Bell Jar.* New York: Harper and Row, 1971; reprint, New York: Bantam Books, 1972. First published 1963.
____. *The Collected Poems.* Ed. Ted Hughes. New York: Harper and Row, 1981.
Plotinus. *Selected Works.* Trans. Thomas Taylor. London: George Bell and Sons, 1909.
Pope, Alexander. *The Rape of the Lock and Other Poems.* Ed. Geoffrey Tillotson. London: Methuen, 1962.
Pounds, Michael C., and Peter H. Salus. "Film Semiotics and Specular Information." *Semiotics 1984.* Ed. J. Deely.
Pym, Barbara. *Crampton Hodnet.* New York: E. P. Dutton, 1985.
____. *The Sweet Dove Died.* New York: Harper and Row, 1980. First published 1978.
Rhys, Jean. *Wide Sargasso Sea.* Harmondsworth: Penguin, 1968. First published 1966.
Riding, Laura. "Miss Banquett, or the Populating of Cosmania." *Progress of Stories.* New York: Dial, 1982. First published 1935.
____. "With the Face." *Collected Poems.* New York: Random House, 1938.
Robinson, Marilynne. *Housekeeping.* New York: Bantam Books, 1982. First published 1981.
Robison, Mary. "Mirror." *The New Yorker* (12 August 1985): 30–34.
Roethke, Theodore. "Fourth Meditation." *The Collected Poems of Theodore Roethke.* Garden City, N.Y.: Doubleday, 1966. First published 1958.
Rossetti, Christina. "Passing and Glassing." *The Poetical Works of Christina Georgina Rossetti.* Ed. William Michael Rossetti. London: Macmillan, 1904.
Rossner, Judith. *August.* Boston: Houghton Mifflin, 1983.
Rubin, Lillian B. *Women of a Certain Age: The Midlife Search for Self.* New York: Harper and Row, 1979.
Sarton, May. *At Seventy: A Journal.* New York: W. W. Norton, 1984.
____. *Mrs. Stevens Hears the Mermaids Singing.* New York: W. W. Norton, 1975. First published 1965.

Sass, Louis A. "Introspection, Schizophrenia, and the Fragmentation of Self." *Representations* 19 (summer 1987): 1–34.

Scarf, Maggie. *Unfinished Business: Pressure Points in the Lives of Women.* New York: Ballantine, 1981.

Schreiner, Olive. *The Story of an African Farm.* Harmondsworth: Penguin, 1982. First published 1883.

Sexton, Anne. "Now." *Love Poems.* Boston: Houghton Mifflin, 1967.

Shakespeare, William. *The Riverside Shakespeare.* Ed. G. Blakemore Evans et al. Boston: Houghton Mifflin, 1974.

Shapiro, Jane. "Life without Martin." *Fine Lines: The Best of "MS." Fiction.* Ed. Ruth Sullivan. New York: Charles Scribner's Sons, 1982. First published 1979.

Shelley, Mary. *Frankenstein.* Ed. James Kinsley and M. K. Joseph. Oxford: Oxford University Press, 1969. First published 1818.

Shulman, Alix Kates. *Memoirs of an Ex-Prom Queen.* New York: Bantam Books, 1973. First published 1972.

Sinclair, May. *The Three Sisters.* Garden City: N.Y.: Dial Press, 1985. First published 1914.

Sitwell, Edith. "Mademoiselle Richarde." *The Collected Poems.* London: Duckworth, 1930.

Smith, Betty. *A Tree Grows in Brooklyn.* New York: Harper and Row, 1968. First published 1943.

Sontag, Susan. "The Double Standard of Aging." *Saturday Review* (23 September 1972): 29–38.

Spackman, W. M. *A Presence with Secrets.* New York: E. P. Dutton, 1982. First published 1980.

Spacks, Patricia Meyer. *The Female Imagination.* New York: Knopf, 1975.

Spenser, Edmund. *Spenser's Faerie Queene.* Ed. J.C. Smith. Oxford: Clarendon, 1909.

Spires, Elizabeth. "Mascara." *The New Yorker* (19 November 1984): 58.

Stafford, Jean. "Between the Porch and the Altar." *The Collected Stories of Jean Stafford.* New York: Farrar, Straus and Giroux, 1969.

Stephens, James. *Mary, Mary.* New York: Boni and Liveright, 1912.

Styron, William. *Sophie's Choice.* New York: Bantam, 1980. First published 1979.

Swift, Jonathan. *The Poems of Jonathan Swift.* Ed. Harold Williams. Oxford: Clarendon, 1958.

Symons, Arthur. "White Heliotrope." *Poems by Arthur Symons.* London: Heinemann, 1902.

Tada Chimako. "Mirror." Trans. Kenneth Rexroth and Ikuko Atsumi. See Barnstone, Aliki.

Talbot, Laura. *The Gentlewomen.* New York: Penguin, 1986. First published 1952.
Tallent, Elizabeth. *In Constant Flight: Stories by Elizabeth Tallent.* New York: Henry Holt, 1987. First published 1983.
Tarkington, Booth. *Alice Adams.* New York: Grosset and Dunlap, 1921.
Tate, Allen. "Last Days of Alice." *Collected Poems 1919–1976.* New York: Farrar Straus Giroux. 1977.
Taylor, Elizabeth. *Blaming.* London: Chatto and Windus, 1976.
——. *A Game of Hide-and-Seek.* New York: Alfred A. Knopf, 1951.
——. *Hester Lilly.* London: Chatto and Windus, 1969.
——. *Palladian.* London: Chatto and Windus, 1969.
——. *The Sleeping Beauty.* New York: Dial, 1982. First published 1953.
——. *The Soul of Kindness.* New York: Dial, 1982. First published 1964.
Tennyson, Alfred. "The Lady of Shalott." *Tennyson's Poetry.* Ed. Robert W. Hill, Jr. New York: W. W. Norton, 1971. First published 1852.
Thomas, Dylan. "We Have the Fairy Tales by Heart." *The Poems of Dylan Thomas.* Ed. Daniel Jones. New York: New Directions, 1971.
Timmerman, John H. "Plath's 'Mirror.'" *The Explicator* 45 (1987): 63–64.
Tolstoy, Leo. *Anna Karenina.* Trans. David Magarshack. New York: New American Library, 1961. First published 1877.
Trollope, Anthony. *Rachel Ray.* New York: Dover, 1980. First published 1863.
Twain, Mark. *Eve's Diary.* London: Harper and Brothers, 1906.
Updike, John. "Mirror." *The Carpentered Hen and Other Tame Creatures.* New York: Alfred A. Knopf, 1982. First published in *The New Yorker,* 1957.
Walker, Alice. *The Color Purple.* New York: Washington Square Press, 1983. First published 1982.
——. "Coming Apart." *You Can't Keep a Good Woman Down: Stories by Alice Walker.* New York: Harcourt Brace Jovanovich, 1980.
Wedekind, Frank. "Pandora's Box." *The Lulu Plays and Other Sex Tragedies.* Trans. Stephen Spender. London: John Calder, 1977.
Weil, Simone. *Waiting for God.* Trans. Emma Craufurd. Intro. Leslie A. Fiedler. New York: Harper and Row, 1973. First published in English 1951.
West, Jessamyn. *Cress Delahanty.* New York: Harcourt Brace, 1948. First published 1945.
West, Rebecca. *The Return of the Soldier.* New York: Dial, 1980. First published 1918.
——. *The Thinking Reed.* Harmondsworth: Penguin, 1985. First published 1936.

Wharton, Edith. *The Custom of the Country*. New York: Charles Scribner's Sons, 1913.

——. *The House of Mirth*. New York: New American Library, 1964. First published 1905.

——. *The Mother's Recompense*. New York: D. Appleton, 1925.

——. *The Reef*. New York: Charles Scribner's Sons, 1965. First published 1912.

——. *Summer*. New York: Charles Scribner's Sons, n.d. First published 1917.

White, Antonia. *Beyond the Glass*. New York: Dial, 1981. First published 1954.

——. *Frost in May*. New York: Dial, 1980. First published 1933.

——. *The Lost Traveller*. New York: Dial, 1980. First published 1950.

——. *The Sugar House*. New York: Dial, 1981. First published 1952.

Wolf, Leonard. "Fifty-Fifty." *Love Stories*. Ed. Martin Levin. New York: Popular Library, 1975. First published 1963.

Wolitzer, Hilma. *Hearts*. New York: Pocket Books, 1982. First published 1980.

——. *In the Palomar Arms*. New York: Farrar/Straus/Giroux, 1983.

Woolf, Virginia. *The Diary*. Ed. Anne Olivier Bell. New York: Harcourt Brace Jovanovich, 1981.

——. *Mrs. Dalloway*. New York: Harcourt Brace and World, 1953. First published 1925.

——. "The New Dress." *A Haunted House and Other Short Stories*. London: Hogarth Press, 1943. First published 1927.

——. "A Sketch of the Past." *Moments of Being: Unpublished Autobiographical Writings*. Ed. Jeanne Schulkind. Sussex: University Press, 1976.

Yeats, W. B. *The Collected Poems*. New York: Macmillan, 1956. First published 1928.

——. "Discoveries." *Essays and Introductions*. New York: Macmillan, 1961. First published 1907.

Young, Emily Hilda. *The Curate's Wife*. New York: Penguin, 1985. First published 1934.

Zola, Emile. *Nana*. Trans. George Holden. Harmondsworth: Penguin, 1982. First published 1880.

Index

Library of Congress Cataloging-in-Publication Data

La Belle, Jenijoy
Herself beheld : the literature of the looking glass / Jenijoy La Belle
p. cm.
Bibliography: p.
Includes Index.
ISBN 0 8014-2202-7 (alk. paper)
1. Mirrors in literature. 2. Literature—Women authors—History and criticism. 3. Women in literature. 4. Self in literature. 5. Identity (Psychology) in literature. I. Title.
PN56.M537L3 1988
809'.93353—dc19 88-47734

P9-CKO-823

IMAGES OF PERSEPHONE

Edited by Elizabeth T. Hayes

FEMINIST READINGS IN WESTERN LITERATURE

UNIVERSITY PRESS OF FLORIDA

Gainesville/Tallahassee/Tampa/Boca Raton
Pensacola/Orlando/Miami/Jacksonville

Quotations from *Two-Headed Poems* (1978) and *Procedures for Underground* (1970), by Margaret Atwood, are reprinted in this volume by permission of the rights holder, Oxford University Press Canada. Quotations from the *Quetzalcoatl* typescript (1923), by D. H. Lawrence, are reproduced by permission of the Houghton Library, Harvard University. An earlier version of chapter 5 was published previously in *Hawthorne's Literature for Children*, by Laura Laffrado (Athens: University of Georgia Press, 1992), and chapter 8 was published in *Beckett and Myth: An Archetypal Approach* (Syracuse, N.Y.: Syracuse University Press, 1988); both are reprinted by permission of the publishers.

Half-title figure: *Supplicant Persephone* (1945), by Ivan Mestrovic, courtesy of the Syracuse University Art Collection.

Library of Congress Cataloging-in-
Publication Data
Images of Persephone: feminist readings in Western literature / edited by Elizabeth T. Hayes.
p. cm.
Includes bibliographical references (p.) and
index.
ISBN 0-8130-1262-7 (acid-free paper)
1. Persephone (Greek deity) in literature.
2. Women in literature. 3. Feminism and
literature. I. Hayes, Elizabeth T.
PN57.P45I46 1994
809'.93352042—dc20 93-37016

The University Press of Florida is the scholarly publishing agency for the State University System of Florida, comprised of Florida A & M University, Florida Atlantic University, Florida International University, Florida State University, University of Central Florida, University of Florida, University of North Florida, University of South Florida, and University of West Florida.

University Press of Florida
15 Northwest 15th Street
Gainesville, FL 32611

for

Helen Simpson Tracy

November 18, 1918–January 16, 1993

mother, teacher

CONTENTS

PREFACE

For more than twenty-five centuries, the Persephone myth has occupied a central position in both the collective unconscious and the collective consciousness of people in Western cultures. Because it is an intensely moving story, embodying so clearly the archetypal "loving and terrible" mother and the archetypal rite of passage for women in patriarchal cultures, the myth is extraordinarily resonant for a great many people, particularly but by no means exclusively for women. Images, or reenactments, of the Persephone myth have appeared in the works of writers both male and female in every Western culture, in every period over the centuries. Not only are these images compelling in themselves, as artistic texts, but they brilliantly illuminate the personal and cultural codes of the writers from whom they spring.

For the past ten years, I have been collecting and teaching in my college classes both images of the myth and related criticism. Though literary images and critical texts on Persephone number in the hundreds, *Images of Persephone* is to my knowledge the first collection of critical essays by different scholars on the Persephone myth in literature. It is also the first collection of feminist / cultural criticism of such images. The individual essays explore female protagonists' relationships and experiences within patriarchal cultures that range from Homer's classical-period ancient Greece to Cixous's postmodern France, from Chaucer's medieval England to Atwood's contemporary Canada, from Quinault's France under Louis XIV to Morrison's 1940s America. Because half the writers discussed are "canonical" male authors, the feminist readings provide fresh insights on gender issues animated in these writers' uses of the Persephone myth. Moreover, four of the six texts by women included in this book have never before been examined as Persephone images. The range of writers—across cultures, periods, genders, and genres—and the range of their treatment of the myth demonstrate the vitality and centrality of the Persephone archetype over twenty-six hundred years of Western thought.

The Persephone myth stands at the crossroads of feminist/cultural, archetypal, and literary/textual study. *Images of Persephone* models an intertextual "criticism at the crossroads" by highlighting the generative convergence of these approaches. It will serve, I hope, as a valuable resource for both scholars and students. The individual essays utilize a range of critical approaches to the myth and its literary images. Some essays are more heavily weighted toward theory, some toward literary criticism, literary history, or biography, and some toward archetypal criticism. All contain feminist or cultural criticism to one degree or another, and all give close intertextual readings of the myth as it resonates in a varied and intriguing group of literary texts.

Putting together a book, even a small book, is a lot like work. I am grateful to the many people who have encouraged and supported me during this book's long gestation period. The Le Moyne Faculty Research and Development Committee's two course-load reduction grants were lifesavers. I am grateful both to the committee and to my department chairs, Dr. Harold Ridley, S.J., and Dr. David Lloyd, who made it possible for me not only to obtain the grants but to use them profitably. For their critical comments on the manuscript, I particularly thank my colleagues Susan Thornton, Julie Olin-Ammentorp, and Amanda Brown and reader Kathleen Ashley. Special thanks to Janet Wolf, who has listened, advised, critiqued, and encouraged from the beginning.

I am grateful to all the contributors to *Images of Persephone* for their unfailing good cheer and patience throughout this process, as well as for their willingness to revise yet again when I asked. We are all grateful to Dr. Walda Metcalf at the University Press of Florida for her faith in this project and her invaluable support. Grateful thanks also go to Sharyn Knight, whose expert technical assistance literally made the manuscript possible.

My husband, David, my son, Timothy, my daughter, Annabeth, my mother-in-law, Ann Hayes, and my father, Charles S. Tracy, have all been staunch in their support, picking up the slack when I was forced to cut back to "part-time" family member. Finally, thanks to my late mother, Helen S. Tracy, teacher extraordinaire, who always said, "You ought to write a book!"

Elizabeth T. Hayes

CHAPTER I

THE PERSEPHONE MYTH IN WESTERN LITERATURE

> Though Persephone resisted fiercely, Hades seized her and carried her off, screaming in shrill voice. Her cries echoed from the mountain peaks to the depths of the sea, and her noble mother Demeter heard her. A sharp pain seized the mother's heart, and she shot out like a bird over land and sea, searching for her daughter. For nine days she searched without rest, stopping neither to eat nor drink. . . .

The myth of Persephone is one of the most emotionally charged narratives ever told. The story of the Maiden's abduction and rape by the god of the dead and the Mother's bitter grief resonates with powerful feeling that touches even casual listeners or readers. Children find in the myth their worst nightmare come to life—forced separation from the mother at the hands of a sexually predatory, deadly stranger—but also find reassurance in the mother's absolute refusal to reconcile herself to the loss of her child and in the reunion of mother and daughter at the end. Adults find in the myth a representation of their own experiences of traumatic loss and grief. Women find their life experiences and emotional responses valorized rather than dismissed because these experiences and responses are presented in the myth as a serious, viable topic for narrative. Both men and women alike find in the myth a compelling evocation of the archetypal Mother, the most numinous of all the archetypal figures. It is easy to understand why this myth should be so frequently recounted and so universally known.

The resonance of the myth extends beyond the personal, however, to the cultural, the locus of so much postmodern inquiry. Tracing the myth from its shadowy beginnings in prerecorded history to its earliest written narratives and beyond, we discover that the mythic text is a fascinating inscription of religious and cultural history. Indeed, it is a palimpsest that reveals vital changes in the relationship between human beings and the natural world, as well as major shifts in the economy of social power over the millennia.

The earliest written narratives of the Persephone myth, from which all subsequent Western versions derive, animate a watershed cultural event: the displacing of the matriarchal worship of the Great Goddess in ancient Greece by the patriarchal worship of the Olympian gods. These classical-era versions of the myth vivify the social codes of patriarchy, brought to Greece by Zeus-worshipping conquerors, codes that have been passed down to Western societies as part of their Hellenic heritage and that form the basis for Western cultural phallocentrism. The strong response of Western women to the Persephone myth arises in large part from its mythic presentation of their story—the story of women's struggle to gain subjectivity and voice in societies dominated by men.

In addition to the religious and social upheavals inscribed in the mythic text, we can also see a corresponding epistemological change. The rationalist, Apollonian epistemology underlying patriarchal cultures embodies a deep distrust of all things nonrational—the natural, the physical, the ecstatic, the intuitive, the emotional—all of which are equated with the feminine. Rationalism, a hierarchical system, relegates the nonrational to the position of inferior "other" —indeed, drives it from consciousness altogether into the unconscious. The result is "psychic monotheism," psychologist James Hillman's term (1972, 265) for the perceived superiority of the ego to the unconscious in Western thought. In compartmentalizing the psyche and creating a hierarchy of the compartments, we hinder the attainment of psychic wholeness, for the psyche comprises both the rational and the nonrational, whether we choose to value the nonrational or not.

In the Persephone myth, we find a paradigm for the restoration of the nonrational to a position of equality in the consciousness. Persephone embodies the life force in the psychic depths, the potential generativity and creativity of the unconscious. When Demeter and Persephone are united and equal, before the abduction, in the upper, "conscious" world presided over by Apollo, the sun god, they function generatively; indeed, Persephone the daughter embodies Demeter the mother's generativeness. When the two are separated and Persephone is forcibly removed to the underworld (significantly, by a male agent operating under Apollonian patriarchal law), creativity and generativeness cease altogether on earth. Only when Persephone is restored to her place in the upper world and reunited with Demeter does generativeness return. (Although Demeter and Persephone cannot be neatly split and compartmentalized, with one representing the unconscious and the other rationality, Demeter does function in the sunlit [i.e. Apollonian] upper world, creating life, while Persephone and her alter ego, Hecate, are associated with the dark underworld realm of shadow and soul.) The path to psychic wholeness lies in a conjunction of the opposites that every psyche contains at least in potential form—consciousness and unconsciousness, rationality and nonrationality, light and dark, life and death. In the Goddess, as she appears in tripartate form in the myth of Persephone and in pre-Olympian mythology, we find such a conjunction—not a blending or merging, but a contiguous positioning of opposite but equal qualities.

A rejection of the tyranny of rationalism and an insistence on a polycentric structuring of consciousness—the return of the repressed feminine—is precisely what the mythic narrative models so strikingly. "Persephone's beauty" is, fittingly, the metaphor used to refer to the unconscious in another myth, the tale of Psyche. Only when Psyche journeys to the underworld and obtains some of Persephone's beauty can she become herself—psyche, soul—and, uniting with Eros, become immortal. Only when Demeter is united with Persephone does she create new life. The origin of creativity and psychic transformation is the unconscious, not the ego, but those who journey to the underworld must return to the conscious world with Persephone's beauty for the transformation to be complete. In valorizing psychic conjunction, the myth points the way for women—and men—to free themselves from an exaggerated reliance on the rational and to draw more fully upon the wealth of the unconscious, so thoroughly denigrated in patriarchal epistemology.

That the Persephone myth reveals something quintessential about the female psyche was early recognized by Carl Jung. He concluded that "the feminine influence [in the myth] so far outweighed the masculine that the latter had practically no significance" (1969, 158); as a result, men might not be psychologically capable of understanding the story fully. Jung's conclusion has been illuminated, interestingly, by recent studies of moral, social, and psychological development in women that give empirical weight to what the Persephone myth has long shown: women's value system or moral code is typically different from men's in significant ways. Most women value relationships over individuation, interdependence over autonomy. Women frequently operate through a context-dependent morality based on responsibility toward others rather than through a context-independent morality based upon a set of rights and laws. By measuring women against male-derived models of morality or psychology or epistemology, we fail to perceive women's differences, or we label those differences inferiorities. In either case, we cast the discussion in terms that prevent us from fully understanding or appreciating the female psyche.

The myth, however, valorizes female ways of being and acting. It explores Demeter and Persephone's response to patriarchal law and power, highlighting the women's valuing of relationship, of unity, of conjunction over the separation and hierarchical ordering valued by the male gods. Demeter does not recognize what Hades and Zeus consider to be their patriarchal right to dispose of Persephone as they choose. Her greatest anger is directed toward Zeus, who treats his daughter—their daughter—as a sexual object to be used to consolidate his power. Relationships are nothing to Zeus the patriarch but everything to Demeter the matriarch. Demeter does everything in her power to rescue her child from death, including laying waste the natural world, a pitiless action that, in this female-centered context, is presented as perfectly justified. It is also politically shrewd, though Demeter appears to be acting solely from grief and anger, from emotion, rather than from any calculated, rational plan. Nothing is as important to her as reestablishing her relationship with her daughter. Similarly, nothing is as important to Persephone as reuniting with her mother. Indeed, Persephone learns painfully the importance of relationships: she discovers that narcissism, as signified by her going off alone to pick the narcissus, leads to death for women (Gilligan 1982, 23), and that only her bond with someone who values connectedness saves her from permanent death. Thus, the myth contextualizes and simultaneously valorizes female standards of moral and social conduct, even implying the superiority of relationship-based morality to rule-based morality.

Clearly, the Persephone myth is an extraordinarily resonant and rewarding text. This wonderful richness is the reason that Western artists of all eras have reenacted it again and again in sculpture, painting, music, opera, drama, poetry, and prose. Writers in particular have been drawn to the Persephone story, from the time of Homer through the present, repeatedly recreating the archetypal events and figures. In these archetypal recreations, or "images" of the archetype, recurrent narrative patterns, imagery, and symbols appear, as one would expect; an archetype is, after all, nothing more than a primordial or paradigmatic form with "ubiquitous reverberations" (Hillman 1972, 217) that manifest themselves through recurrent patterns. In the strictest Jungian sense, the Persephone myth is itself one of many literary images of the archetype. In critical practice, however, the classical-period myth, as the original written narrative of the Persephone story, is the prototype for all later Persephone narratives; the patterns, imagery, and symbols in this first narrative establish the basis for later recurrences. The myth, therefore, has to a certain extent been conflated with the archetypes it animates, especially because the myth is one of our primary sources of conscious knowledge of these archetypes.

In literary works modeled even loosely on the Persephone myth, the recurrent narrative patterns and symbols become the ground for negotiation of meaning among writer, text, and reader. Any image of Persephone in literature, whether consciously or unconsciously created, immediately locates itself in, and plays itself out against, a rich tradition of Persephone images. This book examines some dozen of these images of the Persephone myth in Western literature, giving close intertextual readings of the recurring archetypal patterns and figures resonating in the works of selected writers.

The range of writers discussed in the essays demonstrates the centrality of Persephone in Western cultural consciousness, for the myth has clearly served the purposes of a great many very different writers over the centuries. From Chaucer to Alice Walker, each writer expands the focal image in significant ways, revealing his or her own epistemology, relationship to cultural gender codes, and textual goals and concerns. In this way, *Images of Persephone* is an exploration of a dozen varied literary responses to a central, profoundly evocative, female-centered text.

To hear, read, or study the Persephone myth is to participate indirectly in the oldest form of worship known to the human race. Our early ancestors worshipped the earth, mother of life, represented anthropomorphically as the Earth Mother, from whose womb all living creatures issue. The Mother, or the Goddess—"She of a Thousand Names" (Walker 1985, 68)—was worshipped in one avatar or another all over the ancient world from at least 25,000 B.C.E. on, according to the evidence of clay sculptures, stone carvings, and rock paintings. Because women, the bearers of life, were close to the Mother and shared her cyclical rhythms, they became her sibyls and priestesses. Particularly after women learned to cultivate grain and communities depending on agriculture developed, proper worship of the Mother was considered a necessity of life. Both the growing of grain and the fertility rituals that supported it were the responsibility of women for many millennia.

The earliest ritualistic worship of the Mother involved imitative magic: something fruitful was placed in the earth—an ear of corn, a pregnant sow, or, in Central and South America, a female sacrificial victim—in the belief that this act would cause the earth to be fruitful. In ancient Greece, during the Thesmophoria, a three-day sowing ceremonial at which only women were permitted, suckling pigs, animals sacred to the Mother, were thrown into clefts in the earth, while the fleshly remains of the previous year's pigs were brought up and mixed with the seeds about to be planted. The most influential of all the Goddess rites in Greece were the Eleusinian Mysteries, well established by the mid-fifteenth century B.C.E. (Mylonas 1961, 14).

The worship of the Mother at Eleusis began with a purification rite and the sacrifice of pigs. Next came a symbolic death or descent of the Goddess to the underworld and her return to life (the "going down" and the "coming up"), a revelation of sacred objects ("mysteries"), including in all probability an ear of corn or a sheaf of grain, and a symbolic birth (the "fair birth"). Initiates became one with the Mother and felt spiritually transformed by their new understanding of the mysteries of life and death revealed to them during the rite. The Persephone myth is a metaphoric interpretation of these ancient fertility ceremonies. As Jane Harrison says, the "myth . . . arose from the ritual, not the ritual from the myth" (1903, 124). Beneath the overlay of the actions of the anthropomorphic Olympian deities appears the outline of the older, pre-Olympian worship of the Goddess, a figure whose evolution is instructive.

The many local earth goddesses worshipped all over the ancient world were, quite simply, embodiments of the earth, mother, or Earth Mother, who first appeared as a universal, abstract deity in Greek mythology in the form of Gaia, also called Ga, Ge, or Da. Gaia and her local avatars were chthonic or earth deities, goddesses of not only the soil and everything growing from it, but also the underworld, the depths of the earth beneath the soil. Gaia created life literally from her body and took it back into her body at its death. Thus, the Earth Mother was viewed as the conjunction of opposites; she simultaneously incorporated both life and death, creation and destruction, growth and decay, the upper world and the underworld. She was the loving and simultaneously terrible (or devouring) mother. The Goddess was not distant or removed, but was intimately involved in the life of every animate being on earth. Nature was thus experienced as an active, immediate, maternal presence.

From roughly 2000–1000 B.C.E., first the Ionians, then the Achaeans, and finally the Dorians invaded Greece from the north. These conquerors brought with them their sky god, Zeus, and the Olympian pantheon, deities whose actions and roles reflected the patriarchal social system of their worshipers. The resulting clash of matrifocal and patrifocal cultures is vividly portrayed in the mythology of the classical period, where the usurpation and diminishment of the power of the Goddess is everywhere illustrated. Many of the mythic narratives enact the physical conquering and rape of local embodiments of the Goddess by male gods, especially Zeus, a tireless and wily subjugator of both immortal and mortal females. In other myths, powerful local Goddess figures were killed off, like Medusa, slain by Perseus, or Metis, swallowed by Zeus when she was pregnant with Athena, goddess of wisdom, a clever depiction of Zeus's literal incorporation of the wisdom of the Goddess. Other local Goddesses, like Hera and Aphrodite, were reduced to subordinate wives of male gods, or they were split into two or three goddesses, each with greatly reduced power. Despite the overall success of the conquering Olympians, however, worship of the Mother never entirely died out, as the longevity of the Eleusinian Mysteries and the importance of the Virgin Mary illustrate.

Of the many local Goddesses subsumed and diminished by Olympian worship, Demeter retained the greatest likeness to Gaia. Pictured in classical mythology as Gaia's granddaughter, Demeter was a chthonic deity reduced from Earth Mother to Grain Mother.

Only the fruits of the earth, particularly agricultural produce, were the province of the Demeter of classical times. Her name, however, indicates her pre-Olympian position or function; according to Kerényi, *Da*, like *Ga* or *Ge*, means "earth," and *meter* means "mother" (1967, 28). Moreover, Demeter's preclassical underworldly chthonic powers can be discerned from the fact that the dead were still called "Demeter's people" in old Athens (Harrison 1903, 267).

Demeter was brought to Greece from Crete, one of the last strongholds of Goddess worship. In pre-Homeric Cretan mythology, recounted in classical times by Hesiod in his *Theogony*, Demeter made love to the Cretan hunter Iasios (or Iasion), or in some sources Zagreus, in the furrow of a thrice-plowed field—that is, one ready for sowing (Baring and Cashford 1991, 366). Both Iasios and Zagreus were associated with or were names for the god of the underworld. From this union came the child Ploutos or Pluto, meaning "wealth" or "riches," another name for the underworld god (Kerényi 1967, 30).

These associations specify the pre-Olympian Demeter as a fully chthonic goddess, mistress of both the soil and the underworld. So do the snakes that we frequently see twined about Demeter in pictoral representations, for snakes were chthonic creatures sacred to the Goddess; in Crete, snakes were held to be avatars of the Goddess herself. Similarly, the pig, particularly the sow, was considered a chthonic animal, the "uterine animal of the earth" (Kerényi 1969, 119), and therefore sacred to Demeter and vitally important to her rites. (Indeed, so important was the sacrifice of pigs to the worship of the Mother at Eleusis that the pig became the emblem of Eleusis, stamped on all Eleusinian coins [Gadon 1989, 153].)

In classical mythology, Demeter was the mother both of the fruits of the earth and of Persephone, the Maiden, whose father was Zeus. Persephone as Demeter's daughter was a revision made by classical storytellers for narrative purposes, according to mythographer Jane Harrison (1903, 274). For centuries before the classical period, the maiden was viewed literally as part of the mother, the mother's younger self. This view underlies the many portrayals of Demeter as a victim, like Persephone, of rape by Olympian gods. Pausanius, for example, recounts a tale of Demeter's rape by Poseidon (a name meaning "husband of Da") (Kerényi 1967, 31). In an effort to escape the pursuing god, Demeter turned herself into a mare, but Poseidon turned himself into a stallion and raped her, begetting a daughter and a steed, Arion (Dexter 1990, 127). Another variant has Demeter raped by Zeus when she appealed to him to save her from Poseidon; to escape Zeus, she changed herself into a cow, but Zeus changed himself into a bull (Pratt 1985, 114). Orphic mythology contains a similar rape occurring when both Demeter and Zeus had changed to snakes, from which union a four-eyed, horned Persephone was born (West 1983, 73). That Demeter and Persephone experienced identical patriarchal violence blurs the distinction between the two.

Persephone's story is of course an encoding of patriarchal violence. Her abduction and rape by Hades in the myth supposedly explain her presence as an underworld deity, but because the underworld was her original realm in preclassical mythology, we are really seeing a local Goddess's power usurped by an Olympian god and then partially restored to her, but as derivative of the male god's power. In classical mythology, Persephone was at once the Kore (Maiden), the Queen of the Dead, and the resurrected goddess whose return from death brought new life to the earth. Thus she was fully chthonic, associated with the fertility of the soil as well as with the underworld depths. Her distinctive characteristic was her cyclical movement between the upper and the lower chthonic worlds.

The name *Persephone* is probably a translation into Greek of the name of an ancient, pre-Greek local Earth Mother. "Pherrephata," one of the many variants of Persephone's name, means "killer of suckling pigs" (Gimbutas 1982, 214), associating Persephone with the pigs sacrificed during the Eleusinian Mysteries and other ceremonials dedicated to the Mother. In most worship of the Mother, however, Persephone was not named but was simply called the Kore. (Appropriately for the daughter of the Grain Mother, the word *koura* is also the feminine form of the word for grain sprout.) She was also called "ineffable maiden," the only maiden goddess given that epithet (Kerényi 1967, 26). The Kore is the secret, hidden, ineffable heart of the Mysteries dedicated to the Goddess. She either didn't need to be named or was too sacred to be spoken of among the uninitiated.

That the maiden was an underworld goddess in preclassical times shows through the overlay of the classical myth in a number of ways. Although the classical story has Persephone living in the upper world with her mother for two-thirds of the year, no mythological traveler to the underworld ever found the Queen of the Dead absent. Except for the moment of her reunion with Demeter in the spring, she was always pictured in the underworld, indicating that the underworld was her rightful realm. Black sheep were sacrificed to Persephone, also indicating her underworldly connections (Dexter 1990, 128). Finally, in an Orphic myth, Zeus, not Hades, seduced his daughter Persephone, as he had seduced Demeter, by taking the form of a serpent (or dragon), sacred to the chthonic Mother. From the union of Persephone and the serpent Zeus came the child Zagreus, the early avatar of Dionysus, himself another form of "Zeus Chthonios," Chthonic Zeus (Guthrie 1966, 219), as Hades was sometimes called.

Persephone and Demeter were worshipped at Eleusis and elsewhere as a contiguous Maiden / Mother, the Korai. That two goddesses shared one cult underlines their essential unity. Demeter encompassed the upper-worldly, open, fertile or vegetative aspect of Gaia, whereas Persephone embodied the secret or mysterious underground germinative aspect. What distinguished Persephone from other notable maiden goddesses like Artemis and Athena, Persephone's most conspicuous companions on the Nysian Plain shortly before her abduction by Hades, was her relationship to her mother (Downing 1981, 134). Athena was essentially motherless, having sprung from the forehead of Zeus, and Artemis's relationship to her mother Leto was unimportant, but Persephone's eventual reunion with her mother Demeter was the focus, the point, of the classical myth. Clearly, Demeter lost the part of herself associated with fertility, creativity, when her Kore was stolen away. The two goddesses are really one: the Maiden is the younger form of the Mother, holding within her the potential to become the Mother. When the two are shown together in ancient sculpture and painting, it is frequently difficult or impossible to tell Persephone and Demeter apart (Frazer 1922, 462), a tangible indication that there was no need for the artists to differentiate the Mother from the Maiden.

Often, however, a third goddess is also depicted, indistinguishable from both Persephone and Demeter. Maiden and mother are but two phases of women's life cycle. The third, the postmenopausal "wise crone" stage, is embodied in the goddess Hecate. An ancient form of the Goddess, Hecate was herself originally called "the triple goddess" because, in the days before the advent of the Olympian gods, she herself ruled over the three realms of earth, sky, and underworld. Hecate may be a derivative of Heqit (Hekat), one of the oldest of the Egyptian Goddess figures, whose name comes from *heq*, "intelligence." (*Heq* was also the word for "tribal ruler" in the Egyptian predynastic period [Walker 1985, 50], indicating the kind of power associated with Heqit.)

As a sky goddess, the Greek Hecate embodied the dark phase of the moon's cycle, when the moon is hidden or "underground." Like all moon goddesses, Hecate was a guardian of maidens and also presided over childbirth. As an earth goddess, she was a nurturing mother figure, a double for Demeter, as the classical myth makes clear: Hecate heard the kidnapped Persephone's cries, accompanied (or led) Demeter to Helios to find out where Persephone had been taken, and followed Demeter in greeting the returned Persephone. In other versions of the story, either Demeter or Hecate journeyed to the underworld to seek Persephone (Kerényi 1969, 110), showing the interchangeability of the two as mother goddess. As a chthonic deity, Hecate was Persephone's constant companion in the underworld, almost her alter ego.

Hecate's many associations with things dark, hidden, or underworldly linked her with spirits, ghosts, and magic (Kerényi 1969, 112–13). Coming from the dark underworld or her dark cave (a chthonic space), she was usually depicted holding a torch, another connection to Persephone and Demeter, who were also depicted holding torches. Hecate, however, was given the epithet *phosphoros*, "bringer of light," implying that her torch was figurative; the light of understanding was her gift. For instance, Hecate, bearing "a light," led Demeter to enlightenment from Helios. Hecate lit the pathway to the underworld for the newly dead, helping them cross over from the upper world to the world of shadows, just as she helped newborns cross over from the dark world into the light at birth. The enlightenment she brought was a knowledge of mortality, an understanding that death is always a part of life.

In rituals honoring chthonic deities, three was a sacred number (Harrison 1903, 288). Thus the Thesmophoria, the sowing ceremonial dedicated to the Mother and the Kore, was celebrated for three days and the Eleusinian Mysteries for three times three; the dead were invoked three times; mourning lasted three days; and where three roads met, "the threefold Hecate of the underworld was worshipped" (Harrison 1903, 288). Triple deities developed quite naturally in worship where triplicity was sacred.

Hecate's pre-Olympian triplicity readily merged with the chthonic Maiden / Mother duality. In the ancient triple-goddess Hecate who was depicted as one female body with three faces, we can just as easily see the maiden, mother, and crone as the goddess who ruled the sky, earth, and underworld. Typically, the functions of the individual goddesses in a triple-goddess group were not rigidly separated, with the result that a blending and merging of the three occurred. This was certainly the case with the triple goddess Hecate-Demeter-Persephone. The three were so closely linked, with so many overlapping functions and roles, that significant merging occurred, as is evident from the goddesses' depiction on sacred monuments and in other ancient works of art as three indistinguishable female forms holding one torch (Kerényi 1969, 110). United, this triple goddess, like many of the other goddess trios, embodied all the elements of the original overarching paradigm, the Goddess.

Literary images of the Persephone myth commonly include only one or two of the three figures of the triple goddess Persephone-Demeter-Hecate, depending on which facets of the larger paradigm are central to the text. References in this book to "the Persephone myth" or to "Persephone images" are not intended to erase Demeter or Hecate (though Hecate in particular appears less frequently than the other two goddesses in *Images of Persephone*). These references are merely shorthand for the accurate but cumbersome phrases "the Persephone-Demeter-Hecate myth" or "images of Persephone-Demeter-Hecate." Mention of any one of the goddesses implies the other two, for they are indeed a triple goddess.

Not until the classical period was the myth of Persephone transcribed. The earliest existing written version, probably dating from 650 B.C.E., is the fragmentary Homeric "Hymn to Demeter" (see Appendix A), several translations of which I consulted in composing this chapter's epigraph. (The term *Homeric* does not necessarily ascribe authorship to the poet Homer, who may or may not have actually existed, but rather indicates that the poem is in the Homeric style.) Oral versions of the myth, dating from the establishment of the Eleusinian Mysteries in Greece in the fifteenth century B.C.E. (the Mycenaean period), were no doubt in circulation for at least eight centuries before the composition of the hymn. Although there can never be a definitive text of the Persephone myth or any other myth, the Homeric hymn, as the earliest surviving written version, and the most beautiful, has had a profound influence as a disseminator of the myth.

Other early recorded versions of the Persephone story, also from the classical period, are found in Hesiod's *Theogony* and in hymns and poems ascribed to Orpheus and his followers (Richardson 1974, 5, 77). The Hesiodic version is very similar to the Homeric, but the Orphic differs in important respects (see Appendix B). The Orphic story, for example, provides an explanation of the sacrifice of pigs so important to the Eleusinian Mysteries, but it makes no mention of the terrible famine caused by Demeter that is so prominent in other versions. The Orphic Persephone story was widely disseminated and quite influential. Euripides, for instance, used the Orphic version as a source for his *Helena,* which the American poet H. D. used in turn as a source for her "Helen in Egypt."

The most influential Roman version of the myth comes from Ovid's *Metamorphoses* (see Appendix C), written in the first century C.E. (Ovid also retold the myth in his *Fasti.*) A recent study by British scholar Stephen Hinds, *The Metamorphosis of Persephone,* presents strong evidence that Ovid was familiar with the Homeric "Hymn to Demeter" and used it as a source for his version of the Persephone story (1987, 56). Proserpina's abduction by Pluto, Ceres's frantic search and extensive grieving, and the eventual partial restoration of maiden to mother are the bases of the Ovidian myth, but Ovid has added other elements, such as Cyane dissolving into a pool of water and Arethusa discovering and reporting Proserpina's whereabouts to Ceres. The popularity and availability over the past two millennia of Ovid's *Metamorphoses* has done much to spread the Persephone myth to Western cultures. Many writers, among them Chaucer, Quinault, and Hawthorne, have taken their Proserpinas from Ovid and his successors.

Any story that has survived through so many centuries must be powerful indeed, tapping into the deep wellspring of human emotion and experience that Jung calls the collective unconscious. Yet, as critic Froma Zeitlin reminds us, a myth's "survival is also predicated on its capacity to reproduce the cultural values required for its survival" (1986, 124). One of the patriarchal values reproduced in the Persephone myth is male dominance of women, the subtext of the classical mythic story. The forced separation of daughter and mother through male agency, the violation of the maiden, and the mother's anger are all played out against a backdrop of the politics of patriarchy.

The effects upon women of phallocentric social codes particularly concern feminist and cultural scholars, who find in the Persephone myth one of the most illuminating illustrations in Western culture of these effects. Indeed, the Persephone myth embodies the archetypal experience of women in a patriarchy, for we see in the myth powerful male figures who sexually and emotionally abuse women at will without so much as recognizing their actions as abusive. Even a vitally important goddess like Demeter is pushed out into the margins of political power; although she marshals her forces most effectively to win a well-deserved partial victory over the patriarchs, she is plainly operating from the margins, using the last resort of the weak, nonviolent noncooperation. The subtext of the myth presents rape and abduction of women as perfectly acceptable to the male power structure, with men treating women as objects while reserving subjectivity for themselves alone. The myth also underscores the abridgement of women's control over their own destinies because of their vulnerability to physical and sexual abuse.

Like all texts, literary images of the Persephone myth are located within identifiable cultural constructs that can be examined for their political implications. In addition, a Persephone image reflects where its author situates himself or herself within—or outside of—those cultural constructs, particularly on issues of gender politics. Examination of a Persephone image can also focus on why a writer has chosen to engage this myth in his or her work, pointing discussion toward literary history, psychology, biography, or genre studies. Finally, any critique of an archetypal image in literature will perforce concern itself with textual matters, for how a writer employs Persephone images to create a work uniquely his or her own is always of prime concern to scholars. The intertextual play between myth and image everywhere informs and shapes the reading of the image, as the essays in this book vividly demonstrate.

Marta Powell Harley, for example, in "Chaucer's Use of the Proserpina Myth in 'The Knight's Tale' and 'The Merchant's Tale,'" shows Chaucer wrestling with the issue of female vulnerability to male exploitation through his use of the Proserpina myth. Whereas the male characters in the Knight's and Merchant's tales attempt to mitigate the appearance of violence through renaming or ritualizing, the female characters make covert, ineffectual efforts to maintain or regain control. Harley finds a clear antifeminist strain in these tales despite the sympathy Chaucer creates for the Proserpina figures, an antifeminism she attributes to the romance and fabliau genres Chaucer employs, as well as to the androcentric bias of Chaucer's culture.

Janet S. Wolf's "'Like an Old Tale Still': Paulina, 'Triple-Hecate,' and the Persephone Myth in *The Winter's Tale*" disputes the traditional view that the dominant deity in Shakespeare's play is Apollo, arguing that it is instead the triple goddess Persephone-Demeter-Hecate. Examining the image of each goddess in the play, Wolf finds an overlapping of the roles of Perdita, Hermione, and Paulina that parallels the overlapping of the functions of the goddess trio in the myth. Focusing particularly upon the often-neglected Hecate, Wolf makes a compelling case for reading Paulina not only as a Hecate figure but also as a classical Greek "wise crone" Hecate rather than as the sinister, witch-like Hecate of later tradition.

In "Sexual and Artistic Politics under Louis XIV: The Persephone Myth in Quinault and Lully's *Proserpine*," Michèle Vialet and Buford Norman argue that the opera *Proserpine* was designed to valorize male sexual and political domination of women's destinies in Louis XIV's France. They examine the social and historical circumstances under which *Proserpine* was proposed for Louis XIV's pleasure, as well as the opera's shrewd harmonizing of the aesthetic, the political, and the sexual. In spite of the profound sympathy the text and music create for the goddesses, Vialet and Norman conclude that Quinault and Lully's rewriting of the Persephone myth intentionally moves its audience to embrace the patriarchal, monarchical beliefs and actions of the writers' patron, Louis XIV.

Laura Laffrado's "The Persephone Myth in Hawthorne's *Tanglewood Tales*" examines Hawthorne's revision of the Persephone story in "The Pomegranate-Seeds" to express themes of loss. In creating this children's story, Hawthorne looks to the archetypes of classical mythology for scenarios and themes to help him express the sea change in his vision caused by personal losses and by the contracting of his creative energy as his literary career moved past its prime. By recovering this neglected children's story, Laffrado contributes to studies of children's literature as well as to examinations of Hawthorne's writing and career.

Melissa McFarland Pennell also recovers a valuable neglected text. In "Through the Golden Gate: Madness and the Persephone Myth in Gertrude Atherton's 'The Foghorn,'" Pennell argues that Atherton uses the Persephone myth in "The Foghorn" as a way of exploring the difficulties facing nineteenth-century female artists in their efforts to achieve an independent, authoritative voice despite social ostracism and condemnation. The Persephone figure in Atherton's story functions as an ideal double, allowing Atherton to present the "self-division" of a narrator torn between her desires to rebel against and to embrace values from the patriarchal society that surrounds and eventually entraps her.

Virginia Hyde finds the mythology of Persephone pervasive in D. H. Lawrence's poetry, short stories, novels, nonfiction, and painting, all of which she surveys in "'Lost' Girls: D. H. Lawrence's Versions of Persephone." Lawrence's preference for Pluto, Hyde argues, causes him to advance a theory of depersonalization by which the modern Persephone should lose her individual features of personality and social identity, instead following archetypal patterns that increase her sexual subordination even while seemingly enlarging her responsiveness to cosmic surroundings. In addition, Hyde demonstrates a link between Lawrence's negative version of Persephone and the "Fatal Women" of Pre-Raphaelite and "Decadent" writers and painters, and she provides a pioneering account of the Persephone myth in *Quetzalcoatl,* the long-unpublished first version of *The Plumed Serpent.*

Mary A. Doll's "Ghosts of Themselves: The Demeter Women in Beckett" investigates Beckett's drama of feminine consciousness acted out particularly in *Not I, Footfalls,* and *Rockaby.* Doll argues that the mythos of Beckett's women is a Demetrian one of grief and loss, resulting in a journey inward to find the lost part of the self. Beckett's Demeter women have no control over their grief or their searching, because they are governed by forces beyond the control of consciousness. The pattern of losing, grieving, and searching that the women follow echoes the archetypal pattern found in the Persephone myth, which, Doll concludes, Beckett uses masterfully to enhance his pervasive theme of souls bound by absent presences.

Martine Motard-Noar's "From Persephone to Demeter: A Feminist Experience in Cixous's Fiction" is the first detailed study of Persephone in Hélène Cixous's works. Motard-Noar examines the Persephone myth as a starting point in the development of Cixous's controversial and widely influential feminist position. Focusing particularly on the novel *Illa,* Motard-Noar demonstrates Cixous's radical disruption of and recreation of the myth, through which Cixous elucidates women's struggle against patriarchal ideology and patriarchal language constructs.

In "Dark Persephone and Margaret Atwood's *Procedures for Underground,*" Eileen Gregory discusses Persephone in Atwood's poetry as an imaginal activity rather than as a static figure, a vision of postmodern desubstantiation rather than of romantic reconciliation of oppositions. Unlike many critics, Gregory does not find a bias toward the natural, female, or primitive in Atwood's vision, nor does she discover signs of an ameliorating vision in Atwood's poetry. Instead, Gregory argues that the "underground" voice of Persephone-Hecate dominating Atwood's poetry reiterates transformations gone awry, irreconcilable oppositions, and the imminent danger of the world we live in.

Finally, my own essay, "'Like seeing you buried': Persephone in *The Bluest Eye, Their Eyes Were Watching God,* and *The Color Purple,*" examines the Persephone archetype in three African-American novels, two of which have not previously been recognized as Persephone images. Toni Morrison, Zora Neale Hurston, and Alice Walker have rewritten the myth to illuminate their visions of the African-American woman's struggle for identity and empowerment in a Eurocentric, phallocentric culture. The problematical mother-daughter bond created in these texts and their deconstruction of the natural cycle motif of the myth signify some of the difficulties African-American Persephones must overcome if they are to achieve a strong, positive identity and voice.

The literary texts examined in *Images of Persephone* are only a small sampling from a very large body of Persephone images in literature. Noting the importance of the Goddess to female identity and women's literature, Susan Gubar views the deity in the Persephone myth as perhaps "the central mythic figure for women" (1979, 302). Although Gubar is certainly correct, she underestimates the centrality of Persephone. Many images of the Persephone archetype have been created by men, for whom the myth is also highly resonant and important. Indeed, the Persephone story contains archetypes central to both men and women in Western cultures, as this book illustrates.

Images of the Persephone myth in literature stand at the convergence of three vital areas of study: the feminist or cultural, the archetypal, and the literary or textual. The intertextual readings presented in the following essays explore all three areas in quite different ways. Perhaps just as importantly, the essays showcase a varied group of powerful, marvelously evocative literary texts.

BIBLIOGRAPHY

Baring, Anne, and Jules Cashford. *The Myth of the Goddess: Evolution of an Image.* London: Viking, 1991.

Berger, Pamela. *The Goddess Obscured.* Boston: Bantam, 1985.

Bullfinch, Thomas. *Bullfinch's Mythology*. San Francisco: Harper and Row, 1970.

Cles-Reden, Sibylle von. *The Realm of the Great Goddess*. London: Thames and Hudson, 1961.

Dexter, Miriam Robbins. *Whence the Goddesses*. New York: Pergamon, 1990.

Donovan, Josephine. "Introduction." In *After the Fall: Persephone in Glasgow, Wharton, and Cather*. University Park: Pennsylvania State Univ. Press, 1989.

Downing, Christine. *The Goddess: Mythological Images of the Feminine*. New York: Crossroad, 1981.

———. "The Mother Goddess among the Greeks." In *The Book of the Goddess*, edited by Carl Olson. New York: Crossroad, 1983.

Eliade, Mircea. *The Myth of the Eternal Return*. Translated by Willard R. Trask. Princeton: Princeton Univ. Press, 1954.

Frazer, J. G. *The Golden Bough*. New York: Macmillan, 1922.

Frye, Northrop. *Anatomy of Criticism*. Princeton: Princeton Univ. Press, 1957.

Gadon, Elinor W. *The Once and Future Goddess*. San Francisco: Harper and Row, 1989.

Gilligan, Carol. *In a Different Voice: Psychological Theory and Women's Development*. Cambridge: Harvard Univ. Press, 1982.

Gimbutas, Marija. *The Goddesses and Gods of Old Europe*. Berkeley: Univ. of California Press, 1982.

Gregory, Eileen. "Euripides and H. D.: In Virgo." Unpublished essay, 1988.

Gubar, Susan. "Mother, Maiden and the Marriage of Death: Women Writers and an Ancient Myth." *Women's Studies* 6 (1979): 301–15.

Guthrie, W. K. C. *Orpheus and Greek Religion*. New York: Norton, 1966.

Hall, Nor. *The Moon and the Virgin: Reflections on the Archetypal Feminine*. New York: Harper and Row, 1980.

Hamilton, Edith. *Mythology*. New York: Little, Brown, 1942.

Harrison, Jane. *Prolegomena to the Study of Greek Religion*. Cambridge: Cambridge Univ. Press, 1903.

Hillman, James. *The Myth of Analysis: Three Essays in Archetypal Psychology*. Evanston, Ill.: Northwestern Univ. Press, 1972.

———. *Re-Visioning Psychology*. New York: Harper and Row, 1975.

———. *The Dream and the Underworld*. New York: Harper and Row, 1979.

Hinds, Stephen. *The Metamorphosis of Persephone: Ovid and the Self-Conscious Muse*. Cambridge: Cambridge Univ. Press, 1987.

Hirsch, Marianne. *The Mother/Daughter Plot: Narrative, Psychoanalysis, Feminism*. Bloomington: Indiana Univ. Press, 1989.

Homer. "Hymn to Demeter." In *The Homeric Hymns*, translated by Charles Boer, 91–135. Chicago: Swallow, 1970.

———. "Hymn to Demeter." Translated by Daryl Hine. In *Spinsters and Spiders*, by Marta Weigle. 104–11. Albuquerque: Univ. of New Mexico Press, 1982.

Jung, C. G. *Aspects of the Feminine.* Translated by R. F. C. Hull. Princeton: Princeton Univ. Press, 1982.

———. "The Psychological Aspects of the Kore." In C. G. Jung and C. Kerényi, *Essays on a Science of Mythology: The Myth of the Divine Child and the Mysteries of Eleusis.* Princeton: Princeton Univ. Press, 1969.

Kerényi, C. *Eleusis: Archetypal Image of Mother and Daughter.* Translated by Ralph Manheim. Princeton: Princeton Univ. Press, 1967.

———. "Kore." In C. G. Jung and C. Kerényi, *Essays on a Science of Mythology: The Myth of the Divine Child and the Mysteries of Eleusis.* Princeton: Princeton Univ. Press, 1969.

Larrington, Carolyne. *The Feminist Companion to Mythology.* London: Pandora, 1992.

Lichtman, Susan A. *Life Stages of Woman's Heroic Journey: A Study of the Origins of the Great Goddess Archetype.* Lewiston, N.Y.: Edwin Mellen, 1991.

Matthews, Caitlin. *Sophia, Goddess of Wisdom: The Divine Feminine from Black Goddess to World-Soul.* London: Mandala, 1991.

McLean, Adam. *The Triple Goddess: An Exploration of the Archetypal Feminine.* Grand Rapids, Mich.: Phanes, 1989.

Mylonas, George E. *Eleusis and the Eleusinian Mysteries.* Princeton: Princeton Univ. Press, 1961.

Nilsson, Martin P. *The Mycenaean Origin of Greek Mythology.* Berkeley: Univ. of California Press, 1932.

Olson, Carl. *The Book of the Goddess.* New York: Crossroad, 1983.

Ovid. "The Rape of Proserpine." In *Metamorphoses* V, translated by A. D. Melville, 109–16. New York: Oxford Univ. Press, 1986.

Powers, Meredith A. *The Heroine in Western Literature: The Archetype and Her Reemergence in Modern Prose.* Jefferson, N.C.: McFarland, 1991.

Pratt, Annis. *Archetypal Patterns in Women's Fiction.* Bloomington: Indiana Univ. Press, 1981.

———. "Spinning among Fields: Jung, Frye, Lévi-Strauss and Feminist Archetypal Theory." In *Feminist Archetypal Theory,* edited by Estella Lauter and Carol S. Rupprecht. Knoxville: Univ. of Tennessee Press, 1985.

Richardson, N. J. *The Homeric Hymn to Demeter.* Oxford: Clarendon, 1974.

Sjoo, Monica, and Barbara Mor. *The Great Cosmic Mother.* San Francisco: Harper and Row, 1987.

Walker, Barbara G. *The Crone: Woman of Age, Wisdom, and Power.* San Francisco: Harper and Row, 1985.

West, M. L. *The Orphic Poems.* Oxford: Clarendon, 1983.

Wilshire, Donna. "The Uses of Myth, Image, and the Female Body in Re-Visioning Knowledge." In *Gender/Body/Knowledge: Feminist Reconstructions of Being and Knowing,* edited by Alison M. Jaggar and Susan R. Bordo. New Brunswick, N.J.: Rutgers Univ. Press, 1989.

Zeitlin, Froma. "Configurations of Rape in Greek Myth." In *Rape,* edited by Sylvana Tomaselli and Roy Porter. Oxford: Basil Blackwell, 1986.

Marta Powell Harley

CHAPTER 2

CHAUCER'S USE OF THE PROSERPINA MYTH IN "THE KNIGHT'S TALE" AND "THE MERCHANT'S TALE"

Chaucer's earliest allusions to Proserpina are explicit and uncomplicated. In *The House of Fame*, the impressionable narrator marvels at the pillars celebrating the writers of antiquity, focusing at last on the statue of Claudian, "That bar up al the fame of helle, / Of Pluto, and of Proserpyne, / That quene ys of the derke pyne."[1] The "Proserpyne"/"pyne" rhyme recurs in *Troilus and Criseyde*, in an allusion not found in Boccaccio's *Filostrato;* protesting Pandarus's suggestion that he find another love, Troilus vows to love Criseyde until death parts them: ". . . down with Proserpyne, / Whan I am ded, I wol go wone in pyne, / And ther I wol eternaly compleyne / My wo, and how that twynned be we tweyne" (544, bk. 4, lines 473–76). Chaucer's use of the Proserpina myth in *The Canterbury Tales* is altogether different. Whereas in *The House of Fame* and *Troilus*, the allusions are of marginal importance, serving simply to identify Claudian and hyperbolize Troilus's attachment to Criseyde, in the Knight's and Merchant's tales, Proserpina's complex identity ranges from an unnamed aspect of Diana to a combative Queen of Fairyland. Although Chaucer's use of the myth in the two tales deepens his characterizations of Emelye and May, exposing their vulnerability to male exploitation, Chaucer's climactic vision of female assertiveness and solidarity nevertheless fails to transcend antifeminist clichés.

In "The Knight's Tale," Theseus designates Emelye as the grand prize in an elaborately planned tournament between the Theban cousins, Palamon and Arcite. While Palamon and Arcite pray to Venus and Mars in temples constructed in the east and west walls of Theseus's "noble theatre" (line 1885), Emelye visits Diana's alabaster and coral temple in the north wall. In describing the temple's "lifly" statue of Diana (line 2087), Chaucer's Knight combines the three aspects of the triple goddess Diana-Lucina-Proserpina: on earth, she is Diana, the chaste goddess of the woodlands and the hunt; above, she is Lucina, the bright moon goddess protecting women from the pains of childbirth; and below, she is Proserpina, queen of the underworld.[2] Interweaving the three aspects of the goddess in his description of Diana's statue, the Knight includes nothing extraneous to the conception of this triple goddess:

> This goddesse on an hert ful hye seet,
> With smale houndes al aboute hir feet,
> And undernethe hir feet she hadde a moone—
> Wexynge it was and sholde wanye soone.
> In gaude grene hir statue clothed was,
> With bowe in honde and arwes in a cas.
> Hir eyen caste she ful lowe adoun
> Ther Pluto hath his derke regioun.
> A womman travaillynge was hire biforn;
> But for hir child so longe was unborn,
> Ful pitously Lucyna gan she calle
> And seyde, "Helpe, for thou mayst best of alle!"
> (lines 2075–86)

In her subsequent prayer, Emelye reveals her own awareness of the triple nature of the goddess:

> O chaste goddesse of the wodes grene,
> To whom bothe hevene and erthe and see is sene,
> Queene of the regne of Pluto derk and lowe,
> Goddesse of maydens, . . .
> . . . .
>
> I am, thow woost, yet of thy compaignye,
> A mayde, and love huntynge and venerye,

> And for to walken in the wodes wilde,
> And noght to ben a wyf and be with childe.
> Noght wol I knowe compaignye of man.
> Now help me, lady, sith ye may and kan,
> For tho thre formes that thou hast in thee.
> (lines 2297–2300, 2307–13)

Emelye's similarity to Diana, the chaste hunter, is clear enough. Before hearing Emelye proclaim her commitment to chastity and her love of hunting, we see her roaming in the garden "ful of braunches grene" (line 1067) and participating, with Theseus and Ypolita, in the hart hunt, which may aptly serve here as a metaphor for "the hunt of virtue" (de Weever 1986, 168). Emelye is "clothed al in grene" (line 1686), a detail anticipating the observation that Diana's statue "in gaude grene . . . clothed was" (line 2079). Later at Diana's temple, Emelye appropriately wears an evergreen garland, a "coroune of a grene ook cerial" (line 2290).

Emelye's similarity to Lucina is likewise clearly suggested. In the description of Diana's statue, the moon beneath Diana's feet represents Lucina, and the woman in childbirth summons her by name. Elsewhere in his works, "Chaucer uses five names for the planetary goddess: *Cinthia, Diana, Latona, Lucina, Proserpina*" (de Weever 1986, 155), but the epithets for the moon goddess invariably recall her brightness: in *Troilus and Criseyde*, she is "Lucina the sheene" (bk. 4, line 1591), "Cinthia the sheene" (bk. 4, line 1608), and "brighte Latona the clere" (bk. 5, line 655); in "The Franklin's Tale," the epithet is again "Lucina the sheene" (line 1045). There seems little likelihood that coincidence explains the repeated references to Emelye's brightness: she is Ypolita's "yonge suster sheene" (line 972), "fresshe Emelye the shene" (line 1068), and "Emelye the brighte" (line 1737) with "brighte heer" (line 2289).

If Emelye is, like Diana, a chaste hunter and, like Lucina, remarkably bright, how then is Emelye like Proserpina? We have seen that the explicit references to Proserpina in *The House of Fame* and *Troilus and Criseyde* associate the underworld queen with pain; the allusions in "The Knight's Tale" stress the darkness of the realm, as does Aurelius's allusion in "The Franklin's Tale" to Lucina's "owene dirke regioun / Under the ground, ther Pluto dwelleth inne" (lines 1074–75). To suggest Emelye's likeness to Proserpina, however, Chaucer does not draw on Proserpina's dark, dire existence as Pluto's queen. Rather, he turns to classical accounts of Proserpina's innocent play prior to her ravishment. Although Ovid reports in his *Metamorphoses* that Proserpina "ludit et aut violas aut candida lilia carpit" [was playing, and gathering violets or white lilies] (1925, 264–65, line 392), he specifies in his *Fasti* that she "crocos tenues liliaque alba legit" [plucked dainty crocuses and white lilies] (1931, 220–21, bk. 4, line 442). Similarly, in Claudian's *De Raptu Proserpinae*, Proserpina "aestuat ante alias avido fervore legendi" [beyond her fellows . . . burned with a fierce desire to gather flowers] (1922, v. 2, 328–29, bk. 2, line 137).[3] In "The Merchant's Tale," Chaucer actually cites Claudian's depiction of Proserpina gathering flowers: it was "queene Proserpyna" whom Pluto "ravysshed out of [Ethna] / Whil that she gadered floures in the mede— / In Claudyan ye may the stories rede, / How in his grisely carte he hire fette" (lines 2229–32). Chaucer echoes both Ovid's and Claudian's accounts in his depiction of Emelye, who "hadde hir pleyynge" within a garden (line 1061): "She walketh up and doun, and as hire liste / She gadereth floures, party white and rede" (lines 1052–53). Chaucer's contemporary, John Gower, also employs the formula that Proserpina "wente hir out to plei, / To gadre floures in a pleine" (1980, 245, bk. 5, lines 1286–87). That Emelye picks the flowers "to make a subtil gerland for hire hede" (line 1054) may be a further imitation of Claudian, whose Proserpina, having filled her baskets, "sociat flores seseque ignara coronat,/augurium fatale tori" [twines a wreath of flowers and crowns herself therewith, little seeing in this a foreshadowing of the marriage fate holds in store for her] (1922, 328–29, bk. 2, lines 140–41).

Chaucer returns to the triple goddess in "The Merchant's Tale," a fabliau written several years after the Knight's courtly, philosophical romance. Given Chaucer's knowledge and admiration of Ovid, Ovid's two versions of the myth in his *Metamorphoses* and *Fasti* may have influenced Chaucer's dual treatment in "The Knight's Tale" and "The Merchant's Tale" (see Hoffman 1966 and Fyler 1979). In a recent study, Stephen Hinds terms Ovid's two accounts a "remarkable exercise in cross-reference" and essentially agrees with the traditional classification of the *Metamorphoses* version as "epic" and the *Fasti* version as "elegiac," although Hinds sees "grey areas" and does not consider the distinction "completely clear-cut" (1987, 102, 113–14). Chaucer's perception of the generic differences in the Ovidian tales may have encouraged his inscription of the myth in courtly romance and fabliau. Oddly enough, granting the clear differences between epic and romance and between elegy and fabliau, the broad distinctions in style and characterization that Hinds draws between the "epic" *Metamorphoses* account and the "elegiac" *Fasti* version apply rather well to the Knight's romance and the Merchant's fabliau, and Chaucer's two tales may well reflect the Ovidian tales' contrasting emphases on conquest and lust.

Whereas Diana is the most obvious aspect of the triple goddess in "The Knight's Tale," the dominant aspect in the Merchant's fabliau is Proserpina, whose unsolicited support of May symbolically links the two. The women characters in "The Merchant's Tale" recapitulate those in "The Knight's Tale"; Proserpina replaces Diana, and May becomes the counterpart of Emelye. As Emelye's counterpart, May is the earthly embodiment of not just one aspect of the triple goddess Diana-Lucina-Proserpina, but all three. May's likeness to Diana, the chaste hunter, is tenuous, though the springtime world that May's name suggests may recall the goddess of the grove. The equation of May and Diana depends upon the mediating portrait of Emelye, Diana's devotee. In "The Knight's Tale," Emelye is closely associated with the freshness of a May morning:

> Till it fil ones, in a morwe of May,
> That Emelye, that fairer was to sene
> Than is the lylie upon his stalke grene,
> And fressher than the May with floures newe—
> . . . .
> Er it were day, as was hir wone to do,
> She was arisen and al redy dight,
> . . . .
> To doon honour to May . . . .
> Yclothed was she fressh . . . .
> (lines 1034–37, 1040–41, 1047–48)

The character May in "The Merchant's Tale" is the fulfillment of this natural imagery: May, the Merchant claims, "was lyk the brighte morwe of May" (line 1748), and the epithet "fresshe May" (line 1782) occurs more than a dozen times in the tale.

May's similarity to Lucina also recalls Emelye. Lucina's characteristic brightness, captured in the phrases "Lucina the sheene" and "fresshe Emelye the shene," resurfaces in the Merchant's summary description of May, "This fresshe May, that is so bright and sheene" (line 2328). Further, May's apparent invocation of

Mary is cast in language that suggests the moon goddess, who protects women in childbirth: "Help, for hir love that is of hevene queene! / I telle yow wel, a womman in my plit / May han to fruyt so greet an appetit / That she may dyen but she of it have" (lines 2334–37).[4]

The equation of May and "queene Proserpyna" (line 2229), who is introduced with "Pluto, that is kyng of Fayerye" (line 2227), is anticipated in an early description of May, "that sit with so benyngne a chiere, / Hire to biholde it semed fayerye" (lines 1742–43), but January's similarity to Pluto leaves little doubt that May and Proserpina are linked. Claudian's *De raptu Proserpinae* opens with an account of Pluto's impatience to be married: Pluto "tumidas exarsit in iras / proelia moturus superis, quod solus egeret / conubiis sterilesque diu consumeret annos / impatiens nescire torum nullasque mariti / inlecebras nec dulce patris cognoscere nomen" [blazed forth in swelling anger, threatening war upon the gods, because he alone was unwed and had long wasted the years in childless state, brooking no longer to lack the joys of wedlock and a husband's happiness nor ever to know the dear name of father] (1922, 294–97, bk. 1, lines 32–36).[5] January's desire for a wife is likewise the impetus for action. More specifically, Pluto's "swelling anger" becomes January's "greet corage," and Pluto's appeals to Jove are translated into January's "Preyinge oure Lord":

> And whan that he was passed sixty yeer,
> Were it for hoolynesse or for dotage
> I kan nat seye, but swich a greet corage
> Hadde this knyght to been a wedded man
> That day and nyght he dooth al that he kan
> T'espien where he myghte wedded be,
> Preyinge oure Lord to graunten him that he
> Mighte ones knowe of thilke blisful lyf
> That is bitwixe an housbonde and his wyf,
> And for to lyve under that hooly boond
> With which that first God man and womman bond.
> (lines 1248–62)

January, too, expects offspring; his interest in children precludes his taking an "old" wife, a "womman thritty yeer of age" (line 1421):

> Wherfore I sey yow pleynly, in a clause,
> I wol noon oold wyf han right for cause.

> For if so were I hadde swich myschaunce
> That I in hire ne koude han no plesaunce,
> Thanne sholde I lede my lyf in avoutrye
> And go streight to the devel whan I dye.
> Ne children sholde I none upon hire geten;
> Yet were me levere houndes had me eten
>   Than that myn heritage sholde falle
>   In straunge hand, and this I telle yow alle.
> (lines 1431–40)

Thus, as Proserpina is sacrificed to Pluto's needs, "fresh May" becomes the victim of January's compelling desire to marry.

Chaucer's use of the goddess Diana-Lucina-Proserpina in characterizing Emelye and May in the tales of the Knight and Merchant is especially suggestive, considering the constellation of interrelated and often contradictory ideas swirling about the mythical trio. The three manifestations of the triple goddess comprehend a range of meanings, from idealized desire to inescapable reality. The triple goddess simultaneously represents female assertiveness (in the form of virginal, independent, and vengeful Diana) and vulnerability (to abduction, rape, and the pains of childbirth). The vulnerability is somewhat mitigated by Lucina, who has the power to succor women in labor, and by Ceres, Proserpina's outraged mother, whose tireless quest and protest won the compromise enabling Proserpina to spend a portion of each year on earth. In his characters Emelye and May, Chaucer explores this conflict between vulnerability and resistance, giving particular attention to the conflict between marriage and female sovereignty.

Froma Zeitlin asserts that the Pluto-Proserpina myth, "beyond any others, provides the cultural archetype of marriage as forcible abduction" (1986, 141). Chaucer indeed uses the myth in both the Knight's romance and the Merchant's fabliau to underscore the marital exploitation of Emelye and May. "The Knight's Tale" blunts the Diana myth, wherein Diana avenges Actaeon's voyeurism, and reenacts the Proserpina myth, wherein Pluto's voyeurism leads to Proserpina's abduction and rape. Theseus (having "conquered al the regne of Femenye" [line 866] and subdued in marriage "queene Ypolita" [line 868]) obviates Emelye's commitment to chastity, offering her virginity to the victorious voyeur. As Hope Phyllis Weissman observes, Theseus, rather than "deferring to the decision of the heroine herself, . . . transform[s] personal male emotional activity into a public ritual of the male state" (1975, 100). In effect, Theseus diverts lust into a civilly sanctioned tournament and reconstructs rape as marriage. Especially effective in enlarging our sympathy for Emelye is her appeal to Diana; while at the outset Emelye is "virtually without psychological dimension," she emerges "as a psychological being" when she pleads with Diana to preserve her "freedom and identity," "her body . . . [and] her independent will" (Weissman 1975, 99, 100, 101). Joseph Harrison even finds in the description of the temple of Diana "a note of sympathy" absent from the descriptions of the temples of Venus and Mars (1984, 111).

That May's marriage to January represents a violation of May's desires is beyond doubt. May is seen, seized, and imprisoned. We are told that May "was broght abedde as stille as stoon" (line 1818), and we are forced to see January's sexual ministrations through May's eyes: "But God woot what that May thoughte in hir herte, / Whan she hym saugh up sittynge in his sherte, / In his nyght-cappe, and with his nekke lene" (lines 1851–53). A later episode of "lovemaking" likewise demonstrates the marital rape:

> Adoun by olde Januarie she lay,
> That sleep til that the coughe hath hym awaked.
> Anon he preyde hire strepen hire al naked;
> He wolde of hire, he seyde, han som plesaunce;
> He seyde hir clothes dide hym encombraunce,
> And she obeyeth, *be hire lief or looth.*
> But lest that precious folk be with me wrooth,
> How that he wroghte, I dar nat to yow telle,
> *Or wheither hire thoughte it paradys or helle.*
> (lines 1956–64, my italics)

The alternatives, of course, are rhetorical. January's rape, described in a metaphor unmistakably echoing Pluto's rape of Proserpina, is "helle." To say that May "is no willing partner to her husband's inept playfulness" is to euphemize rape (Donovan 1959, 53). Karl P. Wentersdorf identifies as a primary function of the Pluto-Proserpina episode its "indicat[ion] that the marriage entered into by January is reprehensible because, in view of its very circumstances, it takes on some of the aspects of rape," but Wentersdorf's view "that May, unlike Proserpine, is apparently not under any coercion to marry January" ignores the compelling element of political and social power that January (like Theseus) represents (1965, 525–26).

Chaucer's more direct use of the third aspect of the triple goddess in "The Merchant's Tale" suggests some sensitivity to the other half of the Pluto-Proserpina myth—the "drastic feminine protest in the person of the mother" (Zeitlin 1986, 141). In "The Knight's Tale," there is no "drastic feminine protest." Although Chaucer stirs sympathy for Emelye, Emelye's request for freedom, for divine preservation of her independence, is not granted. Just as Diana fails Proserpina in Claudian's *De Raptu* (1922, 332–35, bk. 2, lines 205–39), Diana fails Emelye in "The Knight's Tale," and Emelye has no Ceres, no mother-protector—only a sister, Ypolita, whose subjugation is just another reminder of the inevitable loss of independence.

The Pluto and Proserpina (Chaucer's "Proserpyna" or "Proserpyne") interlude in the Merchant's narrative is a comic dramatization of the "drastic feminine protest" that Ceres represents in the myth. Pluto and Proserpyna enter the Merchant's narrative at a crucial point. May and January are roaming about January's walled garden; following May's "fynger signes" (line 2209), which simply reinforce the instructions May has already given Damyan in a letter, Damyan climbs up into the pear tree to await May's arrival. Chaucer shifts the scene to the garden's "ferther syde" (line 2226), where Pluto and Proserpyna, the King and Queen of Fairyland, dispute the relative virtues of men and women. Pluto announces his intention to grant January his eyesight "whan that his wyf wold doon hym vileynye" (line 2261), and Proserpyna counters with a pledge to grant May a "suffisant answere, / And alle wommen after, for hir sake" (lines 2266–67).

The irony in this domesticated, Celticized version of the Pluto and Proserpina myth is that Proserpyna, whose rape has just been recounted (lines 2229–32), succeeds in thwarting Pluto's criticism and the effect of his initiative. Just as the Wife of Bath in her prologue had accused clerks of writing tendentious, unflattering accounts of women ("no womman of no clerk is preysed" [line 706]), Proserpyna attacks Pluto's "auctoritees" (line 2276)—in particular, "this Jew, this Salomon" (line 2277)—and concludes, "I sette right noght, of al the vileynye / That ye of wommen write, a boterflye!" (lines 2303–4). Ultimately, Pluto exclaims, "I yeve it up!" (line 2312), although he feels compelled to keep his oath: "My word shal stonde, I warne yow certeyn. / I am a kyng; it sit me noght to lye" (lines 2314–15). In effect, Chaucer fortifies his Proserpyna with the combative and protective impulses of Diana, Lucina, and Ceres.

Because Chaucer earlier parodies the Knight's romance in the

Miller's fabliau, offering Alisoun as a counterpart to Emelye, the Merchant's fabliau stands as a second effort. Although Chaucer minimizes the loss of freedom that Alisoun's marriage brings (the stereotypical old, jealous husband, John, "heeld hire narwe in cage" [line 3224]), Chaucer graphically exposes May's marital experiences and repeatedly speculates on May's accompanying thoughts. The physical details of May's loathsome marriage and the development of the underlying myth of the triple goddess create a counterpart to the virginal Emelye more complex than the randy Alisoun. Building on the predicament of Emelye in "The Knight's Tale," "The Merchant's Tale" affirms that marriage may violate female integrity and that male "auctoritees" (such as Theseus and Solomon) may be charged with bias.

Nevertheless, the sympathy for the unfortunate women cannot surmount the antifeminist constraints of genre and culture. In the romance, Emelye is ultimately Palamon's reward, and in the fabliau, May's rebellion and Proserpyna's intercession are reducible to the classic activities of the fabliau wife, adultery and lying. Like the allusions in "The Merchant's Tale" to Rebecca, Judith, Abigail, and Esther—"four of the most venerable of Old Testament Deliverance paradigms" (Otten 1971, 284)—the underlying myths of the triple goddess Diana-Lucina-Proserpina simultaneously enlarge and undermine the characters May and Proserpyna. In the Merchant's fabliau, deliverance from forced marriage means no more than the freedom to pursue adultery (the pear-tree episode pejoratively suggesting the respite on earth that Jove allows Proserpina), and righteous protest is simply the provision of a prophylactic lie. Conceding that the "emergent viewpoint of the [Pluto-Proserpyna] episode is masculine," Robert M. Jordan speculates that "this is what makes the rendering of Proserpina's victory so amusing—even for a female reader, I should think" (1963, 298). Feminist readers, male and female, may be more disappointed than amused. Although Chaucer's use of the triple goddess Diana-Lucina-Proserpina in his characterizations of Emelye and May clearly raises the issues of female vulnerability and protest, the potential for creating a positive image of female resistance and solidarity dissipates in the disagreeable atmosphere of the fabliau. Ultimately, Chaucer's "queene Proserpyna," the Ceres-surrogate of "The Merchant's Tale," wields only the dubious power that the misogynists readily grant women, the power of verbal deceit.

NOTES

I presented a version of this essay at the Seventh Biennial Conference on Medieval-Renaissance Studies, New College, March 1990.

1. Chaucer, *The House of Fame,* in *The Riverside Chaucer,* 366, lines 1510–12. Subsequent line numbers in parentheses refer to this edition.

2. For other remarks on this *triformis dea,* see Chaucer 1987, 838, n. 2313; Donovan 1979, 60–61; Duffey 1983, 128; and de Weever 1986, 166.

3. On Chaucer's familiarity with Claudian, see Pratt 1947.

4. For interpretations of May's pregnancy, see Chaucer 1987, 889, n. 2330–37 and n. 2414.

5. These lines are likewise quoted in Donovan 1957, 50.

BIBLIOGRAPHY

Chaucer, Geoffrey. *The Riverside Chaucer.* 3d ed. Edited by Larry D. Benson. Boston: Houghton Mifflin, 1987.

Claudian. *De Raptu Proserpinae.* In *Claudian,* edited and translated by Maurice Platnauer, 2:293–377. 2 vols. New York: Putnam's Sons, 1922.

de Weever, Jacqueline. "Chaucer's Moon: *Cinthia, Diana, Latona, Lucina, Proserpina.*" *Names* 34 (1986): 154–74.

Donovan, Mortimer J. "Chaucer's January and May: Counterparts in Claudian." In *Chaucerian Problems and Perspectives: Essays Presented to Paul E. Beichner,* edited by Edward Vasta and Zacharias P. Thundy, 59–69. Notre Dame, Ind.: Univ. of Notre Dame Press, 1979.

———. "The Image of Pluto and Proserpine in *The Merchant's Tale.*" *PQ* 36 (1957): 49–60.

Duffey, Terry. "The Proserpinean Metamyth: Claudian's *De Raptu Proserpinae* and Alan of Lille's *Anticlaudianus.*" *Florilegium* 5 (1983): 105–39.

Fyler, John M. *Chaucer and Ovid.* New Haven: Yale Univ. Press, 1979.

Gower, John. *Confessio Amantis.* Edited by Russell A. Peck. Medieval Academy Reprints for Teaching 9. Toronto: Univ. of Toronto Press, 1980.

Harrison, Joseph. "'Tears for Passing Things': The Temple of Diana in the Knight's Tale." *PQ* 63 (1984): 108–16.

Hinds, Stephen. *The Metamorphosis of Persephone: Ovid and the Self-Conscious Muse.* Cambridge: Cambridge Univ. Press, 1987.

Hoffman, Richard. *Ovid and the Canterbury Tales.* Philadelphia: Univ. of Pennsylvania Press, 1966.

Jordan, Robert M. "The Non-Dramatic Disunity of the 'Merchant's Tale.'" *PMLA* 78 (1963): 293–99.

Otten, Charlotte F. "Proserpine: *Libratrix Suae Gentis.*" *Chaucer Review* 5 (1971): 277–87.

Ovid. *Fasti.* Edited and translated by Sir James George Frazer. London: Heinemann, 1931.

———. *Metamorphoses.* 2d ed. Edited and translated by Frank Justus Miller. 2 vols. London: Heinemann, 1925.
Pratt, Robert A. "Chaucer's Claudian." *Speculum* 22 (1947): 419–29.
Weissman, Hope Phyllis. "Antifeminism and Chaucer's Characterizations of Women." In *Geoffrey Chaucer,* edited by George D. Economou, 93–110. New York: McGraw-Hill, 1975.
Wentersdorf, Karl P. "Theme and Structure in the Merchant's Tale: The Function of the Pluto Episode." *PMLA* 80 (1965): 522–27.
Zeitlin, Froma. "Configurations of Rape in Greek Myth." In *Rape,* edited by Sylvana Tomaselli and Roy Porter, 122–51. Oxford: Basil Blackwell, 1986.

Janet S. Wolf

CHAPTER 3

"LIKE AN OLD TALE STILL": PAULINA, "TRIPLE HECATE," AND THE PERSEPHONE MYTH IN *THE WINTER'S TALE*

It has long been recognized that the Persephone myth plays a role in *The Winter's Tale*, Shakespeare's story of redemption, rebirth, and reconciliation. The earliest and most complete development of the idea was made by W. F. C. Wigston in 1884. He noted that Hermione, with the loss of Perdita, falls like the earth in winter into her death-sleep. She is restored to life at the return of her daughter who, like Persephone, is a lost child and is connected with the spring through the text. G. W. Knight (1958, 106) and Northrop Frye (1986, 161) also touch on the idea. Carol Neely specifically connects the myth to the dominant role of women in the play (1987, 81).

All of these studies quite rightly focus on Hermione as the figure of grieving Demeter and Perdita (whose name means "lost") as the lost Persephone. But there is another grieving woman in the play, Paulina, and Hermione is also lost and brought back from the dead, in one of the most moving and theatrically wonderful scenes that Shakespeare ever wrote. Thus, Paulina could equally well represent Demeter and Hermione could represent Persephone.

The blurring and overlapping of the roles of mother and daughter in the play reflect the blurring found in the Persephone myth and its rituals, for Demeter and her daughter "were a sacred duo, often nameless, each related to the other as past and future" (Wasson, Hofmann, and Ruck 1978, 101) and "merely the older and younger form of the same person" (Harrison 1903, 274). There is, however, a third woman with an important role in the myth, and that is the ambiguous goddess Hecate. I suggest that Paulina represents Hecate, and that the shifting roles among the three women in the play parallel their roles in the myth. If, as Robert Graves maintains, the triad of Persephone, Demeter, and Hecate does indeed represent the three phases of the moon, the seasonal cycle (1957, 1:12, 92), and women at the three main stages of their life cycles (Graves 1957, 1:12; Wasson et al. 1978, 101–2), i.e., woman as maiden, nymph, and crone,[1] then Hermione, Perdita, and Paulina have a similar function in a play so centered around sexuality, thwarted maternity, and fertility, a play whose ending embodies life affirmation and continuity. Although Apollo's oracle certainly plays a role in the play, it is not, as Shakespeare scholars have suggested, the god Apollo who dominates *The Winter's Tale* (Tillyard 1963, 189; Martz 1987, 124) but rather the triple goddess Demeter-Persephone-Hecate.

Shakespeare mentions "triple Hecate"[2] in *A Midsummer Night's Dream,* and this line is usually glossed as referring to Hecate's function as moon goddess along with Artemis and Selene or Luna.[3] The epithet has additional roots, however. According to Hesiod's *Theogony,* the Titan Hecate is honored by Zeus above all others and holds dominion over the three realms of land and sea and sky. In Hesiod's account she can be a beneficent figure, endowed by Zeus with the power of bestowing on mortals any desired gift—success in battle, athletics, fishing, livestock breeding. She is a nurse; *kourotrophos,* "a fostering goddess for all youths," "a nurturer of youths" (Hesiod 1983, lines 404–52). In later tradition, she is commonly referred to as a fertility goddess, sharing attributes with Demeter and with Artemis (all of them, for example, are depicted as carrying torches, a common attribute of goddesses of fertility). One of Hecate's epithets is *phōsphoros,* "bringer of light" (Euripides 1956, 569; Kerényi 1969, 110); another, *euōnymon,* "whom it is good to speak of," she shares with Artemis (West 1966, 281). Like Artemis, Hecate presides over childbirth, and like Persephone, over death. Hesiod hints at the potential for a destructive Hecate when he adds to his account that she has the capability of withholding success from her votaries if she wishes. That power, along with her role as earth or fertility goddess, leads to her eventual connection with the world of the dead, and in later times she is more widely known in her sinister dimension as goddess of witches, "associated with uncanny things" (Hammond and Scullard 1970, s.v. "Hecate") and invoked at crossroads, where three-bodied statues of her on triangular pedestals were set up. She is Medea's patroness, for example, and is invoked in Euripides' play and Apollonius's epic. Her companions are the Erinyes, and her appearances accompanied by them, scourges in hand, were terrifying.

The earlier, benevolent Hecate plays a role in the Homeric "Hymn to Demeter." She hears but does not see the abduction of Persephone, and she approaches Demeter, torch in hand, to report what she has heard. The two goddesses go together to Helios to ask him what he knows, and when Persephone returns, Hecate is the first to greet her, after her mother. The author of the Homeric hymn reports that Hecate "showed much affection" for Persephone (Homer 1970, 130), and from that point on, she is Persephone's constant companion. In the Homeric hymn, Hermes brings Persephone back; but on a vase dating from the time of the Parthenon, Hecate is shown lighting Persephone's way out of Hades (Hammond and Scullard 1970, s.v. "Hecate"). Moreover, Hecate is often confused with Persephone and Demeter. The Erinyes, Hecate's companions, are sometimes said to be Demeter's daughters; and in Euripides' *Ion,* the chorus invokes Hecate herself as a daughter of Demeter (1958, line 1048). Like Demeter, she is a goddess of crops, a torch-bearing goddess, and a driver of a chariot drawn by dragons or serpents (triple Hecate's team in *Midsummer Night's Dream*). As a goddess of the underworld she is often confused with Persephone, invoked in *Aeneid,* book 4, at the death of Dido. In some localities Demeter took on a Hecate-like quality: she was known in Phigalia as "the Black One" (Pausanias 1935, bk. 8, sec. 42) and in Thelpusa as "Demeter Erinyes" (Pausanias 1935, bk. 8, secs. 25, 42). Hecate does not appear in the Homeric epics, but when Persephone is mentioned in the *Iliad,* it is with the epithet *epainē,* "awful" or "dreaded" (Homer 1938, bk. 9, line 457). The Homeric "Hymn to Demeter" blurs the roles of Hecate and Demeter, for Demeter, in her disguise as old woman and then nurse to the son of Keleos and Metaneira, takes on Hecate's role as nurse and crone, and, in her anger, the role of avenging fury.

Overlapping and confusion of the roles of the triad of Demeter,

Persephone, and Hecate were widespread in the Renaissance. Shakespeare was familiar with the Erinyes dimension of Demeter's character, because he draws on it in *The Tempest*. When summoned by Iris to attend Juno at the wedding of Ferdinand and Miranda, Ceres (Demeter) angrily replies that she will come only if Venus and Cupid are not there, because she holds them responsible for Dis's abduction of her daughter and has "forsworn" (4.1.91) their company. In Heywood's *The Silver Age*, Hecate the moon goddess and Proserpine, daughter of Ceres, have become confused. Ceres grieves for the loss of her daughter the moon, and the compromise achieved between Ceres and Pluto results in the phases of the moon rather than in the change of seasons. Proserpine will shine twelve times a year in heaven and be with Pluto twelve times a year.

In *The Winter's Tale*, Perdita compares herself to Proserpina and is the lost daughter; it therefore makes perfectly good sense to regard her as the Persephone figure in the play and to regard Hermione as the Demeter figure. To this duo Shakespeare has added a third woman, Paulina, whose role is similar to that of Hecate in the myths. Although Paulina and Antigonus have young children ranging in age from five to eleven, they are slightly older than Hermione and Leontes: Antigonus has a "beard" that is "grey" and "little blood . . . left"[4] and Paulina in good-natured but wistful self-disparagement refers to herself at the end of the play as "an old turtle" (5.3.132). Like Hecate in the Homeric hymn, she is a good friend to the two women—defending Hermione, protecting the infant Perdita, preserving Hermione, curing Leontes, and rejoicing at the reunion of husband, wife, and daughter.

Moreover, Paulina is regarded by Leontes as a Hecate in her sinister dimension, the "railing Hecate," as Shakespeare refers to her in *I Henry VI* (3.2.64). Leontes calls Paulina "a mankind witch" (2.3.67), "crone" (2.3.76), and "hag" (2.3.107) and threatens to burn her at the stake. Paulina becomes a fury in act 3, scene 2, chastising Leontes for his crimes against his wife, his children, his friends and counselors, and his guest. Several critics have seen Paulina as Leontes' conscience (Knight 1958, 26; Martz 1987, 137). The crimes that Leontes has committed, against a guest, against a mother (not his own mother, admittedly, but a pregnant woman who is the mother of his children), were exactly the crimes for which Hecate's companions the Erinyes, who personified the pangs of conscience, hounded transgressors (see *Oedipus at Colonus, Oresteia*). Then, like the Erinyes in *Oedipus at Colonus*, Paulina becomes a benign figure to the repentant Leontes, curing him of his "lunes" (2.2.30). She in fact becomes a kind of nurse to the reborn Leontes; her "medicinal" words had failed to "purge" (2.3.37–38) Leontes earlier in the play but now succeed. "O grave and good Paulina, the great comfort that I have had of thee" (5.3.1), he says to her toward the end of the play.

And Paulina in the last scene of the play becomes something of a sorceress-magician, in the tradition of the Hecate who is the patroness of witches, although both she and Shakespeare deny it. Leontes speaks of the "magic" in the statue that "conjures" (5.3.39) again a recollection of his crimes and drains the life from Perdita, who looks like stone herself when she sees the statue. Paulina creates a miracle and brings Hermione back from the grave while insisting that she is not "assisted by wicked powers" (5.3.90) or engaging in "unlawful business" (5.3.96) and that her "spell is lawful" (5.3.105). "Be stone no more . . . I'll fill your grave up" (5.3.99, 102) she tells the statue. Paulina is Heracles bringing Alcestis back from the dead, or Medea renewing old Eason, yet she is none of those things but is instead a loving, comforting, nurturing friend whose rectitude and patient faith have repaired Leontes and Hermione's shattered family. She has nursed Hermione back to health and sustained her for sixteen years, cured Leontes, and kept both hopeful that the oracle would be fulfilled. Like Hecate with her torches, she is "the bringer of light" to *The Winter's Tale.* And like the Hecate of the *Theogony,* she has indulged Leontes' dearest wish.

The Winter's Tale, like the Persephone myth, contains three women at the three major stages of a woman's life cycle, each dominating a different section of the play. Hermione is the nymph or matron, the mother, dominating the first section of the play; Perdita is the Kore, the maiden, dominating the second; and Paulina is the crone, presiding over the end of the play. But Shakespeare provides, as does the Persephone myth, a great deal of overlapping among the roles of the three women.

Paulina, for example, briefly replaces Hermione as a nurse to Perdita in act 2, scenes 2 and 3. She replaces Hermione as companion to Leontes for sixteen years. She gets to greet Perdita before her own mother does, and then greets her as if Perdita were her own lost child, as Hecate does in the Homeric hymn. In the statue scene, Paulina watches overjoyed as Hermione embraces Leontes, then bids Hermione turn to acknowledge her daughter: "turn, good lady, / *Our* Perdita is found" (5.3.121, my italics). Leontes at various points in act 3 threatens to burn all three women at the stake. As

Paulina was by Leontes, so Perdita is later accused of witchcraft by Polixenes, who breaks up his son's betrothal ceremony and then turns on the bride with: "fresh piece of excellent witchcraft" (4.4.426–27) and "you, enchantment" (4.4.438).

There are, naturally, many similarities between mother and daughter, some shared by Paulina. Both Perdita and Hermione share Paulina's feistiness, and Perdita shares her mother's charm, beauty, hospitality, and sexual frankness. Her happy world of love and warmth, both familial and sexual, is violated by a tyrannical male figure, just as her mother's was. She resembles her mother physically, as Leontes can see when he first sees her as a sixteen-year-old. (Similarities between mother and daughter have led several directors to have one actress play both roles.)

If Perdita is the Persephone figure, then strictly she is the Queen of Hades, queen of the dead; but it is the two older women in *The Winter's Tale* who are more closely allied to the underworld. Hermione appears as a ghost to Antigonus "in pure white robes" (3.3.21) in a scene with connotations of the Hecate triads. She bows to him "thrice" (3.3.23) (cf. "with Hecate's ban thrice blasted" in *Hamlet* [3.2.258]) and waits until her "fury [is] spent" (3.3.25) before she speaks to him. She is both the grieving mother and a ghostly, scary, vengeful figure:

> 'For this ungentle business,
> Put on thee by my lord, thou ne'er shalt see
> Thy wife Paulina more.' And so, with shrieks,
> She melted into air.
>
> (3.3.16–17)

In a later scene, Paulina imagines herself as the ghost of Hermione, a vengeful fury pursuing Leontes should he marry another woman:

> Were I the ghost that walked, I'd bid you mark
> Her eye, and tell me for what dull part in't
> You chose her: then I'd shriek, that even your ears
> Should rift to hear me; and the words that follow'd
> Should be 'Remember mine.'
>
> (5.1.62–67)

Eventually, of course, Perdita the maiden will become a nymph and then a crone. The joy at the end of the play is tempered somewhat by the knowledge that Hermione, Leontes, and Paulina are reunited with Perdita just as she is about to leave them again; she is betrothed to Florizel and is about to move into her mother's role as matron, as wife and mother. A comparable situation occurs with Polixenes seeing his son reach sexual maturity. Polixenes feels threatened by the change, however, and refuses to accept his son's independence, whereas the women, as Neely has noted, are more tolerant of natural change and growth (1987, 79).

These are the broadest parallels between the Persephone myth and *The Winter's Tale,* with both myth and play enacting the lives of three women, essentially kindred, at three stages of life, through experiences of loss and restoration. But there are many other evocations of myth in *The Winter's Tale,* some closely related to the triad of Persephone, Demeter, and Hecate, some less so. Their cumulative force is to suggest that women dominate the play not only as dramatic characters, which is evident from the plot, but also as presiding deities.

Demeter, Persephone, and Hecate are fertility goddesses, but Hecate is part of another triad controlling fertility, the triple moon goddess Luna-Artemis-Hecate. Among their other functions, both Artemis and Hecate are concerned with childbirth, children, and families. Hecate shares the cult epithet *kourotrophos,* "nurturer of children," with Artemis. In ancient times the moon, not the sun, was thought of as influencing fertility, partly because dew is heaviest on moonlit nights, and dew is an important substitute for rain in warm climates; and partly because of the similar duration of the menstrual and lunar cycles (cf. the "moist star" of *Hamlet* [1.1.118], and "governess of floods" in *Midsummer Night's Dream* [2.1.103]).

The sheepshearing festival combines native English and ancient classical fertility festivals. Martz thinks that the scenes may be indebted to festivals for Apollo (1987, 124). But why should there not be resemblances to the most famous ancient fertility ritual of all, the Eleusinian Mysteries? One characteristic of the Eleusinian Mysteries was their celebration of humanity. In the classical era, women played a much more important role in the ceremonies than they did in Athenian society, and men and slaves were admitted to what began as a women's ritual. The sheepshearing festival is inclusive and communal, welcoming rich strangers like Polixenes and Camillo, male and female, young and old, and even, albeit unknowingly, thieves like Autolycus. It's probably more important, however, that the rituals for Demeter involved a celebration not just of fertility but of human sexuality. Demeter, it must be remembered, was a fertility goddess who never married, and who enraged Zeus when she bore her son Iacchus (or Pluton) after she and the Titan Iasius sneaked away from a wedding to make love in a thrice-ploughed field (Homer 1965, bk. 5, 125–28; Hesiod 1983, 971).

We know we are in a different world from that of Leontes' possessive jealousy when the old shepherd comes in complaining good naturedly about teenagers who *will* get wenches with child and assuming, with no trace of condemnation whatsoever, that Perdita is the product of "trunk work, behind-stair work" (3.3.74). Yet the happy influence of Bohemia will be carried back to Sicily, where evidence of Leontes' "recreation" (3.2.238) is his willingness to stick up for the young lovers. The whole Bohemian episode includes a comfortable acceptance of young love and celebration of sexuality, culminating in Perdita's lament for virgins who die unmarried and her subsequent sexual joking with Florizel about burying him under flowers, not dead, but "quick, and in my arms" (4.4.132) and about pretending that he is a bank to make love on. The spirit of tolerance in the Bohemian community exists even among the puritans in their midst. The entertainment, Perdita's foster brother tells us, includes one puritan, but he sings anyway. In another account of the Persephone story, an Orphic hymn, the grieving Demeter is cheered up by a peasant wife (another version of the crone) named Baubo, who makes ribald gestures and causes Demeter to laugh for the first time since Persephone's disappearance. The Eleusinian Mysteries included a ritual copulation and a lot of coarse games and tales (Kerényi 1967, 40). Autolycus provides those in *The Winter's Tale* with his ballads "so without bawdry" and such "delicate burdens" as "jump her and thump her" (4.4.195–97). In classical myth the tie between Demeter and herders was very close because in the Orphic hymn, a swineherd, shepherd, and cowherd witness the rape and bring Demeter news of Persephone's whereabouts (Kerényi 1967, 171). In gratitude, she rewards one of them by giving him the gift of knowledge of agriculture, which he spreads to all lands by traveling in a chariot drawn by serpents, much like Hecate's team (Graves 1957, 1:92). Singing shepherds played a prominent role in Eleusinian processions. In the Orphic hymn, the name of the shepherd who helps Demeter find Persephone is Eumolpos, "the sweet singer" (Harrison 1903, 555–56). It is entirely appropriate, then, that Perdita's saviors in *The Winter's Tale* should be genial, festive shepherds.

The idea that women in various stages of their life cycle dominate the play as presiding deities is supported by references in the play to fertility of human life and to seasonal changes. The second scene opens with the line "Nine changes of the watery moon" (1.2.1), making explicit the connection between the moon, water, and human pregnancy. The first two and a half acts take place in winter, as Mamillius tells us when he begins his "sad tale" (2.1.25). There is some confusion over the season of the Bohemian episodes, but they certainly take place in spring or summer. Act 4, scene 3 begins with Autolycus's joyous song of praise to spring, to the daffodils, the first flowers of spring, to spring fever in humans and birds, and to spring housecleaning and the opportunities it affords for him to ply his trade. And sheepshearing should take place in spring. Florizel's description of Perdita's dress compares her to Flora "peering in April's front" (4.4.3), again giving the impression that we are in the early spring of the year. But Perdita, in her Proserpine speech, laments that she has no spring flowers and gives Camillo and Polixenes flowers of midsummer (Martz 1987, 135). Leontes tells Perdita, whom he knows only as Florizel's fiancee at this point, that she is as welcome to Sicily "as is the spring to th' earth" (5.1.151), but this remark is symbolic and metaphorical. The mood in the closing act, with Leontes' remarks about his wife's wrinkles and Paulina's about her age, is "autumnal" (Pafford 1976, lxx), but of course it is in this scene that Hermione is reborn and Perdita is found.

Knowing the season of the sheepshearing scene is not critical; with the entrance of the shepherd in act 3, scene 3, we move from the tragic winter world of Leontes' court and Sicily to the spring-summer world of Perdita and Bohemia. All seasons of the year are represented in the play, and Hermione's pregnancy is a visible reminder of her role as earth mother or corn goddess. There are various accounts of where the rape of Persephone took place—in the Homeric hymn, it is near Mt. Nysa. But according to Ovid, it occurred in Sicily, and the explanation given for this location is that Sicily was renowned for the fertility of its soil. Wigston also suggested that Shakespeare changed the name of his heroine from Bellaria in Pandosto to Hermione because Hermione is the name of a city where Demeter had a famous temple.

The Persephone story is about a rape, and no one gets raped in *The Winter's Tale.* But of course the story of the rape of Persephone is about death as well as about sexual violation and forced marriage.

Leontes causes the death of his son and one trusted counselor, and tries to cause the death of his wife, his daughter, his best friend, and another trusted counselor. He has destroyed his family, and in his barbaric treatment of his pregnant wife and his children, he has attacked life itself. Before he begins to repent, he seems bent on becoming an agent of death. His turning against a previously welcome guest violates codes of hospitality; Hades himself is called sometimes "the receiver of many guests" but also "the Inhospitable One" (Wasson, Hofmann, and Ruck 1978, 110). The Stratford (Ontario) Shakespeare Festival's 1986 production of the play presented the scene of Hermione's arrest as a kind of rape. Hermione and her women were dressed in night clothes, Hermione was sleepily putting her son to bed, and into this warm, intimate, and protected atmosphere burst Leontes and six men. According to Colm Feore, who played Leontes, David William, the director, "staged it as a vicious, absolutely vicious infiltration of her chamber . . . her women, her pregnancy and her children. . . . He violates her chamber as he feels she has violated him" (quoted in Gaines 1987, 206).

The Winter's Tale contains many references to tales and stories, beginning with the title. There are Mamillius's tale; Hermione's misery, "which is more than history can pattern" (3.2.35); the stories that the young shepherd can tell his children when "he's dead and rotten" (3.3.81), as the old shepherd puts it in a happy malapropism; Autolycus's "true" ballads (4.4.282); and the marveling of the courtiers over the revelations of the last act. Their astonishment over the unfolding of miraculous incredible events, so "like an old tale" (5.2.62), forestalls any possible audience objection to the denouement. Paulina's announcement that the statue is indeed alive, "That she is living / Were it but told you, should be hooted at / Like an old tale: But it appears she lives" (5.3.115) has a similar function. Shakespeare, as scholars have noted (Goddard 1951, 272), also draws in this play on some old tales of good women who have been tested and proven. The Griselda story is one, the Alcestis myth another.[5] But the oldest tale he draws on is the myth of the grieving mother, the lost child, and the supportive older woman of the Demeter-Persephone story.

Louis Martz has made a good case for Greek influences on *The Winter's Tale.* It should be noted that Hecate does not appear in Ovid's account of the Persephone story, so that if the parallels I have adduced are valid, Shakespeare has chosen Greek rather than Roman versions of the story. Martz makes a case for the scope of a play that begins in a Grecian context and ends in a Christian context, the three sections being a summary of all human history. But the analogues to the Persephone story do more than universalize the experience of the play or pay tribute to Shakespeare's Greek predecessors. The triad of Demeter, Persephone, and Hecate underpins and enriches the portraits of three of Shakespeare's strongest, most attractive, and most triumphantly successful women.

NOTES

1. A nymph is a married woman, a matron; a crone is a woman past the years of childbearing.

2. Shakespeare, *A Midsummer Night's Dream,* in *The Riverside Shakespeare,* act 5, scene 1, line 384. Subsequent act, scene, and line numbers in parentheses in discussions of all plays by Shakespeare except *The Winter's Tale* refer to this edition.

3. See, for example, Kittredge's gloss on the line: "The moon goddess has three names—Diana on earth, Phoebe in heaven, and Hecate in Hades. In the character of Hecate she is the goddess of nocturnal spells and the patroness of witches" (1971, 246, note to 5.1.367). Dr. Johnson wrote that "thrice-crowned queen of night" (3.2.2) in *As You Like It* "allud[es] to the triple character of Proserpine (or Hecate), Cynthia, and Diana, given by some mythologists to the same goddess" (1968, 251).

4. Shakespeare, *The Winter's Tale,* act 2, scene 3, lines 161, 165. Subsequent act, scene, and line numbers in parentheses in discussions of *The Winter's Tale* refer to the Arden edition.

5. The Alcestis story has some connections with Persephone; in Apollodorus's version, Persephone refuses Alcestis's sacrifice and sends her home.

BIBLIOGRAPHY

Euripides. *Ion.* Translated and with an introduction by Ronald Frederick Willets. In *The Complete Greek Tragedies,* edited by David Grene and Richmond Lattimore. Chicago: Univ. of Chicago Press, 1958.

———. *Helen.* Translated by Richmond Lattimore. *The Complete Greek Tragedies: Euripides II.* Edited by David Grene and Richmond Lattimore. Chicago: Univ. of Chicago Press, 1956.

Frye, Northrop. *Northrop Frye on Shakespeare.* Edited by Robert Sandler. New Haven: Yale Univ. Press, 1986.

Gaines, Robert A. *John Neville Takes Command.* Stratford, Ontario: William Street Press, 1987.

Goddard, Harold C. *The Meaning of Shakespeare.* Chicago: Univ. of Chicago Press, 1951.

Grant, Michael. *Myths of the Greeks and the Romans.* Cleveland: World, 1962.

Graves, Robert. *The Greek Myths.* 2 vols. Baltimore: Penguin Books, 1957.

Guthrie, W. K. C. *Orpheus and Greek Religion: A Study of the Orphic Movement.* New York: Norton, 1966.

Hammond, N. G. L., and H. H. Scullard. *Oxford Classical Dictionary.* 2d ed. Oxford: Clarendon, 1970.

Harrison, Jane Ellen. *Prolegomena to the Study of Greek Religion.* Cambridge: Cambridge Univ. Press, 1903.

Hesiod. *Theogony.* Edited by M. L. West. Oxford: Clarendon, 1966.

———. *Theogony; Works and Days; Shield.* Translation, introduction, and notes by Apostolos N. Athanassakis. Baltimore: Johns Hopkins Univ. Press, 1983.

Homer. *The Iliad.* Translated by A. T. Murray. Cambridge: Harvard Univ. Press, 1938.

———. *The Odyssey.* Translated by Richmond Lattimore. New York: Harper and Row, 1965.

———. "The Hymn to Demeter." Translated by Charles Boer. Chicago: Swallow, 1970.

Johnson, Samuel. *Johnson on Shakespeare.* Edited by Arthur Sherbo. Yale Edition of the Works of Samuel Johnson, edited by John M. Middendorf, vol. 7. New Haven: Yale Univ. Press, 1968.

Kerényi, C. *Eleusis: Archetypal Image of Mother and Daughter.* Translated by Ralph Manheim. Princeton: Princeton Univ. Press, 1967.

———. "Kore." In C. G. Jung and C. Kerényi, *Essays on a Science of Mythology: The Myth of the Divine Child and the Mysteries of Eleusis.* Princeton: Princeton Univ. Press, 1969.

Kittredge, George Lyman, and Irving Ribner. *The Complete Works of Shakespeare.* Waltham, Mass.: Ginn, 1971.

Knight, G. W. *The Crown of Life.* London: Methuen, 1958.

Martz, Louis L. "Shakespeare's Humanist Enterprise: *The Winter's Tale.*" In *Modern Critical Interpretations of William Shakespeare's The Winter's Tale,* edited by Harold Bloom. New York: Chelsea House, 1987.

Neely, Carol Thomas. "Women and Issue in *The Winter's Tale.*" In *Modern Critical Interpretations of William Shakespeare's The Winter's Tale,* edited by Harold Bloom. New York: Chelsea House, 1987.

Pafford, J. H. P. Introduction to *The Winter's Tale,* by William Shakespeare. Arden edition. London: Methuen, 1976.

Pausanias. *Description of Greece.* Translated by W. H. S. Jones. Cambridge: Harvard Univ. Press, 1935.

Shakespeare, William. *The Riverside Shakespeare.* Edited by G. Blackmore Evans. Boston: Houghton Mifflin, 1974.

———. *The Winter's Tale.* Edited by J. H. P. Pafford. Arden edition. London: Methuen, 1976.

Tillyard, E. M. W. "Shakespeare's Last Plays." In *The Winter's Tale,* edited by Frank Kermode. New York: New American Library, 1963.

Wasson, R. Gordon, Albert Hofmann, and Carl A. P. Ruck. *The Road to Eleusis.* New York: Harcourt Brace Jovanovich, 1978.

West, M. L. Prolegomena and Commentary to *Theogony,* by Hesiod. Oxford: Clarendon, 1966.

Wigston, W. F. C. *A New Study of Shakespeare: An Inquiry into the Connection of the Plays and Poems, with the Origins of the Classical Drama and with the Platonic Philosophy, through the Mysteries.* N.p.: Trubner, 1884.

Michèle Vialet
and Buford Norman

CHAPTER 4

SEXUAL AND ARTISTIC POLITICS UNDER LOUIS XIV: THE PERSEPHONE MYTH IN QUINAULT AND LULLY'S *PROSERPINE*

The popularity of mythological rapes as subjects in seventeenth-century French profane art offered artists opportunities to heighten sensuality through violence and to test the limits of the representability of sexual desire. Pictorial and sculptural representations of rape, displayed in landscaped gardens and in ornate rooms, were meant to catch the eyes of passersby and to work on their imaginations, spurring more or less daring remarks but always teasing their libidinal desires. Artists strained the expressiveness of paint and marble to give the vividness of a rape actually witnessed by the viewer to their representations of an adult male carrying off a defenseless maiden. The bodies of the participants are captured in the heat of the moment: the muscle tension of the abductor's gnarled arms and legs is reinforced by his determined facial features, the maiden's plump body—largely unveiled by falling garments—counters only with a powerless and disbelieving look and the gesture of its free hand hopelessly reaching for help. Reubens's *Rape of the Daughters of Leucippus* and both Bernini's and Girardon's *Rape of Persephone* seem to give us not only the spectacle of a social transgression but also the feeling that the rape cannot be undone, that it will be carried to its end, no matter what forces attempt to counteract it. Underscoring the realism of these representations is the truncated narrative of a man's victory over a woman's resistance to love.

Beyond the eroticism of the representations, however, we suspect that rape scenes had yet another appeal to male viewers, that of embodying a compelling fantasy of order in relationships between men and women. In that respect, the myth of Persephone is of particular significance. It is one of the few classical myths setting rape in a sociopolitical context: that of the family that Zeus illegitimately created with Demeter, on the one hand, and, on the other, that of the political alliance the god instituted with his brother Hades to gain power. Furthermore, the rape causes the victim's mother to revolt against a social order that conceals her daughter's disappearance beneath a veil of silence. Finally, the myth lent itself to numerous literary treatments throughout the Ancien Régime, thus giving us not only multiple representations of the rape itself but a detailed narrative of the conflicts that different periods recognized in the myth and of the solutions they proposed.

In the following pages, we examine one much acclaimed and influential version of the rape of Persephone, Philippe Quinault and Jean-Baptiste Lully's 1680 *tragédie lyrique, Proserpine.* This baroque opera provides a unique opportunity to investigate the modifications the myth underwent at the hands of Quinault and Lully, presumably because they felt their version was better suited to elicit the admiration and the tears of the public than previous treatments. It also allows us to inquire into the significance that the new treatment had for the society of Louis XIV's most glorious years. It has been suggested that myths and history from the ancient world make possible an investigation of reality while allowing us to move beyond it (Néraudeau 1986, 59). The seventeenth-century public's interest in Quinault and Lully's *Proserpine* can be traced to a kind of collective psychological processing of the practice of male sexual and political domination of women's destinies in Louis XIV's France.

After we briefly situate *Proserpine* in the tradition of musical and sculptural representations of rape, we analyze the libretto with particular attention to the mother-daughter relationship, to the place of this relationship in the society that is reflected in the text and music, and to the work's advocacy of women's submission to men's desire in the name of universal peace. We argue that, in spite of the profound sympathy the text and music create for the fate of Proserpina and her mother, Quinault and Lully's version of the Persephone myth is ultimately designed to have the spectators welcome the law of masculine desire as figured in Proserpina's marriage. In light of the sociohistorical circumstances under which *Proserpine* was proposed for Louis XIV's pleasure, especially the decision to marry Marie-Louise d'Orléans to Charles II of Spain, we point to the shrewd harmonizing of aesthetic, political, and sexual politics demonstrated in Quinault and Lully's rewriting of the classical myth.[1]

PERSEPHONE AND EARLY OPERA

The Persephone myth was already a popular subject on the musical stage by the time of Louis XIV. In the fifty years following the creation of what is considered the first opera, Peri's *Dafne* of 1597, there were four librettos called *Proserpina rapita,* two for operas and two for smaller scale works. Of the two for operas, one libretto was written by Giulio Strozzi in 1630, with music by Monteverdi, and the other was written by O. Castelli in 1645, with music by Pompeo Colonna. There was also a prologue plus four "intermedii in musica," probably by Ridolfo Campeggi with music by Girolamo Giacobbi, published in Bologna in 1613, and an "intermedio per musica" by Benedetto Ferrari dalla Tiorba, first performed at Venice in 1641 (Sartori 1991; Loewenberg 1978; Sonneck 1914, 899).

There was no French opera in France in the first half of the seventeenth century, but there were two plays called *Le Ravissement de Proserpine,* one by Alexander Hardy around 1611, frequently revived, and another, based on Hardy's play, by Jean Claveret in 1639. Claveret's work, with scenes set in heaven and Hades as well as on earth, was especially spectacular and has been seen as a step on the way to opera (see Lancaster 1929–42, vols. 1 and 2, especially 2: 170–71 and 1:58; and Rigal 1989, 419). The existence of these Italian and French works, in addition to the enormous popularity of Ovid's versions of classical myths, makes it hardly surprising that the creators of French opera would eventually turn to the Persephone myth.

Indeed, Persephone's rape had already been the subject of ballets danced by the king earlier in his reign, and Quinault had proposed it as a subject for a machine play in 1670 (the story of Cupid and Psyche was chosen; see Néraudeau 1986, 121–22, 144). Ovid's *Metamorphoses* were read by most educated men in Latin, and by the general reading public in the translation of Renouard (1651). Benserade's adaptation of the *Metamorphoses* in rondeau form, published in 1676 by the Imprimerie Royale, guaranteed that all of Louis's courtiers would be familiar with them (for more information, see Néraudeau 1986, 16–18; Apostolidès 1981, 79; and Gros 1926, 544–52).

One measure of the popularity of the Persephone myth, and especially of Ovid's version, is a long tradition of burlesque versions (Anton 1967). There was an anonymous *Enlèvement de Proserpine* written in 1430 and an anonymous *Ravissement de Proserpine* published in Lyon in 1556. Closer to Quinault's time was a burlesque comedy, *Le Ravissement de Proserpine,* "performed" in Sorel's *Le Berger extravagant* (published in 1627 and revised as *L'Antiroman ou l'Histoire du berger Lysis* in 1633). At the time Quinault was writing his first plays, D'Assoucy, who had already published *L'Ovide en belle humeur* in 1650, published a burlesque poem, *Le Ravissement de Proserpine,* in 1656.

Perhaps the most striking evidence of the popularity of the rape of Persephone and of other mythological victims is found in that epicenter of classical French allegory, the palace and gardens of Versailles. For the area in front of the central facade, dominating the long central axis that includes the king's bedroom, Le Brun designed in 1674 the *parterre d'eau,* a basin that was to have Apollo at the center and, in the four corners, larger-than-life statues of rapes from classical mythology. Each rape was to represent one of the four elements, with the rape of Persephone by Pluto representing fire. The full explanation of the allegorical meanings of these statues is lost, but Nivelon's biography of Le Brun states that the statues were intended to represent the universe and its harmony: "toute la masse de la construction universelle, . . . l'enchaînement de ce qui compose l'univers" [the entire mass of universal construction, . . . the linking together of what makes up the universe] (Marie 1968, 160–61). Le Brun probably took much of his plan from Jean Baudouin's French translation of Cesare Ripa's *Iconologia* (Ripa 1976, 2:5) which, like earlier court ballets, has the same groupings as Le Brun's plan and which follows the presentation of the four elements with: "C'est à peu près ce qu'on peut dire succinctement des quatre Eléments, les principales puissances desquels, selon Empedocle, sont l'amitié & la discorde, dont l'une unit ensemble les choses, & l'autre les sépare" [That is about all one can say succinctly about the four Elements, the principal powers of which, according to Empedocles, are friendship and discord, one of which joins things together while the other separates them] (1976, 2:5).[2] Rape is thus idealized as a representation of separate entities that achieve unity by force—the same elements that are characterized by violence and injustice also contain the potential for ordering the universe and holding it together.

In 1673 Quinault and Lully collaborated on *Cadmus et Hermione*, a *tragédie-lyrique* that inaugurated a tradition of French opera that would last until the end of the eighteenth century. They produced an opera or ballet each year until Quinault's retirement in 1686, except for a two-year hiatus during which Quinault was out of favor because Madame de Montespan, the reigning but fading royal mistress, recognized herself in the excessively jealous Juno of *Isis* (1677). Quinault was restored to his post by the king in October 1679, and his first post-hiatus libretto was *Proserpine*, one of the pair's most successful operas. It opened at Saint-Germain-en-Laye on February 3, 1680, and had nine revivals from 1681 to 1759, with the 1758–59 version running for thirty-six performances (Schneider 1992; Schneider 1982). Only three of Quinault and Lully's eleven operas had revivals after 1758, a time when the traditional French opera of Lully and Rameau was being challenged by Italian composers of *opera buffa*.

The success of *Proserpine* was confirmed by parodies and adaptations. Seventeenth- and eighteenth-century parodies, which were usually of the words rather than of the music, reflected popular success even more than they did commonly perceived flaws. In a period when large numbers of people whistled Lully's tunes and read Quinault's librettos, there were parodies of most of their operas (Grout 1941, 211–19, 514–26; Grannis 1931, 111–45). The *Mercure de France* describes a parody *Les Noces de Proserpine* in April 1727, at the time of the second revival that year. Two other revivals were also followed by parodies: *Farinette*, by Favart, was performed in March 1741, and *Petrine*, a work by an unidentified author performed in January 1759, was probably based on *Farinette* (Sonneck 1914, 900).

In 1803 Nicolas-François Guillard created a three-act version of Quinault's libretto for music by Paisello. In spite of Napoleon's admiration and support of Paisello, the opera had only thirteen performances, and an Italian adaptation made in 1806–8 was never performed. Guillard followed Quinault very closely but made some important changes to the scenes that take place in the underworld. For example, he added a scene in which Proserpina agrees to become Pluto's queen when she realizes how much suffering he has eliminated from his kingdom on her behalf. At about the same time Lorenzo da Ponte (best known for his librettos for Mozart) wrote *Il Ratto di Proserpina,* set by Peter von Winter and performed in London in 1804 (Pitou 1983, 450–51; Loewenberg 1978).

QUINAULT'S LIBRETTO

Quinault's libretto includes an allegorical prologue, with the drama of Proserpine per se divided into five acts. Like most prologues to seventeenth-century French operas, this one contains obvious references to current events at court, thus suggesting to the spectator that the plot of the opera could be seen as reflecting these events. (Quinault's disgrace after *Isis,* mentioned earlier, is a case in point.) Although not directly connected with the plot of the opera, the prologue introduces the motif of world peace with which the opera concludes (see Isherwood 1973; Niderst 1976, 187–212; Duron 1987, 73). This is the most explicit return to the themes of the prologue of all the Quinault librettos, one that is also expressed musically. The *ritournelle* for oboe in the final chorus is quite similar to the one in the final chorus of the prologue, and there are also similar *ritournelles* for trumpets in the prologue and in the last act. The arrivals of Victory and Jupiter, which bring about the final resolution in the prologue and in the last scene, are both preceded by trumpets and in C major ("gai et guerrier" [gay and warlike], according to the *Règles de composition par Monsieur Charpentier* [Cessac 1988, 456–57]).

This allegorical prologue presents Victory, obviously representing Louis XIV, who delivers Peace, Felicity, and Abundance from the cave where Discord has chained them. Discord is in turn put into chains, and Felicity and Abundance gladly prepare to enter into the chains of love, whose time returns now that the weapons have been put away. The Hero's power to bring peace is equated with Jupiter's triumph over the Titans at the beginning of Ovid's version of the Persephone myth and of the opera. The implication is that a new era, based on the newly established power of the Hero, is about to start. The prevailing mood is celebratory and optimistic, but undertones point to the precarious balance in which the conflicting forces are held. Discord is imprisoned but not eradicated; the Hero has used victory to establish peace ("Il s'est servi de la Victoire, / Pour faire triompher la Paix" [He has used Victory / To ensure the triumph of Peace]), although he could have given in to the seduction of Discord and Glory; lovers welcome Love but know it will put them in chains and bring no pleasure without pain ("Il [Amour] n'a point de bien sans peine: / Mais peut-on trop payer ses douceurs?" [Love has no gain without pain / But can one put a price on its pleasures?]).[3]

Quinault's main source for the five acts of the opera is Ovid's *Metamorphoses* (V, 341–641; see Appendix C). Act 1 begins with the celebration of Jupiter's victory over the Titans and shows the departure of Ceres (in a chariot drawn by winged dragons) and the earthquake—caused by the Titans' attempt to continue the war—that prompts Pluto to make a tour of Ceres' Sicily. After several lovers' quarrels among Arethusa, Alpheus, and Ascalaphus (Pluto's confidant), act 2 ends with the abduction of Proserpina: emerging from the underworld, Pluto seizes the unwilling maiden and places her on his chariot (2.9); acts 3, 4, and most of act 5 depict Ceres' and Proserpina's grief. The climax is reached when Ceres, in despair and asking death to relieve her, hears the infernal divinities call for the destruction of the universe and decides to join them in their cry: "Périsse l'univers!" [May the universe perish!] (5.3). News about Proserpina from Alpheus and Arethusa delays Ceres' action until the next scene, where Mercury announces Jupiter's ruling; this ruling is celebrated in the final divertissement, in the presence of the reunited gods, by songs calling for an everlasting peace. (See Appendix D for a more detailed plot summary.)

Departing from Ovid's *Metamorphoses,* Quinault conforms to the seventeenth-century conventions of dramatic *bienséances* by playing down the sexual aspect of the rape. Proserpina is shown to be abducted but respected by an enamored Pluto, who seeks her love rather than physical gratification. However, Quinault retains the reference to eating the fruit that forbids the return of a living being to earth: Proserpina is tricked into tasting seeds of the dangerous fruit and finds herself condemned to remain in Hades (4.3; 5.1). Although the episode can be given a classical sexual interpretation, the libretto explains Proserpina's action as an innocent attempt to quench her thirst. It is unclear whether this remaining element of violence is used to convey the sexual content of the classical myth or if it partakes of a certain cleansing of the myth designed to raise the issue of abduction separately from that of forced sexual encounter. Clearly, the euphemization of rape under the name of abduction would have pleased the sensibilities of the French court in the 1680s.

Quinault also omits two of Ovid's episodes: Ceres' anger at the child who calls her a glutton and the daughters of Achelous turned into sirens. He also rearranges two scenes: the metamorphosis of Cyane is postponed until after Ceres returns to find her daughter missing (3.6); Ceres' prayer to Jupiter, reduced to eight short lines (5.4), comes only after Jupiter has requested Proserpina's release, immediately before his decision is announced. Finally, Quinault expands the roles of Arethusa and Ceres. The courtship of Arethusa and Alpheus, which Ovid describes after Proserpina's fate has been decided, becomes a major subplot, and Arethusa becomes the accomplice of Pluto's rape by thoughtlessly allowing him to approach Proserpina, whom he had found so beautiful moments earlier after receiving a shaft from Cupid's bow. Arethusa's share of responsibility prompts her to visit Proserpina in Hades, where she listens to the captive's complaints and attempts to convince Proserpina to accept Pluto's love. Ceres' relationship to Jupiter is also developed—she mentions her love for him often, especially to Mercury when he comes from Jupiter to ask her to take care of the crops in Phrygia (1.2).

By preferring the version Ovid gives of the myth in *Metamorphoses* to the one in the *Fasti* (4, 417–620), Quinault chose action over elegy. The tone is more grandiose, and divine majesty is presented in a style of solemn dignity. The narration is more objective, with little scope given to the personality of the narrator (Otis 1970, 50). Like its Ovidian model, Quinault's version emphasizes the cosmogonic dimension and consequences of Proserpina's rape. The framework of the opera (including the prologue) features the revolt of the Titans and its effects on heaven, Hades, and earth. Quinault does not include Venus's desire to add Pluto to her list of illustrious victims, but Pluto does mention Cupid's arrow (2.7) and that he is destined to love Proserpina (5.1). His rape of Proserpina affects the balance of power among the three rulers of the universe (Jupiter, Neptune, Pluto) and causes Ceres to devastate much of the Mediterranean world. We are definitely outside of the realm of pastoral and elegy, where the loves of the characters have no effects beyond their personal lives. Because Quinault is frequently criticized for writing lightweight, overly *tendre* texts (Boileau, for example, claimed Quinault said everything tenderly, even "I hate you"; Satire 3, lines 187–88) in which the only topic of conversation is love, the choice of a myth with such cosmic implications is important.

JUPITER'S RULING

Reduced to bare action, the story of Proserpina's rape is a chronicle of brute force legalized by the king of the universe in spite of a mother's opposition. Limited to the instant they seize, plastic representations show just that. As is clear in our overview of *Proserpine,* however, Quinault and Lully provide a more nuanced version of the myth, focusing less on the *raptus* (the abduction) than on the sequence of reactions that culminate in Jupiter's ruling. Important clues for interpreting the opera can be drawn from an analysis of this ruling.

Mercury announces to Ceres the famous decision Jupiter has made in consultation with the assembly of gods:

> Proserpine verra le jour;
> Elle suivra Cérès et Pluton tour-à-tour;
> Elle partagera son temps et sa tendresse
> Entre la Nature et l'Amour.
>
> [Proserpine will see the light of day
> She will follow Ceres and Pluto in turn;
> She will divide her time and her affection
> Between Nature and Love.]
>
> (5.5).

The decision is timely, because Ceres has just been stopped from joining the infernal divinities in the destruction of the universe by the news that her daughter is in Hades (5.3).

Like the classical solution of the Persephone myth, Jupiter's ruling appears both fair and conciliatory to Ceres. In allowing Proserpina to share the year between her mother and Pluto, the god seems to recognize Ceres' claim over her daughter. Mercury stresses that her wishes were heard: "Vous verrez votre fille, et Jupiter lui-même / A pris soin qu'à vos voeux le sort ait répondu" [You will see your daughter, and Jupiter himself / Has made sure that destiny has answered your wishes] (5.5). Jupiter does not seem to deny Ceres' claim when he announces his split decision: "Cérès, que de vos pleurs le triste cours finisse; / Qu'avec Pluton Proserpine s'unisse" [Ceres, may the sad course of your tears come to an end; / May Proserpina be united with Pluto] (5.6). We also recall that Jupiter took the initiative to reclaim Proserpina and threatened Pluto with his troops (5.1). His ruling does punish Pluto's transgression by allowing him only six months per year with his bride, a marital arrangement never imposed on any other god. Finally, the decision also seems to take pity on Proserpina, who will see the daylight again six months per year.

Although these aspects of Jupiter's ruling point to a god moved by a mother's tears, the compromise is marred by ambivalence and may be understood as serving the interests of Pluto rather than those of Ceres. Jupiter upholds Pluto's claim to keep Proserpina as his wife and returns the young woman to her mother for half of the year only. Not only does Jupiter renounce his initial intent to set Proserpina free unconditionally, but he forces the young woman to marry, a destiny she had been spared at her birth.

Although the libretto does not indicate the reasons behind Jupiter's half measures, it presents the compromise as a necessity for the return of peace on earth, in heaven, and in Hades. In other words, Proserpina is sacrificed to politics, to Jupiter's peace politics. Unlike Iphigenia, another sacrificed mythological daughter, whose blood will obtain the gods' support for the Trojan War, Proserpina will guarantee peace between the masters of the universe. The two final scenes emphasize the triumph of political conciliation as the infernal and terrestrial divinities join to call for an everlasting peace. Even the last stage directions specify that the joy of the dancing and chanting divinities comes from seeing "l'intelligence rétablie entre les plus grands Dieux du monde, par le mariage de Pluton & de Proserpine" [understanding restored among the greatest Gods of the world, by the marriage of Pluto and Proserpina] (5.6).

From a political point of view, Proserpina's rape plays a central role in defining Jupiter's power over his allies. His ruling is a model of diplomatic success—given the delay with which he intervened, all can believe their requests were heard. They can also flatter themselves (and thank Jupiter) that they each benefit from the ruling: Pluto gains the bride he loves, Ceres recovers her daughter, Proserpina can leave Hades. With his authority increased by the justice he seems to have given each of his allies, Jupiter is the true beneficiary of Proserpina's abduction. His triumph over the Titans was an effect of military superiority; by his ruling, he establishes that his power will be tempered by diplomacy and justice.

In the libretto, Jupiter's decision is not motivated. Like the characters of the opera, the spectator can only speculate on Jupiter's real motivations. One possible interpretation is that Pluto had the military advantage because of his ability to free the Titans; Jupiter would have given in to military strength. Another is that Jupiter had no desire to wage a war against his brother, preferring instead to maintain peace. A third is that Jupiter wished to satisfy Pluto before Ceres: thus, he would have given the appearance of challenging Pluto (5.1) but had actually secretly negotiated with him a six-month deal. After all, far from being punished for his rape, Pluto is allowed to keep Proserpina in full legality through marriage.

Jupiter's ruling integrates the rape of Proserpina into society by making its legalization (marriage) the keystone of peace between the old allies (earth, heaven, and Hades), but where does it leave Ceres' motherly rights? The sequence of scenes makes clear that Jupiter's benevolence towards Ceres results from her devastation of the countryside. The mother's fight for the recovery of her daughter presents too many risks for Jupiter, especially when Ceres decides to ally with Pluto's troops to destroy the universe (5.3). In other words, Jupiter gives in to Ceres for the sake of his own power. The mother can therefore credit her partial victory to her determination (indeed, to her waging of war) and congratulate herself for not letting the abduction of her daughter go unchallenged. Although she does not undo the abduction, she does challenge the habitual sexual violence of the gods from the viewpoint of her own family unit (itself reduced to a mother-child group by this very type of violence). Only through her power of destruction is she able to maintain her mother-daughter relationship—the only relationship that Jupiter's infidelities allow her to retain—in the face of the gods' unrestrained division of lands and women. Clearly the mother-daughter relationship has had some power to destabilize the gods' tacit agreement to close their eyes to each other's acts of violence against goddesses and female mortals. (Pluto defends his claim by denouncing his brother's numerous love affairs [5.1].) But Jupiter's ruling does not recognize in the mother-daughter relationship a merit of its own. The apparent support it receives when Mercury describes the god's decision can only be attributed to a diplomatic touch, gallantry if you will, that will be reassuring, even flattering, to a mother's ear.

THE ERASURE OF VIOLENCE IN THE NAME OF LOVE

The loving relationship uniting Ceres and Proserpina receives prominent treatment throughout the opera. Yet in spite of a sensitive development of maternal and filial love orchestrated at all levels (lyrical, musical, and visual) to move the audience to sympathy, the opera sanctions the breakup of the mother-daughter couple. The performance ends on the happy mood of Proserpina's marriage as everyone rejoices at the reconciliation of Ceres, Pluto, and Jupiter. The music of the two final scenes is harmonious, cheerful, and celebratory, suggesting neither distress nor an ironic countertone covering Proserpina's sorrow with the joy of the dances. The feelings of pity and fear that Ceres and Proserpina's plight arouses among the spectators vanish as catharsis helps the spectators believe in the happy solution given by Jupiter. What then has made possible the transformation of a tragic separation into a New Greek Comedy? What causes the violence done to Proserpina and Ceres to be erased from the dénouement?

The opera is carefully organized to highlight the distress that Proserpina's abduction causes both mother and daughter. Proserpina's refusal of love is stressed in act 1 by Arethusa's description of Proserpina's pride first to Alpheus ("Si Proserpine est belle / Son coeur est fier et rigoureux" [Even though Proserpina is beautiful / Her heart is proud and severe], 1.5), and later to Pluto:

Cette fière Beauté s'obstine
A fuir les amants et l'Amour.
Dans l'innocent repos de cette solitude,
Elle évite les Dieux
De la Terre et des Cieux

[This proud beauty obstinately
Flees from lovers and Love.
In the innocent repose of this solitary place,
She avoids the Gods
Of the Earth and of the Heavens]

(2.6)

In a duet with her nymphs, Proserpine herself sings of the happiness of not having a sensitive heart: "Le vrai bonheur / Est de garder son coeur" [True happiness / Is keeping one's heart] (2.8). It is true though that she does not go as far as her nymphs in expressing her proud defense against love ("Pour nous défendre / D'un amour tendre / Avec fierté / Nous avons pris les armes" [To protect ourselves / Against a tender love / With pride / We have taken up arms], 2.8). One could interpret her parting from them to gather flowers as a figuration of a subconscious longing for another object of love than the "belles fleurs" [beautiful flowers] and "charmant ombrage" [charming umbrage] (2.8) she described as the only worthy object of love.

When Pluto's infernal divinities emerge from the underworld to abduct Proserpina at the close of act 2, Cyane complains of the eruption of their "barbare violence" [barbarian violence] into the idyllic setting of Ceres' retreat. Proserpina, previously shown gathering flowers for the return of her mother and singing of the simple happiness of her life free from love, calls in vain for help. Cyane is threatened with losing her voice should she denounce Pluto (2.9). The musical treatment contrasts Proserpina's plaintive song, Pluto's firm desire, and Proserpina's cries for help, although the chorus tries to sound reassuring.

To accentuate the sudden disruption of happiness caused by the rape, act 3 contrasts the grief of Proserpina's companions to the sweet anticipation of Ceres, who returns from her mission to Phrygia not suspecting any problem. Looking forward to seeing her daughter, Ceres describes her love as a "tendresse maternelle" [maternal affection] whose "empressement" [zeal] is greatly increased by her love for Jupiter because, as she admits to herself, "C'est Jupiter que j'aime en elle" [It is Jupiter whom I love in her] (3.4). She does not seem, however, to treat Proserpina as a compensation for Jupiter's neglect but rather as a dear proof of Jupiter's past love for her.

The spectators are made to feel for the mother's and the daughter's distress alike. Proserpina's disappearance deeply affects Ceres. She progresses from inquisitive disbelief to affliction (3.5), then to a pitiless devastation of the trees and crops she normally bestows on humanity (in an attempt to have their innocent clamor move the gods), and finally to an alliance with the rebellious forces of Hades (5.3). Her maternal sorrow is exasperated by the silence with which she is met whenever she inquires about her daughter, especially when she witnesses Cyane's metamorphosis into a brook (3.6). This powerful figuration of silence subsumes the other forms of silence her calls receive, starting with Proserpina's literal silence (3.4) and the nymphs' lack of information (3.5). One of the most poignant moments of the opera occurs when musical discord breaks through as Ceres expresses her mounting rage to the air: "Ah! quelle injustice cruelle" [Ah! what a cruel injustice] (3.7). Unable to understand why the gods repay her generosity and rectitude with cruelty and insults, she resolves to burn and devastate the lands she had blessed with crops. No less touching an air is "Déserts écartés, sombres lieux" [remote deserts, dark places] (5.2), which Ceres sings in a setting of bare desolation, as the stage directions indicate ("Le Théâtre . . . représente une solitude"), preceded by a somber prelude. Her jagged melody, marked by the highly dissonant tritone on "cachez" [hide] and the frequently shifting harmonies, emphasizes her distress. Acknowledging her ultimate defeat, she begs deserts and darkness to hide the tears that her immortal condition condemns her to shed forever.

Proserpina expresses in a more reserved, although no less touching, manner her distress at being separated from her mother and companions. However, her burden of solitude differs from that of her mother in that she is lonesome in the midst of the attentive companions Pluto has given her. Her sorrow contrasts sharply with the happy Shades' celebration of Hades' "bienheureuse vie" [blissful life] (4.1), as well as with their advice to accept Pluto's love (4.2–3). Nostalgia and discouragement dominate Proserpina's first air as a captive:

> Ma chère liberté, que vous aviez d'attraits!
> En vous perdant, hélas! que mon âme est atteinte
> De douleur, de trouble et de crainte!
> . . . .
> Faut-il vous perdre pour jamais?
>
> [My dear liberty, what attractions you have!
> In losing you, alas! how my soul is stricken
> With pain, with confusion and with fear.
> . . . .
> Must I lose you forever?]
>
> (4.2)

In the following scene, her grief increases as she discovers that Ascalaphus has betrayed her trust: he has shown her the dangerous fruit that could quench her thirst but failed to disclose the power of the seeds. Her outrage finds expression in her second air, "Je ne verrai jamais la lumière céleste!" [I shall never see heavenly light!], in which she condemns Ascalaphus to live in darkness and fear and changes him into an owl (4.3).

To Pluto, who pleads for a chance to teach her love, the young captive calls forth her right to "le bonheur qui m'était destiné" [the happiness that was intended for me], which is to live "sans amant" [without a lover] (4.5), and she denounces his cruelty. Pluto is moved enough to decide to win Proserpina's love and starts by suspending all pain in Hades.

As it is lived by Ceres and Proserpina, the mother-daughter relationship appears to be a strong bond that has been fed by happy times and a serene independence from other love relationships (this is equally true of mother and of daughter). Deprived of each other's company, they have both lost the source of their happiness: life has become death, an emotional reality for Proserpina and Ceres that the myth expresses with the Hades metaphor on the one hand and the destroyed crops and search for solitude on the other. In spite of its intensity, the mother-daughter relationship seems at quite a disadvantage when the situation calls for voicing it on its own merit. Ceres does not confront Jupiter in Quinault's libretto, as she does in both Ovidian accounts. Rather, she implores him once in absentia after she has learned of his failed attempt to set Proserpina free: "Grand Dieu! c'est votre fille aussi bien que la mienne; / C'est votre fille, hélas! / Ne l'abandonnez pas" [Great God! she is your daughter as well as mine; / Alas, she is your daughter! / Do not abandon her] (5.4). She has given up all hope and merely wishes to die peacefully and end her despair: "Sans troubler votre paix, j'irais suivre ses pas, / Si je pouvais passer dans la nuit du trépas" [Without disturbing your peace, I would follow her steps, / If I could pass into the night of death] (5.4).

One possible interpretation of this departure from the Ovidian account is to view Ceres' silence as pride: she will not stoop to moving Jupiter by her tears. Another approach is to attribute it to a pragmatic analysis of the rape: Ceres will not address Jupiter if she suspects him of complicity with Pluto (after all, her journey to Phrygia, which was made at Jupiter's request, helped make the abduction possible), or if she knows that mothers' rights carry no weight among the gods when opposed to those of a brother in love. Although both explanations could be sustained, our analysis of the happy tone given to the denouement points to a larger frame of interpretation. In renouncing aggressive behavior, Ceres leads the way to the acceptance of Proserpina's new fate. As we will show, Quinault's libretto erases as much violence as it can from the denouement. Whereas the Persephone myth responds to the challenge of a strong mother-daughter relationship by the sheer violence of rape sanctioned by the rule of the father, Quinault emphasizes the possibility of an acceptable compromise. In fact, Quinault's libretto undergirds the treatment of Proserpina's rape with a subtle interpretative subtext that takes the violence away from Proserpina's fate.

The development of Arethusa's love story and of Ceres' discussions of love may help the spectators relinquish a tragic interpretation of Proserpina's forced marriage. These two departures from Ovid serve to prepare, rehearse, and legitimize the marriage of Proserpina to Pluto. Indeed, they provide alternatives to the tragic life that seems to be in store for Proserpina. Far from being digressive fillers that have a detrimental effect on the unity of action, as some critics have argued, these two developments make the denouement psychologically and socially acceptable. Their ties to the action are not causal but interpretational.

At first, Arethusa models the conduct that frees her from fear and gives her happiness. Long attached to "fierté" and "rigueur" toward love (she had obtained Diana's protection to escape her suitor Alpheus, 1.3), she finally gives in to love (1.4) and to Alpheus (2.5). Later on, when she visits Proserpina in Hades, she encourages her to accept Pluto's love (4.3). Pluto himself pleads love as the cause of his abduction and cunningly invites Proserpina to exchange the sorrowful sighs she gives for her mother for the "[doux] soupirs d'amour" [[sweet] sighs of love] (4.4). The pressure to let love transform and redeem the rape extends to the chorus of the nymphs, who argue that "Pluton aime mieux que Cérès. / Une mère / Vaut-elle un époux?" [Pluto loves better than Ceres. / Is a mother / As good as a husband?] (4.5).

Ceres proposes a more complex model in her own relationship with Jupiter. Unlike Arethusa or her own daughter, she takes no stand against love. She is the one to advise Arethusa to "Aimez sans vous contraindre; / Aimez à votre tour. / C'est déjà ressentir l'amour, / Que de commencer à le craindre" [Love without constraint; / It is your turn to love. / One is already feeling love / When one begins to fear it] (1.3). Through her life, she also gives the example of her faithfulness to the unfaithful king of the heavens, stating that she finds happiness in cherishing her daughter, the testimony of the king's love, and suggesting that such behavior can win back a lover's attention. It is, however, her response to Jupiter's ruling on her daughter's rape that is most telling. We recall the words by which Ceres expresses her reaction to the god's decision: "Qu'un bien qu'on avait perdu / Est doux, quand il est rendu / Par les soins de ce qu'on aime!" [How something one has lost / Is pleasant when it is returned / Thanks to the person one loves!] (5.5). In other words, Ceres finds the compromise satisfactory, although as a mother she must renounce both her wish to spend all her days with her daughter and the promise made by destiny that Proserpina would remain unwed. Jupiter's lover takes precedence over Proserpina's mother.

Arethusa's and Ceres' submissions to their lovers' law parallel the submission that is required of Proserpina. Pluto's persistence, combined with the fact that Proserpina's request seems to have been heard although not fully granted, will melt her youthful rejection of love. From a structural point of view, the three female characters developed in the opera are similarly moved from resistance to acceptance of men's love practices. Love is a rhetorical figure for men's desires. What is at stake, of course, goes beyond the fulfillment of male sexuality. It is rather a model of social order based on men's drives where women are to accept (without resistance) the call of love, or "L'Amour qui vous appelle," [Love that calls you], as Ceres puts it to Arethusa (1.3). Our analysis of Arethusa's and Ceres' behavior shows that, in *Proserpine,* to accept the call of love is to admit that a woman is happy when bowing to a lover's ardor but also when retaining her love for him after his ardor has cooled, because maternity can be viewed as an acceptable substitute, so to speak, for the departed father/lover.

Significantly, when Proserpina appears in the final scenes of the opera, she is not given voice either in favor of or against her marriage. Nor does Pluto comment on the ruling, contenting himself with attending the ceremony by the side of his wife-to-be. Her silence can easily be explained by conventions of verisimilitude within the diegetic world of the opera; nonetheless, Proserpina's silence is a powerful rhetorical figure leaving the spectators with no direct information on the heroine's level of acceptance of the decision.

Given this silence, the function of Arethusa's and Ceres' submissions to love is not only to soothe the spectator by removing the certainty of lasting distress for Proserpina but also to propose a consensus on the conditions under which relationships between men and women can harmoniously operate. Thus, by intertwining Arethusa's story with that of Proserpina and by making Ceres an exemplary advocate of love—a departure from Ovidian accounts—Quinault and Lully rewrite the myth of Proserpina. Erasing its violence, they transform it into the prelude to an auspicious marriage that seals peace among all parties while bringing to each his or her measure of contentment.

THE RECEPTION OF *PROSERPINE* AND FORCED MARRIAGES

To a society fascinated by rape scenes, Quinault and Lully's *Proserpine* provides an interpretative grid that applies equally to mythological rapes and to similar handlings of mother-daughter relationships. Quinault and Lully's downplaying of Proserpina's personal drama is in tune with the prevailing mood at Louis XIV's court. To their contemporaries, the rhetorical figure of exile to a kingdom of death could evoke many a marriage made necessary by French diplomacy or family affairs, but such marriages did not become synonymous with cruelty. However unappealing they might have been, they were sanctioned by society. The distressed bride-to-be could only hope for the sympathy of a close relative or her maid. Her entourage, mother and friends alike, would advise her to learn to love her imposed husband; they would represent to her the advantages of her marriage, appealing to her sense of pride and duty and, if necessary, to Christian values. Whether at the highest levels of the court or in the towns and rural areas, women were given by fathers or tutors to husbands they did not choose. Convents provided an alternative only when the families were well off and consenting. Legally, women were dependents of either their fathers or husbands. Unless they chose loose manners, they had to wait for widowhood to be able to have a say in the possession of their bodies or the conduct of their affairs.[4] The consensus extended to literary texts as well. Women's challenges to marriage or resistance to gallantry (as defined by the men)—Madeleine de Scudéry's *Clélie* is a case in point—were portrayed as deviant and ridiculous (e.g., Molière's *Précieuses ridicules* and *Femmes savantes,* Sommaize's *Dictionnaire des Prétieuses*). Even their fear of maternity, often a cause of death, was unlikely to earn them respect or compassion.

With such a convergence of values, *Proserpine* would not stand out by the originality of the solution it proposed to forced marriage. Nevertheless, *Proserpine* moved seventeenth-century French society to an extent not recorded before. Sévigné wrote to her daughter that "L'opéra est au-dessus de tous les autres" [The opera is above all the others] (February 9, 1680). Lully's music was praised, Quinault was said to have outdone himself, and everyone admired the dances, rich costumes, and beautiful scenery (especially the Elysian Fields and Pluto's Palace in acts 4 and 5). It seems, however, that the opera made its strongest and most durable impression with its depiction of the mother's grief over the loss of her daughter. At first, courtiers likened Ceres to Madame de Montespan, whom the king was neglecting somewhat (Sévigné 1974, February 9, 1680). But soon other interpretations took hold. Sévigné reported that her friends said that Ceres and Proserpina represented her and her daughter, while Pluto was M. de Grignan, her son-in-law (March 1, 1680). Shortly afterwards, the Princess Palatine's furious protest against the king and Monsieur, who had decided to marry her son to Mademoiselle de Blois, illegitimate daughter of Louis XIV by Madame de Montespan, brought back the image of Ceres searching for her daughter. It is this metaphor that Saint-Simon recalled when he described the incident in his memoirs: "Madame . . . marchait à grands pas, son mouchoir à la main, pleurant sans contrainte, parlant assez haut, gesticulant, et représentant fort bien Cérès après l'enlèvement de sa fille Proserpine, la cherchant en fureur et la redemandant à Jupiter" [Madame . . . strode along, her handkerchief in her hand, crying unabashedly, speaking rather loudly, gesticulating, a very good figuration of Ceres after the abduction of her daughter Proserpina, furiously looking for her and asking Jupiter to return her] (Van der Cruysse 1988, 346; Saint-Simon 1889–1928, 1:72–73).

However, when the opera was revived in 1727, forty-seven years after its first performance, *Proserpine* had lost much of its power to move the public. French society had lost its sensitivity to the plight of a mother and daughter separated against their will. In his long report, the critic of *Le Mercure de France* writes:

> Nous ne nous arrêterons pas à donner un Extrait de la Tragédie . . . entre les mains de tout le monde . . . . Nous mettrons seulement ici ce qu'on en pense aujourd'hui. On trouve que l'intérêt principal n'en est pas assez vif; les regrets d'une Mère à qui on a enlevé une Fille bien chère, n'ont pas produit sur les coeurs l'effet que l'Auteur en avait attendu.
>
> On est pourtant forcé d'avouer à la gloire de l'Actrice qui représente Cérès, que si quelque chose a dû faire réussir cet Opéra, c'est la manière vive et pathétique par laquelle son rôle est chanté et joué.
>
> [We shall not take the time to give a summary of the tragedy . . . in the hands of everyone . . . . We shall only state here what one thinks of it today. It is thought that the main subject is not vivid enough; the complaints of a mother whose beloved

daughter has been abducted did not touch the heart in the way the Author had expected.

Nevertheless, one has to admit to the credit of the Actress who plays Ceres, that if something could ensure the success of this opera, it is the vivid and pathetic manner in which her part is sung and played.] (February 1727, 349–50)

Contrasted with the reception of *Proserpine* in 1680, this review by *Le Mercure de France,* which clearly distinguishes between the effect of the plot and of the performance itself, suggests an erosion of the public's sensitivity to the plight of a mother whose daughter has been abducted. The personal drama suffered by the individuals involved did not suffice for dramatic interest. Yet there is no evidence that abductions and forced marriages occurred less frequently in the beginning of the eighteenth century. This change in reception leads us to infer, with due caution, that the power of Quinault and Lully's opera to move the 1680 public had to do with a less clearly defined consensus on how to respond to abductions and forced marriages.

In 1680, the law pertaining to abductions and rapes was the 1639 Ordnance on marriages performed without the consent of the parents and proper procedures. Young men and women who had married without parental consent or had chosen partners of inappropriate social status were liable to be punished by death. However, the courts were satisfied with the annulment of the marriage and disinheritance of the youth and all children born out of it. The Ordnance did not allow the abductor or, technically, the parents to legalize the abduction or seduction by a subsequent and lawful marriage, which had been the practice encouraged by the church since the Council of Trent and even the time of Gratian (eleventh century) (see Gravdal 1991, 6–11; Brundage 1987). In the 1660s, General Prosecutor Talon urged that the letter of the law be applied. The courts tried to stop the social disorder fostered by past leniency, but in so doing, they ended up blind to cases in which the families had accepted the facts and shown signs of reconciliation. There was, of course, pressure on the courts to rule in favor of a third party who would benefit should the inheritance be denied to the disobedient child. Nonetheless, some lawyers called for a more sensible interpretation of the spirit of the Ordnance. Although further research might reveal additional reasons for the change of sensitivity between the 1680s and the 1720s regarding the myth of

Persephone, it seems that the public of Lully and Quinault could not close its heart to the plight of women, mothers or daughters, who fell the victims of male decisions.

ART AND POLITICS IN THE SERVICE OF THE KING

Broadening the scope of our inquiry, we now examine how the sociohistorical circumstances under which *Proserpine* was composed for Louis XIV relate to our analysis. Although the seventeenth-century public, especially the court, delighted in finding correlations between classical mythology and current events or people, it is difficult to state with any certainty whether artists were influenced by major political events in the choice of their subjects. It is, however, worth noting that at about the time Quinault and Lully chose to work on *Proserpine* (summer 1679) (see Bussy 1858, 4:395), Louis XIV was asked to marry Marie-Louise of Orléans, daughter of the late Henrietta of England and Monsieur, his brother, to the young but gloomy and degenerate king of Spain, Charles II, son of Philippe IV. Negotiations had started at the end of April 1679, swiftly conducted by the ambassador extraordinary from Spain, Los Balbazes, who had direct orders from Charles II, very much in love with Marie-Louise's portrait, to ask for no territorial concessions or dowry and to hasten the process while the Queen Mother was in political exile. The marriage was part of the Nimwegen Treaties (August 1678–February 1679) with Spain, but Charles's request came as a surprise, given the long-held Spanish distrust of the French. When Louis XIV agreed to the plans on June 30, Monsieur rejoiced at having his daughter become the queen of Spain, but Marie-Louise, who was seventeen and had never imagined leaving the French court she loved (she hoped to marry the Dauphin), cried excessively. She did not move her uncle the king, who entrusted her with the mission to be as good a queen of Spain as Marie-Thérèse of Spain had been of France. Before Marie-Louise's departure on September 20, 1679, the king firmly stated his goodbye: "Madame, je souhaite de vous dire adieu pour jamais; ce serait le plus grand malheur qui vous pût arriver que de revoir la France" [I wish never to see you again. It would be the greatest misfortune that could befall you should you see France again] (Sévigné 1974, September 27, 1679). Louis XIV feared that Marie-Louise would try to obtain a repudiation, thus allowing the Spanish Queen Mother to remarry her son to a Hapsburg and reform the old Hapsburg's encirclement

Pluto Abducting Proserpina (1699), by François Girardon. Reprinted by permission of the Reunion des Musées Nationaux.

Pluto Abducting Proserpina (detail), by François Girardon. Reprinted by permission of the Reunion des Musées Nationaux.

of France (Van der Druysse 1988, 246; Primi Visconti 1988, 134; Basenne 1939, 28; Sévigné 1974, September 27, 1679).

Louis XIV valued highly his role in the Nimwegen Treaties and even more his wise planning for the Spanish succession. No one at the court would have dared take Marie-Louise's side. Sévigné is quite pitiless when she describes the sorrow of the queen of Spain:

> La reine d'Espagne crie toujours miséricorde, et se jette aux pieds de tout le monde; je ne sais pas comment l'orgueil d'Espagne s'accommode de ces désespoirs. Elle arrêta l'autre jour le Roi par delà l'heure de la messe; il lui dit: "Madame, ce serait une belle chose que la *Reine Catholique* empêchât le *Roi Très Catholique* d'aller à la messe." On dit qu'ils seront tous fort aises d'être défaits de cette catholique.
>
> [The queen of Spain still begs for mercy, and throws herself at everyone's feet; I do not know how Spain's pride puts up with these marks of despair. The other day she stopped the King after the time for mass to start; he said to her, "Madame, it would be a fine thing if the *Catholic Queen* prevented the *Very Catholic King* from going to mass." Rumor has it that everyone will be quite happy to be rid of this catholic.] (Sévigné 1974, September 18, 1679; see also September 15, 20, and 27, 1679)

A mother herself who cries her heart out whenever her daughter departs for Provence, she has only one word of sympathy for the young bride: a lasting peace with France's neighbors requires this marriage, and Marie-Louise's happiness is no issue in the balance.

There are conflicting accounts in the seventeenth- and eighteenth-century sources on how Quinault and Lully selected the subjects of their *tragédies lyriques*. The best known is that of Le Cerf de la Viéville:

> Quinault cherchait et dressait plusieurs sujets d'opéra. Ils les portaient au Roi, qui en choisissait un. Alors Quinault écrivait un plan du dessein et de la suite de sa pièce. Il donnait une copie de ce plan à Lully . . . . Quinault composait ses scènes: aussitôt qu'il en avait achevé quelques-unes, il les montrait à l'Académie Française, dont vous savez qu'il était: après avoir recueilli et mis à profit les avis de l'Académie, il aportait ces scènes à Lulli . . . . [Lully] examinait mot à mot cette poésie.
>
> [Quinault sought out and drew up several subjects for operas. He took them to the King, who chose one of them. Then Quinault wrote a plan of the design and sequence. He gave a copy of this plan to Lully . . . . Quinault wrote up his scenes: as soon as he had finished some of them, he showed them to the Académie Française, to which as you know he belonged: after having gathered and put to profit the opinions of the Academy, he took the scenes to Lully . . . . [Lully] examined word for word this poetry.] (Le Cerf 1704–6, 2:212–13, 214)

The other account suggests that Louis XIV left the final choice to the Académie. In the first published proceedings of the Académie Royale des Inscriptions et des Belles-Lettres, we read that "quand M. Quinault fut chargé de travailler pour le Roi aux tragédies en musique, Sa Majesté lui enjoignit expressément de consulter l'Académie" [when Quinault was directed to work for the king in the production of Tragedies in music, His Majesty directly commanded him to consult with the Academy] (*Histoire de l'Académie royale . . .*, 1:4; Donington 1981, 289, after Bonnet 1969, 195 ff.).

As far as *Proserpine* is concerned, it is tempting to infer from Lully's dedication to the king that the composer wanted to celebrate the peace that Louis XIV's victory over Holland, Spain, and the emperor, as well as his generosity at the Nimwegen Treaties, had restored in Europe. Lully says he aims at making his works "dignes, s'il est possible, de l'attention du Vainqueur de mille Nations différentes, du Pacificateur de l'Europe, de l'Arbitre souverain du Monde" [worthy, if possible, of the attention of the Conqueror of a thousand different Nations, of the Pacifier of Europe, of the sovereign Arbiter of the World] (Quinault 1680). Lully had already composed *Bellérophon* (1679) in honor of the king's triumph, but the extraordinary success of this opera could have encouraged him to glorify the king's achievement again (Gros 1926, 128–29; *Le Mercure galant*, January 1680, 300–301). The parallel between Proserpina's marriage and Louis XIV's final peace arrangements with Spain could further seduce the composer or those who had the responsibility to choose the subject, making the Persephone myth a most appropriate choice for the winter's new opera. The choice was ingenious. Not only was it flattering to the king's image because it equated his power to that of Jupiter after his victory over the Titans, but it also demonstrated the authors' esprit, the highest quality a person could have. A half-century later, *Le Mercure de France* complimented the ingeniousness of *Proserpine*'s prologue when the opera was revived in February 1727 (346–47).

The parallel also had the merit of presenting Jupiter–Louis XIV as a ruler concerned with long-term peace and his subjects' happiness. Marie-Louise's marriage also sealed an old promise made to the king of Spain: in 1672, Louis XIV had proposed to engage Charles II to his daughter Marie-Thérèse, who was to die at age five.

Although it is not possible to prove a direct causal relationship between the creation of *Proserpine* and Marie-Louise of Orléans' marriage, it is likely that some of these considerations, especially those that sought to enhance the king's image, favored the final choice of the subject. Needless to say, strict political sense demanded a happy treatment of the parallel, as did any understanding of what art in the service of the king ought to be. Quinault and Lully's opera had to show Proserpina happy, or at least reconciled, with her imposed marriage and her new life as a queen. Similarly, Ceres' grief and anger, which was so pathetically represented in the body of the opera, had to be dissolved in reconciliation and thankfulness. The rape, the violence by which the marriage had been born, could not cast its shadow over the final scene. Jupiter's glory required the happy submission of mother and daughter alike. A woman's fate was not to be an issue in the balance.

Whereas Ovidian accounts of the myth leave Proserpina a victim of brute sexual desire and readers unsure about her feelings and those of Ceres as they submit to Jupiter's ruling, Quinault and Lully make the mother and daughter's defeat acceptable: Ceres tells of her satisfaction, and we are led to imagine Proserpina happy to share her time between Pluto's palace and her mother's flowering fields. Moreover, the opera makes the mother-daughter defeat seem desirable and Proserpina's rape a blessing in disguise. *Proserpine* is so written that it draws the spectators first to identify with Ceres' and Proserpine's protests in acts 3 to 4, and then to withdraw support from them as Pluto readies his troops for war and Ceres goes into a delirium of mourning, a hysteria she channels into destruction. The mother-daughter submission cannot fail to be perceived as a political or rather a universal necessity: any prolonged resistance on the part of Ceres would entail the destruction of the universe. In more everyday terms, the opera prescribes that the two troublesome women reenter society and accept that they will be, if not nonentities, little more than love objects, necessary to soothe men's desires. The patriarchal state can maintain peace and harmony in the world only as long as it is able to keep women from defining their fate independently.

Our view of the power structure of the myth thus differs from the case David McClelland makes for a Demeter-Persephone life style (1975, especially 96–99). Although his perspective finds some support in Cyane's defense of the mother-daughter couple in Ovid's *Metamorphoses* (V, 414–20), Quinault and Lully do not mention this alternative to married life. The primary motivation of Proserpina's rape is the capture and domestication of a woman. Two centuries prior to the grand operas of the nineteenth century, *Proserpine* dramatizes what Catherine Clément calls the "undoing of women" (1988).

Political imperatives, marital practices, and aesthetic catharsis converged to give the myth of Persephone an unusual timeliness, and Quinault and Lully's *Proserpine* appealed both to Louis XIV's court and to the Parisian public in 1680. Astute members of the audiences of Quinault and Lully's opera could easily find in its version of the Persephone myth a tale of prudent sexual politics in a monarchical world.

NOTES

1. Michèle Vialet wishes to thank the Charles Phelps Taft Memorial Fund for its 1989 summer research grant in support of this project. Since this chapter was submitted, several decisive studies of rape in literature have appeared in print, especially the invaluable study by Kathryn Gravdal (1991) and the volume edited by Higgins and Silver (1991). Our analysis of Quinault and Lully's erasure of violence in the interest of a peaceful solution concurs closely with a number of observations Gravdal makes on the use of rape in various medieval genres.

2. Spelling has been modernized in this and other quotations. English translations are our own, as they are of other works quoted, unless otherwise indicated.

On this statuary, see Néraudeau 1986, 225; Marie 1968, 1:160–61; Nolhac 1901, 153–54. On Le Brun's debt to Ripa, see Mâle 1951, 412; Walton 1986, 85; Apostolidès 1981, 91–92. On the presence of disorder in Ovid's portrayal of the gods, see Néraudeau 1986, 16–18, 158, 165. On rape, violence, and social order, see Brownmiller 1975; Bryson 1986; Porter 1986.

3. Quinault 1970, prologue. This is the only edition readily available; there is no edition with line numbers. Subsequent act and scene numbers in parentheses in discussions of *Proserpine* refer to this edition.

4. In Charles Sorel's *Francion*, Agathe and Laurette are examples of the former choice; Célimène in Molière's *Le Misanthrope* and the princess of Clèves in Lafayette's novel represent the latter. For a historical study, see Lougee 1976.

BIBLIOGRAPHY

Anthony, James R. *French Baroque Music from Beaujoyeulx to Rameau.* Rev. ed. New York: Norton, 1974.

Anton, Herbert. *Der Raub des Proserpine: Literarische Traditionen eines erotischen Sinnbildes und mythischen Symbols.* Heidelberg: Carl Winter Universitätsverlag, 1967.

Apostolidès, Jean-Marie. *Le Roi-machine: spectacle et politique au temps de Louis XIV.* Paris: Minuit, 1981.
Bassenne, M. *La Vie tragique d'une reine d'Espagne. Marie-Louise de Bourbon-Orléans, nièce de Louis XIV.* Paris: Calmann-Lévy, 1939.
Boileau-Despréaux, Nicolas. *Oeuvres.* Edited by Georges Mongrédien. Paris: Garnier, 1961.
Bonnet, Jacques. *Histoire de la musique et de ses effets.* Paris, 1715. Reprint. Geneva: Slatkine, 1969.
Brownmiller, Susan. *Against Our Will: Men, Women, and Rape.* New York: Simon and Schuster, 1975.
Brundage, James A. *Law, Sex, and Christian Society in Medieval Europe.* Chicago: Univ. of Chicago Press, 1987.
Bryson, Norman. "Two Narratives of Rape in the Visual Arts: Lucretia and the Sabine Women." In *Rape,* edited by Sylvana Tomaselli and Roy Porter, 152–73. London: Blackwell, 1986.
Bussy, Roger de Rabutin, comte de. *Correspondance avec sa famille et ses amis (1666–1693).* Edited by Ludovic Lalanne. 6 vols. Paris: Charpentier, 1858.
Cessac, Catherine. *Marc-Antoine Charpentier.* Paris: Fayard, 1988.
Clément, Catherine. *Opera, or the Undoing of Women.* Translated by Betsy Wing. Minneapolis: Univ. of Minnesota Press, 1988.
Donington, Robert. *The Rise of Opera.* London: Faber and Faber, 1981.
Duron, Jean. "*Atys: Commentaire Musical et Littéraire.*" *L'Avant-Scène Opéra* 94 (1987): 30–85.
Grannis, Valeria Belt. *Dramatic Parody in Eighteenth-Century France.* New York: Publications of the Institute of French Studies, 1931.
Gravdal, Kathryn. *Ravishing Maidens: Writing Rape in Medieval French Literature and Law.* Philadelphia: Univ. of Pennsylvania Press, 1991.
Gros, Etienne. *Philippe Quinault, sa vie et son oeuvre.* Paris: Champion, 1926.
Grout, Donald J. "Seventeenth-Century Parodies of French Opera." *Musical Quarterly* 27 (1941): 211–19, 514–26.
Higgins, Lynn A., and Brenda R. Silver, eds. *Rape and Representation.* New York: Columbia Univ. Press, 1991.
Histoire de l'Académie royale des inscriptions et belles-lettres, depuis son establissement jusqu'à présent. Edited by M. de Boze. 51 vols. Paris: Imprimerie Royale, 1736–1809.
Isherwood, Robert. *Music in the Service of the King: France in the Seventeenth Century.* Ithaca, N.Y.: Cornell Univ. Press, 1973.
Lajarte, Théodore de. *Bibliothèque Musicale du Théâtre de l'Opéra.* Paris: Librairie Des Bibliophiles, 1878.
Lancaster, Henry Carrington. *French Dramatic Literature in the Seventeenth Century.* 4 vols. Baltimore: Johns Hopkins Univ. Press, 1929–42.

Le Cerf de la Viéville, Jean-Laurent, sieur de Freneuse. *Comparaison de la musique italienne et de la musique françoise.* Brussels, 1704–6. Reprint. Geneva: Minkoff Reprints, 1972.

Loewenberg, Alfred. *Annals of Opera.* 3d ed. Geneva: Societas Bibliographica, 1978.

Lougee, Carolyn. *Le Paradis Des Femmes: Women, Salons, and Social Stratification in Seventeenth-Century France.* Princeton: Princeton Univ. Press, 1976.

McClelland, David. *Power: The Inner Experience.* New York: Irvington, 1975.

Mâle, Emile. *L'Art religieux de la fin du XVIe siècle, du XVIIe siècle et du XVIIIe siècle: Étude sur l'iconographie après le Concile de Trente.* 2d ed., rev. Paris: Armand Colin, 1951.

Marie, Alfred. *Naissance de Versailles.* Paris: Vincent, Fréal, et Cie., 1968.

Négociations Relatives à la Succession D'Espagne sous Louis XIV. Edited by M. Mignet. 4 vols. Paris: Imprimerie Royale, 1842.

Néraudeau, Jean-Pierre. *L'Olympe du Roi-Soleil. Mythologie et idéologie royale au Grand Siècle.* Paris: Belles-Lettres, 1986.

Niderst, Alain. *Regards sur l'Opéra.* Paris: Presses Universitaires de France, 1976.

Nolhac, Pierre. *La Création de Versailles.* Versailles: Bernard, 1901.

Otis, Brooks. *Ovid as an Epic Poet.* Cambridge: Cambridge Univ. Press, 1970.

Pitou, Serge. *The Paris Opera: An Encyclopedia of Operas, Ballets, Composers, and Performers. Rococo and Romantic, 1715–1815.* Westport, Conn.: Greenwood Press, 1983.

Porter, Roy. "Rape—Does It Have a Historical Meaning?" In *Rape*, edited by Sylvana Tomaselli and Roy Porter, 216–36. London: Blackwell, 1986.

Primi Visconti, Jean-Baptiste. *Mémoires sur la cour de Louis XIV, 1673–1681.* Edited by J.-F. Solnon. Paris: Perrin, 1988.

Quinault, Philippe. *Proserpine.* Libretto. Paris: Ballard, 1680.

———. *Théâtre de Quinault, contenant ses Tragedies, Comedies et Opera.* Paris, 1778. Reprint. Geneva: Slatkine, 1970.

Rigal, Eugène. *Alexandre Hardy.* Paris: Hachette, 1989.

Ripa, Cesare. *Iconologie.* Translated by Jean Baudouin. 2 vols. Paris, 1636. Reprint, New York: Garland, 1976.

Saint-Simon, Duc de. *Mémoires.* Edited by A. de Boislisle. 39 vols. Paris: Hachette, 1889–1928.

Sartori, Claudio. *I Libretti italiani a stampa dalle origini al 1800.* 5 vols. Cuneo: Bertold e Locatelli Musica, 1991.

Schneider, Herbert. "Proserpine." *Dictionnaire de la musique en France au XVIIe et XVIIIe siècles.* Edited by Marcelle Benoît. Paris: Fayard, 1992.

Schneider, Herbert. *Die Rezeption des Opern Lullys im Frankreich des Ancien Regime.* Tützing: Hans Schneider, 1982.

Sévigné, Madame de. *Correspondance.* Edited by Roger Duchêne. 3 vols. Bibliothèque de la Pléiade. Paris: Gallimard, 1974.

Sonneck, O. G.-Th. *Catalogue of Opera Librettos Printed Before 1800.* Washington, D.C.: Government Printing Office, 1914.
Van der Cruysse, Dirk. *Madame Palatine, princesse européenne.* Paris: Fayard, 1988.
Walton, Guy. *Louis XIV's Versailles.* Chicago: Univ. of Chicago Press, 1986.

Laura Laffrado

CHAPTER 5

THE PERSEPHONE MYTH IN HAWTHORNE'S *TANGLEWOOD TALES*

Nathaniel Hawthorne's *Tanglewood Tales* (1853), a collection of classical myths retold for children, includes "The Pomegranate-Seeds," a retelling of the Persephone myth. Hawthorne's revision of the myth was emblematic of recent events in his life. In the story, both Ceres and Proserpina are rendered helpless by circumstances, suffer irrevocable loss, and, with altered expectations and the burden of experience, reshape their lives around their new, confined circumstances.

Robert D. Richardson argues that Hawthorne (and Charles Kingsley and Thomas Bulfinch after him) was "not interested in the Greek qualities of Greek myth" and that the use of "Roman sources and Roman names" combined with the popularity of such works "is one reason for the marked Romanizing of Greek myth, which still persists" (1972, 506). Hawthorne's major source for the myths is Charles Anthon's 1841 *Classical Dictionary*, a popular handbook on mythology. Anthon "pieces together all of the classical fragments," drawing from "Homer, Aristotle, Pliny, Appollodorus, Eustathius, Philostratus, and so on" (McPherson 1969, 71, 84). Hugo McPherson's *Hawthorne as Myth-Maker* usefully compares Hawthorne's additions and omissions in the myths with the information given in Anthon's *Dictionary*.

Tanglewood Tales was Hawthorne's last completed book of fiction written in America and his final children's book. Written two years after the successful *A Wonder-Book for Boys and Girls* as a sequel to that work, it is by no means the sunny and happy work that the first collection is proclaimed to be. Nina Baym has stated the comparison clearly: "Unfortunately, when he attempted to replicate his achievement eighteen months later in *Tanglewood Tales,* he lost his magic touch; the second book of children's myths is a much more grim affair" (1976, 179).

Much had happened to Hawthorne during the months between his writing of the two books: the Hawthornes had moved across Massachusetts from Lenox to Concord; Hawthorne's sister, Louisa, on her way to visit them in Concord, had drowned in July 1852; his wife's mother had died in early 1853; pre–Civil War rumblings were becoming increasingly insistent; Hawthorne's friendship with Herman Melville, at its peak during the writing of *A Wonder-Book,* no longer colored his daily life; and, despite Hawthorne's growing fame as a writer, it was increasingly clear that his writing would provide, at best, a slender means of existence. Such events reached to the heart of Hawthorne's worldview and altered the way he had previously approached the use of classical myth in *A Wonder-Book.*

Roy Harvey Pearce has stressed "Hawthorne's insistent belief, one which runs through virtually all of his writing, that childhood is that period of life in which innocence, directness, and clarity are paramount facts. It was a period that had inevitably to be left behind once the child entered upon the tragic rigors of adulthood. Yet it could be remembered, recovered in the imagination, so as to serve as a measure of what the adult had lost and what he had gained" (1972, 306). In *Tanglewood Tales,* Hawthorne looks to classical myth for the scenarios and themes of loss that he could not otherwise express. By privileging the events of the myth, he is able to discover what he "had lost and what he had gained," a discovery allowed by his exploration of the archetype he chooses.

In "The Pomegranate-Seeds," Hawthorne's Proserpina is much younger than most Persephones. She is old enough to pick flowers while her mother ripens the harvest and young enough to be disobeying her mother by doing so. As she tugs at the roots of an enchanted shrub, the ground opens and Pluto drives out, snatches her up, and speeds off in his chariot toward Hades. Neglected by her mother (Ceres is condemned for being away from her child), disobedient, inexperienced (unable to recognize an enchanted shrub

"It is the only one in the world," said the servant. Illustration by Milo Winter, from the 1913 edition of Nathaniel Hawthorne's *Tanglewood Tales.*

when she sees one), and too weak to do more than scream feebly as she is abducted, Proserpina is presented as a victim (had Ceres not been away . . .), a foolish child, and a female in a stereotypical rape scenario (in the arms of a dark, male stranger much larger than she, she screams weakly, drops her flowers, and shields her face with her golden hair). Beyond these common images, however, is the central fact that Proserpina's epistemology was inadequate for her circumstances: she could not read the signs, and so she suffers and learns.

Ceres fails to protect her daughter from this classic separation anxiety come to life, fails to hear her daughter's faint cries, and fails to prevent the abduction of her child. The text encourages a view of Ceres as weak and negligent by showing Proserpina's screaming resulting in "many mothers . . . [running] quickly to see if any mischief had befallen their children."[1] In this retelling of the myth, other mothers are alert to their children's potential danger, but Ceres is not. To promote Ceres' neglect further, toward the end of the journey to Hades, Proserpina actually sees Ceres "making the corn grow, and too busy to notice the golden chariot as it went rattling along! The child mustered all her strength, gave one more scream, but was out of sight before Ceres had time to turn her head" (302). Ceres, the representative of organic life, is too busy with the earth's fertility to notice the product of her own fertility.

In thriving as earth mother, she has apparently neglected to nurture her own child. In Hawthorne's version of this myth, Ceres' concern with larger issues of fertility results in her paying the price always envisioned by a punitive culture for the "bad" mother: she loses her child. Not only does Hawthorne accept this price without question, he revises Anthon (and thus Anthon's classical sources) to assign blame to Ceres for Proserpina's kidnapping. This narrative change increases the pain of Ceres' loss—not only has her child been taken from her (as in classical myth versions), but, Hawthorne implies, she could have prevented it.

Imprisoned in Hades, Proserpina initially clings to the past, refusing Pluto's offer of water from Lethe and refusing to eat or drink. She will not be nurtured without her nurturing mother. She soon adjusts to her enclosure, however, telling Pluto, "I love you a little" (324) and declaring that only fruit would tempt her to eat. Once she is given a pomegranate, "dry, old, withered" though it is, the seeds "somehow or other" reach her mouth, "that little red cave" (325). Her own desire in this clearly sexual scene seals her bond with Pluto.

The reduction of Proserpina's age is intended to desexualize her and thus to sanitize the myth for children. The element of sexuality, however, has not been sanitized; instead, it has gone underground. The sexual innuendo in the pomegranate scene is coded sexuality located in little red caves and significant seeds. Sexuality is hidden, not eliminated. Hawthorne's version also implies that Pluto's desires are platonic. References to Pluto's rape of Proserpina in classical myth are encoded in the abduction, forced stay in Hades, and sexual innuendo. The strategy to desexualize the myth by reducing Proserpina's age fails.

The unappealing condition of the pomegranate that Pluto offers Proserpina (reflecting Pluto's own unappealing sexuality) is the result of Ceres' refusal to nurture the earth while she is unable to nurture her daughter. During Proserpina's stay in Hades, Ceres wanders nearly witless searching for her daughter, having abandoned all other work—the work, indeed, that resulted in her absence during her daughter's abduction. Now, in Proserpina's absence, both mother and earth are barren. Hawthorne's use of the archetype here promotes the barrenness that results from loss: loss of a loved one, loss of hope, loss of identity.

Proserpina is rescued eventually and returned to her mother, who mourns to learn that Proserpina has put six seeds in her mouth and so is only half-restored to her. Proserpina's cheerfulness contrasts with her mother's grief: Proserpina declares, "[I] can bear to spend six months in his palace, if he will only let me spend the other six with you" (329). As the sentence suggests, Pluto now controls Proserpina; he has the power to permit her to spend time with her mother. And Proserpina herself is no longer a baby. She has learned self-control and has acquired a sense of identity.

This new identity is not only separate from her mother's identity but can be read as the antithesis of Ceres' identity. Proserpina's happiness in the enclosure of Hades reveals her betrayal of her mother and her mother's values. She chooses a life—enclosed and thus secure, inorganic and thus barren—that is a kind of death. Her cheerfulness reflects her self-control and newly acquired sense of identity: she is no longer just her mother's child.

Hawthorne's choosing to make Proserpina happy with Pluto and her life in Hades is a significant change from classical versions of the myth and from Anthon's treatment of the myth. Other versions, however, clearly show Pluto as rapist, Proserpina as victim. "The Pomegranate-Seeds" encourages a reading of Pluto as lonely and Proserpina as a sunny child who can change his life with her youthful spirits. Indeed, the text insists on Proserpina's happiness. Yet that happiness is marred by the events that have led up to it (abduction, imprisonment in Hades) and by the restrictions that must follow. The giddy rush of language with which Proserpina responds to her mother's grief ends the story, effectively cutting off any further response by Ceres or any intrusion of mournful facts: "'Do not speak so harshly of poor King Pluto,' said Proserpina, kissing her mother. 'He has some very good qualities. . . . He certainly did very wrong to carry me off; but then, as he says, it was but a dismal sort of life for him, to live in that great, gloomy place, all alone; and it has made a wonderful change in his spirits, to have a little girl to run up stairs and down. There is some comfort in making him so happy; and so, upon the whole, dearest mother, let us be thankful that he is not to keep me the whole year round!'" (329). Proserpina is shown to have come to terms with her losses and to be ready, in her maturity, to proceed with diminished expectations.

This submission, however, need not be overrated. Proserpina's identity may be shaped by a strange, powerful man instead of by her dear, powerful mother, but that does not alter her heritage. Although Hawthorne may chastise Ceres for her inability to protect her child, he cannot alter her inherent power; she is, after all, a goddess. With such a powerful woman as her parent, Proserpina gains enough authority to choose her identity (enclosed as that identity may be), to comfort her mother, to use her archetypal experience to gain self-control and authority over her enclosure in Hades. This model does not allow the possibility of Proserpina's becoming a woman like Ceres (and, of course, in the story Ceres is punished for being that sort of a woman, a working mother, if you will). And Proserpina's empowerment comes only by virtue of her association with Pluto. She is, nonetheless, empowered. One reading of "The Pomegranate-Seeds," then, shows a helpless child becoming a powerful woman, a prison becoming a kingdom, and a classical myth becoming instruction for young, female readers in methods of turning their experiences within a restrictive system into vehicles of power and authority.

Yet "The Pomegranate-Seeds" is also a story that has everything to do with loss: the child's inevitable loss of faith in the parent's omnipotence, the parent's loss of the child to time, and the grief of both at these inevitabilities that read so sadly like betrayals. The story locates Proserpina's loss of her mother in the moment when, locked in Pluto's arms, she sees her mother and utters her unheard cry for help. Ceres' loss of her daughter is located in the moment when she is reunited with Proserpina and, locked in her daughter's arms, learns of the six seeds and Proserpina's good cheer. Both moments promote the unavoidable realization of loss by conflating loss with betrayal: Proserpina literally sees her mother as she figuratively sees her mother's inability to save her; Ceres literally sees

Proserpina as she figuratively sees her daughter's new identity, her adulthood.

Hawthorne's choosing to retell classical myths and his grim consistency in retelling them in *Tanglewood Tales* is highly suggestive of their meaning and resonance in his life and worldview. This suggestion is encouraged by the way Hawthorne's revision of the Proserpina / Ceres myth differs significantly from that of his contemporaries. In one of Margaret Fuller's "Conversations," the Persephone myth is discussed by Hawthorne's neighbors and peers, the leading intellectuals of New England. This wide-ranging discussion, which includes Fuller herself, Ralph Waldo Emerson, William Story, Elizabeth Peabody, George Ripley, and others, at first seems to provide a discourse that also sees loss and betrayal in the myth: "The pilgrimages of the more prominent of these goddesses, Ceres and Isis, seem to indicate the life which loses what is dear in childhood, to seek in weary pain for what after all can be but half regained. . . . This era in Mythology seems to mark the progress from an unconscious state to a conscious state. Persephone's periodical exile shows the impossibility of resuming an unconsciousness from which we have been once aroused, the need thought has, having once felt the influence of the Seasons, to retire into itself" (Fuller 1972, 519). This discussion privileges Proserpina's new consciousness and thus (in a typical Transcendentalist movement) her individuality, her awareness. Proserpina's six months in Hades are read as a painful victory for growth, for thought, for consciousness itself. The separation of mother and daughter *as* mother and daughter signaled in Hawthorne's "The Pomegranate-Seeds" is absent here, as is Pluto's control over Proserpina, the enclosure that is Hades, and the barren state of Ceres and the earth. Fuller and her fellow conversationalists see Proserpina's time in Hades as a necessary exile in which to fulfill a need of the inner, divine self.

Hawthorne carefully distinguishes between Pluto's "letting" Proserpina stay on earth periodically and Proserpina's willing acquiescence to Pluto's desire for her to remain in Hades the rest of the time. For Hawthorne, if Proserpina is asserting her individualism, she is doing so only in confinement, only because Pluto "lets" her do so. Her individualism thus depends on her submission to male authority and her acceptance of her experience. Where Fuller reads the resulting consciousness in the action of the myth, Hawthorne reads the resulting confinement and emptiness.

What Hawthorne invents in his retelling of the myths saves him.

The enactments of scenarios and themes of loss in the Proserpina / Ceres myth allow Hawthorne to make the myth his own, to turn its themes into the themes of his life and his writing. These themes allow his understanding to extend fully, beyond the limits of his own transient existence. Like the children who listen to historical stories in *Famous Old People,* another collection of Hawthorne's children's stories, and thus learn lessons of earthly sin and violence, the recent events of Hawthorne's life had impressed upon him his own mortality. Up until this point, Hawthorne had managed to preserve a portion of his innocence, an ability to call up the childlike side of himself and write it into his fiction, most obviously into his children's books. Provoked by his life's circumstances, provoked by his resulting view of the world, Hawthorne loses that essential innocence, moves beyond that once thriving part of his nature.

In "The Pomegranate-Seeds," Hawthorne focuses on the loss of childhood innocence—the loss that awaits both children and their parents—and ways that that loss can be turned to gain in experiencing the world. Such a gain (Proserpina's identity, Ceres' six months a year with her daughter) comes at a price, the price of experience in an imperfect world. By remembering the experience of childhood in his imagination and by recovering that childhood in the archetypes of the Proserpina / Ceres myth, Hawthorne is able to discover what he has lost and what he has gained, and he finds that loss to be great indeed. In the finding, he airs the inner voices of his depths so that he will not sink under the burden of that loss and can continue in the world in which he finds himself.

Like Proserpina adapting to what is, after all, her fate and Ceres accepting her half-regained daughter in "The Pomegranate-Seeds," Hawthorne, too, adapts and adjusts. He goes on to his consulship in Liverpool, which marks his entrance into the world of rationalism and materialism (the world that he had always seen as deathly for the artist) and his exit from the prime of his literary career. The Proserpina / Ceres myth, pregnant as it is with themes fundamental to the psychological landscape of human nature, allows Hawthorne to express what for him was otherwise inexpressible and, like Ceres, like Proserpina, to move on.

NOTES

1. Hawthorne 1972, 300. Subsequent page numbers in parentheses refer to this edition.

BIBLIOGRAPHY

Baym, Nina. *The Shape of Hawthorne's Career.* Ithaca, N.Y.: Cornell Univ. Press, 1976.

Fuller, Margaret. Selection from "Margaret and Her Friends." In *The Rise of Modern Mythology, 1680–1860,* edited by Burton Feldman and Robert D. Richardson. Bloomington, Ind.: Indiana Univ. Press, 1972.

Hawthorne, Nathaniel. "The Pomegranate-Seeds." In *A Wonder-Book and Tanglewood Tales. The Centenary Edition of the Works of Nathaniel Hawthorne,* edited by William Charvat, Roy Harvey Pearce, and Claude M. Simpson, vol. 7. Columbus: Ohio State Univ. Press, 1972.

Homer. *The Homeric Hymns.* Translated by Charles Boer. Chicago: Swallow, 1972.

McPherson, Hugo. *Hawthorne as Myth-Maker.* Toronto: Univ. of Toronto Press, 1969.

Ovid. *Metamorphoses.* Translated by Frank Justus Miller. Cambridge: Harvard Univ. Press, 1984.

Pearce, Roy Harvey. Historical introduction to *True Stories from History and Biography,* by Nathaniel Hawthorne. *The Centenary Edition of the Works of Nathaniel Hawthorne,* edited by William Charvat, Roy Harvey Pearce, and Claude M. Simpson, vol. 6. Columbus: Ohio State Univ. Press, 1972.

Richardson, Robert D., and Burton Feldman, eds. *The Rise of Modern Mythology, 1680–1860.* Bloomington, Ind.: Indiana Univ. Press, 1972.

Melissa McFarland Pennell

CHAPTER 6 THROUGH THE GOLDEN GATE: MADNESS AND THE PERSEPHONE MYTH IN GERTRUDE ATHERTON'S "THE FOGHORN"

Although many readers associate Gertrude Atherton with novels of old California, few know of her interest in the classical world and her use of its settings and culture for her fiction, as seen in her novels *The Immortal Marriage, The Jealous Gods,* and *Dido, Queen of Hearts.* Recognized for her treatment of feminist themes in historical novels and in novels of manners, Atherton draws upon her knowledge of the literature of the classical world to create a tightly constructed, highly effective Gothic tale of madness and deception in her short story "The Foghorn."[1] Using details from the San Francisco Bay area where she spent her youth to create the physical setting for the story, Atherton infuses this environment with an eerie darkness that evokes the presence of an underworld. At the center of this underworld, a version of the Persephone myth unfolds, and Atherton uses this motif to provide structure and to suggest larger meanings in the events that comprise her tale. By revising the Persephone myth to give her narrator an element of control over her own destiny, Atherton explores a woman's need to create her own story and self-image. However, as her narrator seeks a voice with which to express her own sense of self-worth and her need for freedom, this element of control proves elusive. The journey through the underworld that promises escape from a restrictive social order instead results in the narrator's confinement by and dependence on that order. In the irony of the denouement, Atherton suggests that the woman who by herself attempts to challenge or circumvent the patriarchal values of her society risks ostracism and personal collapse.

An innovative narrative style, shaped by an interior monologue, allows Atherton to bring the reader into the mind of the central character, a mind that no longer functions in the rational world. This narrative form also endows the central character with an element of power by controlling the amount of knowledge shared with the reader. Reflecting a pattern in women's fiction identified by Gilbert and Gubar in *Madwoman in the Attic* (1979), this narrator engages in the projection of an ideal double who embodies many qualities associated with Persephone and who disappears when the narrator's "real" self is revealed at the conclusion of the dream vision. In fact, Atherton's story can be seen as a version of a "failed" Persephone myth, for there is no resurrection at the end, no strong mother who will rescue this Persephone figure from her entrapment. Atherton's narrator is, by the end of the story, an orphan, left to cope with her madness in isolation, to hear her voice only from within as the silence of her "underworld" surrounds her. When the narrator's manipulation and denial collapse, the reader is confronted by the shocking end of the mental and emotional journey and is transformed from observer to deceived participant. The reader's feeling of betrayal is vital to the effect of the story, because by sharing in this emotion with the central character, the reader is brought into closer relationship with her. In writing "The Foghorn," Atherton joins the company of female authors who have grappled with their own feelings of rejection and betrayal, who "dramatize their own self-division, their desire both to accept the strictures of patriarchal society and to reject them" (Gilbert and Gubar 1979, 78).

By opening the story with an interior monologue, Atherton immediately draws the reader into the main character's point of view; the reader has no opportunity to establish an objective standard with which to judge either events or the movement of the narrative. This narrative structure is crucial to the effect of the tale, for as Michel Foucault explains, "The madman has been the one whose discourse cannot have the same currency as others. His words may be considered null and void, having neither truth nor importance" (Foucault 1981, 53; see also Foucault 1973). Although there can be found exceptions to this statement within the body of Western literature, it is an operative element in the story Atherton constructs, for to reveal the narrator's true self at the beginning is to risk the dismissal of her voice. In order to achieve the shock of recognition at the end of the tale, Atherton cannot allow the reader to deny the validity of the narrator's voice or to question too soon the truth of the narrator's vision.

This interior perspective also allows Atherton to delve into the subconscious mind of the nameless narrator, thereby misleading the reader, who initially accepts the narrator's comments as the ruminations of a conscious mind. These operations of the subconscious mind create an interior "dream" time within the narrative that does not correspond to chronological time. Part of the narrative effect hinges upon this dream time, when events happen out of sequence and images are fused in a way that *seems* logical yet cannot withstand conscious scrutiny. Throughout the narrative, Atherton hints that there is something curiously wrong with the narrator's reflections, and the narrator admits that "while not yet fully conscious she had relived all of the old hopes, dreams, ecstasies; reached out arrogantly sure of herself and the man, contemptuous of the world."[2] Not until the reader steps outside the interior monologue at the end of the story is the extent of the deception revealed. The reader suddenly must question all that has been accepted from this unreliable narrator, and all that has been assumed about the verity and rationality of her world.

The deception worked upon the reader relies heavily upon the doppelganger motif as the narrator's dream vision presents an ideal image of herself, physically and mentally. This idealized persona serves two purposes within the story. First, it furthers the deception being carried out on the reader, for the beautiful figure who appears in the dream presents a picture of normalcy and attractiveness, playing upon the reader's assumptions about the face of madness. Second, the projection allows the narrator to present her version of self and the events and attitudes that have shaped her life. Her choice of a figure whose experiences resemble in part those of Persephone reveals the "self-division" to which the narrator is subject, for while she desires to accept and embody certain values from the patriarchal world, she chafes against the restrictions those values place upon her. Part of her attempt at resolving this self-division involves her efforts to redefine the pattern of the myth. In the narrator's subconscious world, the ideal can be regained, but the losses she experiences in the course of her dream—the loss of her lover and of her freedom—remain beyond her control, creating what becomes the never-ending nightmare within which the narrator is trapped. This nightmare is the world of the narrator's madness, and as Shoshanna Felman notes, "madness can only occur within a world in conflict, within a conflict of thoughts" (1985, 36). The narrator's dream encompasses her conflict of thoughts, as she struggles with the vision of self as Other and rebels against what is defined by the larger world as reason itself.

The narrator's projected ideal is a beautiful young woman, a characterization of Persephone. While thinking about herself, the narrator believes that she remains a beauty, carefully recounting each of her features: "her teeth were exquisite" and her hair and eyes were "beyond cavil" (798). Most proud of her hair, the narrator describes "the warm bright waving masses of her hair [that] had never been cut since her second birthday. They too were made for burrowing" (798). In folklore, long luxuriant hair represents the sun's strength in summer, health, and the virgin bride, all meaningful reverberations of the Persephone myth (Jakes 1961). This image of luxuriant tresses further suggests female sexuality and the narrator's sense of satisfaction with her physical self. To complement this physical appearance, the narrator also projects an ideal mental capability, claiming that "she read the Greek and Latin classics in the original text, and attended morning classes over at the university" (799). By acknowledging her role as a reader and therefore interpreter of texts, the narrator claims for herself a role most often forbidden to women in the public sphere. The narrator admits resentfully that society does not accept a woman of her intellectual caliber, that "men didn't mind if you 'adored' music and pictures, but if they suspected you of being intellectual, they either despised or feared you, and faded away" (799). However, the lover in her dream embraces her intellect as well as her physical self, and she does not have "to conceal from him the awful truth" (799) of her intelligence.

To enhance character development and to provide her Persephone figure with the background against which she has rebelled, Atherton inserts bits and pieces of the past in the narrator's thoughts. The narrator alludes to a respectable family past with references to the "old house on Russian Hill" where "her old servants were intimate with all the other servants on the Hill" (801), and the mention of her mother "coming in for Granddad's fortune" (799). Her family is a part of the social establishment, committed to maintaining both the traditions and the status it enjoys, and the esteem her mother commands is not unlike that held by Demeter. The narrator's mother "had always expressed a wish that each of her daughters should wear [her wedding] dress to the altar" (799) and she mourns when she learns of the narrator's broken engagement to an acceptable young man. The narrator also thinks of her sisters as "protected by husbands, wealth, position" (803) and able to experience vicariously the unconventional through her without taking risks themselves.[3]

Recalling her Uncle Ben's mention of the "queer twists in this family since 'way back" (799), the narrator, however, implies that amid this respectability there exists a taint in the family bloodline, a mental and moral weakness. In contrast to the honorable and distinguished maternal family, the narrator's father reveals instability, as he had "taken to drugs" and later had "run off with another woman" (799). His is a lesser pattern of infidelity than Zeus's, but one nonetheless that suggests the father's opportunities to pursue that which he desires. This absence of the father reinforces the mother-daughter bond, an aspect of the Persephone myth, and contributes to the narrator's belief in female authority because there is no dominant male influence in her early development. While the narrator prides herself on her strength and resolution and on the fact that on her mother's side "they were a long-lived family" (804), she attempts to deny any legacy from her father, but she cannot escape her connection to him.

When she thinks about her own illicit relations with a married man, the narrator believes people will say, "Like father, like daughter" (805), and she sees in her father's behavior an unspoken consent to her own choices. She asserts that the "accident" in which her dream vision culminates fulfills a retributive justice, not only for her own behavior but for the actions of her father as well. She believes that the sins of the father must be visited upon the child, and that her own unconventional and openly rebellious choices have brought down upon her a punishment she deserves. This attitude is one of the first alterations in the pattern of the Persephone myth that becomes apparent in the story, for Persephone attests to her own innocence when telling of her kidnapping ("he bore me away all unwilling, beneath the earth" [Hesiod 1964, 319]), while the narrator admits that she willingly accompanied her lover and deserves the consequences. What appear to be contradictions in attitude between the narrator's desire to rebel against social conventions and her sense of shame in both her father's and her own actions are reflections of the neuroses that have developed under the strain of oppression that the narrator has endured. These neuroses, as Karen Horney explains, engender "alternating phases" in which the neurotic is "at times offensively irresponsible in sexual or financial matters, and at others . . . shows highly developed moral sensibilities" (1950, 78). Although the narrator associates the loss of freedom and the loss of reason with punishment for past crimes, she is unable to connect her flight of the mind, her dream vision, with her desire to escape the condemning world. The narrator perceives the oppression that has made her feel an outcast, but she does not see that her own responses to and evaluations of experience have been shaped by these same values of a patriarchal society.

To cope with her own experience of illicit love, the narrator deflates the significance of marriage, associating it with her mother's yellowing, decaying wedding dress, which the narrator refuses to wear. Indicating her rejection not only of family tradition but also of societal expectations, the narrator's description of the dress suggests that the bride about to marry enters a death experience, the end of the virgin self, the end of an individual destiny, again echoing yet modifying the Persephone myth. The narrator instead prefers a situation in which she can maintain control over her own destiny, but she does not admit the problematic nature of her situation: like Persephone, she is drawn away from her mother's sphere, yet the new world she enters is controlled by the lover figure. Her lover does not use flowers or objects of beauty as does Hades to ensnare his victim, but he offers her that which is most attractive to her, a life that seems to defy convention. He invites her to elope, although he cannot expect "legal release" from his wife, who has refused him a divorce. Instead, the narrator must accompany her lover into exile, a "perpetual honeymoon" in which "that solidarity which makes the two as one against the malignant forces of life" (802–3) will shape her future. Like Persephone, the narrator will be drawn into a world that exists "in hidden places," for her a type of social underworld. Though she believes she can achieve freedom and a life of her own by fleeing her mother's social sphere, the narrator cannot anticipate what lies beyond the Golden Gate. Unlike Persephone, a "shy mate" who remains "much reluctant" in the company of Hades (Hesiod 1964, 313), the narrator assumes that with sexual initiation and knowledge will come a new source of power and independence. To emphasize this revision of the Persephone myth, Atherton does not place her narrator in the company of innocent youths like those who surround Persephone before her abduction. Instead, she allows the narrator to compare herself to Mary Stewart, Ninon de L'Enclos, Diane de Poitiers, and Madame Recamier, all women who attained power as mistresses of married men. By linking herself to these women, the narrator attempts to reassert the significance of her individual self and to gain for herself similar access to power and influence over social as well as personal affairs.

While she creates an ideal picture of herself and the potential she has for power and fulfillment, the narrator also describes a setting that introduces an undercurrent of conflict with the vision she attempts to maintain. In classical mythology, Persephone functions as a part of nature's cycle, whereas this Persephone figure believes that the natural world is oppressive, a measure of her displacement in the world. The narrator perceives the world as a hostile place where she becomes diminished as an individual being, much as Persephone feels when she enters the underworld. In this diminished state, the narrator perceives a power in the environment that she would like to embrace. Her own sense of oppression is heightened by the towering redwoods that surround her and her lover as they seek solitude after admiring "the 'ruins' of a Roman temple at the foot of the lawn lit by a blazing moon" (802). These redwoods threaten as "unfriendly trees, but [are] protective, sentinel-like, shutting out the modern world; reminiscent those closely planted aisles were of ancient races . . . godlike races, perhaps" (802). Possibly alluding to the Roman underworld, whose entrance at Lake Avernus was "surrounded by high banks, which in Virgil's time were covered with a gloomy forest" (Bulfinch 1913, 266), this setting overshadows the narrator. Its vastness and intensity reduce the stature of the individual when compared to the world of nature and the history of the human race. The narrator, however, attempts to appropriate the power of this environment, claiming that she and her lover "had felt like gods that night. How senseless to try to stave off a declaration of love . . . to fear . . . to wonder . . . to worry" (802). Her self-confidence blinds her to the power of both the natural world and the social world. In her defiant mood, the narrator cannot fathom the danger that awaits her.

To enhance further the tension between the narrator and her environment, Atherton infuses the setting with additional Gothic elements. All but the last fraction of the narrative evolves during the night, when the subconscious attains freedom, and the story within the story also reaches its climax in a night scene. Frequently the only light in these nights scenes is the moon, the light of irrationality. All of the other lights the narrator sees are repetitions of the yellow moon: the "gliding spheroids of golden light," which indicate the boats on the bay (800); the "pulsing light" of the search beam that sweeps the bay (800); even the stars she sees during her escape that "shed a misty yellow light" (803). Many of these light sources are artificial, suggesting a manufactured quality in the narrator's vision, though this is not emphasized until the end of the story. These eerie lights enhance the threatening atmosphere that pervades the area, as the narrator looks toward the prison island of Alcatraz and senses the "psychic emanation of imprisoned men" (800), a contained yet palpable violence. The narrator perceives this same undercurrent of violence and rage within herself, yet she has not found a way to use or to express it.

In this realm of darkness, the Gothic element of the sublime emerges and controls the development of certain images. When describing San Francisco Bay at night, the narrator concentrates on the Golden Gate, "a narrow entrance between two crouching forts, separating the harbor of arrogant beauty from the gray waste of the Pacific" (800), as she differentiates the known world from the abyss of the ocean. Here the sublime is evoked by the vastness of the ocean that lies beyond the Golden Gate, by the absence of definition and limits, which inspires awe and terror while reinforcing the insignificance of the individual. Here the narrator appears to differentiate between the "arrogant beauty" of her known world and the "gray waste" of uncharted regions of experience she hopes to explore. Her tone reflects ambivalence toward the familiar, defined by limits that remind her of her own feelings of confinement, and she yearns to pass into the realm of freedom. She achieves this passage as she flees with her lover and passes "out through the Golden Gate" (803). This aspect of the story reflects the influence of Ovid's treatment of the Persephone myth in the account of Proserpina, whose abductor carries her "through the deep lakes" and who "smote the pool open to its very depths" to gain entry to the underworld" (Ovid 1969, 119–20). This passage through the narrow door or cave and through the pool of water is also part of the archetypal journey into the unconscious as described by Carl Jung, who suggests that a body of water is commonly the symbol for the unconscious. The Golden Gate becomes a doorway to freedom and the threshold for the abyss of the irrational, for the great emptiness that, like the "ponderous, rather stupid old ocean" (800), the narrator mocks yet chooses as her vehicle for escape.

Adding to the subliminal magnitude of the experience, a fog envelops the narrator and her lover as they flee in the night, forcing her to grope for landmarks and creating a maze through which she drifts with no awareness of external reality. As in the world of the unconscious mind, there are no familiar markers, no known signs that serve to reassure the wanderer. The narrator has described the fog as "that dense, yet imponderable white mass pushing its way through the Golden Gate like a laboring ship" (801) as it seems to point the way toward escape while blocking a clear view of what lies ahead. Although the fog initially appears a benign presence, it becomes during the narrator's flight a "racing mountain of snow-white mist" (803), a menacing, unstoppable barrier that clouds vision. Reasserting the narrator's lack of control over both the natural world and the direction of her journey, the fog manifests the narrator's predicament, for that which appears to offer a path to freedom may be in fact a new form of entrapment.

While seeming to provide concealment for the romantic escape of the narrator and her lover, the fog also suggests the presence of the netherworld, a world set apart from the land of the living, to which this Persephone figure is being drawn. Atherton further develops this impression by using the movement of the fog to suggest spectral images. The fog moves like a "ghostly ship" as it proceeds through the bay, and over land it graces the earth as a "more formless, but still lovely visitant that swirled over the inland water, enshrouding the islands" (801). Even the foghorns sound as though they emanate from the underworld or from the land of the wandering dead with "their long-drawn-out moans of utter desolation" (801). This suggestion of voices from the dead foreshadows the bleakness and apparent hopelessness of the narrator's true situation, for when she and her lover are enveloped by the fog, she again hears the foghorns with their "low, menacing roar" and "wailing siren" cry out in warning. As these sounds seem "to come from new directions" (803) and the fog blocks her vision, the narrator experiences isolation and bewilderment, much like the feeling Persephone had when she no longer "beheld earth and starry heaven and the strong-flowing sea where fishes shoal, and the rays of the sun, and still hoped to see her dear mother" (Hesiod 1964, 291).

These spectral images also enhance the character development of the lover figure. Suspect because "he never came to the house" (801), the lover's existence is known to the narrator alone, suggesting that he may be only a figure in the world of her dreams. Like Hades, who is never called by his proper name, this lover remains unnamed, adding to the aura of mystery about him. The lover assumes a rather sinister aspect as he reveals a "rigid white face" (803), a mask of death, when they are consumed by the fog. In this close association with death and the dead, the lover resembles Hades carrying the maiden into the underworld, for "magnificently he rowed . . . long sweeping easy strokes as he smiled possessively into her eyes" (803). Although the narrator voluntarily leaves with her lover, this scene reenacts the moment in the Persephone myth when "Pluto, Lord of the Dead, issuing from the abyss carried [Persephone] off on his golden car to be his bride and queen in the underworld" (Frazer 1959, 424). The entry into the underworld, like the passage through the Golden Gate, functions as a symbolic movement into the unconscious mind, but because the underworld is associated with death, this movement takes on a more ominous aspect. In what appears to be her daring flight from a restrictive family and society, the narrator reveals that she envisions this as an escape from oppressive confinement; it is her chance to "run away" and to "find completion" (802). For the mind burdened by neuroses, love itself, as Horney explains, "becomes a phantom—like success—carrying with it the illusion that it is the solution for all problems" (1964, 289). In Atherton's story, the reader is forced to question whether the narrator's escape with the phantom lover is only one more illusion in the dream world she creates.

Using revisions of the Persephone myth, Atherton portrays the plight of the maiden fleeing one danger only to encounter another. Thwarted by the fog that engulfs them, the narrator and her lover crash, crushed between two passing ships. The violence of this moment, conveyed through ellipsis and single syllable words, culminates in the narrator "shrieking as she saw his head almost severed," and as she watches, "the very fog turn[s] red" (803), a color that signifies blood and passion. Echoing the condemnation to the underworld that occurred in *Vathek*, the narrator feels as though "she had been screaming since the beginning of time" (803) while incurring the punishment for her endeavor to escape. This nightmarish ending to what had been a dream of hope and liberation is really only the beginning of the horror the narrator must face as she reenters the world of the conscious mind.

When the narrator is thrust back into the world of the conscious mind, there is a marked change in the setting from the exterior to the interior world, from the vastness of the ocean to the confinement of a "bare small room" (803). At the opening of the story, the narrative voice offers observations suggesting that the speaker is in her own bedroom, but when the the interior setting resumes at the end of the dream, it is that of an institution. At first the reader is led to believe that this hospitalization is the result of the crash, but soon the narrative reveals another picture. Feeling isolated and neglected, the narrator remarks that it is "odd that she should be left alone like this" and that surely her family "might have found her a better room" (804). As the sun (a symbol of life and rationality) rises, the narrator "looks up at the high barred window" (805) of her room, gazing from a perspective that suggests her entrapment in an underworld, now one of madness and institutionalization. The barred window also underscores her separation from the rational world and reveals, as Phyllis Chesler explains, how that world views madness as a "shameful and menacing disease, from whose spiteful and exhausting eloquence society must be protected" (1972, 34). Her imprisonment behind bars indicates a caged existence not unlike that which the narrator has associated with Alcatraz and its "dull monotonous existence" (800) and which recalls the imprisonment of the narrator in "The Yellow Wall-paper." The narrator's confinement in a mental asylum creates a painful irony in light of the asylum she has sought in the dream world of the irrational. Instead of an underworld governed by her lover where she will exercise power and influence, the narrator is cast into an underworld guarded by a doctor and nurse, representatives of the social order, upon whom she depends for any care she receives.

As the narrator awakens to consciousness, the reader is confronted by her actual condition. A clue is provided to prepare the reader for what is to come, but the line "Eyepits red with rust of ancient tears" from Edwin Arnold's poem "Light in Asia" is such an obscure reference that it appears insignificant. Arnold's poem recounts the story of Buddha and this line comes from a passage in which Siddhartha, encountering a figure of age and decay, is appalled by the realization that all human beings are subject to the ravages of time and aging. According to Edith Hamilton, this awareness influences Persephone as well, for "after the lord of the dark world below carried her away, she was never again the gay young creature who had played in the flowery meadow. . . . She did indeed rise from the dead every spring, but she brought with her the memory of where she had come from; with all her bright beauty there was something strange and awesome about her" (1942, 64). This same realization appalls the narrator of "The Foghorn," who has envisioned herself as immortal and eternally youthful, a goddess like Persephone, but discovers that she is old and haggard. As Horney explains, "Naturally it would shatter a person's feeling of godlikeness to face the fact that for him, too, life is limited and precarious; that fate can strike him at any time with an accident, bad fortune, illness or death—and blast his feeling of omnipotence" (1950, 46). As the narrator comes to realize the truth of her situation, her awareness undercuts the feeling of power she had gained through her dream and reinforces her sense of a diminished self.

The encounter with the narrator's actual image remains a shocking experience, even though there are subtle clues throughout the story to prepare the reader. Far from the picture of the beautiful woman projected in her dream, the narrator is an emaciated hag. Instead of the images of health and fertility from the Persephone myth with which she associates herself, the old woman bears the marks of decay, as though she has already died. In her waking state she more closely resembles an image of Hecate, goddess of the underworld, who roams only at night, unleashing the terrors of darkness. Clasping her head in an effort to retain either her sanity or her dream, the narrator brushes her hand over her head to find "harsh, short bristles" instead of the "lovely abundant hair" of which she dreamed (804). Although the narrator believes her stubbly hair is the result of a brain fever, the shearing of hair symbolizes both death and a paring away of power and strength that becomes a token of disgrace. It further suggests a loss of sexual power or attractiveness, an added element of punishment for behavior that has been deemed unacceptable. Earlier in the story the narrator felt a toothache, a small sign of decay, but instead of the radiant smile she projected in her dream, the narrator "raised one of those withered yellow hands to her mouth. It was empty" (805). These signs of physical decay are also evident as the narrator peers down into her dressing gown, where she sees "pendent [*sic*] dugs, brown and shrivelled" (805). With this final blow to her idealized image of female beauty, the narrator assumes the appearance of a crone, a withered and often powerless woman who no longer exerts control over her own destiny or even her own body.

Passing through the mental death of madness and the natural course of physical decay, the narrator has degenerated. The only sound she makes in this state is an inarticulate cry, as though language, a sign of rational process, has escaped her. She approaches a state of nonbeing in which her voice as well as her body fails her. Only in her interior monologue does she still rage against the values and expectations of a social order that has attempted to define her, as she recalls "how she hated, hated, hated, self-righteousness, smug hypocrisy . . . illogical minds—one sheep bleating like another sheep" (805). But when she hears the doctor and nurse approaching, "she dropped back on the pillow and closed her eyes and lay still" (805), too exhausted and overwhelmed to continue her struggle. The futility of her effort to surpass the limits her society had established for her becomes apparent and "she understood" (805). As the guardians enter, the doctor's voice is heard, "brisk and business-like and deeply mature," while the nurse sounds "young and deferential" (806). In a final irony, the doctor addresses the nurse: "Don't forget to look in. Good little girl. I know you never forget" (806). It is clearly the good little girl, not the independent woman, who is praised and appreciated by the patriarchal society Atherton wishes to challenge.

Using Gothic motifs and a revision of the Persephone myth, Atherton presents a terrifying portrayal of a woman who seeks to escape one form of oppression only to encounter another. In her autobiography, Atherton admitted her need to escape San Francisco and the confinement society placed on her, so that she could pursue her art. As Elinor Richey notes, "Gertrude Atherton knew the pain of sexist repression, knew the cost of strength required to overcome it, knew its scars—the scars that made her wary of emotional commitment" (1974, 62). This short story reflects Atherton's own concern for the fate of the literary woman who is ostracized and condemned for her efforts to achieve an independent voice, what Gilbert and Gubar have called the "anxiety of authorship . . . built from complex and often only barely conscious fears of that authority which seems to the female artist to be by definition inappropriate to her sex" (1979, 51). Focusing on this concern in "The

Foghorn," Atherton explores the effects of oppression and the toll it takes on a woman who seeks to redefine herself and her world. Having rejected the role of dutiful daughter, Atherton's narrator experiences a journey like Persephone's to an underworld that entails profound and traumatic change. Unlike Persephone, however, this narrator has no one who will negotiate a compromise for her, who will call her back from her inward journey. To cross the threshold into the underworld of madness offers the narrator one type of freedom, but the price it exacts, the loss of voice and presence, defeats the purpose of the journey.

NOTES

1. For discussions of Gertrude Atherton's feminism and its influence in her fiction, see Forrey 1976; Bradley 1986; and Richey 1974.

2. Atherton 1937, 804. Subsequent page numbers in parentheses refer to this edition.

3. Atherton's sisters-in-law enjoyed similar status at the time of Atherton's marriage to her husband George. She came to see herself as the rebel and risk-taker in the family. For a discussion of the relationship between Atherton's life and her fictional heroines, see Leider 1991.

BIBLIOGRAPHY

Atherton, Gertrude. "The Foghorn." In *The Haunted Omnibus,* edited by Alexander Laing. New York: Farrar and Rinehart, 1937.

Bradley, Jennifer. "Woman at the Golden Gate: The Last Works of Gertrude Atherton." *Women's Studies* 12 (1986): 17–30.

Bulfinch, Thomas. *Bulfinch's Mythology.* New York: Grosset and Dunlap, 1913.

Chesler, Phyllis. *Women and Madness.* New York: Doubleday, 1972.

Felman, Shoshanna. *Writing and Madness.* Ithaca, N.Y.: Cornell Univ. Press, 1985.

Forrey, Carolyn. "Gertrude Atherton and the New Woman." *California Historical Society Quarterly* 55 (1976): 194–209.

Foucault, Michel. "The Order of Discourse." In *Untying the Text,* edited by Robert Young. Boston: Routledge and Kegan Paul, 1981.

———. *Madness and Civilization.* New York: Vintage Press, 1973.

Frazer, Sir James George. *The New Golden Bough.* Edited by Theodore H. Gaster. New York: Mentor Books, 1959.

Gilbert, Sandra M., and Susan Gubar. *The Madwoman in the Attic.* New Haven: Yale Univ. Press, 1979.

Hamilton, Edith. *Mythology.* Boston: Little, Brown, 1942.

Hesiod. *The Homeric Hymns and Homerica.* Translated by Hugh G. Evelyn-White. London: William Heinemann, 1964.

Horney, Karen. *Neuroses and Human Growth.* New York: Norton, 1950.

———. *The Neurotic Personality of Our Time.* New York: Norton, 1964.

Jakes, Gertrude. *The Dictionary of Mythology, Folklore, and Symbols.* New York: Scarecrow Press, 1961.

Jung, Carl G. *The Archetypes and the Collective Unconscious.* Princeton: Princeton Univ. Press, 1971.

Leider, Emily Wortis. *California's Daughter: Gertrude Atherton and Her Times.* Stanford: Stanford Univ. Press, 1991.

Ovid. *Metamorphoses.* Translated by Rolfe Humphries. Bloomington, Ind.: Indiana Univ. Press, 1969.

Richey, Elinor. "The Flappers Were Her Daughters: The Liberated, Literary World of Gertrude Atherton." *American West* 11 (1974): 4–10, 60–63.

Virginia Hyde

CHAPTER 7

"LOST" GIRLS: D. H. LAWRENCE'S VERSIONS OF PERSEPHONE

D. H. Lawrence deals recurrently with a character that he sometimes calls the "lost girl." And why is the lady lost? Because she is Persephone, abducted from the daylight world of consciousness, her element, to the alien underground of Plutonic sensuality. Perhaps the most various and persistent treatment of the Persephone myth in the twentieth century appears in his works—in poetry, short stories, novels, nonfiction, and perhaps even painting. It is no coincidence that his works on male dominance, discussed by Judith Ruderman (1984), Cornelia Nixon (1986), and others, often overlap with the Persephone group, featuring a rather sinister Plutonic man. Lawrence, however, utilizes this mythology in a variety of ways—not only to depict relations between the sexes but also to explore archetypes of death and immortality. His sources for Persephone are as diverse as his uses; from Pre-Raphaelite "Fatal Women" to works on ancient religion and fertility rituals, they merge in his own thinking with "the memories of old, far-off, far, far-off experience that lie within us."[1] His blend of the "realistic" and archetypal in female characterization has both fascinated and disturbed women readers and critics.

The Persphone myth itself has evoked a dual response from women, largely because it is twofold, with both patriarchal and matriarchal implications. As Annis V. Pratt and others have pointed out, a myth of primal womanhood (the broken but resurgent union of mother, daughter, and fruitful earth) can not be negated by the tale of male dominance (the rape of Persephone) superimposed upon it (1985, 112–15). Even C. G. Jung considered the story distinctively female at its core, "alien to man" ("Aspects" 1969, 177), and twentieth-century women have increasingly proclaimed its relevance to them (see, for instance, Stewart 1979, 44–50; Scott 1984, 131, 145, 180, 197–99; Westling 1985, 78–92, 167–70; and Donovan 1989). Although Lawrence rather seldom emphasizes the mother-daughter relationship, a good example of it occurs in *St. Mawr* (1924). He would probably not be surprised that feminists can find in his work not only the dark, destructive "male" myth but also the intimations of female divinity that inhere in his preferred metaphors for cyclic rebirth. For example, Sandra M. Gilbert reveals that the deepest theme in *The Ladybird* (1923) is not the vaunted dominance of its autocratic "hero" Count Dionys but the revitalization of men by the Persephone-like Daphne (1985, 130–61). Yet the powers of these two half-mythic figures wax and wane in the course of their story just as Daphne divides her life between a daylight identity and a nocturnal one. The intense contact and cautious alternation between the gendered gods fits Lawrence's vision of life, at once vitalistic and tragic, in which the relations between the sexes lie at the heart of both rapture and agony.

In his hands, such figures take on peculiarly Lawrentian features. Deities like Persephone become reminders of lost human faculties. "How are we to get back . . . Demeter, Persephone, and the halls of Dis?" he asks in a long essay published in 1930, "A Propos of *Lady Chatterley's Lover.*"[2] To "know the earth . . . Plutonic," he adds (512), is to know it according to sensuous awareness, the "blood," the unconscious. The modern overly cerebral individual, having lost sensuality, is especially in need of it to be in touch not only with others but also with a universe that contains, to Lawrence, "male" and "female" creative forces. Thus, the "hierogamous marriage," which Evelyn J. Hinz has defined and located in Lawrence ("Hierogamy" 1976, 900–913; "Rainbow" 1976, 27; see also Hyde 1984)—the marriage between representatives of "upper" and "lower," male and female—appears in Persephone / Pluto figures in many Lawrence works, like psychic dramas in which the two need each other for wholeness. In the poem "Autumn Sunshine" (revised version of 1918), for instance, Lawrence refers to "heaven's pale wine" that is paradoxically distilled by Persephone in "the hell-queen's cup,"[3] thus illustrating a necessary interdependence between the goddess of the daylight and Dis.

The extended significance of these deities, then, gives them a metaphysical dimension beyond the psychological. Perhaps Lawrence's most famous use of them came as he was dying of tuberculosis at age forty-four. While he was ill at a temporary residence in Bavaria, he happened to see flowers—the Bavarian gentians of his poem of that name—and he imagined holding them, as Persephone herself might, as a brilliant torch, a talisman, a symbol of life merging almost imperceptibly with death:

> let me guide myself with the blue, forked torch
> of this flower
> down the darker and darker stairs, where blue
> is darkened on blueness,
> even where Persephone goes, just now, from the
> frosted September
> to the sightless realm . . .
> . . . .
> of the arms Plutonic and pierced with the passion
> of the dense gloom,
> among the splendours of the torches of darkness,
> shedding darkness on the lost bride and
> her groom.
>
> (697)

This Persephone may be half of a psychic unity—the light (as conscious mind) embracing deep, dark color (as unconscious sensuality). But the two mythic figures are also, respectively, soul and body in the final convergence of life with death.

No doubt Lawrence's image of the lost bride as a harbinger of immortality owes something to Gilbert Murray's association of Persephone with "the old liturgy of the dying and re-risen year-bride" and his description of her as a "home-coming Bride" after her ordeal in the earth (1912, 94, 95), for Lawrence had read Murray's *Four Stages of Greek Religion* in 1916. While this passage may hint at ancient rites of human sacrifice (and Lawrence certainly knew of such rites from Sir James George Frazer's *Golden Bough*),[4] it also points to the truth of the earth's perennial renewal (as suggested by the gentians) and thus to the hope of human immortality. One of Lawrence's major sources on mythology, Jane Harrison, had stressed that, in contrast to Demeter, Persephone "withdraws herself more and more to . . . the things below and beyond" (1903, 276). Günther Zuntz, discussing the ancient Persephone in funeral art, describes her as "the Queen of Death who . . . had become the giver of Life" (1971, 176). Similarly, Lawrence's poem looks beyond the "nuptials" of Persephone and Pluto to her triumph over death. Three torches or "flames," common on the goddess's sacred monuments (Kerényi 1969, 111), are among the symbols of immortality in the poem's little-noticed final draft (see also Mandell 1984, 231; and Sagar 1985, 350–52). The "wedding-guest" (evidently the poet) will carry "a flower . . . and three dark flames" to "the marriage of the living dark" (960). In Lawrence's version, the deathly lost bride is paradoxically obliterated and vitalized at the same time by the contact with Dis; indeed, this descent is necessary to the design of rebirth.

Lawrence's poetic version of Persephone's ravishment is seemingly elevated by religious meaning above any social debate on the implications of abduction and forced submission. But he also translates this myth into more realistic fiction, and one of his character types is the fair woman whose Apollonian function it is to represent civilization at its deadliest. But why so? The ancient Persephone is at one with nature in her girlhood, and woman (despite Eve's desire for knowledge) has, historically, been identified more commonly with deep, instinctive faculties than with the civilizing consciousness (see, for example, Jung 1969, 94–96). Lawrence's modern Persephone, however, is long past her old unity with earth, far advanced in Eve's proclivity to know. Lawrence typically associates his women with light (or white) imagery for complex, even conflicting reasons to be explored later (both autobiography and immediate literary influence may play their roles). The association between woman and light is, of course, in some ways conventional, partly based on Persephone's myth itself (she comes from the daylight) and partly on primordial affinities between women and lunar mythology (a tradition Lawrence himself often invokes). But he often has a further meaning, connecting the mental-spiritual woman with "enlightened" society: she may be "pale" because drained of sensual substance (which he often relates to brilliant colors) by civilization. That is, her bodiless spirituality may not be innate but simply symptomatic of an unbalanced social code. Such a modern

Dance Sketch (c. 1928), an oil painting by D. H. Lawrence. Reprinted by permission of the owner, Saki Karavas, and Laurence Pollinger Ltd. for the estate of Frieda Lawrence Ravagli.

woman, according to Lawrence, may have access to earthy ties through her Plutonic opposite, who must often rescue her from the glaring light and plunge her into his own realm of healing darkness. If this doctrine seems to reverse a common claim, often deplored by feminists, that women are "close to nature" whereas men are agents of culture (see, for example, Ortner 1974), it does so in important ways. But this is an area of contradiction in Lawrence (as also in feminism). Besides reversing these poles at times, he also, on the other hand, places the blame for social stagnation and collapse squarely on male figures and "the man's world" (as he terms it in a well-known chapter title in *The Rainbow*), gaining hope for the future from women's special potential for renewal in nature. If it seems frankly paradoxical that this renewal should begin for them with Pluto, yet so it often does in his fiction.

Lawrence characteristically sees Persephone's abduction as a benefit—albeit a mixed one—to the lady, who can thus be saved from emotional death-in-life by a partner who balances out her own traits (as he, too, can be saved by balance). Thus Lettie and George, in Lawrence's first novel, *The White Peacock* (1911), need each other, but Lettie chooses, rather perversely, to move "upward" into higher society, not downward to George's sensuous farm life, and she is only casually, perhaps ironically, termed Persephone. Another "Proserpine" in the same novel is, on the other hand, no modern woman at all but an uncultured and rather slovenly matron who is preferred by her gamekeeper husband over the high-society "peacock" who had once condescended to marry him. The opposites fail to meet in *The White Peacock;* and, in some of Lawrence's most realistic embodiments of Persephone and Pluto, the partly autobiographical parents in *Sons and Lovers* (1913), the benefit of the marriage of opposites is almost indiscernible in the clash: while the mother rigidly upholds the light of the mind and "enlightened" society, the father reacts with "brute force" after laboring manually all day in a dark underground mine (Ford 1965, 38–41). Even a painting from this early period, *The Milk-White Lady and the Coal-Black Smith* (c. 1912), employs somewhat similar figures of light and dark, a fair blonde woman indoors at a window and a dark man in the elemental outdoors.[5]

Several later Lawrence characters who have been identified with Persephone include Alvina in *The Lost Girl* (1920), Dolly in "The Princess" (1924), Kate in *The Plumed Serpent* (1926), and the virgin in *The Virgin and the Gypsy* (1930) (Ford 1965, 31). Gilbert finds Pluto's Hades pervasive in the 1924 poetry book *Birds, Beasts and Flowers* (1980, 73–93), and her discussion of the Persephone references in *The Ladybird* has already been mentioned (1985, 143, 152–53). In addition, P. T. Whelan has related the Brangwen women in *The Rainbow* (1915), especially Lydia, to both Demeter and Persephone, showing Lawrence's complex practice of shifting his emphasis to indicate changing cultural attitudes over time (1988, 23–24). Around the reading world, it seems, Lawrence's Persephone is well recognized (see, for example, Viinikka 1988).

Moreover, *The First Lady Chatterley* (written in 1926) is particularly informative on the alternatives posed by Lawrence's version of this mythology. Connie Chatterley, who explicitly associates herself with Persephone, contrasts her philosophical Plato-quoting husband with her lover, the potent gamekeeper: "And she was an escaping Persephone, Proserpine. Well, she'd rather be married to Pluto than Plato" (Lawrence 1944, 89–90). As in the standard *Lady*

Chatterley's Lover (1928), her escape is from the vapid world of thought and calculated nihilism (in a postwar milieu), with Sir Clifford, to the woods where she experiences, with Parkin, instinctive tenderness for all living things and her own rebirth through sexuality. The first version's explicit references to Plato underline a theme continued in the essay "A Propos of *Lady Chatterley's Lover*," blaming classical and Christian idealism alike for the eventual imbalance in Western thought (511). But the ancient Persephone, Demeter, and Pluto had been poised in interrelationship with each other: hence the necessity for individuals to encounter and incarnate such gods again.

Of course, Connie's story deals with only part of the mythic model, avoiding abduction and rape altogether and securing her place in the natural order rather than wrenching her away from it. Even this idyllic version of a rescued Persephone is, however, rendered complex by real-life elements: despite genuine desire for the gamekeeper's more uncouth lifestyle, Connie cannot really expunge Plato from her own consciousness, for she still desires "to know" the presumably rarefied world of cultural thought—"to read Swinburne again" and even the *Times Literary Supplement*! (Lawrence 1944, 90). Not even in the last *Lady Chatterley* is it certain that the opposites, though less radical there, can meet in any stable rapprochement. The lesson, of course, is preeminently for Connie: although the mental, socially constructed self is not one's essence, it is, Lawrence implies, all but inescapable—yet try to escape it one must.

An even greater difficulty is posed by the Persephone mythology in Lawrence's fiction. Its ugliest elements, from the rape narrative, appear with particular force in "The Princess," in which the title character, after going voluntarily with her Mexican guide into a remote mountain area, is held there against her will in a cold, dark cabin and repeatedly subjected to sex acts that she has initiated but later tried to repulse. However much she may need sensual faculties, she does not develop them from this violent assault by a would-be Plutonic man, and he, profoundly death-committed, is the one who loses his life. The story gains little in tastefulness from its probable mythic underpinnings.

Lawrence's canon as a whole has been charted by Ford in terms of the "'S Curve': Persephone to Pluto" (1965, 26–60), in which the novelist's sympathies presumably shift from the female to the male figure, from the light to the dark. In *Sons and Lovers,* the proud, unbending mother (apparently much like Lawrence's own) may initially seem a more sympathetic figure than the cruder coal-miner father (again, drawn from the author's own background); but this father is at times cast in a life-giving role, and later protagonists like Ciccio of *The Lost Girl* and Cipriano of *The Plumed Serpent* seem in part glorified versions of this earlier coal-stained character.

To a great extent, though, Lawrence's literary, not personal, sources help to account for the turn he gives to his mythology. He was the inheritor of a virtual cult of Demeter and Persephone peaking in the late nineteenth century and the early twentieth, as a number of literary works attest—works like George Meredith's "The Day of the Daughter of Hades" (1883) and Alfred Tennyson's "Demeter and Persephone" (1889). Tennyson's heroine, significantly, is a rather domestic version of Demeter, a Victorian ideal, and Robert Bridges, in 1904, even wrote the masque *Demeter* specifically to honor a "womanly" role to be fostered by inaugurating a new building at the Somerville College for women. If the motherly Demeter could serve as a fitting symbol of the traditional woman, the kidnapped Persephone was a more complex entity, subversive of society because she was removed from the common life and linked with death—being, indeed, queen of Hades. Yet she also might logically appeal to patriarchal fantasies of power because of her subjection to her husband, albeit only seasonal. To some Victorians, she even became a strange sex symbol.

The Pre-Raphaelite vision of the "Fatal Woman"—adopted, too, by late-nineteenth-century "Decadent" writers and artists like Aubrey Beardsley—was well known to Lawrence, for *The White Peacock* relates his teasing, rather callous heroine Lettie to works by Rossetti, Burne-Jones, and Beardsley (Alldritt 1976, 6–10). The tantalizing "fatal" figure took the form of Persephone in poems like A. C. Swinburne's "Hymn to Proserpine," "The Garden of Proserpine," and "Hesperia" (all published in 1866) and in paintings like D. G. Rossetti's seven replicas of *Proserpine* (1877), in which the title figure sulkily, almost coyly, displays the pomegranate that binds her to a yearly term with Pluto. As Rossetti's paintings show visually, the Pre-Raphaelite Proserpine is a pale but sultry-looking queen, vaguely enervated (indeed, lifeless) despite spectacular appeal to the senses. Swinburne associates his goddess with sleep-inducing poppies, languid lips, fatal wines, and the strange pallor that Mario Praz found typical of all "Fatal Women" (1956, 221; see also Marsh 1988 and Dijkstra 1986).

Although opposite to the prevailing domestic ideal, such women reflect to Lawrence, I believe, an intellectualized countervision that he finds shallow. A rebel himself, like Swinburne, against Victorian repression, he sees it still hopelessly present in these figures. While Karen Z. Sproles believes Lawrence's rejection of Pre-Raphaelite ladies comes rather late in his career (1990, 300), I see them consistently representing to him a super-sophisticated civilization that, counterfeiting real emotions, is sapped of nature, almost completely lacking in the sensual quality it seems to flaunt. After this fin-de-siècle, the "times" have not improved but worsened, in his view; in fact, he openly regards history as a degenerative process—even an apocalyptic one—in which only the most radical reversal can allow either communal or individual revitalization. For the individual, the change means such a profound shift of priorities that it can come only in extremis. Thus, his own latter-day Persephone is not languorous because she is in Pluto's Hades; rather, since she is already deadened by civilization, she may avoid world-weary languor only by the "underworld" experience. Although Gilbert refers to Lawrence as "famously misogynistic" (1985, 141), she herself shows that the goddess takes the essential position in some of his work, and this reality, whether conscious or not, motivates his many fictional attempts to restore this sacred dimension in women characters with whose ordeals he generally shows marked empathy (see, for example, Siegel 1991 and Simpson 1982).

Partly from the moribund imagery of the "end of an era," then—specifically, that of the nineteenth century into which he was born—Lawrence's texts sometimes refer to Persephone as the negator of life; Lady Chatterley, for instance, links the nearness of death in a forbidding world to Persephone's breath "out of hell on a cold morning" (1959, 79). This description occurs in an allusion to Swinburne's "Hymn to Proserpine," for Connie has quoted to herself, "The world has grown pale with thy breath" (1959, 79), referring to the "pale Galilean" Christ who, in the poem, has turned the world "grey"; she means to associate her society, Christendom, in a late phase, with death.[6]

Often, however, Lawrence's references to the goddess are charged with more hope of positive transformation. Believing that one's daylight being must merge with hell—with earthy lower faculties and even with the earth itself—he wishes to represent the underworld without any hint of Christian hellfire. As Gilbert points out, the Persephone myth underlying much of *Birds, Beasts and Flowers* allows him a "morally neutral" depiction of hell (1980, 82). He not only associates it with the senses but also renders it significantly appealing by detailing its electrifying colors and allying it with the earth's natural plenitude. Thus, he imagines the flowers that Persephone picks in her lifetime on the fields of Enna as brilliant outcroppings from below, from Pluto's realm of the flesh: "little hells of color, caves of darkness, / Hell, risen in pursuit of her [Persephone], royal, sumptuous / Pit-falls . . . Hell, glamorous and purple" (308). The earth itself rises up personified, like Pluto or his minions.

Alvina, in *The Lost Girl,* wanders similarly in Italian hills through a riot of colors: magenta anemones, indigo grape hyacinths, rose cyclamens, lavender crocuses, blue periwinkle, rose-red gladioli, and black-purple irises—many of these the flowers associated with the ancient Persephone (Frazer 1911–15, 36). A sense of glamour and doom overwhelms her, as if she were indeed the Kore descending into Hades: "She felt that intense sunlight had on her the effect of night: a sort of darkness, and suspension of life. The more she wandered, the more the shadow of the by-gone pagan world seemed to come over her."[7] But that shadow is instinct with strange wonder and beauty of its own, and the situation mingles the extremes of experience: "And a wild, terrible happiness would take hold of her, beyond despair, but very like despair. No one would ever find her. She had gone beyond the world . . . , she had reopened on the old eternity. . . . *She was lost, a lost girl*" (352, 316, my emphasis). Alvina sometimes seems to blend with her setting, almost losing conscious selfhood in it; even her modern time metamorphoses backwards into mythic time. In this process of annihilation, Lawrence is not attempting to deemphasize her essential self but only her socially constructed one, and this distinction is crucial in an assessment of his technique and its meaning.

Lawrence's women characters, encountering the Plutonic, undergo a process of being mythicized—not developing conscious social or personal identity, as in traditional novelistic treatment, but losing it, being modeled according to primordial archetypes, even in apparently nonfabular works. In exchange for individuation, Lawrence merges his modern Persephone both with a mate and with a cosmic or elemental location, thus developing the similitude between Hades or Dis as both a god and a place. One Lawrence painting, *Dance Sketch* (c. 1928), reveals a related technique that might almost be called the "terrestrialization" of a painted subject, something like an inversion of the personification of nature.[8] A Persephone-like figure, luminous-white as light, steps from her own white background into the orbit of a darker Plutonic male. The woman has a "mythic" demeanor because her face is not particularized and her form shares the lighting of surrounding air; meanwhile, the man, ruddy as if from the earth itself, is harmonized with his own dark-blue background yet also seems to merge with her airy light. Both seem released from conscious ego, given over to the elements—along with a delicate white goat that, Pan-like, has joined the dance at a moment of utmost equilibrium.

Lawrence here depicts graphically the relation to the universe that he so frequently advocates: one should, he insists, strive to introject its forces, to be tangibly—and essentially—changed by them, thus knowing "the earth . . . Plutonic." It is remarkable that his painted figures should seem actually tinted visibly, as if by such forces, but Lawrence misses no opportunity to affirm the importance, as he sees it, of stemming the overly conscious personality while augmenting the more elemental being that can partake of the "male" and "female" in the cosmos. If the woman seems in danger of assimilation into the realm of her companion (like Persephone in Dis), Lawrence's nonfiction nonetheless insists that both man and woman must equally interact with the surrounding universe, mysteriously experiencing it through contact with each other. Another painting, *Italian Landscape*, long identified (until recently) as Lawrence's and forming the present cover illustration for the Penguin edition of *The Lost Girl*, employs some similar effects in merging its Persephone-like subject with her surroundings. (This work now appears to be by Lawrence's friend Achsah Brewster, whom he met in 1920, and their possible influence on each other is now a matter of scholarly study.)[9]

Of course, prose fiction as a literary form deals preeminently with the highly developed personality. Thus, when a novelist's message requires that characters (male and female) become depersonalized, virtually mingling with landscape to show their newly opened senses in contact with natural forces, readers inevitably find their expectations disturbed. As we have seen, the problems do not arise to the same degree in Lawrence's poetry. The "lost bride" Persephone in "Bavarian Gentians" is mythically the same "lost girl" of the later novel. But the meanings of this term have real-world reverberations in the novel, as when Alvina loses all that has previously defined her. Her story has features of a novel of manners in describing her staid, comfortable Victorian-style English background—and features of a Gothic novel in tracing her escape from it. She is a literate, middle-class woman who goes to the remote peasant home of her Italian husband Ciccio, moving "down in the darkness . . . to the gulf of darkness below" (305). Here, feeling "quite, quite lost," she has "gone out of the world, over the border." Indeed, "she was lost to Woodhouse [her old home], to Lancaster, to England . . . all lost" (306).

Her condition is in many ways like being dead, for Lawrence's language evokes the shadow of death and the angel of death: "What strange valley of shadow was she threading? What was the terrible man's passion that haunted her like a dark angel?" (321). That very passion provides for emotional rebirth, yet even this salvation is not without its realistic drawbacks. While she has by no means been raped, she is placed in this extreme position by her helpless erotic attachment to Ciccio. And her subjugation in other areas of life *is* distinctly forced upon her. Ciccio and one of his male relatives seem to be "threatening her with surveillance and subjection" (326) and will not speak with a woman about politics, religion, or other topics that have long been staples in Alvina's conversation within her own informed circles back in England. In spite of this treatment, she is, somewhat paradoxically, almost worshiped as a bright opposite to the gloomy men of her new home, who see in her "a fairness, a luminousness" of soul, "something touched with divinity" (325). This divinity, we realize, is that of the daylight Persephone, however attenuated in her present circumstances.

But Alvina is threatened by more than the men in her new life; the land itself seems to be trying to claim her, in some mysterious way, casting over her a sense of heavy darkness (334). As she experiences the "pagan twilight" of her location, she has "a sense of ancient gods who knew the right of human sacrifice" and "she believed she would not live" (351–52). Even to her own mind, "she was lost" so that "no one would ever find her" (314, 316). Her worst moments come when she foresees herself alone in Italy, abandoned there when her husband goes into World War I. She fantasizes in vain about getting away, back to the world of light, as Persephone might return intermittently to her home: "She was always making little plans in her mind—how she could get out of that cruel valley and escape to Rome, to English people. She would find the English Consul and he would help her" (336). But "she knew how easy it would be, once her spirit broke, for her to die and be buried in the

[Italian] cemetery" (336). Meditating thus, she becomes "like a lump of darkness in that doomed Italian kitchen" as "death and eternity were settled down on her" (338). And thus she is left in "Hades." Her story shows Lawrence's complex awareness not only of the value but also of the cost of the Plutonic experience—the radical trauma of losing one's accustomed home and social identity, even for the compensation of rich new experience.

Some characters in Lawrence's fiction are even more explicitly related to Persephone than is Alvina. In *Quetzalcoatl* (written in 1923), the first version of *The Plumed Serpent* that forms an independent creative effort while also illuminating some features of the published novel (Clark 1987, xxv; Martz 1990, 287–98; Martz 1993), the Mexican leader, Don Ramón, directly acknowledges that the protagonist, Kate, is in Persephone's role while in Mexico with himself and a Mexican Indian general, Cipriano: "Poor Persephone. You can be queen in hell, with us," says Ramón (Lawrence 1923, 333).[10]

"Hell," Lawrence states in *Apocalypse*, is the repository of all superseded ancient powers (109). Fittingly, then, a religious and political movement in Kate's Mexican setting attempts to restore the old Aztec gods in the place of ascetic Christianity. In *Quetzalcoatl*, Ramón quotes from Swinburne's "Hymn to Proserpine," in which the "pale Galilean" has displaced the old classical gods: "You have triumphed you Galileans" (1923, 337), he explains that a reversal is due to occur—Mexico is to be the inversion of modern, white Christendom, and the ancient Aztec deities are to preside over an era that renews the dark, sensuous faculties. Ramón taxes the moderns with their sterility, likening them to corn chaff that will be harvested by apocalyptic flames. Besides echoing the Bible, such imagery is partly applicable to fertility mythology. The desolation of the earth, with its blasted crops, suggests Demeter's grieving neglect of it or Pluto's more aggressive invasion of it. The corn is, of course, peculiarly associated with both Demeter and Persephone, as Lawrence would have known from Frazer's *Golden Bough* (1911–15, 37–41, 61–67). In this case, its barrenness suggests the shortcomings of the modern dispensation, no doubt including Kate as long as she is its representative.

Just as the world is to know a newly pagan era, Kate is to be transformed from a dissatisfied modern woman into the avatar of an ancient goddess—with help from Ramón and the militant Cipriano, who desires her for a wife. Somewhat suggesting Pluto in his tempestuous chariot, Cipriano, in *The Plumed Serpent,* is "like a dark whirlwind column" and "a potency on the face of the earth."[11] In *Quetzalcoatl,* moreover, Kate is in danger of literal kidnapping. Both Ramón and Cipriano, who claim to be gods themselves, want her to assume an Aztec identity and stay in Mexico as a member of their pantheon. Although Kate has originally gone there on her own initiative, Cipriano strongly asserts his right to hold her there against her will. The final *Plumed Serpent* modifies this theme of the earlier novel but does not completely obliterate it. When Kate considers leaving Mexico in the later book, Cipriano "was thinking that if he liked, he could use the law and have her prevented from leaving the country" (437). At the end, Kate stays in Mexico, crying out to him ambiguously, "You won't let me go!" (444). The Aztecs replace the Christians, standing, in this analogue to the classical design, in the place of the chthonic Greek deities. Although the setting is certainly Mexico, the Irish Kate is reminded, too, of "the old, old Europe" (202): Cipriano comes to seem to her "like an old god," and she eventually associates one scene with "Dionysus with a vine sprouting" (426). On one mythic level, then, this is clearly the old Greek world.

The setting is also explicitly the underworld: "They say the word Mexico means *Below this*!" says Ramón (183). Cipriano is cast as a netherworld figure with "dark pinions"—not only as the bloodthirsty Aztec Huitzilopochtli and the sinister Pluto but also as the "god-demon Pan" and perhaps even Lucifer (362, 312). Extensively related to snake images, he represents, among other things, male power. When Kate finally marries him (as she does not do in *Quetzalcoatl*), the wedding rituals require her to kiss his feet and ankles; in the new Church of Quetzalcoatl, moreover, all women must kneel while men stand. Ramón's wife, Teresa, tries to give Kate lessons in female humility. In a remarkably awkward exchange that Lawrence, fortunately, discarded in the final version of his novel, Teresa in *Quetzalcoatl* tells how her husband "takes charge" of her soul: "If thou sayst thou art a god [she tells him], then it is true. If thou art not a god, there are no gods. And if thou wishest me to be a goddess, I will be it. Always at your service" (1923 typescript, 317).

But Kate is a sturdier version of Persephone, declaring her independence: "I think I am myself, and perhaps a good deal more myself, and more of a woman, when I am alone, than when I am submitting to some man," she says (1923 typescript, 315). Even here, however, Teresa gets a last word, claiming that what looks like woman's submission is really something else. Language proves predictably inadequate for such Lawrentian complexities, and this impasse continues to some extent in *The Plumed Serpent*. Despite such controversial exchanges on male dominance, however, an ideal of gender mutuality is prominent in the broad design of both versions, for Kate's own outspoken dissent and her careful accommodation of the new ideology to her own needs mark Lawrence's most innovative direction in the use of his Persephone myth.

Late in the final novel, nonetheless, Kate makes her sexual submission to Cipriano in scenes now famous for his apparent dislike of female orgasm (see, for example, Nixon 1986, 205; Storch 1990, 22; Spilka 1990, 176–88; Widmer 1989, 157–58)—although, it must be said, she seems a happy mate and a partner able to provide welcome counters to his most negative traits. As she settles into this marriage, though, she endures a fear of invasion from the land itself, causing physical change: "The sense of menace that Mexico put over her, and the feeling of inner nausea, was becoming too much to bear" (419). Both her mind and her body are affected: "She could feel it, the terrible katabolism and metabolism in her blood, changing her even as a creature, changing her to another creature" (421). Her condition is like Alvina's, each feeling that the land can penetrate and kill her. As Kate loses the individualistic self and assumes another (but evidently innate) self, she increasingly fills a mythic role that will bind her to her Pluto and his land: her "hard and finished, accomplished" self that has been "curiously invulnerable and insentient" begins to yield to a "sensitive, desirous self" that is "vulnerable, and organically connected with Cipriano" (428). She shares, with Persephone, a dual existence: "When Cipriano was away, Kate was her old individual self. Only when Cipriano was present, and then only sometimes, did the connection overwhelm her" (411). Her sexual relations with him are invariably in darkness; yet in the daytime world, too, she seems like Persephone reborn.

Despite the "unbearable nausea of change," she sinks "to a final rest, within a great, opened-out cosmos" (421), and "the green furrows of the mountain-sides were as if in her own hand" (423). Such passages suggest Persephone's seasonal return to the fertile daylight world; and, indeed, Mexico now has unwonted rain and fruitfulness explicitly attributed to Kate. Cipriano has associated her with "morning, of the time of the rains," and her presence explains why "the northern mystery [of moist cool] seemed to have blown so far south" (405). At last, in the Mexican autumn—which is "like a strange, inverted spring"—she can "hardly remember now the dry, rigid pallor of the heat, when the whole earth seemed to crepitate viciously with dry malevolence: like memory gone dry and sterile, hellish" (426). In Lawrence's reworking of the Persephone myth, Kate is both the bride of Pluto and the fertility goddess.

In the novel's duality, Lawrence intends, once again, to unite upper and lower, male and female, light and dark. Even in the sunlight, Kate thinks about "all the unseen things in the hidden places of the earth," feeling "a certain reconciliation" with the serpent (425). Cipriano is curiously associated with this serpent imagery when Kate, threatening to leave Mexico, imagines him "turned into a sort of serpent, that reared and looked at her with glittering eyes, then slid away into the void, leaving her blank, the sense of power gone out of her" (438). Lawrence is playing, in part, with the Edenic myth, but he may also recollect Madame Blavatsky's report of one Persephone whose mate was a "Dragon Bridegroom" (1931, 2:505).[12] Kate is perhaps "lost" to her English home, but she makes at least a tentative choice to stay in her "underworld," apparently accepting her Persephone identity because she sees it as an alternative to an even less appealing role: "Without Cipriano to touch me and limit me and submerge my will," she thinks, "I shall become a horrible, elderly female" (439). While this reasoning may strike the reader as less than persuasive (and far less than enlightened), it is clear that Lawrence is working with mythic forms of the "triple goddess" or Great Mother, including the aged crone as well as the girl and mother. Repudiating this deathly third figure, Kate has a sense of renewed youth and maidenhood like a rejuvenated Kore. Lawrence suggests, then, that the very loss of some of Kate's socially constructed identity has prepared for her newness of life. Despite this intention, the text never thoroughly dispels the feeling that the setting is a less-than-pleasant Hades, ambiguous at best.

One further character, whose story is also set in Mexico, must be considered in a study of Lawrence's Persephones, for she is the most thoroughly and pointlessly "lost" of all his heroines and her fate most clearly fulfills the fertility sacrifice that the author perceived at the heart of the Persephone myth. This is the unnamed woman in "The Woman Who Rode Away" (published in 1928). She is described both as a maiden—a "rather dazzling Californian girl from Berkeley"—and as a wife who has been drained of vitality not by a Plutonic mate but by a husband who represents the sterile white civilization.[13] This modern Persephone, who has already known death-in-life with him near a "dead, thrice-dead" Mexican town, rides "away" to wild Indians who, she hopes, may offer new life to her (2:547). Of course, she is already in "hell" before she leaves, being far removed from her maiden setting. Although she is taken by the Indians as a sacrificial victim, her story departs from that of Persephone (and from most Lawrentian tales of this format) when she is not even sexually desired (or desiring). Nevertheless, her death at the winter solstice suggests, if not the myth of Persephone in Hades, then a tale that is partly cognate with it. The Indians expect the death to result in better crops and in a new era of dark power. Completely depersonalized, even in her namelessness, she is the "year-bride" dying—though not, as I read the story, reborn. Despite its evident standing as a fable, it strangely fails to suspend Lawrence's "realistic" mode and is the more disturbing for this fact.

The title of an essay by Mark Kinkead-Weekes, "The Gringo Señora Who Rode Away," points up (for consideration and question) the way the story has often been read: as if Lawrence must be on the "side" of the Indians (1990). Mabel Dodge Luhan (who believed herself a model for the woman) referred to it as the tale in which Lawrence "thought he finished [her] up" (1932, 238), and Kate Millett saw the Indians as surrogates for the author, who, she charged, revelled in the "sadistic pornography" of their actions (1969, 410). L. D. Clark finds in this tale an affirmation of "some region of the soul" that is "symbolized by the Indians" (1980, 311), and James C. Cowan, while casting the woman in a Christ-like role as a savior to redeem the sins of her race, reads the story partly in terms of the Indians' worldview (1970, 70–78). Yet a divergent view is gathering force (see MacLeod 1985; Balbert 1985–86, 271; Balbert 1989, 130–31; Kinkead-Weekes 1990, 258–63); and I, rather than assuming that Lawrence sanctions these particular "dark" characters (the Indians), consider the story a parody of his usual treatment of the fair lady's encounter with the Plutonic male. The woman never clearly experiences revitalization, as do most other Lawrentian Persephones. She rides through flowers that she sees "shadowily . . . as one who is dead must see them" (2:559). Feeling herself "dead already," she queries, "What difference does it make, the transition from the dead I am to the dead I shall be, very soon!" (2:579). Her weary despair remains with her to the end. Lawrence makes the Indians not godlike but savage, brutalizing her horse with "resounding" blows and regarding her with "a steely covetous intent" (2:555–56, 560). Only when drugged—when administered an herb that "would numb her mind altogether, and release her senses into a sort of heightened, mystic acuteness"—does she fail to feel "victimised" (2:572). Although we are told that she "wanted" her death (2:577), it is necessary to question her supposed voluntarism. By this strange inverted parable, Lawrence himself seems to point up the horror implicit in his Plutonic myth when carried to its extreme in this fiction.

It may have been clear to him, then, that Persephone and Pluto are more problematical in the tales than they are in his metaphysical theories and related poetry. We have seen that the myth makes a late appearance in his works in the poetry of "Bavarian Gentians." In another poem, "Climb Down, O Lordly Mind," he states, "The blood knows in darkness, and forever dark," adding that it is the "dark heart" to which the gods are real (474). In a pattern of vital (if precarious) mutuality, however, this sensuous center also requires mental and spiritual light. This is why he continually sends his cerebral maidens into the Plutonic arms, expressing the necessity of balance between faculties. This is why Persephone is one of his favorite mythological figures, being one of the "souls that are at home in both homes" (light and dark, life and death), as another poem puts it, praising the double view of "the scarlet and purple flowers at the door of hell" (711). How different is this vivid sight from the dull prospect glimpsed by the victim in "The Woman Who Rode Away," seeing flowers "shadowily," as if dead! All of Lawrence's works mean to convey the double vision, the intensifying juxtaposition of opposites. He would have agreed with one of his sources on Persephone, Gilbert Murray, that "there is the very heart of life in this home-coming Bride of the underworld," life as "a thing continuous and unchanging but shot through with parting and death, life as a great love or desire ever torn asunder and ever renewed" (1912, 85). All of his "lost" girls, whether in realistic fiction or not (and whether disturbing us or not), embody something of this twofold human experience.

NOTES

1. Lawrence 1983, 54. Subsequent page numbers in parentheses in discussions of *Apocalypse* refer to this edition.

2. Lawrence 1970, 511. Subsequent page numbers in parentheses in discussions of "A Propos of *Lady Chatterley's Lover*" refer to this edition.

3. Lawrence 1971, 697. Subsequent page numbers in parentheses in citations of Lawrence's poems refer to this edition.

4. See, for example, *Spirits of the Corn and of the Wild*, 7:236–69, in the third edition (1911–15), the edition available to Lawrence.

5. This watercolor painting is in the Harry Ransom Humanities Research Center, the University of Texas at Austin.

6. For Swinburne's original line, see "Hymn to Proserpine," in Swinburne 1972, 1:69.

7. Lawrence 1981, 365. Subsequent page numbers in parentheses in discussions of *The Lost Girl* refer to this edition.

8. This oil painting is part of the Saki Karavas collection, Taos, New Mexico.

9. I owe this information to Keith Cushman, the Lawrence and Brewster scholar.

10. I have consulted the holograph manuscript of *Quetzalcoatl* (Harry Ransom Humanities Research Center, the University of Texas at Austin), and the typescript (Houghton Library, Harvard University, Cambridge, Mass.), both 1923. Page numbers in parentheses in discussions of *Quetzalcoatl* refer to this typescript. I gratefully acknowledge the permissions of Laurence Pollinger, Ltd., the Frieda Lawrence Ravagli Estate, and the Houghton Library, Harvard, for the use of material in this chapter.

11. Lawrence 1987, 310, 389. Subsequent page numbers in the parentheses in discussions of *The Plumed Serpent* refer to this edition.

12. Lawrence knew Blavatsky's *Isis Unveiled* by 1919.

13. Lawrence 1972, 2:547. Subsequent page numbers in parentheses in discussions of "The Woman Who Rode Away" refer to this edition.

BIBLIOGRAPHY

Alldritt, Keith. *The Visual Imagination of D. H. Lawrence*. London: Edward Arnold, 1976.

Balbert, Peter. "Snake's Eye and Obsidian Knife: Art, Ideology, and 'The Woman Who Rode Away.'" *D. H. Lawrence Review* 18 (1985–86): 255–73.

———. *D. H. Lawrence and the Phallic Imagination: Essays on Sexual Identity and Feminist Misreading*. New York: St. Martin's, 1989.

Blavatsky, Helena. *Isis Unveiled: Master-Key to the Mysteries of Ancient and Modern Science and Theology*. 2 vols. in one. Los Angeles: Theosophy, 1931. Reprint of the London edition, 1901.

Clark, L. D. *The Minoan Distance: The Symbolism of Travel in D. H. Lawrence*. Tucson: Univ. of Arizona Press, 1980.

———. Introduction to *The Plumed Serpent*, by D. H. Lawrence. Cambridge Edition of the Letters and Works of D. H. Lawrence, edited by James T. Boulton and Warren Roberts. Cambridge: Cambridge Univ. Press, 1987.

Cowan, James. *D. H. Lawrence's American Journey: A Study in Literature and Myth*. Cleveland: Case Western Reserve Univ. Press, 1970.

Dijkstra, Bram. *Idols of Perversity: Fantasies of Feminine Evil in Fin-de-Siècle Culture*. Oxford: Oxford Univ. Press, 1986.

Donovan, Josephine. *After the Fall: The Demeter-Persephone Myth in Wharton, Cather, and Glasgow*. University Park: Pennsylvania State Univ. Press, 1989.

Ford, George. *Double Measure: A Study of the Novels and Stories of D. H. Lawrence*. New York: Norton, 1965.

Frazer, Sir James George. *Spirits of the Corn and of the Wild. The Golden Bough: A Study in Magic and Religion*, vol. 7. 3d ed. London: Macmillan, 1911-15.

Gilbert, Sandra M. "D. H. Lawrence's Uncommon Prayers." In *D. H. Lawrence: The Man Who Lived*, edited by Robert B. Partlow, Jr., and Harry T. Moore, 73–93. Carbondale: Southern Illinois Univ. Press, 1980.

———. "Potent Griselda: 'The Ladybird' and the Great Mother." In *D. H. Lawrence: A Centenary Consideration*, edited by Peter Balbert and Phillip L. Marcus, 130–61. Ithaca, N.Y.: Cornell Univ. Press, 1985.

Harrison, Jane. *Prolegomena to the Study of Greek Religion*. Cambridge: Cambridge Univ. Press, 1903.

Hinz, Evelyn J. "Hierogamy versus Wedlock: Types of Marriage Plots and Their Relationship to Genres of Prose Fiction." *PMLA* 91 (1976): 900-913.

———. "*The Rainbow:* Ursula's Liberation." *Contemporary Literature* 17 (1976): 27.

Hyde, Virginia. "Architectural Monuments: Centers of Worship in *Women in Love*." *Mosaic* 17 (1984): 73–92.

Jung, C. G. "The Psychological Aspects of the Kore." In *Essays on a Science of Mythology: The Myth of the Divine Child and the Mysteries of Eleusis*, by C. G. Jung and C. Kerényi, 156–77. Princeton: Princeton Univ. Press, 1969.

———. "The Psychology of the Child Archetype." In *Essays on a Science of Mythology: The Myth of the Divine Child and the Mysteries of Eleusis*, by C. G. Jung and C. Kerényi, 70–100. Princeton: Princeton Univ. Press, 1969.

———. *The Risen Adam: D. H. Lawrence's Revisionist Typology*. University Park: Pennsylvania State University Press, 1992.

Kerényi, C. "Kore." In *Essays on a Science of Mythology: The Myth of the Divine Child and the Mysteries of Eleusis*, by C. G. Jung and C. Kerényi, 101–55. Princeton: Princeton Univ. Press, 1969.

Kinkead-Weekes, Mark. "The Gringo Señora Who Rode Away." *D. H. Lawrence Review* 22 (Fall 1990): 251–65.

Lawrence, D. H. *Quetzalcoatl*. Holograph, 1923. Harry Ransom Humanities Research Center, Univ. of Texas, Austin.

———. *Quetzalcoatl*. Typescript, 1923. Houghton Library, Harvard Univ., Cambridge, Mass.

———. *The First Lady Chatterley*. New York: Dial, 1944.

———. *Lady Chatterley's Lover.* New York: Signet, 1959.
———. "A Propos of *Lady Chatterley's Lover.*" In *Phoenix II: Uncollected, Unpublished, and Other Prose Works by D. H. Lawrence,* edited by Warren Roberts and Harry T. Moore, 487–515. New York: Viking, 1970.
———. *The Complete Poems,* edited by Vivian de Sola Pinto and Warren Roberts. New York: Viking, 1971.
———. "The Woman Who Rode Away." In *Complete Short Stories,* vol. 2. New York: Viking, 1972.
———. *The Lost Girl,* edited by John Worthen. Cambridge Edition of the Letters and Works of D. H. Lawrence, edited by James T. Boulton and Warren Roberts. Cambridge: Cambridge Univ. Press, 1981.
———. *Apocalypse and the Writings on Revelation,* edited by Mara Kalnins. Cambridge Edition of the Letters and Works of D. H. Lawrence, edited by James T. Boulton and Warren Roberts. Cambridge: Cambridge Univ. Press, 1983.
———. *The White Peacock,* edited by Andrew Robertson. Cambridge Edition of the Letters and Works of D. H. Lawrence, edited by James T. Boulton and Warren Roberts. Cambridge: Cambridge Univ. Press, 1983.
———. *The Plumed Serpent,* edited by L. D. Clark. Cambridge Edition of the Letters and Works of D. H. Lawrence, edited by James T. Boulton and Warren Roberts. Cambridge: Cambridge Univ. Press, 1987.
———. *Quetzalcoatl,* edited by Louis Martz. Redding Ridge, Conn.: Black Swan Press, 1993.
Luhan, Mabel Dodge. *Lorenzo in Taos.* New York: Knopf, 1932.
MacLeod, Sheila. *Lawrence's Men and Women.* London: Heinemann, 1985.
Mandell, Gail Porter. *The Phoenix Paradox: A Study of Renewal through Change in the 'Collected Poems' and 'Last Poems' of D. H. Lawrence.* Carbondale: Southern Illinois Univ. Press, 1984.
Marsh, Jan. "Pale Ladies of Death." In *Pre-Raphaelite Women: Images of Femininity,* 135–47. New York: Harmony Books, 1988.
Martz, Louis. "*Quetzalcoatl:* The First Version of *The Plumed Serpent.*" *D. H. Lawrence Review* 22 (Fall 1990): 287–98.
———. Introduction to *Quetzalcoatl,* by D. H. Lawrence. Redding Ridge, Conn.: Black Swan Press, 1993.
Millett, Kate. *Sexual Politics.* New York: Ballantine, 1969.
Moynahan, Julian. *The Deed of Life: The Novels and Tales of D. H. Lawrence.* Princeton: Princeton Univ. Press, 1963.
Murray, Gilbert. *Four Stages of Greek Religion.* Oxford: Clarendon, 1912.
Nixon, Cornelia. *D. H. Lawrence's Leadership Politics and the Turn Against Women.* Berkeley: Univ. of California Press, 1986.
Ortner, Sherry B. "Is Female to Male as Nature Is to Culture?" In *Woman, Culture and Society,* edited by Michelle Zimbalist Rosaldo and Louise Lamphere, 67–87. Stanford: Stanford Univ. Press, 1974.
Pratt, Annis V. "Spinning Among Fields: Jung, Frye, Lévi-Strauss and Femi-

nist Archetypal Theory." In *Feminist Archetypal Theory: Interdisciplinary Re-Visions of Jungian Thought,* edited by Estella Lauter and Carol Schreier Rupprecht, 93–136. Knoxville: Univ. of Tennessee Press, 1985.

Praz, Mario. *The Romantic Agony.* Translated by Angus Davidson. Cleveland and New York: World [Meridian], 1956.

Ruderman, Judith. *D. H. Lawrence and the Devouring Mother: The Search for a Patriarchal Ideal of Leadership.* Durham, N.C.: Duke Univ. Press, 1984.

Sagar, Keith. *D. H. Lawrence: Life into Art.* New York: Viking, 1985.

Scott, Bonnie Kime. *Joyce and Feminism.* Bloomington: Indiana Univ. Press, 1984.

Siegel, Carol. *Lawrence among the Women: Wavering Boundaries in Women's Literary Traditions.* Charlottesville: Univ. Press of Virginia, 1991.

Simpson, Hilary. *D. H. Lawrence and Feminism.* DeKalb: Northern Illinois Univ. Press, 1982.

Spilka, Mark. "Lawrence and the Clitoris." In *The Challenge of D. H. Lawrence,* edited by Michael Squires and Keith Cushman, 176–88. Madison: Univ. of Wisconsin Press, 1990.

Sproles, Karen Z. "D. H. Lawrence and the Pre-Raphaelites: Love among the Ruins." *D. H. Lawrence Review* 22 (Fall 1990): 299–305.

Stewart, Grace. *A New Mythos: The Novel of the Artist as Heroine, 1877–1977.* Monographs in Women's Studies, edited by Sherri Clarkson. St. Alban's, Vt.: Eden Press Women's Publications, 1979.

Storch, Margaret. *Sons and Adversaries: Women in William Blake and D. H. Lawrence.* Knoxville: Univ. of Tennessee Press, 1990.

Swinburne, Algernon Charles. *The Poems.* New York: AMS Press, 1972. Reprint of the London edition, 1904–5.

Viinikka, Anja. *From Persephone to Pan: D. H. Lawrence's Mythopoeic Vision of the Integrated Personality.* Turku, Finland: Turun Yliopisto Julkaisuja, 1988.

Westling, Louise. *Sacred Groves and Ravaged Gardens: The Fiction of Eudora Welty, Carson McCullers, and Flannery O'Connor.* Athens: Univ. of Georgia Press, 1985.

Whelan, P. T. *D. H. Lawrence: Myth and Metaphysic in 'The Rainbow' and 'Women in Love.'* Ann Arbor, Mich.: UMI Research Press, 1988.

Widmer, Kingsley. "Lawrence's Cultural Impact." In *The Legacy of D. H. Lawrence: New Essays,* edited by Jeffrey Meyers, 156–74. New York: St. Martin's, 1989.

Zuntz, Günther. *Persephone: Three Essays on Religion and Thought in Magna Graecia.* Oxford: Clarendon, 1971.

Mary A. Doll

CHAPTER 8

GHOSTS OF THEMSELVES: THE DEMETER WOMEN IN BECKETT

Samuel Beckett's work conveys the sense of what it is like to search and to wait, endlessly. It is like myth, a story that has no ending. Ever in need of retelling, myth eludes finality; any search for the ultimate meaning of myth is elusive, haunting. The Beckettian search is similarly mythic, through and through. Quests to and from, characters who are archetypes, not stereotypes, variations upon sames: all imply an insistence like that of myth to return to the ground of being. The effect on the reader is extra-audenary.[1] Readers and viewers of Beckett's work find it impossible to respond only intellectually to the texts. Like dreams, these texts require us to live in them. Deepest feelings get riled, truths get contradicted, uncertainty prevails. Beckett brings from below rhythms of the past, the purpose of which was then, and is now, to let in the dark side. The recent presence of women in Beckett's plays deepens this mythic sense by giving it feminine consciousness. Beckett presents what poets and mythmakers have always known: that feminine consciousness takes us "back in" and "right down." The haunted females of his recent plays show living souls whose suffering is chthonic but strangely poetic.[2]

It should come as no surprise, then, that allusions to Demeter are woven into the very fabric of Beckett's texts. Demeter's paired relation with her daughter Persephone taps an archetypal structure of the psyche that Beckett has portrayed in various configurations (mother-daughter, father-son, old man–young boy, self-self). Demeter's story, primarily one of loss, is Beckett's basic story. The journey to find the lost one, paradigmatic of the Beckettian search, becomes at the same time a journey to find the lost part of the self. It is an anxious quest, a way of sorrows, a *via dolorosa,* forcing the quester to live as never before—on the edge. A usual way of being is invaded, suddenly, without provocation, bringing new relations, establishing new terms of need. Even Beckett's titles capture the travail of *Lost Ones,* living *All Strange Away,* in a *Come and Go* pattern *Ill Seen Ill Said.*

Four qualities make mythic drama its own distinct type. Each of these qualities overturns the dominant philosophical, Aristotelian requirements of Western drama. Not plot, but image; not action, but rhythm; not subjects but objects; not character, but ghosts: these four negatives clear the way for Beckett's new drama of myth. And what better myth to give structure to such qualities than the myth of Demeter and Persephone? The myth that explores the dynamic between mother and daughter also explores the dynamic between body and soul, ground and undersurface, seen and unseen, sudden action and long, long suffering. Significantly, although the central event of the myth is Persephone's abduction, the central impact of the abduction is on the mother, Demeter. Goddess of pigs and corn, Demeter has always been oriented to earth and its bounty. Suddenly this orientation shifts with the disappearance of her daughter. Demeter becomes consumed by absence. At the core of the myth is a mystery, for it is Demeter—not Persephone—who is led away (ab-ducted). Consciousness, not flesh, is abducted. The rape of Persephone is myth's metaphor for the thrust of an Other world, and for the unwillingness of ego to be led down to the dark side.

We could say that Demeter reveals a potency of mind's imaginings. The mother feels her daughter's absence not intellectually, abstractly, but sensually, concretely. Her grief becomes bodied forth as felt grief: in the feet (she wanders the earth for nine days); in the mouth (she never tastes ambrosia or nectar); and in the flesh (she never washes). When her daughter is returned to her, the joy of the reunion is muted, for a pattern has been set of ever-present absence. Unlike the quest of the father, who captures and retains his boon, the quest of the mother never ends. Demeter must forever share Persephone with the king of the underworld. She must live in her soul as one lives in spring and winter.

But there is specific reference, as well, to the myth of Demeter in the Beckettian corpus. In the early 1937–39 collection of poems, the twelfth poem refers to the plains of Enna, Proserpine and rape:

> jusque dans la caverne ciel et sol
> et une à une les vieilles voix
> d'outre-tombe
> et lentement la même lumière
> qui sur les plaines d'Enna en longs viols
> macérait naguère les capillaires
> et les même lois
> que naguère
> et lentement au loin qui éteint
> Proserpine et Atropos
> adorable de vide douteux
> encore la bouche d'ombre[3]

Basic to this (untitled) poem, as to the "Homeric Hymn to Demeter," is a dynamic tension between sun (*sol*) and shadow (*ombre*), maiden hair (*capillaires*) and Proserpine, cavern and mouth (*bouche*) —a tension that focuses on the central image of "raped maidenhair" (*en longs viols macérait naguère les capillaires*). Subject-object ambiguities so pervade the poem that language obscures rather than clarifies meaning. If *longs viols*, or long rapes, refers to a relation of light to maidenhair fern, the phrase functions merely metaphorically to suggest sunlight raping the meadows of Enna (*les plaines d'Enna*) with a fierce intensity of light. But if the image refers to specifics of the Demeter myth, it functions both literally (to suggest an invasion of maidenhair) and metaphorically (to suggest a violent thrusting together of life and death patterns).

Obscurities of meaning are further built into the fabric of this poem with unpunctuated endlines, repeated *ands*, and with the final *encore*. Sky and sun form, at first, a cavern, seeming to make the outer world a smaller part of a larger "hole." At the end of the poem the cavern forms a new shape, a mouth of shadow (*la bouche d'ombre*), as if the hole of the cavern's darkness were now swallowing itself. Beckett suggests that the big world of sky's cavern will again become the little world of shadow's mouth—perhaps that sky fathers will yield to earth mothers, that is, be reborn (metaphorically) from the speakings of women (*les vieilles voix, la bouche d'ombre*). Or that the macrocosm (*d'outre-tombe, la caverne ciel et sol*) will be eaten up by the microcosm (*la bouche d'ombre*)—the big world entombed by the small world. Instead of rape of the female (the structuring metaphor of the poem), there is the suggestion of engulfment by the female, alongside the suggestion of metaphorical rebirth.

Light and dark symbolism, consequently, exchanges its traditional association—light with pure or unadulterated good, dark with pure or unadulterated evil—and complicates meaning. Light (*la même lumière*) becomes a natural violator, canceling out the shadow world. The old voices (*les vieilles voix*) live in the shadow world; they will be slowly and inexorably extinguished (*et lentement au loin qui éteint*) like rays of light by the darkness inside the skull or cavern of the sky (*la caverne ciel*). Such extinguishing of the ancient voices in the context of the poem functions metaphorically (*les mêmes lois*) like rape in that too much light or clarity ruins that which cannot be explicated clearly.

This poem of Beckett's sets the stage for a feminine mythos that celebrates the various shades of darkness and intensifies the power of metaphor. Beckett presents forces that "macerate" an otherwise "exquisite feminine greyness" such as that held by Proserpine and Atropos (see Cohn 1980, 270). Yet paradoxically, these mythic women are capable of their own macerating, or raping, functions in their searches to inhabit strange territory. Atropos (the thread cutter) and Proserpine (the raped one) are two terrifying female mythic figures who, because they sever or are severed from connection with the earth, bind themselves more deeply into darkness.

The four mythic qualities—image, rhythm, ghosts, and objects—can be seen in those Beckett plays in which women chart a movement from fleshly, sunny substantiality toward ever more greying ghostliness. Winnie, in *Happy Days* (1962), illustrates the beginning of this movement. Discovered in blazing light, surrounded by an expanse of scorched grass, Winnie shows the devastating effect on feminine consciousness when it is exposed to too much light. Implanted too firmly in the earth, Winnie is stuck—cut off from *memoria*. Her speech, filled with empty words and snippets of song or story, is not at all a mingling of soul with image. It is, rather, a grab bag of literary allusions, like the brushes and combs she removes from her bag—objects, merely, to pass through boredom. When

Winnie tells her story of a young girl's descent down the stairs and sudden seduction, however, she is beginning a descent into imagination. The story could be considered a parody of Persephone, with reference to "the scream" and "underthings." The seductor, a mouse, is hardly the horsedrawn god, and yet the function of the animal is animating to the soul. The mouse disturbs Winnie's boredom out of its normalcy, interrupting "the old style" of plot as a forward series of actions seeking resolution. Winnie's story halts at image, which works like a rat of the unconscious gnawing at the psyche.[4]

In image as well as in theme, the myth of Demeter and Persephone touches the core of Beckett's work. His plays, particularly *Not I, Footfalls,* and *Rockaby,* bear an astonishing similarity to the motifs of Demeter. All follow a rhythm of Demeter's sorrowful search as a cycle of finding and losing. All connect the seasons of winter and spring with states of being. All show that unconscious life is more powerfully intense than conscious life. And, in all, a questing pattern of Beckett's characters takes on new urgency as women search literally for the metaphors that ground them.

In *Not I,* for example, a female character called Mouth takes us back to the "mouth" or source of suffering. The play, which lasts only fifteen to seventeen minutes, throws us into a Demeter situation of barren grief. We hear of a hellish life lived without the springs of emotion, "always winter some strange reason."[5] But, just when life seems most lost, at rock bottom, the wellspring gushes forth from Mouth's lips. It is, in accordance with Beckett's design, a play with "blubbering lips" that works "on the nerves, not the intellect" (Harvey 1970, 212). Life that had contained no feeling on one level is suddenly assaulted by another life buried in another level. Buzzings and flickerings in the head spew forth as if from a burst dam. Broken fragments of sentences, interruptions, corrections, and frenzy thrust themselves upon Mouth unannounced. Something, a "dull roar in the skull" (16) begging to be let in, simply refuses to dry up.

The Persephone-Demeter motifs in *Not I* are too numerous to mention individually, because they occur on every page of the play's text. Nevertheless, the following examples give an idea of the pattern, which ushers an audience, as well as the silent character called Auditor, into a strange place of mind. Persephone motifs include references to a grassy meadow, found in Beckett's use of "field," "Croker's Acres" (15, 20); references to the suddenness of the rape event, found in Beckett's phrases "suddenly she felt" (18) and "sudden flash" (16, 19, 21, 22); and references to the scream, as in Beckett's use of "dull roar" and "screaming" (16, 17, 21, 23). Demeter motifs include references to constant walking, as in Beckett's phrase "ferreting around" (21) and words like "on" and "back" (22, 23); references to anguish, as in Beckett's mention of tears (20) and madness (22); references to sitting and staring, as found in Beckett's phrase "long hours of darkness" (22) and his description of Mouth's insentience (15), motionlessness (18), and speechlessness (21). A further dynamic both of the myth and of Beckett's play is the need of opposites to combine, as in Beckett's winter-spring images (17, 22, 23). Also, the specific Demeter mythologem of dry streams is transposed in Beckett as a "flaw in her make-up" that so disconnects the "machine" that Mouth becomes "powerless to respond," "numbed," until "all that moisture" stills the brain (17). It is also transposed as her attempt to "tell . . . then rush out stop the first she saw . . . nearest lavatory . . . start pouring it out . . . steady stream . . . mad stuff . . . half the vowels wrong . . . no one could follow" (22).

In keeping with the Demeter mythos, what happens to Mouth in *Not I* is also what happens to us: we are made to experience differently. We become the objects of "involuntary memory." This is not like Winnie's memory, which she selects from the bank of intelligence and clears of the shadow. It is, rather, as Beckett says, "explosive," and choosing "its own time and place for the performance of its miracle" (1931, 20–21). Here in the *Proust* passage of 1931 Beckett redefines what in 1929 the Verticalists had called "a new mythological reality," neither classical nor positivistic ("Poetry Is Vertical," 148). He insists that images are not of our own making and "real" feelings are not governed by conscious rhythms. The miracle that is performed by involuntary memory is its turning subjects into objects, ideas into images, characters into ghosts, and actions into rhythms so that the self can be created.

A very different rhythm from that in *Not I* pervades *Footfalls* (1976), a rhythm that taps the sounds of words. We see on stage a character visibly saddened at the same time we hear a rhythmic tread of feet. Only a strip of stage is lighted, so that as we strain to see, understanding comes to us through hearing basic sounds. A measured touching of feet to the ground transforms a sight of anguish into a sound of beauty. What we see is a slow dance, what we hear is a cadenced pace, drawing our listening eyes in to its

Billie Whitelaw as May in the Royal Court Theatre production of *Footfalls*, London, 1976, directed by Samuel Beckett. Reprinted by permission of John Haynes, photographer.

rhythm, the beauty of which is strangely at odds with the vision of despair.

May creates space beyond the center by pacing nine steps and making left-turn circles. A woman with dishevelled grey hair, wrapped in long grey tatters, she walks up and down. By so doing she reenacts the mystery rite of Eleusinian initiates, who themselves reenacted the pattern of Demeter's grieving. Theirs was the way of the wrong direction, a *via negativa,* a counterclockwise move into the sinister realm of left-footedness. Initiates prepared themselves for their search to understand grief patterns by imitating the precise actions of Demeter's search. Like her, they fasted for nine days, dressed in long robes, sat on stones. On the fifth day of the nine-day mystery ceremonial, a procession wound its way dancing and singing from Athens through the pass of Daphni onto the Eleusinian Plain, circling around, until at evening the initiates arrived at the temple of Demeter. There, a grief dance was performed by moving to the left. In a recent study of these rites, the circle to the left is described as follows: "First, we come to the Virgin's well, called the Kalichoron, 'well of the beautiful dances.' The circular well, protected by the outer wall of the sanctuary, is surrounded by stone pavement. Here, circle dances are performed. Surely, the form of the dance is a circular movement to the left, counter to Demeter's upperworldly sense" (Sardello 1982, 44).

Needing to feel grief as a left side of being, controlled by right-brain activity, Eleusinian initiates needed to counter ego or upperworldly sense. The point is emphasized by Patricia Berry: "Demeter consciousness tends to live life in a natural, clockwise direction; whereas to connect to her daughter she must begin to live in a contra-naturam, counter-clockwise manner as well. Kerényi (*Essays on a Science of Mythology,* p. 134) remarks how the rituals 'if danced in honor of Persephone would have to go as it were in the *wrong direction,* that is, to the left, the direction of death'" (1975, 197–98).

Indeed, May draws her circle of nine steps in a sequence Beckett makes specific: *Strip: downstage, parallel with front, length nine steps, width one metre, a little off centre audience right. Pacing: starting with right foot (r) from right (R) to left (L), with left foot (l) from L to R. Turn: rightabout at L, leftabout at R. Steps: clearly audible rhythmic tread.*[6] Beckett's carefully choreographed stage directions serve an ancient mystery function of directing audience attention to where it may not wish to go: namely, in the direction of death. May's deliberate pacing to the left for nine steps acts as a kind of invocation, leading us also back and down (*se-ducit*) into a nocturnal regime of soul. Needing to hear—not simply to move—her feet, May, too, must fully sense the space she is creating. She must get (back) in touch with underworld life. When she paces and circles on a narrow strip of stage, she draws a circle of herself: she is May, daughter-mother in one; May, whose anagram Amy forms another character in the play world that confronts us. But she is also May, the real mother of Beckett; May, the springtime that disappears and comes again; May, the lost youth of ourselves that is our wellspring and our despair.

Mother and daughter thus echo each other: one seen, the other heard. Heard in the play as Voice, the mother tells a story about her daughter, seen in the play as the walking image of despair. Oddly, the daughter embodies the image of Demeter, dressed in her dark cloak cast down from both shoulders, walking over the land and sea like a wild bird (Homer 1964, 42–43). Even what we see in this play suggests more than what is "there." In our capacity as auditors and viewers we become transposed into listening receptacles, hardly able to sort out threads of plot, able only to let them in.

It is precisely the echoing sense of distance that connects Beckett's women to Demeter-Persephone. May's pacing, a Demeter dance of despair, reflects a need to move about the night until its claim can be registered in her body, felt deeply in her mind. The story she tells is this: an old Mrs. Winter one autumn evening sits down to supper, for which she has little appetite, and asks her daughter her opinion on the Evensong service. Was it not strange? Her daughter disagrees: "Mrs. W: You yourself observed nothing . . . strange? Amy: No, Mother, I myself did not, to put it mildly. Mrs. W: What do you mean, Amy, to put it mildly? . . . Amy: I mean, Mother, that to say I observed nothing . . . strange is indeed to put it mildly. For I observed nothing of any kind, strange or otherwise. I saw nothing, heard nothing, of any kind. I was not there" (48).

This chilling tale of nonunderstanding and dead-end communication contains in the middle the daughter's question: "Just what exactly, Mother, did you perhaps fancy it was?" (47–48). The word *exactly* juxtaposed with the word *fancy* and then *perhaps* is fecund. It suggests, at the center of this bare-bones world, at the heart of autumn's night, that "fancy," only a "perhaps," nevertheless energizes psychic departure. This becomes apparent as May slips out "at nightfall and into the little church" (46), where she takes on the image of Demeter: "The semblance. (*Pause. Resumes pacing. Steps a little slower still. After two lengths halts facing front at R.*) The semblance. Faint, though by no means invisible, in a certain light. (*Pause.*) Given the right light. (*Pause.*) Grey rather than white, a pale shade of grey. (*Pause.*) Tattered. (*Pause.*) A tangle of tatters. (*Pause.*) A faint tangle of pale grey tatters. (*Pause.*) Watch it pass—(*pause*)—watch her pass before the candelabrum how its flames, their light . . . like moon through passing . . . rack" (47). Such happenings of "fancy" transport events and turn them into images. Calling her story a *semblance,* May knows it tells of an experience only half understood, ill seen ill said, about things not there (the Holy Ghost at Evensong, the daughter Amy's absent presence). Even so, in telling it, May is nourished, for images feed her soul.

In his rehearsal notes on *Footfalls,* with Beckett directing, Walter Asmus taped Beckett's comments to the actress playing May, Hildegard Schmahl: "You are looking for the words, you correct yourself constantly."[7] Asmus also conveys some wonderfully telling comments by Beckett, namely, that May is in the play "exclusively for herself. She is isolated. The costume will look like a ghost costume. . . . It is the costume of a ghost" (85). This comment coincides with Beckett's earlier explanation to the actress that May is like the girl in Jung's lecture (at the Tavistock clinic) who existed but was not actually living because she hadn't been born (83). Asmus writes, "There is the connection with the Jung story. A life, which didn't begin as a life, but which was just there, as a thing" (84). When Beckett called May's sequel a pun, "Sequel = seek well," we get further insight into the deeply mythopoetic basis of the play's mother-daughter relationship, in which seeking well is also seeking by the well and seeking from the wellspring.

As a fourth mythic quality in Beckett's recent plays, a valuing of the thing turns orthodox patterns and hierarchies upside down. Objects rather than subjects contain the "more"; objects take the place of language, since they are ringed with embedded layers of meaning that call forth the centuries and bring back the ghosts. What communicates is not language heard serially, in sentences; exactly, in definitions; or fictionally, in stories. Rather, what communicates is a language of thingness that presents itself dumbly to our senses.

Rockaby's Woman is case in point. The subjects in her world have all deserted her. Left by herself in her rocking chair "*slightly off centre audience left,*"[8] she is like Winnie twenty years later, whose search down the steep stairs of memory seduces her into the depths of myth, into the realm of Persephone, into her own imaginal space.

Down she must go if she is to recover her soul, which lies buried in her shell; for her life lies in death, where the seeds of rebirth are stored. Demeter's myth shows us, as does Beckett, that what must die is the old ego, with its dry, literal way of seeing.

In *Rockaby,* Woman is placed in a Demeter situation of dry search. Day after day at her window, Woman looks for a face in the pane. She is a ghost rather than a character, for, like a window pane, she enables us to see through her. In her bodied self she is expressionless, insubstantial, unreal—a conduit for an Other reality. Voice paces Woman through nine sequences. Like May's feet, Woman's voice turns back on itself at a precise point, which prohibits the story from getting ahead of itself and forces images to do rightabouts and leftabouts. The phrase that signals Voice's turn, repeated nine times in the text, is "all eyes / all sides," each turn seeming to locate the eyes progressively lower, until seeing (and hearing) become sensed no longer in the head but in some lower region of bodily awareness, in the feet, perhaps. The first three times, the voice turns on the phrase "going to and fro / all eyes like herself / all sides" (10–11); whereas the ninth and final turn of phrase is "she so long all eyes / famished eyes / all sides" (19). Each turning of the text, no matter which variation, contains the phrase "high and low" to suggest a synchronistic movement both of eyes searching high and low and of chair rocking high and low. The effect is curious, for although Woman's eyes remain unblinking, Voice tells us they are constantly active, and although the chair is inanimate, it comforts with encircling arms. These regressive Beckettian moves of sensory awareness downward from mind into body and from subject into object thicken the dimensions of soul, giving soul new body, racking body with soul.

Voice's final utterance creates further depth dimension by the word *down,* repeated twenty-one times in four different segments, as if calling Demeter down to join Persephone. The harshness Woman sees and feels—"going down / right down" to where life is "fucked"—is made more complicated by encircling repetitions. Yet with each *down,* the meaning changes slightly, until finally a different kind of meaning is felt, one less mean, more kind:

> So in the end
> close of a long day
> went down
> in the end went down

down the steep stair
let down the blind and down
right down

. . . .

close of a long day
went down

. . . .

down the steep stair
let down the blind and down
right down
into the old rocker
and rocked
rocked
saying to herself
no
done with that
the rocker
those arms at last
saying to the rocker
rock her off
stop her eyes
fuck life

(17, 19, 20)

Words rocked from their literalness in noun permanence become fluid, as here. *Down* becomes not just a deep place but a soft place, composed of the small, light stuffings of memory and regret. Chair becomes fleshlike, capable of lulling or fucking.

Accordingly, Woman's "sole" companions are windows and chairs. The windows, blinded, do not provide eyes to the soul but rather mirror back a stark and barren truth: "a blind up / like hers / a little like / one blind up no more" (15–16). Facing other windows, Woman faces only blind sightedness, like her own, and other panes, like her own pains: "behind the pane / another living soul" (16). Beckett suggests that only in pain can soul be seen, as through a glass, clearly. Yet, for Woman, it is time she stopped searching, for the "only" windows of *Rockaby,* like the "perhaps" fancy of *Footfalls,* yield only further confusion.

And yet, con-fusion is a beginning point in depth. There can be no stopping. Woman pronounces the need to stop; but to hear Billie

Whitelaw pronounce Woman's phrase, "time she stopped," a one-syllable word, *stopped*, extends on the lips for three syllables and a miracle is performed. The point is crucial, at the crux of Beckett's mythic intention: for precisely when it is "time to stop" another time sequence takes over, with a mythos, not a Logos, and a world of deeper time dimension floods the gates.

So is it any wonder, really, that Woman's chair should offer Woman something more? For it is tangible, unlike the fleeting others. Inside her rocking chair, dressed in "best black" (17), Woman derives comfort from its encircling arms. As in the French *pain* for bread, the object world becomes the very staff of life. Comfort denied by subjects is given freely by objects, as Beckett's stage directions indicate: "*Chair: Pale wood highly polished to gleam when rocking. Footrest. Vertical back. Rounded inward curving arms to suggest embrace*" (22).

What it means to "be a living soul," the ghost of a person, relates to the basic grounding myth of feminine consciousness, the myth of Demeter and Persephone. The "Homeric Hymn to Demeter" ends with the poet's referring to a joy that can be gained by understanding loss: "Happy is he among men upon earth who has seen these mysteries."[9] In other words, those who glimpse the dark know that happiness in "no-ing," traveling the pathway of the void. To know "nothing" is to experience the ins and outs of one's own shadow until one knows happiness as "no thing"—just a flowing inside a well. In *Rockaby*, Woman's search for "another like herself / a little like" (14) is not successful. At the "close of a long day" (14) there can be no stopping. Forever in chronological time, the orientation of Woman will be psychological and mythological: back and down. If, as is the doom of Woman, physical life must be lived facing "other only windows / all blinds down" (15), this is a comment on those who have not found the mystery of feminine consciousness: the grace to breathe that void.

It is not enough, finally, to recognize the many similarities between the Demeter myth and Beckett. Nor is it enough to comment on myth's orientation toward image, rhythm, ghosts, and objects. As modern souls, we must re-cognize our own images and ghosts, for our own famished eyes and ears. Beckett urges us to see, hear, feel, and touch the world of feeling, not There, but Here, in the shadows of the self.

NOTES

This essay, now revised, originally appeared in two of my previous publications, reprinted with permission, according to the following citations:

"Measures of Despair: The Demeter Myth," in *Beckett and Myth: An Archetypal Approach* (Syracuse, N.Y.: Syracuse Univ. Press, 1988), 53–69; "The Demeter Myth in Beckett," *Journal of Beckett Studies* 11 and 12 (1989), 109–22.

1. Beckett puns on the extraordinary fund of meanings that can be extracted from sound with his word *extra-audenary* in Beckett 1938, 293.

2. For the connection between suffering and art, see Beckett 1931, 16.

3. Beckett 1977, 51. This poem is one of the few not translated by Beckett from the original French into English. For whatever reason Beckett chose not to translate it, I would like the original to stand, with explication arising from textual discussion.

4. For Winnie's story about the mouse, see Beckett 1961, 54–59. For comment on the rat as a psychic image, see Jung 1976, 106.

5. *Not I,* in Beckett 1976, 22. Subsequent page numbers in parentheses in discussions of *Not I* refer to this edition.

6. *Footfalls,* in Beckett 1976, 42. Subsequent page numbers in parentheses in discussions of *Footfalls* refer to this edition.

7. Asmus 1977, 86. Subsequent page numbers in parentheses in discussions of Asmus's notes refer to this text.

8. Beckett, *Rockaby,* 1981, 9. Subsequent page numbers in parentheses in discussions of *Rockaby* refer to this edition.

9. This line, from "The Homeric Hymn to Demeter" (1964, 480), is echoed in Beckett's play *Ill Seen Ill Said* (1981) in an ironic, even extra-audenary, way with his phrase "know happiness," which follows his phrase "Grace to breathe that void" (59).

BIBLIOGRAPHY

Asmus, Walter. "Practical Aspects of Theatre, Radio and Television: Rehearsal Notes for the German Première of *That Time* and *Footfalls*." Translated by Helen Watanabe. *Journal of Beckett Studies* 2 (Summer 1977): 82–95.

Beckett, Samuel. *Proust*. New York: Grove Press, 1931.

———. "Denis Devlin." Review of "Intercessions," by Denis Devlin. *transition: Tenth Anniversary* 27 (April-May 1938): 289–94.

———. *Happy Days*. New York: Grove Press, 1961.

———. *Ends and Odds: Eight New Dramatic Pieces*. New York: Grove Press, 1976.

———. *Collected Poems in French and English*. New York: Grove Press, 1977.

———. *Ill Seen Ill Said*. New York: Grove Press, 1981.

———. *Rockaby and Other Short Pieces*. New York: Grove Press, 1981.

Berry, Patricia. "The Rape of Demeter/Persephone and Neurosis." *Spring: An Annual of Archetypal Psychology and Jungian Thought* (1975): 186–198.

Cohn, Ruby. *Just Play: Beckett's Theater*. Princeton: Princeton Univ. Press, 1980.

Doll, Mary A. *Beckett and Myth: An Archetypal Approach.* Syracuse, N.Y.: Syracuse Univ. Press, 1988.
———. "Measures of Despair: The Demeter Myth in Beckett." *Journal of Beckett Studies* 11 and 12 (Fall 1989): 109–22.
Harvey, Lawrence E. *Samuel Beckett: Poet and Critic.* Princeton: Princeton Univ. Press, 1970.
Homer. "The Homeric Hymn to Demeter." In *The Homeric Hymns and Homerica,* translated by Hugh G. Evelyn-White. Cambridge: Harvard Univ. Press, 1964.
Jung, C. G. "The Functions of the Unconscious." Translated by R. F. C. Hull. In *The Symbolic Life, The Collected Works,* 18:267–80. Princeton: Princeton Univ. Press, 1976.
"Poetry Is Vertical." *Transition* 21 (March 1932): 148–49.
Sardello, Robert. "The Landscape of Virginity." In *Images of the Untouched,* edited by Joanne Stroud and Gail Thomas, 39–47. Dallas: Spring Publications, 1982.

Eileen Gregory

DARK PERSEPHONE AND MARGARET ATWOOD'S *PROCEDURES FOR UNDERGROUND*

In the tale of Amor and Psyche told by Apuleius, Venus imposes a final ordeal upon Psyche: to descend to the underworld and return with a portion of Proserpine's beauty. Not many return from the depths, so a helpful guide gives Psyche procedures for her journey underground. The world of the dead observes laws of which the living are ignorant. Psyche is strictly to follow certain precise directives—to give coins to Charon, sops to raging Cerberus; to avoid an old woman's web and Persephone's ghostly food. One taboo seems especially shocking to human instincts: as Psyche makes her way across Acheron in a boat, a floating corpse will ask to be taken in. She is to refuse it, for, as her guide says, in this place, "pity is unlawful" (Apuleius 1951, 138). In this Stygian darkness, cool singlemindedness must govern, because simple survival is at issue in every gesture. The guide says: If you are not ruthless, you will die.

Similarly, in Margaret Atwood's "Solstice Poem," a mother imagines instructing her young daughter within a world where death apparently predominates: where in the minds of politicians "wars bloom . . . like flowers / on wallpaper," while eyes of soldiers "flick from target / to target: window, belly, child"; and where women live this violence through their own bodies and those of their children, though not wishing to see: "Each has a mirror / which when asked replies Not you" (1978, 81–82).

What gifts might allow one's daughter to survive in such a world?

> How can I teach her
> Some way of being human
> that won't destroy her?
>
> I would like to tell her, Love
> is enough, I would like to say,
> Find shelter in another skin.
>
> I would like to say, Dance
> and be happy. Instead I will say
> in my crone's voice, Be
> ruthless when you have to, tell
> the truth when you can,
> when you can see it.
>
> Iron talismans, and ugly, but
> more loyal than mirrors.
>
> (1978, 83)

Evidently, there are paths to avoid, commonly accepted "ways of being human" that will destroy: myths of the sufficiency of love, hope of sustaining the momentary release of happiness or of finding safety by losing oneself in another. These are dangerous precisely because they are evasions of the danger; they are forms of the "mirror" that conceals precisely what one wishes not to see. Thus, instead of mirrors, the "crone's voice" would give the daughter the "iron talismans" of her words, to act as countercharms in an ominous and deceptive world. These prescriptions for "being human" paradoxically appear inhuman, pitiless, ugly. One directive acknowledges danger ("Be / ruthless when you have to"), the other the limits of utterance ("tell / the truth when you can") and the limits of perception ("when you can see it"). "Being human" appears to have something to do with "telling the truth," "truth" understood as something at once elusive and inexorable; and survival apparently necessitates the "loyalty" or faithfulness of one's guides. Both of the crone's directives necessitate a kind of self-consciousness allowing one to navigate a territory of lethal illusions, not the least of which is blindness to one's own complicity.

This crone's voice predominates in Margaret Atwood's poetry—

the voice of one reminding herself, and the reader, of sinister negotiations constantly to be engaged. The predominance of that voice might explain what Judith McCombs has described in the reception of Atwood's poetry—the resistance of reviewers to the "temperature" of her poems, the recurring dismay at her "coldness," her lack of emotional "warmth" (1988, 28 ff.). One might grasp some of the implications of this voice by considering it in light of the figure of the crone—Double Persephone or Diana / Hecate—traditionally residing at the threshold of the realm of death. The centrality of this figure, described in Atwood's first volume of poems, *Double Persephone* (1961), is highlighted by her comments in *Survival* concerning the prevalence of "Ice-Virgin-Hecate" in Canadian writing (1972, 199–210). The prominence of the mythic Persephone is evident as well in patterns noted by critics of Atwood's poetry and fiction—patterns of descent, of underground, and of ghostliness, as well as explicit echoes of the Eleusinian pattern, the transference between mother and daughter, in *Surfacing*.[1]

But in Atwood's poetry Persephone may be understood not merely as a mythic paradigm but as a governing perspective. This psychological disposition is suggested in part in Eli Mandel's description of the "ruthless unsentimentality" of the "mirror voice" and the oracular aspects of Atwood's poetry (1988, 115 ff.); in Sherrill Grace's exploration of duplicity as an essential, natural aspect of vision (1980, 56 ff.); and in Kathryn VanSpanckeren's delineation of the "death orientation" of shamanism (1988). These critics and others recognize the highly mercurial and indeterminate consciousness rendered in Atwood's poems.

The Persephonean perspective comes from an orientation with regard to the underworld or underground—but what is the nature of this territory in Atwood's poetry? Most critics concur, implicitly or explicitly, with Frank Davey's linked oppositions, associating the underground with nature or biological process versus artifice; with temporal change versus permanence; with wilderness or "the green country" versus civilization; and thus analogously with "female" versus "male" space, and with unconscious versus conscious life. Thus, John Wilson Foster speaks of the wilderness in terms of the opposition of unstructured space versus imprisoning form (1988, 161), and Grace indicates repeatedly Atwood's representation of nature as "curved, positive, and closely identified with female processes" (1983, 13). In these readings, the descent to the underground or to the interior in Atwood's poetry is understood in more or less traditional (romantic / archetypal) terms, associated with the reconciliation of opposites, with regeneration or individuation.[2]

In Atwood's narratives some of these associations do pertain. However, the underground in Atwood's poetry seems antithetical to such constructs and the teleological vectors they imply. A few critics grasp the complexity of the underground, sensing that it cannot be comprehended in terms of clear oppositions and that it permeates self and other, female and male, wilderness and city (Stevens 1988; Ross 1974). Indeed, in Atwood's poetry, the underground represents an ineluctable aspect of all fictions and constructs, including the illusion of the poem: their tendency to waver and warp at the edges, to desubstantiate and disappear. The vision of Persephone / Hecate is the perception of the threshold quality of things, desires, and images, and of the indeterminacy of projections and apparent fixities.

To define this recurrent perspective in Atwood's poetry, one might examine her volume *Procedures for Underground*, in which, in its title poem, a voice similar to that of Psyche's guide gives instructions for a descent to the underground (1970, 24–25). The underground as envisioned in the title poem seems to be a literal place (Northwest Coast), but it is actually an orientation. The guide can tell you not where it is but how it seems: this is how one will know she is there, she says, in the country "beneath": there, things "are the same / as they are here, but shifted." But what has altered things is no more than the light in which they are seen, the light of a "green sun."

This "green country," however, should not be confused with a place of fertility or organism, or with an idealized female space, as Davey would have it. Its cool, even cold, green light is like that in "The Shrunken Forest" (18), another poem in this volume: "it was too green / for us it was like living / on the surface of the sun (green) only not / burning." This light renders transparency, a loss of corporeal dimension: "we were clear / as ice," the voice in that poem says, "we looked at each / other and saw nothing but a / bending in the air and through / us that element extending placid / as water but it was not water." When out of this place of green light, "we wonder / whether we were ever there / at all, here light / is so hard and different." Ordinary light shows believable, substantial things. However, these too can disappear in certain lights, as the skull disappears in a radiated "diagram," revealing another ghostly territory, "intensely green and shining / transparent even on this paper." "Green" vision is something like X-ray: substances dissolve in an invisible medium—ice, air, water, the paper on which one writes—and one can *see through* things.

To ask what exists "beneath" in "Procedures for Underground" is to ask about the hidden aspects of things—particularly the ruthless aspects of human need. "Those who live there are always hungry": the shades are marked by absence or emptiness within their desire. Especially in light of the other poems in this volume, however, this hunger clearly is not simply "other." One is implicated in the neediness of those beneath: they are "familiars," those "once your friends," though "changed and dangerous." From them, if one survives, one "can learn / wisdom and great power." But the power received from them is not especially magic: it resides in knowledge of their names, which is to say their craving and anger. Here one learns the ravenous absences. Like the corpse asking for Psyche's pity, these souls are to be resisted ruthlessly—though entertained forever, once one has returned to the surface. In the sense that one carries this burden always, one never returns safely from the underground.

Atwood consistently presents in this poem and in the volume *Procedures for Underground* an underworld perspective such as the psychologist James Hillman explores in *The Dream and the Underworld* (1979).[3] The underworld, as he suggests in examining this locus in classical mythology, is not distinct from but simultaneous with daily life; each moment contains the duplicity of surface and depth. The presence / absence of the underworld is a trick of light, a play of mirrors; it is a matter of the light in which one sees. "Entering the underworld," Hillman says, "refers to a transition from the material to the psychical point of view. Three dimensions become as two as the perspective of nature, flesh, and matter falls away, leaving an existence of immaterial, mirror-like images, *eidola*. We are in the land of soul" (51). His description of this play of vision suggests the perspective in much of Atwood's poetry. Seeing in this way, he says, is like "trying to sense the movement of one's own shadow"; this consciousness "is reflective, watching not just the physical reality in front of the eyeballs . . . but seeing into the flickering patterns within that physical reality, and within the eye itself. It is a perception of perception" (52). This self-reflexive vision persistently desubstantiates, deliteralizes, exposing illusions and absences within ordinary moments. Hillman emphasizes, too, that the classical locus of Hades is sinister and cold, ruled by Stygian hatred. This is not the place of fertility and change, not the "living protean world of biological process," as Davey defines Atwood's "underground" (1984, 43), but rather the place of changeless, timeless, shadow-life.

Though Hillman emphasizes the god Hades in relation to the underworld perspective, the realm of Hades is equally ruled by Persephone, and their union defines the order of this world. In the underworld described by Homer and by Virgil, as well as by Apuleius in his story of Psyche's descent, Persephone holds the keys of chthonic power. In the *Odyssey*, a recurring source of allusion in Atwood's work,[4] terrible, proud Persephone sends the shadowy images (eidola) of the dead souls to Odysseus and then scatters them, and she can at any moment send up out of Hades some "gorgonish head" to terrify (Homer 1967, bk. 11, line 635; see also lines 47, 213, 226, 385, 634). For Homer, Persephone is mistress of images in the underworld, the shady outlines signifying bodies but composed of nothingness. Odysseus clearly recognizes that she orchestrates the illusion of what appears to him.

Persephone may be seen not merely as one half of a dual deity (Demeter / Persephone or Hades / Persephone) but, in her power over images, as the problematic figure of a poet. Indeed the "Persephone" in Atwood's *Double Persephone* (1961) suggests such a significance. Persephone here, as Grace has pointed out, is double in suggesting a cycle of life and death and double as well in her duplicity, her control of the world of illusion (1980, 8–9). Persephone elicits desire but stands outside it, witnessing the deathliness within it: the amorous body of the shepherd disintegrating to bone ("Pastoral," 6); the apparent animation of her spring disguising death: "Though her deceptive smile / Lures life from earth . . . / It hides a wicked sickle" ("Persephone Departing," 8). Persephone is the "girl with the gorgon touch" ("Formal Garden," 5) because she is the site of mortal desire and thus of inevitable, lifeless reifications. She witnesses and exposes the deathliness within hieratic gestures of supplication and fictions of desire. She oversees the "marbled flesh" and "fixing eye" of lovers, frozen in "attitude of outstretched hands / Curved in an all-too-perfect grace" ("Formal Garden," 5). And in "Iconic Landscape," her brooding absence and the light of her "cold sun" sustain the many fictions of loss and longing. Double Persephone is within and without desire, drawing it out yet withdrawing; within and without body, life, and process; within and without artifice. Atwood in *Double Persephone* describes the figure of Persephone from an ironic distance, as the "she" upon whom illusions of desire depend, clearly drawing upon Robert

Graves's elaboration of the "white goddess."[5] In her later lyric poetry, however, she explores this doubleness more intimately and more viscerally. The Persephone of her poetry is the "I": she is never "without" desire and death, except perhaps in the problematic gesture of the poem itself. She is profoundly complicit with the gestures and fictions whose human insufficiency she perceives and exposes.

To consider Atwood's *Procedures for Underground* through this lens suggests a consistency in orientation in the volume as a whole. For though the voice in these poems varies in its proximity to the underground—sometimes appearing to speak in daytime and its language of temporal gestures, sometimes entirely within hallucination or dream—still throughout the volume is the persistent attempt to account for the underground dimension within life. The highly analytical and cerebral character of Atwood's poetry is not alien but is essential to this perspective. As Hillman says, "The innate urge to go below appearances . . . shows itself in the analytical mind, which makes psyche by taking things apart" (1979, 27). The poetic eye in these poems, regardless of its phobia or neurosis, is always seeing through its own seeing.

The poems of the volume not only render the complexity of this orientation, but in their rough sequence they suggest as well something like the provisory directives described in the title poem. The volume is divided into three untitled groupings of poems, each of which has a kind of unity and a significant initiation and closure. Each part begins on a note of fear and ends with a qualified and tentative sense of release or recognition. Part one opens with "Eden Is a Zoo" (6), with a painfully constructed image of childhood, and many of the poems in this section concern the intimate territory of memory and dream. They present involuntary omens or "reminders"—as one of the poems expresses it—of what one wishes not to see: forgotten needs, paralyzing fictions, visitations of the dead, the danger of death itself. The first part ends with "Procedures for Underground" (24–25), pointing to the fact that the underground is the interior and that one's survival of the descent requires self-consciousness of one's own desperation and duplicity.

That such awareness is difficult to maintain in the "upperground" is suggested in the second section. It begins with the poem "The Creatures of the Zodiac" (29), describing the defensive schizophrenia characterizing many of the poems in this section. In the daylight world of rational control and of mundane things, "there are no omens," but at night the ferocious underground presences possess one, and "ordinary hatreds" become "predictions," determining a fatal course, like the creatures of the zodiac. The poems of this section concern the daylight world, the featureless cityscape, where the unreal haunts the overreal. The section concludes with "84th Street, Edmonton" (52–53), which suggests the necessity, within the blank, flat abstraction of the city—"more / nothing than I've ever seen"—for some kind of courage that would allow for a primitive act of creation.

Indeed, the poems of the third and final section predominantly concern attempts at elemental making—constructing a marriage, gathering or making totems, willing the poetic image into being—all these constructions drawing upon an awareness of danger and illusion. The first poem, "Highest Altitude" (56), describes the vertiginous fear of two lovers traveling in the mountains, aware of the precarious, life-and-death quality of the path they are attempting. The last poem of the section and of the book ("Dancing Practice," 77–79) returns to the opening image of parents in "Eden Is a Zoo," although the parents are now old and now moving in time, not paralyzed in the past; and indeed, the poem, in the image of the dance, precisely concerns the poetic desire aroused through awareness of the awkward motions of "moving in time." The last poems of the volume especially insist on the gesture of the poem itself as an act of will—which, as such, has its own dangers and limits that the poet cannot ignore.

A poem in the first portion of *Procedures for Underground,* "Two Gardens" (16–17), suggests the character of the double vision that informs the volume as a whole. The first garden in the poem is the one carefully cultivated by a process of inclusion and exclusion: "What stands . . . / is there because I measured, placed, reached / down . . . and pulled out." It is the world of civilized artifact—"fabric- / textured zinnias," chintz-colored asters, "pot-shaped marigolds," and shiny sunflowers. This garden is so stolid and material as to verge on the immaterial—indeed, it is bounded by the unreal. Outside its fragile borders is a ghostly "undergrowth"—a shadow garden haunting the overrealized images of the first:

> but outside the string borders
>
> other things raise
> themselves, brief
> motions at the path's edge

the bonewhite
plants that grow
without sunlight, flickering
in the evening forest
certain ferns; fungi
like buried feet
the blue-
flags, ice flames
reflected in the bay
that melt when the
sun hits noon

these have their roots
in another land

they are mist

if you touch them, your
eyes go through them.

These images, like the chthonic eidola, are the incorporeal nocturnals. They live by a blanched light, in icy temperatures. This garden of antimatter rooted in another land gives an image of the underworld in Atwood's poetry. The ghostly ground is always at the edge of the measured, delimited, known ground—it represents the play (rather than the fixity) of images: images that are "brief / motions at the path's edge," "flickering" in the evening, images that are "ice-flames reflected in the bay." In this garden, apparent substances hide absence: "if you touch them, your / eyes go through them." The two gardens, though seemingly distinct, are simultaneous in experience—their distinction merely a matter of apprehension. Atwood suggests that any firm body, any contrived artifice, may metamorphose into shadowy mist.

In Atwood's topology, the locus of this underworld is suggested in a number of different spatial images. How do you know you are there? Well, the light is cool and luminous, silver, blue, green: "in the wash of new neon / light, the shadowy faces / including your own, float / silently, go under" ("Return Trips West," 51). Images flatten out and waver: "your face / ripples like water where did you go" ("Girl and Horse, 1928," 10). Bodies lose substance: "Your outline, skin / that marks you off / melts in this light" ("A Soul, Geologically," 58). Horizons are lost and space collapses: here "there are / no pleasant views, no distances / . . . everything crowds close to the skin" ("Interview with a Tourist," 23). Boundaries gain numinous significance: "impermanence / makes the edges of things burn // brighter" ("Highest Altitude," 56).

This other world is located underground in the title poem; it is underwater in "Interview with a Tourist," the place where the light "is always the same colour," where the men look "starved and silver / and have goggle eyes / and . . . the women are cold tentacled flowers" (23). This underground orientation is also suggested in images of human *dis*orientation. It is suggested in the vertiginous scale of the wilderness ("Highest Altitude," 56), in the vast stony dimension of geological features ("A Morning," 57). And within erotic animation, the body—with its surfaces, liquids, contours, and caves—is also the landscape of "descent," taking on geological metaphors for the hidden dimension: "from behind your face / the unknown areas appear: // hills yellow-pelted, dried earth / bubbles, or thrust up / steeply as knees // . . . these spaces you fill / with their own emptiness" ("A Soul, Geologically," 58).

The differences among these images of the underground delineated by the Persephone of the poems lies, as the title poem suggests, in one's willingness to name them as one's own. In the first portion of *Procedures for Underground,* memories and dreams are the central locations of the underground dimension. In many poems, memory seems to offer images similar to those of a mirror—having neither depth nor the possibility of revelation. Fixed and static in some artificial construction of nostalgia or of rage, images are denied the animation that a link with the other world might allow. In "Eden Is a Zoo" (6) the image of parents is trapped as in a child's crude drawing, encapsulated in memory by impassable barriers: "Do they see me looking at them / from across the hedge of spikes / and cardboard fire painted red / I built with so much time / and pain." In this poem images of memory are immobilized as in a snapshot, such as that of "Girl and Horse, 1928" (10): "years ago you were caught by light / and fixed in that secret / place where we live, where we believe / nothing can change, grow older." Similarly, in "Frame" (21), the voice of the poem describes a framed window into the past, containing cardboard cutouts of houses and of previous selves, actively constructed in a compulsion necessitated by betrayal and anger: "Who left me here? Who gave me / these scissors? I dream / always of getting outside. / Nothing opens, / I don't know who to forgive."

In these poems, memory seems paralyzed in some state of traumatic amnesia: "Once, when there was history / some obliterating fact occurred, / no solution was found" ("Interview with a Tourist," 23). That fact, like a conflagration or a flood, which wipes away all traces of habitation, fixes a pocket of time in memory and compels desperate efforts of reconstruction. To attempt to dwell in that obliterated landscape is to become—as in "Interview with a Tourist" —one of the shadowy dead. In that two-dimensional landscape, there are no vistas or horizons and no air to breathe.

In the first part of the volume, however, dreams give omens of double life, reflective and complex reminders of the presence of death within things. In "Dream: Bluejay or Archeopteryx," the mirror-like surface of a pool reflects something other than the corporeal self: "my four hands gathering / in either world, the berries / in the dish glowed blue / embers." In the midst of this dreamed image, "a bird / lit on both branches" and, looking up, "against the sun I saw / his lizard eye" (8–9). Then the dreamer, looking down into the pool, the negative image upon the retina, sees an outline beneath her shadow. The mirror becomes a depth, out of which the eidolon of a bird/man/god begins to surface, his head "crested with blue flame" (9). The primordial image is in a sense a trick of light, coming from one's being imprinted by light so that the darkness is illumined.

In another poem, "Midwinter, Presolstice" (20), dreams bring recognition of the connection between the world of life and of death. In the midst of frigid winter, "I dream of . . . / repeated weddings with a stranger, wounded / with knives and bandaged, his / face hidden." The Persephone-like image of union with the hidden stranger (Hades?) is overlaid or doubled with an image of an ordinary man, appearing in another dream: "my gentle husband" is "guarding / a paper bag / which holds / turnips and apples and my / head, the eyes closed." The husband holds her sleeping, "detached" head, abstracted and lost in dreams of death.

If the underworld is perspective and not place, these visitations from another land can happen anywhere. There are no sacred or profane spaces, such as nature versus culture, wilderness versus city. In Atwood's poems, the wilderness or the natural is certainly not the privileged site of the uncanny. As one sees in the rigid artifices of memory, the rational and schematic image given by camera, map, and mirror, as well as the flat and featureless landscapes of Toronto or Edmonton, suggest the world of bodiless images as much as do dreams and memories. The purely rationalized or fixed world is so fully overrealized as to be de-realized: it allows hallucinatory—and involuntary—access into the unchartered territory. In a sense, as in "Dream: Bluejay or Archeopteryx," the brilliance of light on the eye creates a negative image transposed as a shadow in the dark.

If the first part of *Procedures for Underground* explores largely the territory of memory and dream, the second part focusses on surreal revelations within the city. When the city is a set of hypotheses, a disembodied set of premises governing life but entrapping one in fear, then the radically hypothetical—a flood of disembodied images —can drown one: "my eyes diffused, washing / in waves of light across the ceiling" ("Hypotheses: City," 37). When in "End of the World: Weekend, Near Toronto" (32) the city empties itself into the flat silent green countryside in a metallic glitter of cars, the drivers intent on escape, "getting / away from something / they carry always with them," then amid such desperation one can imagine an end of the world, perhaps the soundless fallout of a holocaust: "out of the blue sky . . . something is falling   falling / gently on them like invisible rain."

The means of negotiating the underground is through self-consciousness—and vigilant remembrance—of duplicity and danger, even within gestures that carry the authority of "safety." The poems in the last section concern the problematic character of making a "habitation"—a marriage, an image, a poem—in which one can safely reside. Several critics have noted the predominance of artifices in this last section: "The progression in the book," Peter Stevens says, "is towards a fundamental belief in the prerogatives of poetry in a threatening, tense world" (1988, 38). But if this were true, one could suggest that the seer in "Procedures for Underground" betrays herself in these last poems by taking refuge in art or willed constructions, arguably versions of the self-deceptive mirror (Grace 1981, 57). Indeed, many of these last poems do claim a crucial significance for the gesture of making. But in light of the volume as a whole, one notes the careful, self-conscious qualification of those claims, even as they are made. How are we to take the last gesture in "Woman Skating" (64), for instance? After constructing an elaborate image of her mother in the past, the speaker then goes even further in freezing that image: "Over all I place / a glass bell." A similarly self-conscious artifice occurs in "Carrying Food Home in Winter" (73), where, having admitted the deceptiveness of desire and language in creating illusory "islands of warmth / in winter, in summer / islands of coolness," the speaker herself exerts the power of language over the mundane: "I say I will transform / this egg into a muscle / this bottle into an act of love." Finally, and most notably, in "Dancing Practice" (77–70), the last poem of the volume, the speaker, having witnessed the awkward motions of her parents' dancing, constructs the image of an ideal dance, wherein the dancers are "transformed / for this moment / always / (because I say)"—and, of course, the poem itself, like the ideal dance, is a moment of perfect timing. These assertions of will are not meant to persuade one of some achieved resolution or escape from the problems of duplicity, but quite the contrary: they call attention in a troubling way to the always optative and hypothetical character of poetic utterances.

In the context of this volume, and of Atwood's poetry generally, the making of images and constructs is clearly problematic. In "For Archaeologists" (72) Atwood suggests an "archaeology" of human image-making that is far from romantic. Prehistoric petroglyphs of the hunt, animals running "with spears in their backs," are willed gestures within a ritual of killing, and the drawings are made with blood and smoke. These images are deadly. But nevertheless, for all its violence, the making of these images is part of necessity, coming from hunger and the need to survive; it is "the link between / the buried will and the upper / world of sun and green feeding, / chase and the hungry kill." Such ambiguous, potent images are "part of us now / part of the structure of the bones."

The last section of *Procedures for Underground* suggests that creation is necessary to survival, to the negotiation of the underground—but not heroic creation, asserting in the face of chaos an inhabitable, measured world mirroring one's wish. Rather, in the view presented in Atwood's poetry, the necessity to survive compels one to live at the edge, always to assume the bare possibilities of life, moments in which "genesis descends / here also or never" ("84th Street, Edmonton," 53). The metaphors from archaeology in Atwood's work do not represent nostalgia for some lost origin, as Cheryl Walker suggests (1987, 156); rather, the *arche* to be arrived at is the *arche* of the edge—the "transitional [sliver] of doubt between hazard and security" (Foster 1988, 159)—where everything is vivid in recognition of impermanence. In "Habitation" (60), marriage, like all overrealized images, must allow its danger, or it will not survive: It "is not / a house or even a tent // it is before that, and colder: // the edge of the forest, the edge / of the desert . . . // the edge of the receding glacier." Marriage is a habitation on the edge of the known world, "where painfully and with wonder / at having survived even / this far // we are learning to make fire."

The perspective of Dis or Dark Persephone defines in part the extraordinary power of these poems, and at the same time it sheds light on some of the critical reaction to Atwood's poetry, the complicity as well as the defensive tactics of readers. One who travels the cold "depths" carries unwelcome wisdom: "Few will seek your help / with love, none without fear" ("Procedures for Underground," 25). One is mistaken to search in these poems for expressions of warmth—here "pity is unlawful," and here the truths are cold—and one is mistaken to look here for release, a poetic voice free of the awareness of constraint and duplicity in every utterance and gesture. And, finally, one lends fond hope in attempting to read plots of "positive" development within Atwood's poetry, some "progression [throughout her writing] . . . to [an] apparently satisfying resolution" (Wagner 1981, 82). Critics persistently attempt to see in Atwood's volumes of poetry some amelioration of perspective, some sign that "the poet is on her way toward creating a viable inner order" (Ross 1974, 61).[6] Thus, many greeted with enthusiasm her *Two-Headed Poems* because of the "expansiveness of [a] humane vision" that the poems suggested (Barbour 1988, 212), because of their seeming reconciliation of contraries and their dependence on natural cycles and generation (Grace 1983, 10 ff.; Weir 1983; Irvine 1981). But George Woodcock rightly notes that in the context of the next volume, *True Stories* (1981), this earlier volume represents "a relatively benign interlude" within Atwood's themes of "tenacious survival and constant metamorphosis" (1983, 141); and Walker finds in both of these volumes a darker recognition of the illusion of wishing for any absolutes beyond language (1987, 157–58). Individual volumes of Atwood's poems each move to points of modest and tentative epiphany; but each successive volume invariably begins by insisting on some pitiless aspect of the place where we live.

The "crone's voice" is reiterative: reiteration, indeed, is part of what one wishes not to see. This voice insists on repetitions, unchanging patterns, transformations gone awry, imminent danger. "We Don't Like Reminders"(22), we don't like dangerous edges, don't like to see ghostly outlines glimmering from behind faces. But Margaret Atwood gives omens and reminders, "their roots / in another land."

NOTES

1. Many critical works explore patterns of descent and rebirth, especially in relation to narratives. See, for example, Grace 1980, 105 ff.; Pratt 1988; Piercy 1988; and VanSpanckeren 1988, 189 ff. For discussions of the meaning of the underground in Atwood's poetry, see Rosenberg 1984; Davey 1984; Stevens 1988; and Grace 1980, 49 ff. On the ghostliness of Atwood's writing, especially narratives, see Mandel 1988 and McCombs 1981. Grace (1988) and Thomas (1988) explore echoes of the Eleusinian pattern in *Surfacing*.

2. Delineations of these journeys toward psychological wholeness generally pertain to Atwood's narratives, especially *Surfacing;* see Thomas 1988 and VanSpanckeren 1988. Some of these readings pertain to volumes of poetry, however; see especially Simmons 1987, Brown 1988, and Piercy 1988.

3. VanSpanckeren 1988, 201–2, speaks of Hillman's treatment of the underworld perspective in her discussion of the "death orientation" of shamanism.

4. See Buchbinder 1988 for a discussion of the importance of the *Odyssey* in Atwood's writing.

5. Atwood discusses Graves's *The White Goddess* (1966) extensively in *Survival* (1972, 199 ff.).

6. See also Stevens 1988, 38. For other, largely feminist readings emphasizing positive development, see Piercy 1988, Blakely 1983, and Irvine 1981.

BIBLIOGRAPHY

Apuleius. *The Transformations of Lucius Otherwise Known as The Golden Ass.* Translated by Robert Graves. New York: Farrar, Straus, and Giroux, 1951.

Atwood, Margaret. *Double Persephone.* Toronto: Hawkshead Press, 1961.

———. *Procedures for Underground.* Boston: Little, Brown, 1970.

———. *Survival: A Thematic Guide to Canadian Literature.* Toronto: Anansi, 1972.

———. *Two-Headed Poems.* New York: Simon and Schuster, 1978.

Barbour, Douglas. Review of *Two-Headed Poems,* by Margaret Atwood. In *Critical Essays on Margaret Atwood,* edited by Judith McCombs, 208–12. Boston: G. K. Hall, 1988.

Blakely, Barbara. "The Pronunciation of Flesh: A Feminist Reading of Atwood's Poetry." In *Margaret Atwood: Language, Text, System,* edited by Sherrill Grace and Lorraine Weir, 33–51. Vancouver: Univ. of British Columbia Press, 1983.

Brown, Russell. "Atwood's Sacred Wells." In *Critical Essays on Margaret Atwood,* edited by Judith McCombs, 213–29. Boston: G. K. Hall, 1988.

Buchbinder, David. "Weaving Her Version: The Homeric Model and Gender Politics in *Selected Poems.*" In *Margaret Atwood: Vision and Form,* edited by Kathryn VanSpanckeren and Jan Garden Castro, 122–41. Carbondale: Southern Illinois Univ. Press, 1988.

Davey, Frank. *Margaret Atwood: A Feminist Poetics.* Vancouver: Talonbooks, 1984.

Davidson, Arnold E., and Cathy N. Davidson, eds. *The Art of Margaret Atwood: Essays in Criticism.* Toronto: Anansi, 1981.

Foster, John Wilson. "The Poetry of Margaret Atwood." In *Critical Essays on Margaret Atwood,* edited by Judith McCombs, 153–67. Boston: G. K. Hall, 1988.

Grace, Sherrill. *Violent Duality: A Study of Margaret Atwood.* Montreal: Véhicule Press, 1980.

———. "Margaret Atwood and the Poetics of Duplicity." In *The Art of Margaret Atwood: Essays in Criticism,* edited by Arnold Davidson and Cathy N. Davidson, 55–68. Toronto: Anansi, 1981.

———. "Articulating the 'Space Between': Atwood's Untold Stories and Fresh Beginnings." In *Margaret Atwood: Language, Text, System,* edited by Sherrill Grace and Lorraine Weir, 1–16. Vancouver: Univ. of British Columbia Press, 1983.

———. "In Search of Demeter: The Lost, Silent Mother in *Surfacing.*" In *Margaret Atwood: Vision and Form,* edited by Kathryn VanSpanckeren and Jan Garden Castro, 35–47. Carbondale: Southern Illinois Univ. Press, 1988.

Grace, Sherrill, and Lorraine Weir, eds. *Margaret Atwood: Language, Text, System.* Vancouver: Univ. of British Columbia Press, 1983.

Graves, Robert. *The White Goddess: A Historical Grammar of Poetic Myth.* 2d ed. New York: Farrar, Straus, and Giroux, 1966.

Hillman, James. *The Dream and the Underworld.* New York: Harper and Row, 1979.

Homer. *The Odyssey.* Translated by Richmond Lattimore. New York: Harper and Row, 1967.

Irvine, Lorna. "One Woman Leads to Another." In *The Art of Margaret Atwood: Essays in Criticism,* edited by Arnold Davidson and Cathy N. Davidson, 95–106. Toronto: Anansi, 1981.

McCombs, Judith. "Atwood's Haunted Sequences: *The Circle Game, The Journals of Susanna Moodie,* and *Power Politics.*" In *The Art of Margaret Atwood: Essays in Criticism,* edited by Arnold Davidson and Cathy N. Davidson, 35–54. Toronto: Anansi, 1981.

———. "Country, Politics, and Gender in Canadian Studies: A Report from Twenty Years of Atwood Criticism." *Canadian Issues/Thèmes Canadiens* 10 (1988): 27–47.

———. *Critical Essays on Margaret Atwood.* Boston: G. K. Hall, 1988.

Mandel, Eli. "Atwood Gothic." In *Critical Essays on Margaret Atwood,* edited by Judith McCombs, 114–23. Boston: G. K. Hall, 1988.

Mendez-Egle, Beatrice, ed. *Margaret Atwood: Reflection and Reality.* Living Author Series, no. 6. Edinburg, Tex.: Pan American Univ., 1987.

Piercy, Marge. "Margaret Atwood: Beyond Victimhood." In *Critical Essays on Margaret Atwood,* edited by Judith McCombs, 53–70. Boston: G. K. Hall, 1988.

Pratt, Annis. "*Surfacing* and the Rebirth Journey." In *Critical Essays on Margaret Atwood,* edited by Judith McCombs, 139–57. Boston: G. K. Hall, 1988.

Rosenberg, Jerome H. *Margaret Atwood.* Boston: Twayne, 1984.

Ross, Gary. "The Circle Game." *Canadian Literature* 60 (Spring 1974): 51–63.

Simmons, Jes. "'Crept in upon by Green': Susanna Moodie and the Process of Individuation." In *Margaret Atwood: Reflection and Reality,* edited by Beatrice Mendez-Egle, 39–153. Living Author Series, no. 6. Edinburg, Tex.: Pan American Univ., 1987.

Stevens, Peter. "Dark Mouth" [Review of *Procedures for Underground*]. In *Critical Essays on Margaret Atwood,* edited by Judith McCombs, 37–38. Boston: G. K. Hall, 1988.

Thomas, Sue. "Mythic Reconception of the Mother/Daughter Relationship in Margaret Atwood's *Surfacing.*" *Ariel* 19 (April 1988): 73–85.

VanSpanckeren, Kathryn. "Shamanism in the Works of Margaret Atwood." In *Margaret Atwood: Vision and Form,* edited by Kathryn VanSpanckeren and Jan Garden Castro, 183–204. Carbondale: Southern Illinois Univ. Press, 1988.

VanSpanckeren, Kathryn, and Jan Garden Castro, eds. *Margaret Atwood: Vision and Form.* Carbondale: Southern Illinois Univ. Press, 1988.

Wagner, Linda W. "The Making of *Selected Poems,* the Process of Surfacing." In *The Art of Margaret Atwood: Essays in Criticism,* edited by Arnold Davidson and Cathy N. Davidson, 81–94. Toronto: Anansi, 1981.

Walker, Cheryl. "Turning to Margaret Atwood: From Anguish to Language." In *Margaret Atwood: Reflection and Reality,* edited by Beatrice Mendez-Egle, 154–71. Living Author Series, no. 6. Edinburg, Tex.: Pan American Univ., 1987.

Weir, Lorraine. "Atwood in a Landscape." In *Margaret Atwood: Language, Text, System,* edited by Sherrill Grace and Lorraine Weir, 143–53. Vancouver: Univ. of British Columbia Press, 1983.

Woodcock, George. "Metamorphosis and Survival: Notes on the Recent Poetry of Margaret Atwood." In *Margaret Atwood: Language, Text, System,* edited by Sherrill Grace and Lorraine Weir, 125–42. Vancouver: Univ. of British Columbia Press, 1983.

Martine Motard-Noar

FROM PERSEPHONE TO DEMETER: A FEMINIST EXPERIENCE IN CIXOUS'S FICTION

Hélène Cixous is one of the most controversial thinkers and writers in France. Despite her unwillingness to be labeled a "feminist"—a reductive categorization, according to her, just another "ism"-ending word[1]—she is considered a representative of one of the major creative and critical drives in the New French Feminist movement. She has developed her avant-garde practice of writing in numerous genres and forms, such as the bilingual novel *To Live the Orange* (Cixous 1979), and the play *Portrait of Dora* (Cixous 1979), her revision of Freud. Her most significant theoretical essays include the now classic manifesto "The Laugh of the Medusa," and collaborative projects such as *The Newly Born Woman* (Cixous and Clément 1986).

In 1980, Cixous published *Illa*, which works precisely on this central concept in her works—the newly born woman. In *Illa*, Cixous paradoxically introduces a story apparently opposed to the idea of a newly born woman—the ancient myth of Demeter, goddess of the earth and fecundity, who roams the earth in search of her daughter Persephone (or Kore) throughout the text. The paradox is, however, explained by the narrator's insistence that women must work their way through myths again to situate themselves in the past and present and to examine enigmatic accounts about their own sisters, past and present. In fact, in an interview, Cixous clearly explained why her exploration of the feminine must privilege myths in general: "I am passionately interested in myths, because they are always . . . outside the law, like the unconscious" (Andermatt Conley 1984, 155–56). It is not surprising that images of Persephone/Demeter are present in *Illa,* especially because Persephone represents one of the greatest Greek goddesses. In actuality, the goddess soon disappears as a specific historical figure, to be metamorphosed into a general figure of women that will then freely circulate in the text. As one of the many narrators in *Illa* admits, "There is nothing left in me that is not impregnated with her" [Il ne reste rien de moi qui ne soit imprégné d'elle].[2] It is in such a broad context that the inclusion of the myth of Persephone in *Illa,* a fictional work, can be understood. Nowhere is there a reference to or even a particular historical definition of the Persephone myth, which has known widely different interpretations, as documented, for instance, by Barbara Walker (1983, 786–87). This free adaptation of the myth by Cixous cannot surprise, for it is consistent with the general pattern in her writing, which the author has explained in interviews and essays. For her, the issue at stake is both political and ideological—Cixous's "feminist" writing will not accept any canonical form or any mythological story/"his"tory determined by a particular variation of the myth. She has already formulated a clear critical theory about the necessity of such disruption and recreation: "One never questions enough the traditions of interpretation of myth, and all myths have been referred to a masculine interpretation. If we women read them, we read them otherwise" (Cixous 1984, 156.) On the contrary, in all of the identities given to her in variations of the myth, Persephone often lives, in the overall image of the Woman, an unwilling participant in the constitution of her own myths. Following Michel Foucault's theory that "the real political task in a society such as ours is to criticize the working of institutions which appear to be both neutral and independent; to criticize them in such a manner that the political violence which has always exercised itself obscurely through them will be unmasked, so that one can fight them" (1992, 1). Cixous decides to "discover and create our [women's] myths in the process of a-mazing tales that are phallic" (Daly 1978, 129). In that way, the character of Persephone belongs to a global corpus of myths about women. But Cixous finds her specificity in the fact that her central figure binds them all together in the image of the Mother.

In fact, the accent is immediately put on Demeter's identity as Mother at the beginning of the fiction, because she is defined, when entering the narrative scene, as a mother searching for Kore, her daughter. For that reason, she "runs along the earth, the sea. . . . Roams outside of herself" [Court au bord de la terre, la mer. . . . Erre hors d'elle] (7). Although there is no mention of a cult surrounding "Illa" ("that woman"), it is interesting that Cixous first develops the figure of Demeter in relation to the earlier cults, where Demeter defined the feminine in both its sexual and reproductive aspects, in much the same way as patriarchy has defined the feminine. The text accumulates symbols relating Demeter to images of fertility (wheat) and bluntly affirms Demeter's figurative role: "the mother who comes back" [la mère qui revient] (12–13). The allusion to the maternal relationship in the myth is even more direct farther on: "GODDESS DECIDES NO LONGER BE DIVINE UNTIL RETURN HER DAUGHTER, HER DIVINITY." [DEESSE DECIDE NE PLUS ETRE DIVINE JUSQU'A RETOUR SA FILLE, SA DIVINITE.] (17). Demeter's presence can thus be immediately identified as the tale of the search for a daughter by her mother in the first few pages of the novel. Cixous, unlike most French feminist writers except for Chantal Chawaf, has always recognized and in some way glorified the figure of the mother and maternity, which French feminist writers like Monique Wittig have tried to escape or deny, keeping away from the dangers of heterosexual and patriarchal discourses. Cixous, however, both for personal and political reasons, has written along bisexual lines to express a multiple discourse that encompasses both lesbian desire and the acknowledgment of the need for "materrenelle" (1981, 9) language, a French portmanteau word bringing together the concept of mother and of earth to the heart of her quest.

Beyond any easy categorization, Cixous sets an example of what other figures can accomplish as well in terms of allowing mothers and daughters to create a relationship of their own: "One And becomes real and opens up each time that a woman gives birth back to one of her mothers. And each time that a woman asks to receive the light from another woman" [Un Et devient réel et s'ouvre chaque fois qu'une femme rend naissance à une de ses mères. Et chaque fois qu'une femme demande à recevoir la lumière d'une autre femme] (202). It has become, indeed, a movement back and forth between mothers, women of the origin, and daughters, who stand also as the images of the narrator. Demeter being the traditional image of the mother and even more specifically, of the mother of daughters, it is now the daughter's/narrator's duty to recreate her for the sake of self-knowledge and better understanding of women's oppression by men, as well as for a possible elucidation of feminist struggle. Reverence for women's "Ur-story" is present in a tale-like narrative in which women are compared to potatoes, an image obviously related to that of roots, origins, and earth. The potato stands as the "metaphor for Cixous's persistent search for feminine identity" (Shiach 1991, 93). Therefore, what could be seen as a humorous or at the very least ironic comparison is actually a serious attempt on her part to deconstruct the biblical story of Woman and the apple, or *pomme* in French, and reconstruct it under the sign of the potato/earth apple (*pomme de terre*) or concept of germination, and even better, self-germination from potato/woman to another, that is to say rebirth, despite its/her burial. In fact, Cixous gives the following definition to her reconstitution of women's epic:

> Different from other vegetables, the potato is not a plant, it is an expression from the earth as original matter. . . . Like Cretan civilization, potatoes are the most refined and repressed fruit. Potatoes in culture as in the cult are closely linked to the love-life association which make up for the first First Woman and her daughter the second and third. They are sometimes called Demeter and Persephone, often simply called "the Goddesses" or the potatoes. The potatoes are worth venerating: thus we do not disdain them, but we often make it so we can send them back into that dark oblivion in which they can stay quietly for thousands of years. The story of the potatoes constitutes the tender and crumbly matter, veiled with very fine, brown scrapings, of the central myth hidden in the heart of the universally known legend which tells of the origin of women, and the metamorphosis of potatoes.

> [À la différence des autres légumes, la pomme de terre n'est pas une plante, c'est une expression de la terre en tant que matière originaire. . . . Comme la civilisation crètoise, les pommes de terre sont les fruits les plus raffinés et les plus refoulés. Les pommes de terre dans la culture comme dans le culte sont étroitement unies au couple amour-vie que forment la première Première et sa fille la deuxième et troisième, parfois appelées

Déméter et Perséphone, souvent simplement appelées "les Déesses" ou les pommes. Les pommes de terre sont vénérables: nous ne les méprisons donc pas, mais nous nous arrangeons fréquemment pour les renvoyer à l'enfouissement dans lequel elles peuvent se tenir coites des millénaires. L'histoire des pommes de terre constitue la matière tendre, friable, voilée par de très fines pelures brunes, du mythe central caché au sein de la légende universellement répandue qui raconte l'origine des femmes, et la métamorphose des pommes de terre.] (203)

Demeter and Persephone carry out the chant of oppression as its archetypes. Nonetheless, several other "potatoes" join them in the narrative, as if Cixous felt the need to exemplify her theoretical proposal. This may explain the presence of a character like Cordelia, a clear allusion to Shakespeare's Cordelia, one of King Lear's daughters, who decided to "Love, and be silent" (1961, 983) when faced with the lies blinding her father's love. The fiction also opens with a direct quotation from Virgil's *Georgics* that alludes to Eurydice's lost chance to leave Hades, after Orpheus looks back at her.[3] These characters, although they introduce a male variant to the mother/daughter story, all converge toward an implicit accusation of male dominance, the power to throw women into oblivion. Women's love-giving (whether it comes from a mother like Demeter, a daughter like Cordelia, or a wife like Eurydice) ends up being buried deeply.

Illa ends up accusing all caught in such social conditioning, apparently both men and women, of repressing women's instinctive drives. And women's feeling of unity throughout the myths and the ages paradoxically grows out of the story of their oppression: "We too, in a way, are potatoes together. The goddesses came like us from the southern hemisphere. They lived happy among the other earth nymphs, far from any concept of marriage, until the primitive abduction whose grave and sorrowful consequences for us are still perceptible all along the paths in this text" [Nous aussi nous sommes d'une certaine manière pommes de terre ensemble. Les déesses étaient originaires comme nous de l'hémisphère sud. Elles vivaient heureuses parmi les autres nymphes de terre, loin de toute idée de mariage, jusqu'à l'enlèvement primitif dont les conséquences endeuillantes pour nous sont encore perceptibles tout le long des chemins de ce texte] (203). Despite the presence of other potato stories, the particular choice of the Persephone / Demeter pair in *Illa* indeed raises the question of the ultimate act of male oppression of women—ravishment or rape. Demeter's wrath ("dies illa dies irae" [52]) becomes that of the narrator and of all women in the face of Persephone's brutal abduction by Hades into the chasm as she was gathering flowers. Although the narrator is using the particular myth of Persephone / Demeter, her wrath is globally targeted at most myths, created by men for men in their unconscious need to reveal their perverse desires against women, and young women in particular. Exasperation spreads over Demeter's rage:

> The whole series of grotesque appearances under which the old perverse saw themselves forced to be in order to abduct the vigilant virgins, with a sharp shuttle she represents the gang of those insect-like reduced to their true aspect, as in themselves the rape drive changes them forever, with the entire zoo they put together, here they are, underneath their hair, leather, scales, as they are revealed in dreams, in the horror of their nature, with a look able to disgust leda, demeter, kore, melantho, ariadne, asterie, medusa, theophane, you my friend, angela, or you deo, or you, memory, my sister, or illa, as well as all the women who find no charm in being bitten, torn apart, stabbed in the back, caressed with ram's and bull's horns, and snakes' and eagles' claws, hooves and beaks, and have no libidinal interest in being unveiled by a satyr.
>
> [Toute la série des grotesques apparences sous lesquelles les vieux pervers se sont vus contraints de se présenter dérobés pour enlever les vierges vigilantes, d'une navette aiguë elle figure la bande des insectueux réduits à leur véritable aspect, tels qu'en eux-mêmes la pulsion de viol les change pour l'éternité, leur zoo entier tout craché, les voilà rendus, sous poil, sous cuir, sous écailles, tels qu'en rêve ils sont révélés, horreur nature, avec leur aspect propre, à dégoûter léda, démèter, koré, mélantho, ariane, astérié, méduse, théophané, toi mon amie, angela, ou toi déo, ou toi, mémoire, ma soeur, ou illa, ainsi que toutes les femmes qui ne trouvent aucun charme à se faire mordre, déchirer, poignarder dans le dos, caresser à coups de cornes de bélier, de boeuf, de serres de serpents, d'aigles, de sabots, de becs, et aucun intérêt libidinal à se faire connaître par un satyre.] (71)

The narrator's interest in the Persephone / Demeter pair exemplifies a general need to strike all myths. Because it is impossible to cancel the past, Cixous's political goal is to stress at least the feminine component in each myth to undercut the male violence and perverse sexuality expressed in mythological deeds. In fact, neither Hades nor Zeus, Persephone's father, who tacitly consented to her abduction, appears in *Illa*. They are now finally made impotent in the fiction written by a woman. Bitterness and sorrow now follow in close parallel with Demeter's own reaction: "We no longer love the titans who used to hold the main roles in our passions, the gods we loved. . . . They are keeping away a lost child, about whom we keep thinking with loving sorrow, with sad and peaceful tenderness, a child who leads an unknown existence in our unconscious" [Nous n'aimons plus les titans qui détenaient les rôles principaux dans nos passions, les dieux que nous avons aimés. . . . Ils ont la garde d'un enfant perdu, auquel nous pensons avec une tristesse aimante, avec une tendresse triste et paisible, et qui mène parmi nos inconscients une existence inconnue] (120). Thus, Demeter's wrath finds a more positive outlet, beyond aggression, death, and revenge, for Cixous has started to put together a new poetics of women, a new mythical body characterized by a drive for life. In a direct allusion to *Prometheus Unbound* and an open feminization of Shelley's canonical test, Cixous explains the reasons for Demeter's final restraint in a chapter entitled "Illa unbound": "Because a woman does not surrender to death unless she has forgotten the secret of her strength; . . . because there is in every woman a great passion which does not surrender" (84). Wrath is then replaced by a specific sense of communion with the feminine victims, to whom Cixous obviously belongs. The feminine anger characterized by Cixous's use of the myth can be found and reaffirmed in another work, published one year after *Illa, With ou l'art de l'innocence,* which has not yet been translated into English. In a continuing search for the presymbolic wealth represented by ancient Greek mythology, Cixous uses the story of Eurydice in a presentation that parallels that of Persephone and Demeter quite remarkably and is alluded to in *Illa* in the Latin quotation from Virgil's *Georgics.* In *With,* however, she might be considered as going further than in *Illa,* as there is no mention whatsoever of the male figure, Orpheus. Somewhere between indifference and accusation, the many women narrators of the fiction appear to have expelled or "decentered" the masculine as the eternal culprit in the Eurydice story. To make her point even clearer, Cixous has Amina, a character and one of the women narrators in the book, successfully rescue Eurydice from Hades. The path from the masculine to the feminine in Cixous's works resounds with bitterness, love, and, in the end, hope for radical change.

Persephone and, by extension, Demeter, thus become the representation of love and innocence still present in women's hearts, according to Cixous. Fiction, rewriting of the myth, and/or memory actually attempt to make up for the abduction of the maiden. Therefore, the dynamic principle of the text is an absence/presence dichotomy, Persephone's presence being found in her very absence, one that keeps accusing her oppressor. Cixous, unlike other writers (such as Monique Wittig), finds a feminist tune of reparation that does not entail forgiveness but rather a personal search for the maiden in each woman, while conjuring up in the background the father/male figure, who is also faced with an absence/presence dichotomy.

One of Cixous's narrative talents in *Illa,* and in many of her other fictions as well, is to weave traditional Greek mythology into her own invented mythology. As a French feminist writer, she is not the only one to do so. Her interest in Greek mythology and her gestures away from its determinism reminds one of Monique Wittig, who, in her very personal version of a woman's dictionary, attempts to recapture women's history in a partially fictional manner. In this work, culture, mythologies, oral tradition, personal imagination, and projection are gathered to constitute a purely feminine and lesbian domain, which women have been indirectly prohibited from defining. These motives explain why the subconscious and the imaginary in both Cixous's and Wittig's texts participate in the identification and fictional representation of women's realm. Wittig also stresses the importance of the female couple in the following entry from her dictionary: "DEMETER AND PERSEPHONE—Famous ancient goddesses, companions and lovers from Pelasgia. One was born from the other. When Persephone had to part from her, Demeter would show her sorrow by destroying everything alive on the surface of the earth until Persephone returned. From this come the winter and the autumn, it is said" (Wittig and Zeig 1979, 42). The violence and impact of female love—a representation typical of Wittig's writing—do not appear in Cixous as images of external destruction but rather of self-destruction. Nevertheless, for both Cixous and Wittig, the female couple evokes a privileged topos and a possibility for mythical recreation.

As for the possibility of self-destruction, it is depicted in *Illa* in a passage written with a semi-autobiographical overtone. The narrator, drawing a parallel between herself and Cixous's identity as a Jewish woman, reaffirms the concept of loss and rapture, this time in modern terms, although in very similar fashion to the Persephone / Demeter situation. In a somewhat nightmarish scene, the narrator evokes having to leave abruptly to be taken to a concentration camp. Just like Persephone, she is a wanted woman, a "Jewoman" (*juifemme*)—as Cixous likes to write in many texts. This time, it is the mother who is forced to leave her daughter, in an exchange of female roles. The mother says, "I am afraid, I hurt, I didn't say goodbye, I didn't have time to think intelligently, I didn't tell my mother to take my children to England, I didn't call my love to say 'I love you' before I die, I didn't ask you who is not a jewoman to give my life to my daughter" [J'ai peur, j'ai mal, je n'ai pas fait mes adieux, je n'ai pas eu le temps de penser intelligemment, je n'ai pas dit à ma mère d'emmener mes enfants en Angleterre, je n'ai pas téléphoné à mon amour pour lui dire qu'avant de mourir je l'aime, je n'ai pas demandé à toi qui n'es pas juifemme de transmettre ma vie à ma fille] (166).

At this point of the fiction, the narrator manages to encompass both roles—that of mother and that of daughter—in a gesture of indifference toward the traditional notion of specific roles and characters. For Cixous's fiction strips the notion of character from its capitalist economy, from all its usual attributes, in favor of a notion of characters' free exchange.[4] She is both Demeter and Persephone in a movement of appropriation of total existential anguish, as conveyed in the Persephone / Demeter myth. And again possible self-destruction (caused by the Jewish woman's inability to act before leaving for a concentration camp) is the result of outside oppression. The narrator, just like Persephone, is taken away, in danger of losing her own self, together with the self known to those who love her; the danger of self-destruction is therefore extended to the narrator's daughter and to Demeter herself. The precarious condition in which women find themselves, and their paradoxical feeling of guilt when faced with their own victimization, are here reintroduced by Cixous in a personal light, using a modern background to the tragic myth. The account is nonetheless to be taken in the broad ideological context defined earlier, as the account of a particular woman's condition echoing in its own way the general condition of women as witnessed in Persephone and Demeter.

The question of forced separation in *Illa* has been so obvious to critics that they have discerned a desire for revenge, but only in

Cixous's choice of words. Verena Andermatt Conley notes that Cixous's use of the name of Koré for Persephone has separatist undertones: "Cixous changes the Greek name Persephone, which had been used by male theoreticians to allude to problems of voice (*phonè*), to the more material Koré (*corps-ai*), substituting the masculine letter K for the more commonly used C" (1984, 107). There exists an undeniable interest on Cixous's part to undermine any traditional acceptance of the myth and to distort all clichés about Persephone's fragility as a female object. Becoming Koré, Persephone seems and literally sounds as if she is finally able to struggle on even ground, since Koré sounds like *corps-ai* or "body-[I] have." The glorification of women in the Persephone myth in Cixous cannot therefore be conflated with the cult of femininity, a potentially controversial matter, because the concept of femininity is transformed in her use of the myth. For, in the end Koré, by her name alone, can announce her presence and deny her symbolic oppression.

Despite the change in spelling from C to K and the revelation of her strong identity, Koré cannot prevent Persephone from being present in the text in allusions to problems of voice. A whole syncretism is in process in *Illa,* relating the voice to, in the end, the Female: "The voice is the uterus. The voice contracts and gives birth, gives birth, and for each new joy, breaks into laughter, and gives a name" [La voix est l'utérus. La voix se contracte et met au monde, met au monde, et à chaque nouvelle joie, éclate de rire, et met un nom] (168). Persephone loses her voice by being abducted, yet she is still alive in the underworld. It is now Demeter's grief that speaks of her daughter and speaks for her daughter. In this way, Persephone's voice is immortal as it runs through women, her mother, and then others who give birth to it. As for Demeter, she is allowed to hope for the strength of a female voice of iron, which the narrator conveys in a direct quotation from Virgil, *"Non, mihi si linguae centum oraque centum"* (Cixous 1980, 8; the quotation is from Virgil 1990, 2:43), which is followed in Virgil by an allusion to the possibility of having a voice of iron in addition to one hundred tongues and one hundred mouths. There is hope therefore for "Illa," the third person, the narrator, who roams the earth, like Demeter, in search of herself and all women—she too, as a woman, is given a voice in the fiction. Another source of hope resides in the meaningful sounds made by the actual name used by Cixous to allude to Persephone, as Andermatt Conley suggests. Koré, alias Persephone, is definitely not lost; her absence-presence is voiced by many women, for those who in turn pronounce the word *corps-ai* actualize themselves in the discovery of a body they now themselves own. Similarly, Persephone's body is given back to her in the shape of Koré through *Illa.*

Ultimately the Persephone / Demeter question and that of a / the narrative voice are one and the same, for writing is directly related to the earth and the voice in the sensual quality of their fertility, their creation. For that reason, "the daughter unable to get help from her mother any more stays away from her own life, resembles a writing without a feather in its hands" [la fille n'ayant plus le secours de sa mère reste en deçà de sa propre vie, ressemble à une écriture qui n'a pas de plume entre les mains] (196), and, similarly for Demeter, "who has not seen the moment when her daughter was stolen—she resembles a mouth without a tongue" [qui n'a pas vu l'instant où sa fille a été volée: elle ressemble à une bouche qui n'a pas de langue] (196). It is then easy for the narrative figure, which is, by definition, a writing figure, to assimilate herself as a woman with Persephone / Koré ravished away from the mother tongue, from the only possibility to speak out and give form (*corps*) to words: "May I remember how I came from a first woman, may I remember just once at least one mother, just once an all giving mother with an absolutely faithful and natural voice from birth, please!" [Puissé-je garder en mémoire comment je suis venue d'une première, puissé-je une seule fois ne pas oublier une seule mère, rappeler une seule fois toute donnante d'une voix absolument fidèle et natale et naturelle, puissé-je!] (196). The loss of the daughter's voice, leading to all women's loss of voice(s), causes the mother's wrath as well as the impossibility of her living as a mother, woman, daughter herself, and goddess. The dissolution of her being is stressed in a telegram-style passage: "GODDESS DECIDES NO LONGER BE DIVINE UNTIL RETURN HER DAUGHTER, HER DIVINITY. NO LONGER LIVE. SEARCH. SURVIVE. DEMETER." [DEESSE DECIDE NE PLUS ETRE DIVINE JUSQU'A RETOUR SA FILLE, SA DIVINITE. PLUS VIVRE. CHERCHER. SURVIVRE. DEMETER.] (18).

Demeter's despair and love are, in the end, the only feminine response that can pressure the (masculine) world into Persephone's release. Women's alliance, although multivoiced, still remains powerless and only serves as an intermediary phase. Demeter's direct power over events is limited to the identity given to her by her very name: pronounced in French, Demeter is homonymic of *d'aimer terre*, or "to love the earth," a play on words used by Cixous in *Illa*

(18). Demeter chooses not to love the earth, with the result that she threatens the world and, at the same time, is threatened in her own power to love, which Cixous stresses in the description of Demeter's desperate wandering.

Demeter's wandering, however, leaves no room for any dispersion or disintegration of the self. Her wandering soon becomes a method, an account of and a search for love with no specifically targeted objective, contrary to what is commonly involved with a heterosexual relationship, according to Cixous. The wandering becomes a fictional experience in the plural, as the title of the book underlines. *Illa*, a singular and plural Latin demonstrative pronoun used here in the feminine, evokes a concept for which there is no word in French or in English. *Illa*, meaning "that woman *or / and* those women," announces the core principle of the text, encompassing the singular *and* the plural under woman's / women's general history. Moreover, this pronoun is often used in Latin in a positive and emphatic way, which seems perfectly to fit with the intention of the text.

On the other hand, the pronoun may convey as well a notion of distance both in time and space, like a finger pointing at a third person, probably the woman narrator: "Who? Am? The third woman. . . . Whos? Am we? Who? I? We? Wanders out of herself. *Illa*. A young person. The third woman [my italics]." [Qui? Suis? La troisième. . . . Quis? Suis nous? Qui? Je? Nous? Erre hors d'elle. Illa. Une jeune personne. La troisième] (7). The narrator of *Illa* thus opens the book declining the pronoun from the feminine singular to the feminine plural, from "Who? Am?" to "Whos? Am *we*?" [my italics] and soon after, into a general feminine gender crying out for a solidarity found in the distancing enforced upon it by male discourse. *Illa* thus represents women's position parallel to that of Persephone.

The quality of patriarchal discourse represented by the word *illa* as expressing women's unwilling marginality has also been recognized by writers other than Cixous, particularly feminist psychoanalytic critics. Jane Gallop notes that, in Freudian discourse, woman becomes a third person, the Other, about whom men speak, used as an object of analysis and experimentation; woman is *Illa* for Freud according to Gallop's analysis of one of his speeches: "Although Freud begins his lecture 'Ladies and Gentlemen,' a few pages later he says, 'Nor will *you* have escaped worrying over this problem because *you* are men; as for the *women among you* this will not apply, *they* are themselves this riddle' [my italics]. When he explicitly addresses the audience as sexed beings, he reserves the second-person pronoun for men and refers to women with the third-person pronoun. Freud talks *to* men *about* women" (1985, 38).

Illa, character(s) and title, struggle against the same ambiguity—closeness and distancing. *Illa* represents the closeness among women and, at the same time, women's separation, which paradoxically allows them to gather together under the identity of the persecuted. To counteract any attempt to keep Persephone / women in exile, however, *Illa,* as a fiction, tries to stay close to any movement, transformation, or sensation of women in its narration. The narrator even initiates a conversation about a third person: "Her or me? Me or oneself? Illa?" [Elle ou moi? Moi ou soi? Illa?] (79). The chiasmus playfully points to a tension between women ("her" as opposed to "me"), to be resolved in another entity, that of "Illa." By extension, in this search for "oneself" (*soi*), which could also be translated as "herself," the narrator reestablishes a distance that, in the image of Persephone's condition, appears to be the only historical and chronological path toward a possible feminine reunion. Within this framework, the myth of Persephone can be understood in *Illa* as both a thematic and narrative construction.

Cixous, however, could not totally build her text on such a dual pattern. As a binary movement, it would disqualify her previous theoretical stance against all binary constructs in our patriarchal society. In *The Newly Born Woman,* Cixous questions precisely the dual opposition upon which our society has been based: "Dual, hierarchical oppositions. Superior / Inferior. Myths, legends, books. Philosophical systems. Everywhere (where) ordering intervenes, where a law organizes what is thinkable by oppositions (dual, irreconcilable; or sublatable, dialectical). And all these pairs of oppositions are *couples.* Does that mean something? Is the fact that Logocentrism subjects thought—all concepts, codes and values—to a binary system, related to 'the' couple, man / woman?" (Cixous and Clément 1986, 64). After accusing logocentrism and phallocentrism, she allows herself to dream of a way out of the masculine order and, most importantly, out of the masculine order of dreaming and writing: "If some fine day it suddenly came out that the logocentric plan had always, inadmissibly, been to create a foundation for (to found and fund) phallocentrism, to guarantee the masculine order a rationale equal to history itself. . . . When they [women] wake up from among the dead, from among words, from among laws" (Cixous and Clément 1986, 65).

Cixous's fiction indeed discovers a path leading out of such alienating dichotomy. *Illa* may in fact point to this third pronoun as a third element in a trinity that escapes traditional religious boundaries. This third party accounts for a newly found serenity in the text after the rage expressed immediately following the tale of Koré / Demeter at the beginning of the fiction and even after the quiet disdain and resolution of female rebirth. The real revelation arrives with an *illa*—"the Clarice-voice" [la voix-Clarice] (131). Clarice, who stands for the Brazilian fiction writer Clarice Lispector, whose fiction Cixous read in the late 70s and immediately fell in love with, opens up a new "calm school of approaches" [Calme école d'approches] (134).

Illa-Clarice not only provides for a possibility out of the binary situation in which the book is placed; it / she also actually heals the world of women. Exaltation explodes throughout the very end of the book. Clarice embodies Demeter's attributes—creation, nature—and is therefore able to return the earth back to its original condition, before Persephone's abduction and rape and before Demeter's wrath and need for revenge: "Then the day goes by. But leaves behind a symphony, and sometimes a new species of flowers, and a promised future" [Puis le jour passe. Mais laisse en partant une symphonie, et parfois une nouvelle espèce de fleurs; et un futur promis] (181). *Illa* is thus a piece of "remembrement" (195), a neologism with a double meaning—the action of putting all parts of the body back together, and the English meaning of remembering. In fact, the book claims to be reinventing none other than Demeter by being *livres-terres* ("books-earths") (186), as opposed to *démet-terres* ("undoes-earths"), another homonym of Demeter.

Cixous finds a way past the binary structure that encompasses proximity and distance toward Woman and the Other thanks to the renewed sanctity she gives to the number three, which was sacred in ancient pre-patriarchal worship of the Goddess. She entitles the last section of *Illa* "The new beginning begins by three . . ." [Le recommencement commence par trois . . .] (198). These words might be considered an allusion to a concept that Cixous has always advocated—bisexuality instead of homosexuality. Another possibility would be that the number three, standing for mother–daughter–woman friend, is more restrictive, and thus this movement could be criticized as a reduction to a unitary world. Yet *Illa* is probably to be taken as a preliminary step toward a new beginning, as mentioned in the above quotation. Thus, a triplicity that would hide sexual limitations can be seen as a springboard toward the liberation of feminine libidinal economy. Besides, it is also important to note that Cixous never characterizes the feminine by women and the masculine by men, knowing that the masculine economy can be assumed by women and that, in some cases, men can do the opposite. Therefore, the number three may symbolize a variety of gender choices in hope for reparation.

It is then clear that the use of the myth of Persephone in *Illa* could summarize much of Cixous's writing as well as much of the attitude taken in the last twenty years by feminist writers and critics. They seem to show a chronological evolution from the formal study of ancient myths to freer and more directly contemporary allusions. Both ends of the spectrum demonstrate women's slavery and, at the same time, challenge of slavery throughout the centuries, starting with representative figures such as Persephone / Koré and Demeter. As the depiction of the unconscious, however, the myth of Persephone and Demeter stands as the first recognized set of ideas on which to build an interpretation. Cixous's interpretation, which often uses poetic language for subversive reasons, "proposes [a] mythic construct as a possibility—and even the only possibility—for all women" (Sankovitch 1988, 146). For Cixous and many other feminists, interpretation has recently led to a more global quasi-prophetic understanding of feminism. Women's "remembrance" in no way constitutes an inward movement; it extends to all women in the world for all times, the way it extends to the Brazilian writer Clarice Lispector who comes to rescue Persephone and Demeter. In that sense, euphoria can exist again in women's minds and bodies—in the belief in the possibility of a renewal for women, and in general for the feminine, of creative, expanding (as opposed to binary) relationships in the image of Demeter and Persephone / Koré.

NOTES

1. Cixous, like several other French women writers, has always denied being a feminist. Her hostility to the term seems to result from semantics (feminism would be defined as the exclusion of men and the replacement of their power by another tyranny—that of women) and from her desire to distance herself from any specific political group or agenda. The words

feminism and *feminist* will still be used in this chapter for the same practical reasons as those mentioned by Marks and Courtivron in *New French Feminisms:* "There is as yet no better word to account for the phenomenon" (1981, x). My definition of feminism, much broader than Cixous's, is closer to Marks and Courtivron's: "An awareness of women's oppression-repression that initiates both analyses of the dimension of this oppression-repression and stategies for liberation" (1981, x).

2. Cixous 1980, 37. Subsequent page numbers in parentheses refer to this edition. Unless otherwise specified, all English translations of Cixous's texts in this article are mine. The original French text will follow the translation to convey the richness and complexity of the original, which my translation may simplify.

3. "Illa: 'Quis et me' inquit 'miseram et te perdidit, o tu, quis tantus furor?'" (7). The quotation is from Virgil 1990, 4:494–95.

4. For a good analysis of this phenomenon in Cixous's work, see Sankovitch 1988, 140–41.

BIBLIOGRAPHY

Andermatt Conley, Verena. *Hélène Cixous: Writing the Feminine.* Lincoln: Univ. of Nebraska Press, 1984.

Cixous, Hélène. *Portrait of Dora.* Translated by Anita Barrows. London: Calder, 1979.

———. *Vivre l'orange/To Live the Orange.* Paris: Ed. des femmes, 1979.

———. *Illa.* Paris: Ed. des femmes, 1980.

———. *With ou l'art de l'innocence.* Paris: Ed. des femmes, 1981.

———. "Appendix." In *Hélène Cixous: Writing the Feminine,* edited by Verena Andermatt Conley. Lincoln: Univ. of Nebraska Press, 1984.

Cixous, Hélène, and Catherine Clément. *The Newly Born Woman.* Translated by Betsy Wing. Minneapolis: Univ. of Minnesota Press, 1986.

Daly, Mary. *Gyn/Ecology: The Metaethics of Radical Feminism.* Boston: Beacon Press, 1978.

Foucault, Michel. Quoted in Laurie Finke, *Feminist Theory, Women's Writing.* Ithaca, N.Y.: Cornell Univ. Press, 1992.

Gallop, Jane. *The (M)other Tongue: Essays in Feminist Psychoanalytic Interpretation.* Ithaca, N.Y.: Cornell Univ. Press, 1985.

Marks, Elaine, and Isabelle de Courtivron, eds. *New French Feminisms.* New York: Schocken Books, 1981.

Motard-Noar, Martine. *Les fictions d'Hélène Cixous: une nouvelle langue de femme.* Lexington, Ky.: French Forum, 1991.

Sankovitch, Tilde. *French Women Writers and the Book: Myths of Access and Desire.* Syracuse, N.Y.: Syracuse Univ. Press, 1988.

Shakespeare, William. *The Complete Works of Shakespeare.* Edited by Hardin Craig. Glenview, Ill.: Scott, Foresman, 1961.

Shiach, Morag. *Hélène Cixous: A Politics of Writing.* London: Routledge, 1991.
Virgil. *Georgics.* Edited by R. A. B. Mynors. Oxford: Clarendon, 1990.
Walker, Barbara. *The Women's Encyclopedia of Myths and Secrets.* San Francisco: Harper and Row, 1983.
Wittig, Monique, and Sande Zeig. *Lesbian Peoples.* New York: Avon, 1979.

Elizabeth T. Hayes

CHAPTER 11

"LIKE SEEING YOU BURIED": PERSEPHONE IN *THE BLUEST EYE, THEIR EYES WERE WATCHING GOD,* AND *THE COLOR PURPLE*

The story of Persephone and Demeter (Proserpina and Ceres in Roman mythology) is one of the most widely known of the ancient Greco-Roman myths. It is simultaneously the tale of a daughter abducted, raped, and married against her will to the god of the dead and of a mother, grief-stricken and furious over the loss of her daughter, who ceases to nurture life on earth. One of the few female-centered myths, it focuses on the resistance of Persephone and Demeter, who, by refusing to acquiesce to Persephone's sexual and emotional abuse, pit themselves against the male rulers of the pantheon, with the maternal bond as their chief strength and the political tactic of refusal as their chief weapon. Thus, this myth is vitally concerned with the politics of power: how the marginalized gain a voice within a social system, how women achieve strong, positive identities in a culture that wants to define them only as objects of male ownership.

Because Demeter does succeed in freeing Persephone from death, this myth has long been viewed as a celebration of women's power, for not only is Persephone restored to the world of the living, but new life springs from the dead earth when Persephone returns from the underworld. Certainly no one would deny that the awesome strength and redemptive force of the maternal bond is an important theme of the mythic story. A deconstructive reading is also possible, however. Such a reading undercuts the traditional celebratory view of the mythic text by emphasizing the difficulties Persephone and Demeter experience in gaining a voice within the patriarchy.

The women's victory over Death is, after all, only partial, because Persephone must return to her abuser/"husband" for part of each year. Moreover, Persephone loses her identity as "the Maiden" the moment she is abducted and raped. Alone and powerless in the underground where the god of the dead rules, she is forced to take on a new identity determined by her abuser: she becomes Hades's "wife," Hades's possession, a sexual object. "Marriage" initiates Persephone's lifelong subservient relationship to men and her disenfranchisement from any real political power or voice. One need only look at the ending of the myth to realize how incomplete is the women's victory: Hades is rewarded for his abusive actions by gaining a sexual servant and companion for part of the year, while Persephone and Demeter, the victims, must suffer forever the pain of Persephone's abduction and abuse, as well as live with the bitter consciousness of Persephone's impending mortality even during the months they are together.

Women's political disenfranchisement and their abuse by men within patriarchal cultures are also prominent themes in African-American women's fiction. For this reason, it is not surprising that the Persephone myth should prove extremely useful to African-American writers as they examine the efforts of women of color to gain an effective voice in a society that tries to silence them at every turn. Toni Morrison, Zora Neale Hurston, and Alice Walker in particular have created fascinating reenactments, or images, of the Persephone myth in their fiction, images whose differences from the archetype are as significant as their similarities to it.

The disenfranchisement and silencing that Demeter and Persephone experience, though shared by all women in patriarchal cultures, are especially severe for African-American women, who have long suffered domination both within the minority culture by African-American men and in the dominant culture by all European-Americans. Indeed, the correlation is so strong between the treatment of African-Americans by European-Americans and the treatment of women by men in patriarchal societies that the term *patriarchy* in this essay signifies both sexual and racial domination. *The Bluest Eye, Their Eyes Were Watching God,* and *The Color Purple* relate the experiences of abused African-American girls who suffer a prolonged ritual death as they grow up painfully in the American patriarchy. The Persephone myth, embodying as it does the archetypal rite of passage for women in phallocentric cultures, provides a generative framework for Morrison, Hurston, and Walker as they explore in their fiction the profound effects of patriarchal dominance upon the mother-daughter bond and African-American female identity.

A glance at any version of the myth (see Appendixes A, B, and C) reveals a patriarchy in flagrante delicto, pushing even strong women out into the margins of power. For example, in the Homeric "Hymn to Demeter," the most powerful figures in the story are the king of the gods, Zeus (Persephone's father), and his brother Hades, ruler of the underworld. Their voices override all others, including even that of their sister Demeter, the Grain Mother, probably the most influential goddess in the pantheon. We see illustrated in the myth that what a patriarch wants, he gets—by force, if necessary. Hades sexually desires Persephone, and because he is a powerful male in a male-dominant society, he simply seizes her and makes her his own, by right of eminent domain. Zeus is clearly allied with Hades rather than with Demeter or their daughter Persephone, even allowing Gaia (Mother Earth) to grow a special flower to lure Persephone away from her companions so that Hades can seize her.

That Demeter and Persephone might object to Persephone's abduction, rape, and death, or that they might suffer great anguish at their sudden permanent separation, weighs not a jot with Hades or Zeus, before, during, or after the seizing of the maiden goddess. Indeed, the intense suffering of the women is not the reason Zeus finally orders Hades to release his captive; instead, Zeus simply wants to effect the resumption of the sacrifices human beings make to the gods when the earth is fruitful. Clearly, a deconstructive reading of the myth highlights the patriarchal structure of the world in which Persephone and Demeter's story takes place, a world strikingly similar to the one in which Morrison's Pecola, Hurston's Janie, and Walker's Celie live.

The experiences of Pecola, Janie, and Celie closely parallel Persephone's in many ways. Of course, Morrison, Hurston, and Walker need not consciously have intended to animate the Persephone myth to create images of it in their fictional texts. The archetypes of the Mother and the female rite of passage in the Persephone story embody fundamental human experiences and emotions, part of the collective unconscious of writers and readers alike. Archetypes and other metaphors are the language of art, of the unconscious. We can understand them, respond to them, and use them artistically without ever bringing them to consciousness. Furthermore, although archetypes can affect both writer and audience on a purely unconscious level, some, like the Persephone archetype, are deeply embedded as well in Western cultural consciousness.

There is, moreover, every likelihood that the three writers under discussion came in direct contact in adulthood with this well-known myth. Hurston was a cultural anthropologist and folklorist who studied under Franz Boas at Barnard and Columbia; Toni Morrison earned her master's in classics at Cornell; and Alice Walker not only read *The Bluest Eye* and *Their Eyes Were Watching God* before writing *The Color Purple* (indeed, Walker herself is largely responsible for the present Hurston revival), but she received her undergraduate education at Sarah Lawrence when Joseph Campbell was teaching and popularizing mythography there.

At a seminar session at Syracuse University in 1988, I asked Toni Morrison, the author of the novel most explicitly an image of the myth, if she had consciously set out to write a reenactment of the Persephone story. Interestingly, she replied that although a number of people had pointed out to her the parallels between *The Bluest Eye* and the Persephone myth, she had most assuredly not set out to create an image of the myth; that is not the way she writes. She allowed, however, that as a classics major, she was certainly familiar with the story, and she concluded that the myth had no doubt influenced her subconsciously on some level as she wrote *The Bluest Eye* (Morrison 1988).

Morrison might have been speaking as well for Hurston and Walker or any other artist, for an artist draws from both the unconscious and the memory in creating a work of art. Explaining artistic creation recently, Morrison said the artist uses "what's already there. . . . It doesn't matter if it's 10 seconds, 10 minutes, or 10 years" ago that he or she stored the information. The artist goes to a place in the mind where the information is fresh for him or her, and "something click[s]" (1992, 65). Archetypes, then, can operate subliminally, through the unconscious, as well as through rational thought: that is precisely what gives them their astounding resonance, their numinosity.

The Persephone archetype embodies the prototypical rite of passage for women, whose sexual maturation has long marked the beginning of their greatest vulnerability to male power. The presence of this archetypal rite of passage undoubtedly contributes to the singular resonance the myth holds for Westerners. In fact, images of the Persephone archetype have appeared repeatedly in Western literature for more than two thousand years, in the works of male and female writers in many cultures. Whether or not Toni Morrison, Zora Neale Hurston, and Alice Walker draw explicit attention to or are even conscious of their use of the Persephone myth in their fiction, they have created distinctive, powerful, and revealing African-American images of Persephone.

Probably the most elaborate Persephone image in African-American fiction is Toni Morrison's evocative first novel, *The Bluest Eye,* where the myth shapes, both structurally and thematically, Morrison's exploration of the effects of racism and sexism on women of color. A conspicuous parallel between *The Bluest Eye* and the myth is the centrality of the natural cycle to each. The Persephone story has so often been viewed as an anthropomorphic explanation of the change of seasons that any reference, no matter how slight, to the seasonal cycle in a text dealing with women immediately calls up the Persephone archetype as the model. When a writer titles the four major sections of a novel "Autumn," "Winter," "Spring," and "Summer," as Morrison does in *The Bluest Eye,* she underlines the natural cycle as the structural foundation of the text. Together with the deliberate association of Pecola with the earth's fertility in the italicized prologue (discussed below), the division of the text into seasons signifies the Persephone archetype at work in *The Bluest Eye*.

Whereas the myth begins its seasonal cycle in the spring, the novel ironically opens with autumn, a sign that this text will turn upside down the "standard" archetype, just as it turns upside down middle-class European-American norms and standard English in the Dick-and-Jane primer prologue and the chapter headings. In the Autumn section, Pecola's rite of passage begins, appropriately enough, with the arrival of her first menstrual period. Pecola's entering puberty, however, heralds not the cyclical springing forth of new life after a ritual death of sexual initiation, but the downward linear progression from ritual death to death of the self: she is raped by her father at the end of the Spring section; and in the

Summer section, we learn of the death of Claudia and Frieda's magic seeds, the birth and death of Pecola's baby, and Pecola's irrevocable slide into insanity. The natural cycle in *The Bluest Eye* moves from death to death, not from life to renewed life.

The Persephone archetype is important to *The Bluest Eye* thematically as well as structurally. On the first page of the text, Morrison introduces an eleven-year-old Persephone figure who has been raped by an older man—her father. Persephone, the Kore, symbolized in ancient rites by an ear of seed corn, enters her period of death when Hades forces upon her first his seed, through rape, and then later (according to the Homeric hymn), the pomegranate seeds that guarantee her return to the underworld. Similarly, Pecola is associated with seeds, both her father's seed, forced upon her by rape, and the marigold seeds that Claudia and Frieda plant to insure the life of Pecola's baby. Pecola's association with the earth is made concrete by Claudia, who says that she and Frieda "had dropped our seeds in our own little plot of black dirt, just as Pecola's father had dropped his seeds in his own plot of black dirt."[1] Just as nothing grows on earth during the time that Persephone is subject to Hades's abuse, so Claudia and Frieda's magic marigolds do not grow—indeed, we are told that no marigolds at all grow in Lorain, Ohio, in 1941—because Pecola has been abused by her father.

Unlike Persephone's sexual initiation, which eventually leads to renewed life after a period of death, Pecola's leads only to death, both the figurative death of insanity, and actual death: "Cholly Breedlove is dead: our innocence too. The seeds shriveled and died; her baby too" (9). From all this planting of seed, in the end "nothing remains but Pecola and the unyielding earth" (9). Thus, instead of being a symbol, like Persephone, of periodic renewed fertility after a journey to the underworld, Pecola embodies the modern Waste Land, barren, isolated, sterile. She becomes, in fact, a scapegoat absorbing (in Claudia's words) "all of [the community's] waste which we dumped on her" (159).

The ironic contrasts between Persephone's story and Pecola's point up Morrison's bitter vision of what it was like to grow up black and female in America in the forties. While Persephone is valued and loved by all, including of course Demeter and Hades, Pecola is valued by no one, loved by no one, and blamed by nearly everyone for her own victimization. Only Claudia and Frieda, two powerless children, genuinely sympathize with Pecola and try to help her. Like Persephone, Pecola is in no way responsible for being raped;

she simply happens to be female, and she unwittingly happens to catch the eye of Hades. Unlike Persephone, however, Pecola never escapes from hell after her forced sexual initiation. She never becomes "the resurrection goddess"; indeed, the only identity she manages to accrue, that of a person with the bluest eyes, is both a figment and a sign of her insanity.

Pecola's father Cholly is, like the god of death, a man whose "touch was fatal" and who "filled the matrix of her agony with death" (159). Just as Pecola is an ironic Persephone, Cholly is an ironic Hades. The lord of the underworld is a dominant figure, one of the three rulers of the universe. Cholly, on the other hand, rules nothing, not even himself. A poor African-American man in a European-American society, Cholly has learned that he is powerless in every way; he can't even get his money back for a sofa ruined by careless delivery men. Pecola is the only person whom Cholly can truly dominate. Furthermore, unlike Hades, Cholly doesn't even rape his Persephone because he is powerfully attracted to her. He feels "revulsion, guilt, pity, then love" (127) for Pecola before the rape, and hatred, mixed with tenderness, after it. He rapes her because he has no idea how to be a father, because he feels guilty and angry that Pecola loves him as a father when he is such a bad one, because Pecola scratches her leg the way Pauline once did, because the thought of breaking the incest taboo sexually excites him, because he is drunk—in short, Cholly rapes Pecola because he can.

Though his effort is totally misguided and destructive, Cholly at least tries to give his daughter "something of himself" (159) when he rapes her. Pauline, Pecola's mother, is a failed Demeter who withholds love, affection, and support from her daughter during the time of Pecola's greatest need. It is painfully obvious that Pecola has been raped by Cholly, yet Pauline refuses to believe Pecola when her daughter recounts what has happened, even beating Pecola severely, according to Mrs. MacTeer's friends, when the girl is found to be pregnant. Pauline gives her daughter no protection from Cholly's sexual abuse, thus tacitly condoning the incestuous rape, which apparently happens a second time before Pecola goes mad.

This striking contrast to the behavior of the archetypal Mother helps explain an interesting phenomenon: many college-age readers are more outraged by Pauline's failure to protect Pecola than by Cholly's brutal rape of his own child. Because they are familiar with the archetype, these readers, although not condoning rape, nevertheless expect it and thus accept it from a Hades figure, but they do not expect, nor are they willing to accept, a Demeter figure who refuses to nurture, love, or fight for her child. They angrily condemn Pauline as unnatural, a monster, horrible, while they merely shake their heads over Cholly's devastating abuse. This response is yet another example of the "blame the mother" syndrome so common in our post-Freudian culture, a response Morrison does not share.

Morrison presents a cogent explanation of Pauline's behavior. So imbued is Pauline with European-American standards of beauty and assessments of worth that she, like the society around her, devalues anything not European-American, including herself and her daughter. Although she has, without realizing it, rejected Pecola emotionally at birth because she views her daughter's dark skin as "ugly" (100), Pauline considers herself a good mother because she feeds, clothes, houses, and takes care of Pecola for years. Pauline's emotional distance from Pecola shows distinctly in the name Pecola calls her mother: not "Mama" or even "Mother," but always "Mrs. Breedlove." Her mother is the last person from whom this Persephone can expect emotional support or nurturance. In almost every way, Pauline is an ironic Demeter, denying Pecola the love and support the girl needs to develop a strong identity, leaving Pecola trapped in the hell of incest and patriarchal domination, from which her only escape is insanity.

Zora Neale Hurston's finest novel, the lyrical *Their Eyes Were Watching God,* is, like *The Bluest Eye,* an image of the Persephone myth. Because Hurston's treatment of the myth avoids the bitter irony of Morrison's, *Their Eyes Were Watching God* ends on a much more affirmative note than does *The Bluest Eye.* Although adolescent Janie's two marriages to domineering older men initiate an extended figurative death, Janie, like Persephone but unlike Pecola, eventually achieves freedom from hell. *Their Eyes Were Watching God* details Janie's growth to selfhood, to a strong identity, and her concomitant attainment of freedom from patriarchal dominance.

Janie's first two marriages closely resemble Persephone's marriage to Death. At sixteen, Janie is a veritable "maiden of springtime" associated with fertility through her sexual awakening under the blossoming pear tree with which she identifies ("She had glossy leaves and bursting buds. . . . Where were the singing bees for her?").[2] She is married off to a much older man, Logan Killicks, a farmer of relative wealth and power who owns his sixty acres, unusual for an African-American in the Jim Crow South. A widower, he lives alone on his isolated farm, "a lonesome place like a stump in the middle of the woods where nobody had ever been" (39), in a house "absent of flavor, too" (39), a land of the dead to which he carries off his new bride in his chariot, a springless wagon pulled by mules.

As in the archetypal story, Logan has desired the adolescent Janie for some time, and Janie, like Persephone, is a most unwilling bride. Janie is a young romantic whose experience under the pear tree has made her yearn for a man who "represent[s] . . . pollen and blooming trees" (50), "a bee for her bloom" (54). She is repulsed by the elderly Logan, who "desecrat[es] the pear tree" (28) by looking to her "like some ole skullhead in de grave yard" (28), a description emphasizing the connection of Logan with Hades. Indeed, this marriage is a figurative death to Janie, who feels that the days before the wedding are "the few days to live" (38), and that marriage to Logan is "destructive and mouldy" (38).

Though she protests to her grandmother that she does not love Logan nor find him in any way attractive, Janie does not refuse the marriage. In truth, Janie, like Persephone, has little voice in the matter. Logan has spoken not to Janie but to her grandmother, the head of the family, who, desperate to see Janie settled in life, insists that Janie marry Logan. Logan does not rape Janie, but once she is his wife, he treats her as his possession, expecting subservience from her in all matters. Lonely and isolated, Janie suspends her emotions and waits for love to arrive.

Logan does not have the power of a Hades, however, to keep his Persephone captive in hell. When Logan threatens to kill Janie with an axe for refusing to do farm work in addition to all the housework, Janie places Logan's words "beside other things she had seen and heard" (54) and dissolves the marriage by walking out the front gate without a word while Logan is in the barn. She is not running away specifically to be with Joe, who has been courting her on the sly, but rather to free herself from her bondage to Death. Her first action after leaving Logan is to throw off her apron, symbol of that bondage, as she "walk[s] on, picking flowers and making a bouquet," thinking that "even if Joe was not there waiting for her, the change was bound to do her good" (54). She has silently escaped one patriarchal marriage, but she has not developed a voice or an identity strong enough to resist a second. Joe *is* waiting for her, and before sundown on the first day of her freedom from Logan, Janie has married Joe.

Joe Starks, like Logan, is also a Hades figure. He is twice Janie's age, rich, and powerful; within a week of their marrying, Joe has become the mayor and most important man in Eatonville. Several times he is described as a king (92, 114), an emperor (136), or a ruling figure (75, 79, 134), and Janie is compared to a queen or empress (67, 143). Her role as queen is purely ornamental, though, for Janie, like Persephone, is merely the king's consort, his possession, with no power of her own and no voice. Although Janie finds Joe attractive when she meets him and she marries him willingly after leaving Logan, she has not anticipated Joe's intense need to dominate her completely and deny her her own identity and voice. When she discovers this fact very early in her marriage to Joe, "a feeling of coldness and fear took hold of her. She felt far away from things and lonely" (74). Her severely prescribed existence with a jealous Hades is symbolized by Joe's insistence that she bind up her luxuriant hair lest any other man touch it or enjoy its beauty.

Like Persephone in hell, Janie is denied her own voice, for Joe forbids her to participate in the verbal games, the storytelling, the mule's funeral, and the other community activities of Eatonville, most of which revolve around wordplay of some kind. Joe thinks that Janie ought to be proud and happy to be the number-one woman in town—"the bell-cow" (66), as he tellingly phrases his vision of her—but that position holds no charm for Janie, just as being queen of the dead holds none for Persephone, because the price is nearly complete isolation. Janie also becomes increasingly isolated from Joe, who doesn't want her to be herself but instead to be "*Mrs. Mayor* Starks," an appendage whose function is to glorify Joe. She is allowed to speak out only once, after Joe buys Matt Bonner's mule, and only then because she publicly praises Joe's action. She often wants to argue or fight with him, but "disagreement and confusion . . . mak[e] it hard tuh git along" (90). Janie's response to Joe's patriarchal dominance, then, is silence: "Ah better not talk" (90).

When Joe physically abuses Janie seven years into their marriage for serving a meal not to his liking, she begins a deliberate retreat inward, hiding her thoughts and emotions so that Joe cannot dominate them. The remaining ten or eleven years of her marriage to Joe are a death in life for Janie, with her real self below the surface, entombed alive. She becomes almost schizophrenic, consciously watching "the shadow of herself going about tending store and prostrating itself before [Joe], while all the time she herself sat under a shady tree with the wind blowing through her hair and her clothes" (119). Like Persephone, Janie longs for air, sunlight, the natural world, freedom from the shadowy half-life she is living, bounded by the store and the house, her Hades. She wants to be able to voice her inner life, not to exist as a "rut in the road" with her "life beneath the surface," continually "beaten down by the wheels" (118). For Janie, as for Persephone, marriage means death of self.

To maintain his domination, Joe continually criticizes and belittles Janie. When, after nearly two decades of accepting his verbal abuse, Janie spears Joe publicly with a sharp, clever rebuttal to one of his disparaging comments about her body, Joe is shocked and humiliated. He feels that Janie's words have fatally compromised his civic power because the townspeople will no longer respect a man whose wife makes fun of him. So completely does Joe's self-image depend on the subservience of "his" woman that when Janie gains a voice, Joe essentially ends the marriage. When he dies some months later, refusing to the end to listen to what she has to say, Janie's very first action is to let free her bound hair, symbol of her bondage to this Hades, as her apron was the symbol of her bondage to her first Hades, Logan.

The Demeter figure in *Their Eyes Were Watching God*, Janie's grandmother Nanny, loves Janie dearly but has been deeply scarred by the patriarchal society around her: born a slave, she was forced to become her master's concubine and bear his child ("Ah didn't want to be used for . . . a brood-sow. . . . It sho wasn't mah will for things to happen lak they did" [31]). Her daughter, Janie's mother, was raped and impregnated as a teenager by a trusted male teacher; as will be discussed more fully below, Janie's mother is a Persephone never reclaimed from hell. Nanny begs and pushes Janie to marry Logan, believing that Logan's social position and wealth will provide the protection the grandmother believes Janie needs in this world. She also believes that romantic love is harmful, "de very prong all us black women gits hung on" (41). Her experience has been that love never brings equality in a relationship but only willing rather than forced submission by women. For her, male domination is a fact of life, a given. Therefore, a woman should protect herself by marrying a rich man so that she will gain social status and be spared the evils of poverty.

In valuing wealth and possessions, Nanny shares the materialism of Janie's first two husbands (Cooke 1984, 73), and thus she allies herself with Hades rather than with Persephone. Like Demeter, Nanny loves, nurtures, and protects her child as best she can, and she is heartsick that Janie is unhappy with Logan, but because she believes that women have no choice but to submit to domination by men, Nanny sees life in hell as normative—not desirable, but normative. When a miserable Janie comes to visit a few months after her wedding, Nanny immediately asks if Logan has "beat mah baby *already*" (40, my italics), as if physical abuse is to be expected in marriage. Though one of Nanny's own dreams had been to attain respectability through marriage, she herself never did marry despite many opportunities "cause Ah didn't want nobody mistreating mah baby [Janie's mother]" (36). Plainly, Nanny believes that women are powerless to prevent abuse—and indeed, she has submitted to her own abuse, her daughter's, and Janie's. Loving and well-intentioned though she may be, Nanny cannot guide Janie toward the self-fulfillment or self-expression that might save her from patriarchal abuse.

After Joe's death, when Janie is finally free of male domination, she realizes that she "hated the old woman [her late grandmother] who had twisted her so in the name of love" (138). Nanny's "mislove" (138) had "pinched [the horizon] into such a little bit of a thing that she could tie it about her granddaughter's neck tight enough to choke her" (138). This Demeter does not use her voice to free Persephone from hell; she binds Persephone, in the name of her love for the girl, and hands her over to Hades. To free herself, Janie must escape from both Hades *and* Demeter. In renouncing Nanny as well as Joe and Logan, Janie's budding voice gains strength.

Of the important people in Janie's life, only Tea Cake helps Janie discover and express who she is. Unlike Joe or Logan, Tea Cake encourages her to "have de nerve tuh say whut you mean" (165). With his help, Janie becomes reintegrated into society, participating in communal activities and developing her voice by joining in storytelling sessions. Janie grows and blossoms through her relationship with Tea Cake, who acts in some ways as a masculine Demeter figure. Tea Cake is even associated with seeds and fertility: a "package of garden seed that Tea Cake had bought to plant . . . reminded Janie of Tea Cake more than anything else because he was always planting things" (283). Though his relationship with Janie is certainly a sexual one, Tea Cake is not associated with the forced seeds of rape, the seeds signifying Death's dominance over his captive bride, but rather with Demetrian seeds of life that he plants and nurtures.

Nurturing though Tea Cake is before he contracts hydrophobia, Janie only fully gains herself, ironically, by killing Tea Cake. Although she loves him surpassingly and would gladly sacrifice herself to save him, she is not willing simply to die at his hydrophobia-crazed hands for no reason. Moreover, he comes to represent the patriarchal marriage conventions against which she has so long struggled, for in his madness Tea Cake accuses Janie of sexual unfaithfulness and tries to shoot and kill her. A man's ownership of a woman once again becomes an issue in this text, and Janie must protect herself from the ultimate abuse—death—by shooting Tea Cake in self defense. Even her fulfilling relationship with Tea Cake, then, becomes a marriage to Death from which Janie must escape.

Not until after the shooting does Janie learn the full power of her voice. At her trial for Tea Cake's murder, Janie explains her husband's death in her own words so movingly and eloquently that the judge immediately finds her not guilty, the white women in the audience weep, and Tea Cake's friends shamefacedly apologize for accusing Janie of wronging Tea Cake. Although Houston Baker calls Janie "a blues artist par excellence" (1984, 14) for her larger narration that comprises the text of the novel, the trial marks Janie's first successful blues performance, a tour de force. Janie's days of silence and subservience to patriarchal codes are finished forever. It is apparent by the end of the novel that for Janie, there will be no Persephone-like returning to hell.

The most affirmative of these African-American images of Persephone is Alice Walker's *The Color Purple*. Despite the lengthy and terrible abuse Celie suffers, she not only achieves freedom from patriarchal domination, but she brings about changes in the very fabric of the society in which she lives, helping also to free those immediately around her from patriarchal constraints.

Like Persephone, Celie is brutally forced to become the "wife" of Hades. She is fourteen when her father (who later turns out to be her stepfather) first rapes her; for five or six years, he sexually abuses her, fathering two children. Both physically and emotionally, Celie's relationship with the abusive Pa is a marriage to Death. Permitted no further schooling or intellectual development, worked literally like a slave, and disparaged constantly by Pa, Celie suffers a loss of identity, a death of self, signified with brilliant economy by her act of crossing out the first words of the text, "I am" (Abbandonato 1991, 1110). After being raped by her mother's husband, she is no longer Celie the "good girl"[3] but a sexual object forced into horrified complicity with incest. She upholds Pa's injunction to silence (except in her letters to God) because she wants to protect her ill mother from knowledge of the abuse, but also because she is so completely in Pa's power that she sees silence as her only means of surviving at all.

Celie's figurative death is hastened by the emotional abuse that Pa heaps upon her. She soon comes to believe what Pa repeatedly tells her: that she is ugly, stupid, and fit only for slave labor. The babies she bears and loves are dead to her, for Pa takes them against her will and kills them (or so he says). Moreover, the sexual abuse Celie suffers destroys the only part of her female identity that she cherishes, the ability to create life, for after the birth of the second baby, Celie ceases to menstruate and becomes infertile. (Not surprisingly, the Death figures in the novel, Pa and Mr. ______, view Celie's infertility as one of her few positive attributes.)

Mr. ______, to whom Pa marries off Celie when he tires of her, is simply a second avatar of Hades. Celie is completely subservient to this Hades also, living an isolated, severely restricted existence, with no voice and no power, not even the modicum of power that Hades's love gives Persephone. For twenty more years, Celie's painful ritual death continues as she is emotionally, physically, and sexually abused by her husband. The only way she can survive is to kill off her emotions, refusing to let herself feel anything. Already denied her place as a subject in the phallocentric narrative she is living, Celie takes her objectivity one step farther by imagining herself to be inanimate, a piece of wood, when Mr. ______ abuses her. That Celie is a Persephone living a death in life in the underworld is underlined by Nettie when she tells Celie that seeing her living with Mr. ______ is "like seeing you buried" (18).

Celie's unlikely Demeter is the blues singer Shug Avery, Mr. ______'s longtime lover, a woman bursting with vitality and sexuality (and vituperative jealousy toward rivals). Shug's stage name, "the Queen Honeybee" (76), connects her directly with Demeter, for the queen bee was worshipped in ancient Greece as an avatar of the Goddess, and priestesses of Demeter were called "Melissae," "bees" (Baring and Cashford 1991, 73, 118). Not only do bees fertilize flowers and trees, but the queen bee creates all the new life in a hive; she is the only female in the hive who lays eggs, and she wins her position as queen by killing off her rivals. Shug's stage name, then, is singularly appropriate in its dual suggestion of female power and fertility.

Shug is literally a mother, having borne Mr. ______ three children, but she shows her life-giving, nurturing powers most fully when she befriends Celie after Celie has nursed Shug through an unspecified but life-threatening illness. Shug's love, including sexual love, and her high valuation of Celie revive Celie's withered self-esteem. Gradually, Celie comes to believe in her own worth as a person and to feel emotion again. As Shug's lover, Celie attains sexual fulfillment—indeed, sexual feeling—for the first time in her life.

Shug's recovery of Nettie's letters, which Mr. ______ has for years been intercepting and hiding, precipitates Celie's full return to feeling. Angry enough to slit Mr. ______'s throat yet unable to overcome years of repressing all feeling, Celie can't speak, can't sleep, can't cry; she feels so cold that "pretty soon I think maybe I'm dead" (125). Shug brings life back to the "dead" Celie by teaching her to accept and express her feelings, to speak out, to refuse to be an object. As Marianne Hirsch suggests, "To be angry is to claim a place, to assert a right to expression and to discourse" (1989, 169). Shug validates Celie's anger and encourages Celie to claim a place, to claim her subjectivity, by leaving Hades and living with Shug in Memphis, where Celie finds identity, artistic fulfillment, and economic independence designing and sewing pants.

Shug is an effective Demeter figure, but she cannot singlehandedly rescue her Persephone from hell, as Demeter can; her redemptive powers are not that strong. Shug can act as a model, can nurture, can advise, can love, but she can't *be* Celie's voice, as Demeter is Persephone's voice when Persephone is silenced in the underworld. Celie can escape from hell only by finding her own voice. She does so by publicly reviling Mr. ______ for his treatment of her, placing a curse on him, and announcing that she is leaving him. Mr. ______ tries to reassert his dominance by destroying Celie's newfound self-esteem, telling her mockingly "You black, you pore, you ugly, you a woman. Goddam, . . . you nothing at all" (213). But Celie, with Shug's nurturance, has built herself a positive identity out of these facts of her existence. She even gives up her long-held belief in a white, male God, the patriarch who "act just like all the other mens I know. Trifling, forgitful and lowdown" (199), because, in Shug's words, "You have to git man off your eyeball, before you can see anything a'tall" (204). By refusing to accept any longer the patriarchal vision of her society, and with Shug as a role model and supporter, Celie empowers herself.

The end of *The Color Purple* finds Celie, like Persephone, sharing herself with both Hades and Demeter. Celie has allowed a reconciliation with a much-changed Mr. ______, accepting his company, getting to know and like him, and helping him overcome the restrictive vision of masculine and feminine roles handed down to him by society. He has even proposed marriage—"this time in the spirit as well as in the flesh" (290)—and though she turns him down, she counts him as one of her close friends, "somebody I can talk to" (283). Celie and Shug are still intimate even though they are apparently no longer lovers, with Celie now giving as much emotional sustenance to Shug as she receives.

The difference between Celie and Persephone, however, is that Celie never returns to bondage once she has escaped, as Persephone must. The relationship between Celie and Mr. ______ resumes on Celie's turf—the house she has inherited—and on her terms. Celie quite literally wears the pants: as the creator and owner of Folkspants Unlimited, she sews pants designed uniquely to suit the individual male or female wearer, including herself. She also has inherited a store, and in a radical action for the time, she has hired an African-American woman, Sofia, as clerk. She has taken on much of the economic and social power previously reserved for men in her society. Fittingly, Celie decorates her own bedroom in purple and red, colors she has long associated with strength and power, especially in women (22, 223).

Mr. ______ has also changed. Having gone through a "dark night of the soul" and emerged with new respect for and understanding of women, he is finally able to dispense with restrictive patriarchal codes of "masculine" behavior and take on some "feminine" traits (Walker 1986, 28). He demonstrates his new freedom by learning to cook, clean house, and sew, the latter being something he has always wanted but never dared to do for fear of ridicule. Most importantly, though, he learns compassion, and he becomes an extremely kind and nurturing person, a transformation Walker presents without irony.

Whereas Persephone must divide her time between the male-dominated land of the dead and the female-dominated world of springtime, between her husband and her mother, by the end of *The Color Purple* Celie has done away with the inhibiting divisions between male and female, creating an androgynous world where power is shared and neither sex is devalued or subservient. As Annis Pratt has noted, some women's fiction explores an alternative to patriarchy by creating a new society "where 'maleness' and 'femaleness' no longer undermine the development of the human personality" (1981, 70). This is what we see in *The Color Purple,* where Celie leads the other characters beyond patriarchal strictures to social and spiritual transformation.

One of the most unusual chapters in *The Color Purple* introduces the natural cycle motif that is so important a feature in the myth. Although Celie is associated with infertility and Shug with fertility/sexuality early in the text, little further connection is made with the natural cycle until this chapter, two-thirds of the way through the text. When Celie learns from Nettie's letters that Pa is not her natural father, she immediately wants to find out from him what she can about her father. She and Shug drive over to the farm where Celie suffered such dreadful abuse at Pa's hands. Celie's narrative specifies that "it was a bright Spring day," a Sunday, with a chill "like it be round Easter" (184), placing the action in the season of resurrection and regeneration.

Celie and Shug immediately notice as they turn into Pa's lane that his property is strangely "different from the rest of the country us drive through" (185), so different that "it make us real quiet" (185). Amazingly, magically, everything is green at Pa's, much greener than anywhere else, including the land just outside the lane. Wildflowers, Easter lilies, and daffodils bloom everywhere, birds are singing all along the flowering hedge and in the many blooming fruit trees, and even the sun seems stronger and more direct. The house, painted yellow and green—spring colors—is beautiful. None of this looks at all familiar to Celie, who thinks that they must have made a wrong turn, until Pa himself appears and gives them their biggest surprise. Shug and Celie are both shocked by how young he looks. Although he must be close to fifty, he looks not much older than the fifteen-year-old bride hanging on his arm.

This land, once Celie's hell, clearly has magical regenerative powers. Its unexpected fertility suggests the springing up of flowers and plants in Persephone's footsteps as she returns from the underground. Significantly, at this moment in the novel, Celie is on the verge of making her own departure from hell. She has just discovered who her father was and what her heritage is, freeing her from any hold her stepfather/Hades has on her, and she is so angry at Mr. ______ for all his abuse that within a day or two of her visit to

Pa, Celie leaves her second Hades and makes a new life with her Demeter.

The fertile land she and Shug visit is actually Celie's and Nettie's land, stolen from them by their stepfather, Pa, but later returned to them upon his death. Within a few years of this visit to Pa, Celie is living in the beautiful green-and-yellow house surrounded by the birds and fruit trees and flowers, her children and her extended family around her, a Persephone returned from death to a new, fruitful life in the place where her life began. She, like Persephone, travels full circle from life, through a long figurative death, and back to life again. The fertile land is an emblem of Celie's own incipient resurrection and regeneration, just as renewed life on earth in spring signifies and accompanies Persephone's resurrection.

In the Persephone myth, Demeter's high position as goddess of fertility gives her a strong bargaining position in her efforts to rescue her beloved daughter. Persephone herself, in most versions, remains resisting but powerless to the end, unable to stop Hades from forcing upon her the pomegranate seeds that guarantee her return to the underworld, just as she was unable to stop the original forcing of seeds, Hades's rape. Nevertheless, Demeter is able singlehandedly to bring about Persephone's release from hell. That Persephone must return to Hades for part of each year results from the daughter's weakness, not from any loss of the mother's power or weakening of the mother / daughter bond.

What is striking about the three African-American Persephone images examined here is that they all make problematical the Demeter / Persephone relationship. The bond that in the myth brings salvation to the daughter is, in these works, uncertain or diminished. The chief contrast between the archetype and the archetypal images is that African-American Persephones lack effective maternal support for their resistance to patriarchal domination, a fact illustrated in these texts by Demeter figures, both mothers and substitute mothers, who are unwilling or unable to bargain their Persephones out of hell.

In her essay "Daughters in Search of Mothers," Harryette Mullen theorizes that Alice Walker uses "the absent mother as a recurring figure [in her work] to suggest that mothers in the patriarchal family are in a significant way absent to their daughters" because in a patriarchy, "there would never be any mother strong enough to protect her daughter from the devaluation that is intrinsically part of her social status as a female, which the mother herself shares" (1986, 48). In the whole of *The Color Purple,* Mullen finds "no significant bond between a mother and a daughter" (1986, 47).

Mullen's finding applies equally well to Janie in *Their Eyes Were Watching God* and Pecola in *The Bluest Eye,* for the mothers of these Persephone figures are also absent to their daughters. Pauline is what psychologists call a custodial mother, one who provides for the physical needs of her child but is emotionally distant or absent. Janie's mother Leafy is literally absent: not long after bearing Janie, she severs her relationship with both her daughter and her mother by running away, never to be heard from again. The kidnapping and rape by her schoolteacher have devastated her, both physically and emotionally; she is herself a lost Persephone, unreclaimed from hell. After Joe's death, Janie considers returning to her old home and trying to find her mother, but she decides upon reflection "that she had no interest in that seldom-seen mother at all" (137). There is no bond whatever between Janie and her natural mother.

The mere physical presence of the mother is, of course, no guarantee of her assistance or support, as is plainly illustrated in *The Bluest Eye* and *The Color Purple.* Although both Pecola's mother Pauline and Celie's nameless mother are aware of their husbands' sexual abuse of their daughters, they simply refuse the knowledge, an efficient way of circumventing any obligation to aid their children. Pauline, as previously discussed, refuses to believe Pecola's report of incestuous rape despite the incontrovertible evidence. Celie's mother, who appears briefly in the early pages of *The Color Purple,* is weak and ill—dying, in fact—from childbirth complications. When Celie reports, in her very first letter, that her mother "fuss at me an look at me" (2) with suspicion as Celie experiences morning sickness after Pa has impregnated her, and when she later states that her mother "scream at me" and "cuss at me" (3), she also reports that her mother is nonetheless "happy, cause [Pa] good to her now" (2), i.e., he makes no more sexual demands on Celie's mother. The mother does ask who fathered Celie's first baby (3), and she "*finally* ast how come she find [Pa's] hair in the girls room if he don't never go in there like he say" (117, my italics). It is apparent that Celie's mother knows what her husband is doing. Refusing to acknowledge that her husband is sexually abusing her daughter saves the sick woman from having to intervene in Celie's behalf—and she could intervene if she wished, ill as she is. The mother does, after all, have some power over Pa: when she refuses sexual relations after the birth of their last baby, Pa reluctantly accedes. Moreover, Pa lies to his wife about the abuse, and he expressly forbids Celie to tell her mother, clearly apprehensive that she will find out. Celie's mother, however, is unable, unwilling, or both to protect her daughter, instead cursing and screaming even on her deathbed not at the abuser but at the victim.

Celie admits that she was for a while angry at her mother ("Maybe cause my mama cuss me you think I *kept* mad at her" [6, my italics]). Celie is, after all, first raped because her mother refused sexual relations with Pa. Moreover, Celie keeps silent to protect her mother, believing quite literally Pa's threat that learning of the abuse would "kill your mammy" (1). Though Celie resents her mother's anger and refusal to help or protect her, she also recognizes her mother's weakness within the patriarchal social structure and pities her mother. Indeed, Celie concludes forgivingly that trying to believe Pa's lies about his secret abuse of Celie was what actually killed her mother.

The only mother in any of these texts who comes to the aid of her daughter is Mrs. MacTeer in *The Bluest Eye,* who unhesitatingly throws out Mr. Henry, the boarder, for touching Frieda's breast, even though the family counts heavily on Mr. Henry's board money. Frieda is a potential Persephone included in *The Bluest Eye* as a contrast to Pecola. Her case illustrates how active support from a vocal Demeter can rescue a girl before she becomes a Persephone lost to patriarchal domination.

Nanny, Pauline, and Celie's mother fail as Demeters because they have largely accepted patriarchal norms, leading them to force or to allow their Persephones to fill the damaging role of sexual object. Pauline doesn't aid Pecola after the rape by Cholly because she doesn't value her "ugly" daughter; in addition, she can enhance her chosen role as suffering martyr through this new evidence of Cholly's degradation. Celie's mother is angry that the abuse is occurring, an anger she takes out on Celie, but she is also relieved to be free of her sexual and procreative duties. Nanny, Janie's substitute mother, is certainly much more nurturing and helpful to Janie than is her absent natural mother, but Nanny's advanced age, physical weakness, and acquiescence to patriarchal codes have rendered her ineffectual as a Demeter figure, both for Janie and for Janie's mother Leafy, the lost Persephone in *Their Eyes Were Watching God.*

Shug Avery is the most effective of the Demeter figures in these texts because she has learned to turn her back on the role assigned her by the patriarchy and to take on masculine power. She refuses to be devalued, and she refuses to be silenced. The force of her voice derives in part—but only in part—from the fact that Celie's husband Mr. ______, the most important "patriarch" in the novel, loves Shug deeply. Shug is a feisty, independent thinker who has, since reaching adulthood, operated outside of the social strictures and customs, and she rescues Celie by teaching her to do the same. Shug's effectiveness as a Demeter thus rests not in her self-sacrificing maternal qualities, but in the strong role model she provides as she pushes Celie to assert her subjectivity in the face of patriarchal objectification.

Although Shug rescues Celie from abuse because she loves and values Celie, Shug is not a mother figure to Celie, nor is she a maternal woman. Shug, like Demeter, is admirably strong, but unlike Demeter, she does not singlemindedly pursue the release from hell of her Persephone or make any personal sacrifice in the process of rescuing the lost loved one. Shug is essentially self-concerned and self-centered, despite her great capacity to love. In the process of enfranchising herself by taking on "masculine" roles and refusing "feminine" ones, she has refused to be a nurturer, even to her own children. Indeed, Celie teaches Shug to value nurturing and bonding, inspiring Shug to seek out her own long-ignored, now-grown children. (In some ways, Celie is as much a Demeter figure to Shug as Shug is to Celie.) As a Demeter, Shug cannot show Celie how to gain a strong voice within the patriarchy and at the same time develop her best "feminine" qualities: her ability to set other people's needs before her own, her deep affections, her great capacity for nurturance, and her ability to forge and maintain lifelong nonsexual emotional bonds.

The Color Purple, as Mullen implies, makes a statement about the maternal bond largely through the absence of that bond in the text. Shug is not, of course, Celie's mother or grandmother or even a protective or motherly older woman; she is roughly Celie's contemporary. Moreover, she is Celie's lesbian lover. Because she is also Celie's husband's lover, the emotional configuration of the novel is considerably less traditional and more complicated than that of the myth. Indeed, Celie's and Mr. ______'s love for Shug creates a bond between this Hades and this Persephone, the only real bond that exists between them until the novel's end. Though Shug takes on a number of the important functions of the mother goddess and does restore Celie to life, she is nonetheless a problematical Demeter.

Because these three Persephone images are stories of daughters without mothers, their primary focus is not on the mother or the maternal bond, as in the myth, but rather on the Persephone figures, particularly their self-discovery and assertion of self in a society accustomed to assigning them a place as objects rather than subjects. The absence of mothers and the presence of weakened mother-substitutes force these women to rely chiefly on themselves. They must endure whatever ritual death is meted out to them by a patriarchal system, and they must at the same time somehow preserve or develop a strong identity, an articulate voice. If they are as weak and silent as Persephone, they will be lost.

Pecola is the quintessential example. She simply cannot defend herself—against other children's taunts, against Geraldine's hatred, against her mother's love of white children, against her father's sexual abuse—instead "fold[ing] into herself, like a pleated wing" (61). Although Pecola does tell her mother that Cholly has raped her, she does not try to tell someone other than her mother when Pauline refuses to believe her, and she never reports and cannot prevent the apparent second rape. Her silence, which both stems from and contributes to her victimization, in the end dooms her to a living death of madness. Her fervent wish for blue eyes is an expression of her desperate need for valuation, for love, but only Soaphead Church ever hears her wish expressed; she is even silent in her madness. Claudia's assessment is devastatingly accurate: "the horror at the heart of her yearning [for blue eyes] is exceeded only by the evil of fulfillment" (158). In Pecola's case, as in Janie's and Celie's, the victim must not remain silent. How Persephone learns to speak out against patriarchal domination—or whether she learns to speak out—is the focus of these texts.

Just as Morrison's, Hurston's, and Walker's treatments of the maternal bond motif differ from that of the myth, so do their treatments of the natural cycle motif. Indeed, these writers virtually deconstruct the traditional reading of the archetypal story, which is grounded in the myth's metaphoric connection to the natural cycle. Living things, this reading implies, must undergo a period of ritual death, a sojourn in a dark, closed place, before they sprout or are born. From a seemingly lifeless seed in the dead earth or the dark womb springs new life; without fertilization, germination, and gestation—"death," a period spent "underground"—no new life is possible.

Persephone's sexual maturation, including the capacity to bring forth new life, occurs when she is taken to the underworld and is raped by the god of the dead. This forced initiation into adult sexuality, or "marriage," is synonymous with death for Persephone, but ritual death for women is viewed as a necessary part of the natural cycle. Persephone's return to life heralds and symbolizes the renewed fecundity of the earth in spring, after a season of death brought on by the distraught, angry Demeter. According to some ancient storytellers, Persephone bears a child each spring upon her return to the earth or, alternatively, bears Zagreus (prototype of Dionysus), the product of Persephone's rape by her father Zeus (Frazer 1922, 450). The Maiden in this way becomes the Mother, who later becomes the Crone—the reproductive life cycle of women. Thus, Persephone's abduction and rape are encoded as "natural" events, approved and ordained by the masculine higher powers, to insure the continuation of life on earth. The traditional reading of the mythic text, then, implies that women, the child-bearers, have to suffer in order for life to continue, and that is just the way things are.

Morrison, Hurston, and Walker reject this implicitly patriarchal notion. They refuse to assume that abuse and domination of any kind are either natural or ordained. Indeed, they render Persephone's domination unnatural, highly repugnant, and destructive. *The Bluest Eye*, for instance, presents Pecola's sexual initiation graphically as a brutal rape. Worse, it is the brutal rape of a helpless child of eleven—by her own drunken father. In making this sexual initiation eventually result in complete loss of self, sterility of the earth, and death, Morrison deconstructs the traditional reading of the myth, particularly its implied valorization of social codes that permit and even sanction such destructive domination of women.

Similarly, *The Color Purple* opens with a graphic description of the incestuous rape of an adolescent girl by her father; only much later in the text is this horrifying event defused into "mere" rape by a stepfather. Walker, like Morrison, uses incest to probe the limits of our acceptance of patriarchal codes. The incestuous concubinage Celie suffers at the hands of Pa is shocking and damaging; like Pecola's abuse, Celie's results in infertility and figurative death. Destructive as the incestuous abuse is to Celie, the sexual abuse and domination she suffers within her legally and morally sanctioned marriage to Mr. ______ are clearly just as destructive. Furthermore, there is nothing natural about it: men like Mr. ______ and Harpo have to change their natures to become dominators, and the change is damaging to them, to their families, and certainly to the women they dominate, or try to dominate. Patriarchal culture damages all who live according to its reductive, hierarchical codes.

Their Eyes Were Watching God also paints a picture of the destructiveness to both men and women of patriarchal beliefs and attitudes. Janie's first two husbands do not know or want to know the real Janie; each sacrifices his relationship with Janie the person in order to "own" Janie as a possession. Furthermore, Janie does not attain self-knowledge until after Joe's death. Acquiescence to patriarchal authority isolates a woman even from herself, a state that Hurston depicts as unnatural and unhealthy in passages showing Janie schizophrenically leading two lives, a surface life and an inner "real" life.

Morrison, Hurston, and Walker have created their own versions of the Persephone myth in response to the unique position of African-American women in American culture. Their Persephone images focus not on the natural cycle nor on redemptive maternal love, but on minority women's struggle for identity and empowerment in a Eurocentric, phallocentric culture. Establishing the Persephone archetype as central to their texts enables Morrison, Hurston, and Walker to explore through contrast the rite of passage of African-American girls entering womanhood in twentieth-century America. The problematizing of the mother / daughter bond and the deconstructive reading of the natural cycle motif of the myth are ways of signifying some of the difficulties these women face in their struggle.

An African-American Persephone must forge for herself, in the heat of hell, an identity and a voice powerful enough to overcome the forces of white domination and male domination arrayed against her. This task is arduous, as *The Bluest Eye, Their Eyes Were Watching God,* and *The Color Purple* palpably demonstrate. That two of the Persephones in these texts (and one potential Persephone, Frieda) do eventually achieve freedom from the destructive bonds of patriarchal domination underscores Morrison's, Hurston's, and Walker's cautiously affirmative vision of the possibility for positive change in African-American women's status in American society.

NOTES

1. Morrison 1970, 9. Subsequent page numbers in parentheses in discussions of *The Bluest Eye* refer to this edition.

2. Hurston 1978, 25. Subsequent page numbers in parentheses in discussions of *Their Eyes Were Watching God* refer to this edition.

3. Walker 1982, 1. Subsequent page numbers in parentheses in discussions of *The Color Purple* refer to this edition.

BIBLIOGRAPHY

Abbandonato, Linda. "'A View from Elsewhere': Subversive Sexuality and the Rewriting of the Heroine's Story in *The Color Purple*." *PMLA* 106 (Oct. 1991): 1106–15.

Baker, Houston. *Blues, Ideology, and Afro-American Literature*. Chicago: Univ. of Chicago Press, 1984.

Baring, Anne, and Jules Cashford. *The Myth of the Goddess: Evolution of an Image*. London: Viking, 1991.

Cooke, Michael. *Afro-American Literature in the Twentieth Century*. New Haven: Yale Univ. Press, 1984.

Frazer, Sir James George. *The Golden Bough: A Study in Magic and Religion*. New York: Macmillan, 1922.

Gubar, Susan. "Mother, Maiden, and the Marriage of Death: Women Writers and an Ancient Myth." *Women's Studies* 6 (1979): 301–15.

Hamilton, Edith. *Mythology*. New York: Little, Brown, 1942.

Hirsch, Marianne. *The Mother/Daughter Plot: Narrative, Psychoanalysis, Feminism*. Bloomington: Indiana Univ. Press, 1989.

Homer. "The Hymn to Demeter." In *The Homeric Hymns*, translated by Charles Boer. Chicago: Swallow, 1970.

———. "Hymn to Demeter," translated by Daryl Hine. In *Spinsters and Spiders*, by Marta Weigle. Albuquerque: Univ. of New Mexico Press, 1982.

Hurston, Zora Neale. *Their Eyes Were Watching God*. Chicago: Univ. of Illinois Press, 1978 (J. G. Lippincott, 1937).

Miner, Madonne M. "Lady No Longer Sings the Blues: Rape, Madness, and Silence in *The Bluest Eye*." In *Conjuring: Black Women, Fiction, and Literary Tradition*, edited by Marjorie Pryse and Hortense Spillers. Bloomington: Indiana Univ. Press, 1985.

Morrison, Toni. *The Bluest Eye*. New York: Washington Square Press, 1970.

———. Seminar session, Jeanette K. Watson Distinguished Professor Lecture Series. Syracuse University, October 1988.

———. Quoted in David Gates, "Same Twain, Different Time." *Newsweek Magazine* (July 20, 1992): 64–66.

Mullen, Harryette. "Daughters in Search of Mothers, or A Girl Child in a Family of Men." *Catalyst* 1 (Fall 1986): 45–49.

Phillips, E. D. "Persephone." In *Man, Myth, and Magic: The Illustrated Encyclopedia of Mythology, Religion, and the Unknown*, edited by Richard Cavendish. New York: Marshall Cavendish, 1983.

Pratt, Annis. *Archetypal Patterns in Women's Fiction*. Bloomington: Indiana Univ. Press, 1981.

Richardson, N. J. *The Homeric Hymn to Demeter*. Oxford: Clarendon, 1974.

Walker, Alice. *The Color Purple*. New York: Pocket Books, 1982.

———. "In the Closet of the Soul." *Ms. Magazine* (November 1986): 28–41.

APPENDIX A

Summary of the Homeric "Hymn to Demeter"

Persephone, the Maiden (Kore), was the daughter of Demeter, goddess of the fruits of the earth, and her brother Zeus, king of the gods. Their brother Hades, god of the underworld, saw Persephone and desired her, and with Zeus's help, he stole away the maiden goddess. While Persephone was picking flowers on the Nysian Plain with Athena, Artemis, and other daughters of Oceanus, she was lured apart by a beautiful narcissus, specially grown for Hades by Gaia, the Earth Mother, with Zeus's permission. As Persephone reached to pick the wondrous flower, the earth suddenly gaped open and out of the chasm galloped Hades in his golden chariot pulled by his immortal horses. He seized Persephone and carried her off to his underworld kingdom, even though she resisted fiercely, screaming in shrill voice.

Only Hecate in her dark cave and Helios, the sun, heard the Maiden calling out for help to her powerful father Zeus, but as Persephone's cries echoed from the mountain peaks to the depths of the sea, her noble mother, Demeter, heard her. A sharp pain seized the mother's heart, and she shot out like a bird over land and sea, searching for her daughter, but Persephone was nowhere to be found. For nine days, bearing a torch in her hand, Demeter searched frantically for her child without rest, not even stopping to eat, drink, or wash herself.

On the tenth day, Hecate, holding a light (a torch?), came to tell Demeter that she had heard Persephone's screams. Together, Demeter and Hecate visited Helios, who told them that with Zeus's permission, Hades had abducted Persephone to be his wife. Helios tried to comfort Demeter by reminding her of how powerful and important her daughter's husband was, but the goddess was not to be comforted.

Outraged at Zeus's action and grieving for her lost child, Demeter refused to return to Olympus. Disguised as an old woman, she wandered the earth, stopping at Eleusis, where she mournfully sat on a rock beside a well. When the daughters of King Celeus came to the well for water, they spoke respectfully to her and took her home with them to the palace, where Demeter was engaged as nurse for the baby prince, Demophōon, by Queen Metaneira. Demeter refused Metaneira's offer of food and wine, requesting instead a simple drink of barley and water. Iambe (a servant?) made the grieving goddess smile with her jokes and clowning.

Intending to make her nursling Demophōon immortal, Demeter placed him in the heart of the fire each night. One night, Metaneira spied on Demeter, and when the queen saw her baby placed in the fire, she ran in and snatched him from the flames. Furious, Demeter threw off her disguise and revealed herself as the goddess, chastised Metaneira and all people for their stupidity, and commanded that the people of Eleusis build her a temple to win back her favor.

When the temple was finished, Demeter stayed in it, grieving for Persephone. She refused to let anything grow on earth. Soon, earth became a wintry wasteland, and people began to starve. With the threat of annihilation of the human race looming, and the concomitant disappearance of offerings to the gods, Zeus sent the gods, one after another, to beg Demeter to let the earth be fruitful once more, but she refused to let anything grow until her daughter was returned to her. Finally, to appease Demeter, Zeus ordered Hades to release the captive goddess. Before letting Persephone go, however, Hades secretly slipped her a pomegranate seed and forced her to eat it, thus guaranteeing her return to the underworld.

When Persephone returned to the earth, she was joyfully reunited with her mother, who immediately asked if she had eaten anything in the underworld. She reported to Demeter that Hades had violently forced her, unwilling, to eat the pomegranate seed. Demeter was then sad amidst her rejoicing, for she knew that Persephone could not remain with her always but must return to Hades. Hecate next greeted Persephone affectionately, and became Persephone's constant companion from that day on.

Zeus decreed that Persephone should spend a third of each year with Hades and two thirds with Demeter, a bargain that Demeter accepted. Demeter caused the earth to bloom again with flowers and crops, and she taught her rites and mysteries to the Eleusinian princes, who then taught them to other human beings. When this was accomplished, Demeter returned at last to Olympus to dwell with the other gods.

APPENDIX B

Summary of the Orphic Persephone Myth

The Orphic story of Persephone and Demeter is scattered throughout a number of poems and poem fragments. In this version of the myth, Demeter, searching the world for her missing daughter, was entertained by a poor man, Dysaules, and his wife Baubo (*belly*), who made the grieving goddess laugh by doing some obscene clowning. The couple's sons Triptolemos and Eubuleus reported to Demeter that they knew where her daughter had gone: they had inadvertently witnessed the abduction of Persephone when their herd of pigs had fallen down the chasm opened by Hades as he came from the underworld to seize the maiden. Demeter rewarded the sons by teaching them her mysteries, including the growing of grain, charging them to teach mankind.[1]

The Orphic version makes no mention of Demeter's refusal, in her grief over the loss of her daughter, to let anything grow on earth, or of the famine that resulted from her action.

NOTE

1. W. K. C. Guthrie, *Orpheus and Greek Religion* (New York: Norton, 1966), 135.

APPENDIX C

Summary of "The Rape of Proserpine," from Ovid's *Metamorphoses* V

Pluto, checking the foundations of Sicily for signs of potential damage to the roof of hell, was seen by Venus, who decided to extend her empire to the underworld and at the same time remove a potential maiden goddess from the ranks of the forever chaste. Venus instructed Cupid to shoot his best arrow deep into Pluto's heart, whereupon the god of the dead straightway fell in love with Proserpine, daughter of his sister Ceres and his brother Jove.

Proserpine was gathering flowers with her friends when Pluto seized her. Terrified, she cried out for her mother as Pluto carried her away in his chariot. The nymph Cyane tried to stop Pluto, but the lord of the dead hurled his scepter at the bottom of Cyane's pool. A chasm opened up, and down to hell the chariot plunged. Cyane, heartbroken over Proserpine's rape, wept until she dissolved into her pool.

Ceres, carrying torches, searched day and night for her daughter. She was given a sweet barley-flavored drink by an old crone in a thatched cottage, and when a saucy boy laughed at her, she changed him into a newt. In her wanderings, Ceres came to Cyane's pool, where she found Proserpine's sash floating on the water. She then realized that her daughter had been abducted. Angry and grieving, Ceres caused crops to die and the land to become infertile. The earth became barren, and people began to starve.

The nymph Arethusa told Ceres that she knew where Proserpine was: she herself had seen Proserpine in hell as the consort of the god of the dead. Ceres, outraged, went immediately to Jove and indignantly pleaded for better treatment for their daughter. Jove tried to calm Ceres by reassuring her that her new son-in-law was powerful and worthy: after all, he was Jove's brother, a splendid thing to be. Jove also reminded Ceres that Proserpine could not be freed if she had eaten any food while in hell.

Alas, Proserpine had eaten seven pomegranate seeds while wandering through an orchard in hell. Ascalaphus had seen her eat the seeds and had spitefully reported the action, for which Proserpine changed him into a screech owl. Jove decreed that Proserpine spend half the year with Ceres and half with Pluto. When her six months in hell were over each year, Proserpine was transformed with joy as she went to join her mother in the upper world.

APPENDIX D

Summary of Quinault and Lully's *Proserpine*

Act 1 begins with the evocation of the pastoral pleasures that follow Jupiter's victory over the Titans. Mercury brings Jupiter's request (at the instigation of Juno) that Ceres increase the fertility of Phrygia and tries in vain to convince her that Jupiter still loves her. Bitter but still in love, she prepares to leave. The important subplot of the love between Arethusa and Alpheus is introduced: Arethusa is trying to avoid her persistent suitor, but Ceres recognizes the dawning of love and counsels Arethusa to accept the all-too-rare constant lover. The last three scenes are devoted to Ceres' departure (in a chariot drawn by winged dragons) and to the celebration of Jupiter's victory.

In act 2 Ascalaphus, who has left Hades with his master Pluto to see if the earthquakes accompanying the revolt of the Titans have opened any entrances into the underworld, presents himself as Alpheus's rival. Alpheus pretends to be in love with Proserpina, but he and Arethusa finally admit their love for each other. Pluto arrives in scene 6, asking Arethusa to allow him to see Proserpina, with whom he had fallen hopelessly in love moments earlier after receiving a shaft from Cupid's bow. The scene changes to show

Proserpina and her friends happy to be free from love, but when they separate to pick more flowers, Pluto carries Proserpina away in his chariot. Only Cyane witnesses the rape, and Pluto threatens her with the loss of her voice if she speaks.

In act 3 Arethusa suspects the truth, and she and Alpheus descend into Hades to search for Proserpina. Ceres returns, and no one can tell her what has happened. Cyane tries, but she is changed into a brook. Ceres and her followers begin to express their anger by ravaging the earth.

Act 4 takes place in a remarkably pleasant underworld, where Ascalaphus and the Happy Shades try to convince Proserpina to accept Pluto's love. Arethusa and Alpheus arrive and also sing the praises of love. Proserpina learns that Ascalaphus has tricked her into eating the fatal seeds, and she changes him into an owl. Pluto presses his suit in person, but a tearful Proserpina pleads for her release from the underworld. Pluto decides to win her love, and in the final scene (divertissement), Pluto suspends all suffering in his realm. The shades and infernal divinities praise Proserpina and try to convince her of the joys of being their queen.

In act 5 the infernal judges rule that Proserpina must remain in Hades and that Jupiter does not have the right to take her away. Pluto and the Furies are prepared to fight Jupiter and destroy the universe. Ceres learns Proserpina's fate from Arethusa and Alpheus, and she implores Jupiter to free their daughter. Mercury announces the split decision of the gods, and the heavens open to reveal Jupiter in his majesty. Pluto and Proserpina come out of Hades on a throne, on which Ceres takes her place next to her daughter. In a return to the themes of the prologue, Jupiter ordains that Discord and War remain chained forever, and that heaven, earth, and Hades enjoy eternal peace.

CONTRIBUTORS

Mary Aswell Doll is associate professor and chair of the English Department at Holy Cross College in New Orleans.

Eileen Gregory is associate professor of English at the University of Dallas.

Marta Powell Harley is associate professor of English at Florida State University, Tallahassee.

Elizabeth T. Hayes is assistant professor of English at Le Moyne College, Syracuse, N.Y.

Virginia Hyde is professor of English at Washington State University, Pullman.

Laura Laffrado is assistant professor of English at Western Washington University, Bellingham.

Martine Motard-Noar is associate professor of French at Western Maryland College, Westminster.

Buford Norman is professor of French and chair of the Department of French and Classics at the University of South Carolina, Columbia.

Melissa McFarland Pennell is associate professor of English at the University of Massachusetts, Lowell.

Janet S. Wolf is assistant professor of English at the State University of New York, Cortland.

INDEX